AUTISM

AUTISM

A Comprehensive Occupational Therapy Approach

Heather Miller-Kuhaneck
MS, OTR/L, BCP
Editor

 **AOTA**® The American
Occupational Therapy
Association, Inc.

Mission Statement

The American Occupational Therapy Association advances the quality, availability, use, and support of occupational therapy through standard-setting, advocacy, education, and research on behalf of its members and the public.

AOTA Staff

Joseph C. Isaacs, CAE, Executive Director
Karen C. Carey, CAE, Associate Executive Director, Membership, Marketing and Communications
Jennifer J. Jones, Director of Publications

Krishni Patrick, MA, Editor, Books
Suzanne Seitz, Production Editor
Barbara Dickson, Editorial Assistant
Carla A. Kieffer, Publications Assistant

Robert A. Sacheli, Manager, Creative Services
Sarah E. Ely, Book Production Coordinator, Cover and Text Design

The American Occupational Therapy Association, Inc.
4720 Montgomery Lane
PO Box 31220
Bethesda, Maryland 20824-1220
Phone: 301-652-AOTA (2682)
TDD: 800-377-8555
Fax: 301-652-7711
www.aota.org
To Order: 1-877-404-AOTA (2682)

Disclaimers

This publication is designed to provide accurate and authoritative information in regard to the subject matter covered. It is sold or distributed with the understanding that the publisher is not engaged in rendering legal, accounting, or other professional service. If legal advice or other expert assistance is required, the services of a competent professional person should be sought.
—From the Declaration of Principles jointly adopted by the American Bar Association
   and a Committee of Publishers and Associations

It is the objective of The American Occupational Therapy Association to be a forum for free expression and interchange of ideas. The opinions expressed by the contributors to this work are their own and not necessarily those of either the editors or The American Occupational Therapy Association.

ISBN: 1-56900-109-X

Composition by Maryland Composition Company, Inc., Glen Burnie, Maryland
Printed by Victor Graphics, Inc., Baltimore, Maryland

Table of Contents

Foreword

Autism. It is a diagnostic term that we are hearing more and more about. Families with a young or an adult child with autism enter into a world full of terms and treatments that can be helpful, yet baffling, and unfortunately, sometimes even unhelpful and unethical.

Occupational therapists have a responsibility to understand what autism is and what it is not. We have a responsibility to broaden our understanding from the neurodiagnostic term to its application in the realm of occupation. That is, expanding the meaning of autism to include the effect of the diagnosis on one's roles, life goals, support system, and community membership.

This book provides the occupational therapist, as well as other interested professionals and family members, an opportunity to begin to gain this understanding. Ms. Miller-Kuhaneck has edited an invaluable resource full of perspectives that will foster a richer understanding of autism. The chapters' authors are experts in the field; with extensive combined clinical experience and the ability to apply research findings to clinical practice. This book will help the field of occupational therapy examine and expand its role in the treatment of individuals with autism spectrum disorders. The book looks not only at the lifeskills and sensory integration aspects of the development of children with autism, but provides a framework for understanding the role of occupational therapists in intervention across the spectrum. The volume includes a solid discussion on the social, communicative, and play skills for individuals with autism.

A variety of interventions are discussed; some are from the empirical perspective. Other interventions stem from long and varied clinical experiences. This book is an important contribution to the occupational therapy literature on autism.

Tracy Murnan Stackhouse, MA, OTR
Assistant Professor, Department of Rehabilitation
Medical Investigation of Neurodevelopmental
Disorders Institute
University of California Davis Medical Center

Preface

On an ongoing basis, occupational therapists are faced with a multitude of challenges as they go about their business of assisting people in achieving the skills for living. No challenge may be greater than keeping abreast of the most current information on the wide range of subjects that impact our practice. This book was born out of my own personal search for information as my caseload of children diagnosed with autism expanded greatly during the last 10 years. I found significant amounts of important, but fragmented literature from many related fields, with very little specific to the practice of occupational therapy. I also found documentation of a significant increase in the number of children being diagnosed with a pervasive developmental disorder (PDD) and wondered why there was an increase. My own questions, and the knowledge that it has become common for many occupational therapy practitioners to provide services to children with a PDD and their families, led me to this project. Until recently, information to guide occupational therapy practice for children with a PDD has been lacking. Therapists new to treating children with a PDD might therefore feel overwhelmed and unprepared when faced with this challenge. Clearly a comprehensive resource for occupational therapists was needed. It is my hope that this book will provide the knowledge necessary for occupational therapy practitioners to feel comfortable working with children with a PDD and their families. Families have become savvy in the age of the Internet, and are extremely knowledgeable regarding the multitude of options available to them. They may therefore expect their therapists to be well versed in these alternative options as well. Therefore, a second purpose of this book was to provide a starting place, an overview, of some of the many intervention strategies that are purported to benefit children with autism.

The DSM IV currently places five disorders within the spectrum of the Pervasive Developmental Disorders. Autism is only one of these, however it is most common to see research reported specifically for subjects with autism. Therefore, many of the chapters focus primarily on autism rather than the entire spectrum. The reader should consider that much of the information presented throughout this work may be relevant to the other disorders as well.

The text was created through the collaborative efforts of many experts in the field. It is organized in two sections: Chapters 1 through 3 present the basic knowledge one should be familiar with regarding this diagnostic category. Information on diagnostic criteria, the typical range of behaviors and symptoms seen, and the impact of having a child with this diagnosis on family functioning are included. Chapters 4 through 14 expand on this first section by becoming more specific to assessment and intervention. Tools and techniques for assessment are discussed in chapter 4 and the importance of a comprehensive team approach due to the pervasive nature of these disorders is stressed in the chapter on transdisciplinary intervention. The remaining chapters present specific intervention strategies and commonly offered alternatives. Chapter 14 summarizes what we currently know about this diagnosis and treatment effectiveness through research to date.

The appropriate audience for this book may be students, entry-level practitioners, or advanced practitioners new to this area of practice. Practitioners may have many questions regarding their intervention with this population. The compilation of material included within this text will provide many answers; however, it will not provide all of the answers. This text is intended to be merely a starting place for therapists interested in working with children with a PDD. The rapid pace of new research makes it impossible to become complacent with our level of knowledge. As our families will, we must also continually keep abreast of new developments in the field and frequently search for the latest information available. Therefore, included in many of the chapters are extensive reference lists as well as resources and contact information for a variety of organizations that also supply information specific to autism. I hope these will stimulate practitioners to continue their own search for answers that will make a difference for the children and families that they serve.

Heather Miller-Kuhaneck, MS, OTR/L, BCP

Acknowledgments

A work of this size requires the efforts of a multitude of people, many of them potentially unrecognized. Therefore, I would like to express my gratitude to many wonderful therapists and colleagues who provided encouragement, assistance, suggestions and thoughtful chapter reviews. In addition, the staff and leaders at AOTA have, from the beginning, been of the utmost importance to this undertaking. To Maureen Muncaster, Jane Case-Smith, Suzanne Seitz, Krishni Patrick, Terri Heaphy, Julie Lake, Karen Feltham, Kristin Miller, Grace Baranek, Diana Henry, and Yvonne Swinth, a sincere thank you for all of your help.

Of course the book could not have come into being without the contributions of all of the chapter authors whose knowledge, clinical expertise, and insight afforded significant offerings to this labor of love. I am forever indebted to them for their patience and willingness to continually improve on their work through revision after revision. Lastly, I thank my husband, Shayne for his acceptance and understanding during all of the time that I spent working on this project.

About the Authors

Lisa R. Audet, PhD, CCC-SLP, is the co-creator and co-director of Integrations Treatment Center and Integrative Alternatives in Ohio.

Karin Berglund Bonfils, OTR, is the owner of a private practice called Neuro-Rehab: The Affolter Concept Occupational Therapy for Children and Adults in Grass Valley, California.

Jane Case-Smith, EdD, OTR/L, FAOTA, BCP is the Associate Professor of the Occupational Therapy Division in the School of the Allied Medical Professions at The Ohio State University.

Debra Galvin, PhD, OTR/L, is a pediatric occupational therapist, educator, and child psychologist. Her private practice in Kentucky specializes in serving young children and their families.

Tara J. Glennon, MS, OTR/L, BCP, is Assistant Professor of Occupational Therapy at Quinnipiac University, Connecticut, and owner of several pediatric therapy clinics in Connecticut providing services to children in local school districts, outpatient offices, and the home.

Sandra Greene, MA, OTR, has a private practice in Santa Monica, California.

Barbaralyn Harden, MS, CCC-SP, is currently both a speech-language pathologist and assistive technology specialist for a Washington State school district as well as a private consultant for assistive technology.

Lois Hickman, MS, OTR, FAOTA, is the Director of Jen-Lo Therapy Farm in Longmont, Colorado.

Mary Alhage Kientz, MS, OTR/L, is an occupational therapist at the St. John of God Community Services in Westville Grove, New Jersey. She is also a New Jersey state trainer for the Building Futures Positive Behavioral Support Project.

Patricia S. Lemer, MEd, NCC, MS, BUS, is an educational diagnostician and nationally certified counselor practicing in metropolitan Washington, DC. She is a co-founder and the Executive Director of Developmental Delay Resources.

Zoe Mailloux, MA, OTR, FAOTA, is the Director of Administration at the Pediatric Therapy Network in Torrance, California.

Heather Miller-Kuhaneck, MS, OTR/L, BCP, works as a clinical supervisor at The Connecticut Center for Pediatric Therapy in Wallingford, Connecticut.

Meira L. Orentlicher, MA, OTR/L, is an Assistant Professor in the Occupational Therapy Program at Touro College in New York, New York.

Lynette Scotese-Wojtila, OTR/L, is a Clinical Specialist and the Co-Director at Integrations Treatment Center and Integrative Alternatives in Warrensville Heights, Ohio.

Susanne Smith Roley, MS, OTR, is on staff at the University of Southern California as the project director for the Comprehensive Program in Sensory Integration. She is in private practice in Orange County and is Coordinator of Education and Research at Pediatric Therapy Network.

Anne Trecker, MS, OTR/L, is the Director of Public Relations at the Occupational Therapy Associates in Watertown, Massachusetts.

Renee Watling, MS, OTR/L, is a graduate student who works in the Division of Occupational Therapy in the Department of Rehabilitation Medicine in the University of Washington in Seattle, Washington.

CHAPTER 1

An Introduction to Autism and the Pervasive Developmental Disorders

Heather Miller-Kuhaneck, MS, OTR/L, BCP, and
Tara J. Glennon, MS, OTR/L, BCP

Dr. Leo Kanner first introduced the term autism in 1943, initiating the psychological profession's interest in this condition. As a labeled condition, autism is a relatively recent addition to the disorders described by the psychological profession. However, knowledge of the disorder has grown steadily during the 50 years it has been studied. Much has been learned about diagnosis, intervention, and outcomes, although a definitive etiology of autism remains elusive. As scientists have developed new methods for studying the brain, the neurological basis of the disorder has been well established, refuting early psychological theories of causality. Consequently, a comprehensive understanding of the neurobiological and neurophysiological foundations of the disorder is essential to identify both etiology and options for intervention. Fortunately, the idea that individuals with autism share certain common neuropathological features continues to motivate researchers. Determining the etiology of autism and the Pervasive Developmental Disorders (PDDs) may lead to additional intervention possibilities or perhaps even prevention. Considering the reports of a growing number of children being diagnosed with autism and the extensive intervention requirements for these children, improved treatment and prevention strategies will benefit not only individual children and families but also society as a whole.

This chapter will review historical trends in diagnosis and theories of etiology since the introduction of the term *autism*; describe basic characteristics of the disorder that are used for diagnosis; and document neurobiological findings related to symptomatology, discussing findings related to neuroanatomy, neurophysiology, and neurochemistry as reported by expert researchers in the field. In addition, the chapter will discuss factors that researchers have noted as potential contributors to neurological alterations.

Historical Perspectives

Henry Maudsley, the first psychiatrist to pay specific attention to very young children with severe difficulties in developmental processes, considered these issues to be psychoses, espousing the prevailing thought of the time (Kaplan & Sadock, 1998). When Dr. Leo Kanner (1943) published a paper titled "Autistic Disturbances of Affective Contact," which described and named the Autistic Disorder, the clinical features of the disorder were considered to be also

1

psychological in origin. Kanner was then a psychiatrist at Johns Hopkins working with a group of 11 patients who demonstrated remarkable similarities in their symptoms. The identified behaviors included extreme aloneness, failure to assume anticipatory postures, delayed or deviant language, excellent rote memory, and a limited range of spontaneous activities. This paper generated great interest and established the hallmarks of the disorder.

Originally, the disorder was described as a child's lack of responsiveness to environmental input and inability to relate to people and situations. Kanner suggested that the syndrome had been previously misclassified as mental retardation or schizophrenia. In fact, before the 1970s, children with any PDD were often classified as having a type of childhood schizophrenia (Petty, Ornitz, Michelman, & Zimmerman, 1984). Early theories regarding the origins of autism placed fault with parenting strategies (Bettelheim, 1967). Mothers of children with autism were labeled "refrigerator mothers" and were blamed for cold, unfeeling, relationships leading to the social withdrawal of their children. Theories such as this one led to a host of inadequate and minimally helpful interventions as well as to feelings of guilt in many parents.

Interest in the neurological basis of the disorder finally blossomed in the late 1970s with the advent of tools to measure neurological functioning. The advances in the technique and application of neuroimaging tools greatly contributed to the medical community's understanding of this disorder. Physicians, pediatricians, clinicians, and psychologists who are current with the literature understand now that autistic spectrum disorders are neurobiological disorders. Despite the wealth of information available to the medical and educational communities, however, there is still much to learn. For example, researchers continue to explore questions of etiology, while debating the prevalence of the disorder.

Prevalence

The incidence of autistic spectrum disorders has been reported to be as high as 1 in every 500 births (Ritvo et al., 1989). However, rates are more commonly reported in the range of 1 case per every 2,000 individuals (Tanguay, 2000). The DSM-IV-TR reports prevalence in the range of 2 to 20 cases per 10,000 individuals (APA, 2000). These numbers imply that autistic spectrum disorders are as common as other pediatric diagnoses including diabetes, leukemia, cystic fibrosis, and Down's syndrome (please refer to the website for Cure Autism Now. The Consensus Group Statement: www.cureautismnow.org; Cohen & Volkmar, 1997). Because the symptomatology ranges from mild to severe, documenting a true incidence of the disorder is difficult. Researchers Sugiyama, Takei, and Abe (1992) cited 1.3 cases in every 1,000 that are diagnosed with what would be classic autism in its more severe form and .7 cases per 1,000 that show autistic-like traits. Although some areas are reporting what appear to be significant increases in cases of autism, it is not yet clear whether the reports actually reflect a higher incidence or whether they reflect improved diagnosing techniques (Powell, Edwards, Edwards, Pandit, Sungum-Paliwal & Whitehouse, 2000; Hillman, Kanafani, Takahashi & Miles, 2000). In California, recent reports from the state's Department of Developmental Services show a rapid increase in the rates that autism is being diagnosed, now up to almost six new cases per day (please refer to the website for the California Department of Developmental Service: www.dds.ca.gov). The U.S. Department of Education's annual reports to Congress on its progress to carry out the Individuals with Disabilities Education Act (IDEA) of 1990 [PL 101–476, 20 U.S.C., Ch 33] and its 1991 amendments [PL 102–119, 20 U.S.C. § 1400] show significant increases in the number of children being served with the label "autism." Between the 16th and the 20th annual report to

Congress (1992–1997), the number of children across the country who are labeled with autism and who are being served under IDEA has increased by 178.86%. Nationwide, in a one-year period (1997–1998), the 21st annual report to Congress reported a 26% increase in the number of children with autism who are attending school. Certain individual states are reporting increases ranging from 15% to more than 3,000% during the period from 1992 to 1997, and many states are reporting increases of 20–30% in the year between 1997–98 and 1998–99. Between 1991 and 1996 in the United Kingdom, increases of 18% per year of classic autism and of 55% per year of other autistism spectrum disorders have been reported in preschool populations (Powell, et al., 2000). Many parent groups across the country are using the word *epidemic* to describe the alarming rise in the number of children being diagnosed within the autistic spectrum. Further data gathering certainly needs to be done in this area to determine the true prevalence of the disorder.

Diagnosis

Dating from 1869, psychology professionals within the United States have been able to refer to classification systems to make accurate diagnoses. In 1952, the American Psychiatric Association's Committee on Nomenclature and Statistics published the first formalized and universal nomenclature, the first edition of the *Diagnostic and Statistical Manual of Mental Disorders*, referred to as *DSM* (Kaplan and Sadock, 1998). Subsequent editions were published as criteria were revised: *DSM-II* (1968); *DSM-III* (1980); a revision, *DSM-III-R*, (1987); *DSM-IV* (1994) and the current manual of text revisions *DSM-IV-TR* (2000).

The purpose of the manual's system of classification extends beyond distinguishing one diagnosis from another. First, specific diagnostic criteria, which must be present, are provided to increase the reliability of a clinician's process of diagnosis. Second, though not specific to the causes of a disorder, descriptions of the disorder's clinical features provide information that fosters the exploration of the causes. Additionally, the description of clinical features assists with the development of the most effective treatments.

Historically, the changes within the *DSM* manual in the area of autism provide us with a window to examine what was current thought and knowledge in each of those areas. We can then reasonably attempt to understand the revisions throughout each edition. These changes have been critical to our fully appreciating the diagnosis and the possible outcomes of intervention for the individual with a condition within the autistic spectrum. Significant changes in our knowledge base have occurred within the last 10–15 years. Therefore, a practitioner may find specific help by comparing diagnostic criteria between various recent editions of the *DSM*. The time period between 1987 and 1994 does not seem that substantial; however, the extent of the manual's changes between *DSM-III-R* and *DSM-IV* are significant. The current version, the *DSM-IV-TR* has not been significantly changed in the section of Pervasive Developmental Disorders (APA, 2000).

DSM-III-R (APA, 1987) made great strides in identifying many possible characteristics within the spectrum of autism and PDD. Four main categories were identified:

1. qualitative impairment in reciprocal social interactions,
2. qualitative impairment in verbal and nonverbal communications and imaginative play,
3. a markedly restricted repertoire of activities and interests, and
4. onset during infancy or childhood, with the clinician encouraged to note the age of onset if after 36 months (1987).

Within these four categories, a child must demonstrate 8 out of the 16 identified items. In the first category, a child must meet at least two of the five descriptors; in the second, at least one of the six items; and in the third, at least one of the five descriptors.

DSM-IV (APA, 1994) provided subtle revisions in the category headings for autism and PDD and more specificity within the related category items. Additionally, only six of the total items need to be demonstrated, with at least the same number in each of the first three categories. With respect to the age of onset, *DSM-IV* and *DSM-IV-TR* criteria specifies onset prior to the age of 3. An additional criterion was added to aid in differentiating between Rett's Disorder or Childhood Disintegrative Disorder.

One of the primary drawbacks of *DSM-III-R* (APA, 1987) criteria was that only two subtypes of the autism and PDD spectrum were available to the diagnostician: Autistic Disorder or Pervasive Developmental Disorder, Not Otherwise Specified (PDD-NOS). Autistic Disorder, also known as infantile autism and Kanner's Syndrome, met all of the combinations of criteria specified. However, this disorder simply appeared to be the more severe end of the autistic spectrum. PDD-NOS was described as a condition that met the general description of autism but that did not include the specific number or combination of criteria required for an Autistic Disorder diagnosis.

New Diagnostic Options Within the DSM-IV

Many would agree that another important clarification within the *DSM-IV* (APA, 1994) criteria included the identification of five diagnostic options under the heading of Pervasive Developmental Disorder (Sponheim, 1996). These include Autistic Disorder, Rett's Disorder, Childhood Disintegrative Disorder, Asperger's Disorder, and PDD-NOS. The Autistic Disorder modifications between the revised third edition and the fourth edition of the *DSM* were identified previously. Changes within the use of the PDD-NOS diagnosis also occurred between *DSM-III-R* and *DSM-IV*. Rather than group all of the other combinations of autistic-like features into the PDD-NOS category, as was done in *DSM-III-R*, the *DSM-IV* edition identified specifications. The PDD-NOS diagnosis requires (a) severe and pervasive impairment within the stated categories but not at the level of the specific combinations that are required for autism, (b) a late onset of symptomatology, or (c) both. Generally, these children with a PDD-NOS condition have better language skills and more self-awareness (Kaplan and Sadock, 1998) as well as a more positive prognosis than do children with autistic disorder.

Rett's Disorder, identified by Andrea Rett in 1965, was first identified in 22 girls who initially appeared to have normal development. However, devastating developmental deterioration follows this initial period of at least 6 months of normal development (Bird & Gascon, 1988). The differential diagnostic criteria for Rett's that are identified in *DSM-IV* (1994) and *DSM-IV-TR* (2000) also include a deceleration of head growth up to age 4, loss of previously acquired purposeful hand skills, and poorly coordinated gait or trunk movements. In addition, children with Rett's Disorder often demonstrate respiratory irregularities, and seizures usually appear early on. There are unusual writhing hand movements associated with this diagnosis. With reference to prognosis, Rett's Disorder is progressive, and cognitive level does not typically surpass that of a 1-year-old.

Childhood Disintegrative Disorder (CDD) is characterized by marked developmental regression in several areas of functioning after at least 2 years of apparently normal development (Kaplan and Sadock, 1998). The diagnosis of CDD, based on features that match the specified age of onset and clinical course, requires regression in bowel and bladder control, language, and social skills as well as regression in play skills, motor skills, or both. Although both Rett's and CDD demonstrate regression or deterioration, CDD occurs much later and children with CDD do not demonstrate the stereotypical hand characteristics common to Rett's. Comparing CDD to Autistic Disorder, the differences in language skills are marked. Before the onset of CDD, children are often able to produce full sentences, and after the deterioration, they typically can produce no language. However, neurobiologically, there may be little difference between CDD and autism (Mouridsen, Rich, & Isager 2000).

Another significant change in *DSM-IV* and *DSM-IV-TR* was the inclusion of Asperger's Disorder as a separate entry. Hans Asperger first described the disorder in 1944, one year after Kanner identified infantile autism. Although previously considered a variant form of autism, Asperger's Disorder is now considered to be a related but separate disorder. Restricted patterns of behavior, interests, and activities as well as impaired social functioning are markers. However, a criterion specifies no clinically significant delay in language, cognitive development, self-help skills, or adaptive behavior.

The last diagnostic point to be addressed regards severity. A wide range of disabilities falls under the diagnosis of PDD, and these are based on the combination of symptoms and the severity of each symptom. For example, one child may be intellectually average, or even superior, but may experience several communicative and interactional limitations. Another child may function in the mentally deficient range with no ability to participate in self-care activities. With so many possible combinations of characteristics, researchers and clinicians have speculated that different etiologies may also exist.

Etiology and Neurological Basis of Symptomatology

Discovering the etiology of autism is important because it may lead to new avenues for prevention or to more effective interventions. The effort to determine the neurological basis of the disorder has been supported by developments in neuroimaging and neurochemical analysis. Techniques such as magnetic resonance imaging (MRI), computerized tomography (CT), and positron-emission tomography (PET) scanning have revolutionized our knowledge of the brain in general and of autism in particular. See Table 1.1 for information on neuroimaging techniques. Early studies regarding neurological functioning in autism focused on the limbic system, medial temporal lobe, thalamus, basal ganglia, and vestibular system (Boucher & Warrington, 1976; Coleman, 1979; Darby, 1976; Damasio & Maurer, 1978; DeLong, 1978; Maurer & Damasio, 1982; Ornitz & Ritvo, 1986; and Vilensky, Damasio, & Maurer, 1981). The multitudes of findings that have been reported by a variety of researchers using a variety of measurement methods have produced some confusion and conflicting information. These researchers have not yet reached consensus regarding etiology but have at least confirmed the widespread alterations in neurological functioning in individuals with autism. In an attempt to organize the recent findings, this chapter will divide neurological functioning into anatomy, physiology, and chemistry. However, these areas are completely interrelated in the working brain and cannot truly be thought of as functionally separate.

Neuroanatomy

Bauman and Kemper (1985) reported that the brains of individuals with autism are generally bigger and heavier than most brains of typical subjects. Although they identified that children with autism have increased brain weights of approximately 100 grams; they identified decreased brain weight in adults with autism (Kemper & Bauman, 1998). Piven et al. (1995) supported significantly greater total brain volume after controlling for height, sex, and performance IQ. In a follow-up study, Piven, Amdt, Bailey, and Andreasen (1996) found significant increases in total brain volume in autistic males but not in autistic females. Several other authors (Bailey et al., 1998; Fidler, Bailey, & Smalley, 2000; Lainhart et al., 1997) also sup-

Table 1.1
Neuroimaging Techniques

Technique	Description	Purpose
X-ray Computerized Tomography (CT)	Produces a single-plan X-ray of the brain tissue	Measures structural parameters such as bone and brain tissue; distinguishes between gray and white matter
Magnetic Resonance Imaging (MRI)	Based on the CT scan and produces 3-plane images and offers higher contrast and resolution	Can distinguish different body tissues, can explore anatomical structures, and also can be used to examine the function of structures
Electroencephalogram (EEG)	Records electrical activity of the neurons in the cortical areas under the electrodes	Examines arousal levels, wakefulness and sleep, epilepsy, and coma
Event Related Potential (ERP)	Examines specific components of the EEG recordings related to a specific sensory stimulus in time	Used to examine sensory responsivity
Regional Cerebral Blood Flow (RCBF) Studies	A measure of blood flow in the brain and specific brain tissues conducted through observation of a radioisotope tracer in the blood; measures energy metabolism within anatomical structures	Used to detect changes in blood flow that can indicate changes in brain activity
Positron Emission Tomography (PET)	Combines CT and radioisotope imaging	Provides images of brain activity reflecting the distribution in tissue of a radioactive isotope; maps glucose use in brain tissue, and provides images of neurotransmitter density

Note. The information in this table is synthesized from several useful references:
Martin, J. H. (1991) "The Collective Electrical Behavior of Cortical Neurons: The Electroencephalogram and the Mechanisms of Epilepsy" (pp. 776–791) *Principles of Neural Science* (3rd ed.) Norwalk, CT: Appleton & Lange.
Martin, J. H., Brust, J. C., Hilal, S., Kendel, E. R., Schwartz, J. H., and Jessell, T. M. (1991) (pp. 309–324) *Principles of Neural Science* (3rd ed.) Norwalk, CT: Appleton & Lange.
Pawlik, G., Heiss, W. D., in Bigler, E. D., Yeo, R. A. and Turkeimer, E. (Eds). (1989) "Positron Emission Tomography and Neuropsychological Function" (pp. 65–138) *Neuropsychological Function and Brain Imaging* New York: Plenum.

port that the brains of individuals with autism are often larger than normal, and between 20–24% of individuals with autism have macrocephaly. Macrocephaly is also more common in first degree relatives of individuals with autism (Fidler, Bailey, & Smalley, 2000). However, other researchers have found macrocephaly to be rare (Courchesne, Muller, & Saitoh, 1999).

Cortex

Dawson (1987, 1988) and Dawson et al. (1986) explain that although the two hemispheres of the brain begin as functionally and anatomically asymmetric, the propensity for certain functions to be lateralized to the right or left is probably present at birth. While current views of brain development hold that increasing specialization occurs as an individual acquires functional capacities, this kind of brain development alone cannot account for an autistic individual's deviant pattern of lateralization. In fact, researchers have noted reversed asymmetry and abnormal lateralization of the cortical hemispheres (Lotspeich & Ciaranello, 1993). Researchers have also found evidence that the pattern of hemispheric activity is not only deviant in direction but also deviant in magnitude (Dawson, Finley, Phillips, & Galpert, 1986). Note, however, that those researchers who have developed hypotheses as to the cause of the lateralization concerns indicate that not all autistic individuals exhibit abnormal patterns of lateralization (Dawson 1987, 1988; Dawson et al., 1986). Dawson et al. (1986) and Dawson (1987, 1988) suggest that the specific issue is abnormal activation of both hemispheres rather than an actual difficulty with specialization of one hemisphere.

The ventricles of the brain have also been an area of investigation in individuals with autism. Enlargement of the lateral ventricles *has been found inconsistently.* Damasio (1984) theorized that, in autism, the enlargement of the lateral ventricles was largely related to groupings of study subjects that included not only individuals with autism but also individuals with brain damage. Since this theory was presented and supported by CT investigations (Creasey et al., 1986; Prior, Tress, Hoffman, & Boldt, 1984), a screening procedure has been used to exclude individuals with brain damage from studies. A few studies have investigated the enlargement of the 3rd and 4th ventricles in individuals with autism (Campbell et al., 1982; Hoshino et al., 1984, Piven et al., 1992). In a study by Campbell et al. (1982), enlargement of the 3rd ventricle was associated with moderate enlargement of the lateral ventricles. Enlargement of both the 3rd and 4th ventricles was found by Gaffney et al. (1987). Jacobson, LeCouteur, Howlin, and Rutter (1988) also observed an increase in size of the 3rd ventricle. Hoshino et al. (1984), however, found no

statistically significant difference in ventrical size with their subject group as a whole but did see an increase in ventricle size within the teenage subgroup. When assessing the size of the 4th ventricle, Minshew and Dombrowski (1994) were unable to determine whether the enlargement represented a localized change, suggesting abnormalities restricted to adjacent brain structures, or whether it was associated with generalized enlargement.

There have been multiple findings of irregularities in various lobes of the brain and in the posterior corpus callosum, to which parietal lobe fibers are known to project (Egaas, et al. 1995, Piven et al., 1997; Hardan, Minshew & Kesharan, 2000). However, recent studies of the corpus callosum demonstrated size reductions in anterior areas as well, consistent with frontal lobe dysfunction (Hardan, Minshew, & Keshavan, 2000). Recent research has suggested a relationship between increased frontal lobe volume and cerebellar abnormalities (Carper & Courchesne, 2000), and examined localized dysfunction in the temporal lobes of individuals with autism (Zibovicius, et al., 2000). Various abnormalities have been found in the frontal regions of the brain by some (Bauman & Kemper 1985; Gaffney, Kuperman, Tsai, and Minchin (1989). Jacobson et al. (1988) however, found no abnormalities in the frontal lobes, and Piven et al. (1996) did not find a regional pattern of enlargement in the frontal lobes of subjects with autism. Zilbovicius and Garreau (1995) suggested that autism may be characterized by a delay in frontal maturation, as they found hypoperfusion in the frontal region of the brains of their subjects. In children with autism, hypoperfusion occurred at age 3–4 years whereas it occurs at a younger age in children who develop normally.

Limbic System

In individuals with autism, cells in the limbic system, where emotions are processed, are a third smaller than normal and are found in excessive numbers (Bauman & Kemper, 1985). These small neurons with increased cell density were found in the hippocampus, amygdala, mammillary bodies, anterior cingulate cortex, and medial septal nuclei (Bauman & Kemper, 1985, 1988, 1994). These cells are also noted to be more immature, with stunted dendrite formations and connections (Bauman & Kemper, 1994). In a recent MRI study comparing 15 high-functioning individuals with autism to 15 control subjects, the volume of gray matter in the area around the amygdala was significantly different in the subjects with autism (Abell et al., 1999). Decreased tissue volume in both the amygdala and the hippocampus were found recently by some researchers (Aylward et al., 1999) while others found enlarged amygdalas in subjects with high functioning autism (Howard et al., 2000).

Cerebellum

Documented by researchers in multiple cases and in multiple labs, brains of individuals with autism have been found to have abnormalities within the cerebellum, a structure that helps in making predictions about what will happen next in terms of movements, thoughts, and emotions. Deficiencies have been found in the numbers of Purkinje cells and granule cells, neuron shrinkage has been found in the inferior olive, and the vermal lobes VI and VII have been found to be smaller as well (Bauman & Kemper, 1985, 1986, 1994; Courchesne, Yeung-Courchesne, Press, Hesselink, & Jennigan, 1988; Kemper & Bauman, 1993; Murakami, Courchesne, Press, Yeung-Courchesne, & Hesselink, 1989; Ritvo et al., 1986; Rodier, Ingram, Tisdale, Nelson, & Romano, 1996). The number of Purkinje cells in brains of individuals with autism are reportedly 30–50% fewer than in typical subjects (Bauman & Kemper, 1985; Rapin & Katzman, 1998). A region that is repeatedly identified as abnormal in imaging studies is the vermis, lobules VI and VII (Courchesne et al., 1988; Gaffney et al., 1987; Hashimoto et al., 1995). However, MRI studies by Haas et al. (1996) have found both hypoplasia and hyperplasia in the areas of the vermal lobes VI and VII in individuals with autism. These two distinctly different findings are both significantly different from those of control subjects. More recently, research has demonstrated a relationship between the magnitude of cerebellar hypoplsia of vermal lobules VI–VII and limited play exploration in children with autism (Pierce & Courchesne, 2001).

In subjects with Fragile X Syndrome, a genetic disorder with symptomatology that is similar to autism, the posterior cerebellar vermis is also reduced in size (Reiss, Freund, Tseng, & Joshi, 1991). Those with Rett's Disorder may also have a decreased number of Purkinje cells (Percey, 1993). Cerebellar dysfunction, particularly cerebellar vermal hypoplasia, has been related to the presence of a developmental disability (Shevell & Majnemer, 1996). Not all researchers agree that there are consistent cerebellar abnormalities in the brains of individuals with autism however (Minshew & Dombrowski, 1994).

Brain Stem

Bauman and Kemper (1985) found brain-stem abnormalities, such as decreased cell size, in their autopsy studies of individuals with autism. Gaffney, Kuperman, Tsai, and Minchin (1988) found, through MRI, that the overall brain-stem area, particularly the pons, was smaller in the autistic subjects examined. On MRI scans, the brain stems of children with autism have been noted to be smaller than those of control subjects (Hashimoto et al., 1992). Although reports of size reductions in the brain stem have been inconsistent (Gaffney et al., 1988; Hsu, Yeung-Courchesne, Courchesne, & Press, 1991), a larger study that was documented by Hashimoto et al. (1995) suggests that the midbrain, pons, and medulla are smaller in autistic subjects than in control subjects.

Neurophysiology

Neurophysiological studies to date have focused on both cortical and subcortical areas. Cortical studies have included investigations of hemispheric lateralization, patterns in readings of metabolism and electroencephalograms, and event related potential studies. Subcortical researchers have examined brain stem auditory evoked responses, autonomic responses, vestibular system function, and patterns of metabolism.

Cortical Physiology

Evoked potential studies have demonstrated arousal irregularities and unusual response patterns to novel stimuli (Courchesne, 1987; Courchesne, Lincoln, Kilmar, & Galambros, 1985; Fein, Skoff, & Mirsky, 1981; Hashimoto, Tayama, & Mayao, 1986; Kemmer et al., 1995; Ornitz, 1987; and Wong & Wong, 1991). There is some evidence of diminished hemispheric lateralization in subjects with autism (Ornitz, 1987). Abnormal electroencephalogram (EEG) recordings have been found; however, no specific cite of abnormality has been consistently distinguished (Golden, 1987; Hynd & Hooper, 1992; Lotspeich & Ciaranello, 1993; Ornitz, 1987). EEG differences have been noted in the frontal and temporal regions when children with autism were compared to control subjects, and these differences were more marked in the left than in the right hemisphere. EEG differences were also found between subgroups of children with autism (Dawson et al., 1995). Approximately 20–35% of individuals with autism present with a seizure disorder (Bailey, Phillips, & Rutter, 1996; Fisher, VanDyke, et al., 1999). Regional cerebral blood flow has also been reported to be reduced in the frontal and temporal areas in subjects with autism (Hashimoto et al., 2000) and this reduction has been related to IQ.

Subcortical Physiology

Irregular patterns of metabolism have been found in various limbic structures (Haznedar et al., 2000) as well as between cortical and subcortical structures (Horwits, Rumsey, Grady & Rappaport, 1988). Specifically, when compared with control subjects, subjects with autism have demonstrated metabolic reductions in the anterior and posterior cingulate gyri (Haznedar, et al., 2000). Increased heart rate variability and increased respiration, suggesting disregulation of autonomic nervous system (ANS) responses related to faulty mechanisms in the brain stem have been noted by some (Ornitz, 1987; Zahn, Rumsey, & VanKammer, 1987). James and Barry (1980) report an inability in people with autism to habituate to stimuli. A review of the studies on the brain stem and vestibular system of people with autism demonstrates that although brain stem auditory evoked potential studies have been inconclusive, a variety of vestibular studies have demonstrated abnormal nystagmus responses (Ornitz, 1987). Recently, brainstorm auditory evoked responses were found to be abnormal in both individuals with autism and their relatives (Maziade et al., 2000).

Neurochemistry

Neurochemical studies include neurotransmitters and neuroendocrine systems. Neurochemicals have diffuse areas of action and widespread influence. Three major neurotransmitters have been identified (serotonin, dopamine, and norepinephrine) along with a variety of smaller transmitters, enzymes, and peptides. These neurotransmitters are primarily measured by means of urine or blood specimens and may not be measured directly. Often, the actual measurement is of the chemicals' metabolites or by-products.

Many different chemicals have been studied in many different ways. Across the studies, the most consistent finding related to autism is that of alterations in serotonergic function, particularly, an increase in serotonin levels (Anderson & Hoshino, 1987; Chugani et al., 1999; Hoshino et al. 1984; Schain & Freedman, 1961; Volkmar & Anderson, 1989). However, researchers have also reported a relative decrease in serotonin levels in relation to dopamine (Cohen, Caparulo, & Shaywitz, 1978). Serotonin functions in the release of prolactin, which has been found to be reduced in individuals with autism (Hoshino et al., 1983, 1984). Other neurochemicals also may be involved in subjects with autism. Norepinephrine metabolite levels have been found to be reduced (Young, Cohen, Caparulo, Brown, & Maas, 1979), and the dopamine system may also be affected (Anderson & Hoshino, 1987).

Gingell, Parmar, and Sungum-Paliwal, (1996) provide a brief review of studies showing a variety of abnormalities in hypothalamic-pituitary-adrenal function, and they theorize that neuroendocrine dysfunction may be related to the clinical manifestation of autism. These researchers present a case report of a child with autism and multiple pituitary deficiency. They suggest that perhaps the relationship between the limbic lobe and the hypothalamic pituitary adrenal axis may be important in the development of autistic symptoms in some children. Some authors believe that dysfunction of the endogenous opiod system of the brain is a contributing factor to the pathogenesis of autism (Panksepp, 1979; Panksepp & Sahley, 1987; Sher, 1997). This hypothesis is based on research in which infant animals that have been given opiates demonstrate autistic-like symptoms, research in which the development of infants exposed to opiates in utero is abnormal, and research showing abnormal levels of endogenous opiods in the plasma and cerebral spinal fluid of individuals with autism. The opiod system interacts with multiple neurotransmitter systems, producing widespread neurological effects. Perhaps other peptides such as oxytocin and vasopressin are related to the features of autism. In animal studies, these substances have been shown to be related to the expression of species-typical social behaviors, communication, and rituals (Insel, Obrien, & Leckman, 1999). In studies of mice, oxytocin has also been shown to be related to social memory by means of smell (Ferguson et al., 2000). Oxytocin and vasopressin transmission might be altered through genetic mutations, which supports the genetic hypotheses of etiology.

Discussion of Neurological Findings

Some researchers believe that the cerebellar abnormalities and faulty mechanisms in the brain stem are related. Purkinje cell deficits in the cerebellum can lead to an overexcitation of the brain stem and thalamic systems that are spontaneously stimulated by deep cerebellar nuclei. These nuclei are normally inhibited by Purkinje cells (Courchesne, 1989; Courschesne, Lincoln, Yeung-Courchesne, Elmasian, & Grillon, 1989). Vermal lobes VI and VII of the cerebellum are connected to the fastigal nuclei and the hippocampus. The fastigal nuclei are believed to have a role in arousal, motor initiation, coordination, vestibulo-occular activity, as well as serotonin and dopamine activity (Courchesne, 1987). In situations where cell loss in the deep cerebellar nuclei does not involve damage to the dentate nucleus, the dentate may take over some of the connections of the other nuclei. Without Purkinje cell inhibition, these connections could lead to abnormal activation of the reticulo-thalamic-cortical activating system where the dentate sends excitatory signals. The dentate also has excitatory connections with the raphe nuclei, connections that are related to serotonin production and that may explain the increase in serotonin levels (Courchesne, 1987; Courchesne et al., 1988). The reduction of Purkinje cells suggests a prenatal onset, probably prior to 30 weeks gestation (Bauman & Kemper, 1994).

Vermal lobes VI and VII are areas of the cerebellum where auditory and visual senses connect, suggesting that the cerebellum is a site of sensory modulation. The cerebellum is the oldest mammalian part of the brain, perhaps involved in behaviors that differentiate mammals from lower animals, such as nursing and maternal care. In children with autism, important synchronous mother-infant interactions may be disrupted by cerebellum irregularities, and this disruption may lead to social deficits (Maurer, undated). The social deficits commonly seen in autism may also be related to limbic system abnormalities. Animal studies have supported the connections between limbic system functioning and social behavior. A disorder similar to autism has been created in primates that have had medial temporal lobe structures removed (Bachevalier, 1996). Limbic system abnormalities may be common to all disorders on the spectrum of autism and the PDDs, with expression depending on the severity and location of abnormality (Bauman, 1996).

Another theory states that autism is related to familial affective psychopathology and is a severe affective disorder (DeLong, 1999). This theory is based on the frequency of autism in families that have histories of affective disorders such as depression, bipolar disorder, and obsessive-compulsive disorder as well as on the results of studies suggesting that people with autism have differences in serotonin levels. Serotonin is important in the developing brain because it modulates the development of cortical afferent fibers, and DeLong believes that a low serotonin state that is localized to the left hemisphere could exist in people with autism. Serotonergic reuptake inhibitors do tend to improve autistic symptomatology. DeLong offers much research in support for his theory, and other authors have also reviewed research regarding the association between individuals with autism and familial affective disorders (Rutter, Bailey, Simonoff, & Pickles, 1997).

Summary of Neurological Findings

It is well documented that multiple neurological abnormalities are found in the brains of individuals with autism. Although these alterations potentially explain many of the symptoms of the disorder, they do little to help us understand the actual cause of autism. What leads to the neurological abnormalities is currently unknown. Perhaps the neurological changes are related to genetic factors, or perhaps they are caused by adverse pre- or perinatal events such as exposure to infectious or other toxic agents. Further research is needed to enhance our understanding. However, many scientists are beginning to believe that the etiology of autism is a complex interaction between genetics and environmental factors (London, 2000; Trottier, Srivastava, & Walker, 1999).

Factors Related to Etiology

The neurological differences that lead to the symptoms present in autism may also be common to other disorders and may be caused by a variety of factors. Autism has been reported to co-occur in children with fetal alcohol syndrome (Aronson, Hagberg, & Gillberg, 1997) and in children whose mothers took medications that could damage a fetus (Williams & Hersch, 1997). Autism has also been associated with genetic disorders such as congenital rubella (Chess, Korn, & Fernandez, 1971) and Fragile X. These associations have prompted researchers to study genetic and environmental possibilities for the etiology of autism.

Genetics

Studies have demonstrated a genetic component to the etiology of autism and Asperger's Disorder (Folstein & Piven, 1991; Lamb, Moore, Bailey, & Monaco, 2000; Rutter, 2000; Turner, Barnby, & Bailey, 2000; Volkmar, Klin, & Pauls, 1998). A number of chromosomal alterations have been found in individuals with autism, although these alterations have not typically clustered on any one chromosome (Gillberg & Coleman, 1992). However, a linkage between autism and chromosomes 7 and 15 has been recently suggested, (Bass et al., 2000; Maddox et al., 1999; Fisher, Vargha-Khadem, Watkins, Monaco, & Pembrey, 1999; International Molecular Genetic Study of Autism Consortium, 1998; Ashley-Koch et al., 1999; Schroer et al., 1998). In general, family and twin studies of individuals with autism support a genetic link. Autism does aggregate in families, affecting 2–6% of the siblings of subjects with the condition (Lotspeich & Ciaranello, 1993). Twin studies in the United States and other countries have demonstrated greater concordance for autism in identical versus fraternal twins (Bailey et al., 1995; Cook et al.,1998; Folstein & Rutter, 1977; Ritvo et al., 1985b; Steffenburg, Gillberg, & Holmgren, 1986). These studies suggest that, for identical twins, concordance is high—more than 90% (Bailey et al., 1995; Rutter et al., 1997). In contrast, for fraternal twins, concordance is less than 10%.

A pattern of inheritance has also been demonstrated. In some families, autism appears to be a recessively inherited disorder, but in other families, it appears dominant. Inheritance appears to be paternal rather than X linked (Ritvo et al., 1985; Ritvo, Brothers, Freeman, & Pingree, 1988). However, the preponderance of males with the disorder, suggesting an X-linked, dominant condition, needs to be studied further (Skuse, 2000). Paternal inheritance may be especially strong in the Asperger's subtype of PDD (Gillberg & Coleman, 1992). Research to date, however, has not conclusively demonstrated a primary genetic etiology for autism.

For a variety of reasons, many researchers look to environmental causes rather than to genetics. First, the studies on twins do not show 100% concordance. Second, parents commonly report a typical developmental course for their infant that is followed by regression when their children are toddlers (Davidovitch, Glick, Holtzman, Tirosh & Safir, 2000; Rogers & Di-Lalla, 1990; Tuchman & Rapin, 1997). This regressive pattern has been found by some researchers as well (Maestro, Casella, Milone, Muration & Palacio-Espasa, 1999). Numerous areas of this country and other countries are reporting incredible increases in prevalence and some parents, clinicians, and professionals in the field of autism are calling the increase an epidemic. Epidemics cannot typically be caused by genetics. All these reasons suggest that an environmental component may be part of the etiology of autism (London, 2000).

Environmental

Pre- and perinatal factors such as maternal history, abnormal presentation in labor, low birth weight, low apgar score, and postmaturity (late birth after 40 weeks) may play a minor role in etiology (Nelson, 1991). However, some researchers believe that exposure to a toxin early in fetal development, perhaps at the time of neural tube closure, may play a role in the genesis of autism (Rodier, 1995; Rodier et al., 1996). Studies have shown that adults who were exposed in utero to thalidomide had malformations that must have occurred during fetal development at about 20–24 days when the fetus has only a brain stem. In the past, scientists believed that damage at this early age would prove fatal, but these recent findings have challenged that assumption. Rodier et al. also theorize that early assaults to development such as the damage caused by thalidomide could lead to a chain reaction of problems as a variety of brain cells and nerves develop. Although exposure to thalidomide did not cause many cases of autism, perhaps other unknown toxic substances could cause symptoms of autism if the timing were similar. Rats exposed to valproic acid, an anticonvulsant medication, have been shown to demonstrate cerebellar changes similar to those found in human subjects with autism (Ingram, Peckham, Tisdale, & Rodier, 2000).

Other potentially serious neurotoxins include the hormone disrupters such as pesticides and polychlorinated biphenyls (PCBs) (Needleman, 1995; Tilson, 1998). Many of these chemicals, such as the pesticide DDT, function like estrogen within the human body

(Colborn, 1995). Estrogen is extremely important in the proper development of the fetus. Perhaps chemicals that mimic estrogen have the potential to alter typical developmental processes.

Research links behavioral and learning disorders to chemicals that disrupt the endocrine system and thyroid hormones in particular (Colborn, Dumanoski, & Peterson Myers, 1996; Golub & Jacobson, 1995). Although these chemicals have not yet been specifically linked to autism, the thyroid hormones do help orchestrate the process of normal brain development, and, consequently, chemicals that disrupt them might be linked to the condition. Thyroid hormones stimulate the growth and proliferation of nerve cells as well as their orderly migration to appropriate areas of the brain. When thyroid levels are too low or too high, permanent damage can occur, which can lead to mental retardation or more subtle learning problems.

PCBs and dioxins alter the thyroid system in complex ways, perhaps by binding to receptors and mimicking hormonal action or by altering the number of receptors. Their effect is worrisome because these chemicals persist in the environment for years even though production of many of them has ceased in many countries. These chemicals accumulate in fatty tissue and fat-rich foods, which allows high levels of exposure for humans and wildlife (Colburn, Dumanoski, & Peterson Myers, 1996). These chemicals can also be passed on to infants in utero or through breast milk (Al-Saleh, Echeverria-Quevedo, Al-Dgaither, & Faris, 1998; Golding, 1997). Exposed infants and children have been shown to demonstrate deficits in gross- and fine-motor coordination (Gladen et al., 1988; Guilette, Meza, Aquilar, Delia Soto, & Garcia, 1998), poorer cognitive development (Patandin et al., 1999), lower IQs and poorer reading comprehension (Jacobson & Jacobson, 1996), poorer memory and poorer ability to draw a person (Guilette et al., 1998),

and greater incidences of middle ear disease (Chao, Hsu, & Guo, 1997). Studies of animals that have been exposed to these chemicals also show evidence of hyper-reactivity to unpleasant events, which researchers believe may be paralleled in children (Daly, 1992). In studies with human subjects who have been exposed to these chemicals, behavioral changes such as poor habituation and abnormal reflexes have been found (Daly, 1995).

Are children with autism overly exposed to toxins early in development? Subjects with autism have been shown to have abnormal liver detoxification profiles, which suggests an abnormal exposure to toxins. In one study, 16 of 18 children with autism showed levels of toxic chemicals that exceeded maximum adult tolerances, and the other two children also demonstrated abnormal liver detoxification (Edelson & Cantor, 1998). Although promising, the environmental toxin theory may not adequately explain the cases where regression is seen at approximately 18 months of age in children who were previously developing typically.

Regression can be explained, however, by those who believe that autism is caused from childhood vaccinations. Recent research, which has created quite a controversy, suggests that vaccinations may be involved in the etiology of autism (Wakefield, 1998). Wakefield found a relationship between the measles, mumps, rubella (MMR) vaccination, inflammatory bowel disease, and autism. Other researchers have found in one study involving 48 children with autism and 34 control subjects, that while the children had similar levels of antibodies to two specific viruses: measles and virus 6 (Singh, Lin, & Yang, 1998), the children with autism also had brain autoantibodies, and none of the control subjects had these. The strongest link was between the measles virus antibodies and anti-MBP, an antibody to myelin basic protein (MBP). MBP is a protein found in the myelin sheaths around nerve fibers. The researchers suggest that perhaps exposure to the measles virus triggers an unusual immune system response that interferes with the development of myelin (Singh, Lin, & Yang, 1998). Their theories might mesh with those who believe that the MMR vaccination triggers autism in some children. Perhaps the vaccine is the method of introduction to the measles virus. However, other researchers have not come to the same conclusions (Taylor et al., 1999) when examining the relationship between the MMR vaccine and autism.

Bernard et al. (2000) suggest that vaccinations may be providing significant exposure to mercury because most vaccines contain thimerosal, a preservative composed of 50% ethylmercury by weight. These researchers are theorizing that autism may be a form of mercury poisoning that is caused by receiving too many vaccinations as an infant and young child. Other researchers have examined seasonal and annual patterns of autistic births and suggest that a viral pandemic may be an etiological factor (Barak, Kimhi, Stein, Gutman, & Weizman, 1999; Stevens, Fein & Waterhouse, 2000; Ticher, Ring, Barak, Elizur, & Weizman, 1996).

Certain researchers believe that a bacterial infection, not a viral infection, may cause the onset of autism (Bolte, 1998). A significant number of children with autism have a history of extensive antibiotic use. Bolte suggests that the use of these medicines disrupts the intestinal bacteria levels, harming the "good" bacteria and leaving the child vulnerable to colonization by opportunistic pathogens such as *Clostridium tetani*. This pathogen can produce a neurotoxin that may disrupt the release of neurotransmitters in the brain. Some children with autism have shown improvements when treated with antimicrobials (Sandler et al., 2000). Bolte hypothesizes, therefore, that autism may be one of the sequelae of a chronic subacute tetanus infection or another neurotoxin producing bacteria.

Some researchers suggest that familial predisposition, the preponderance of males diagnosed with autism, and the concerns regarding exposure to viruses and the associated immune abnormalities point to autism as an autoimmune disorder (Comi, Zimmerman, Frye, Law, & Peeden, 1999; Gupta, 2000; Van Gent, Heijen, & Treffers, 1997). Autoimmune abnormalities such as differences in T cells, in percentages of lymphocytes, and in antibodies to myelin basic proteins have been demonstrated in subjects with autism. Autoimmune disorders are more prevalent in families that have a child or family member with autism (Comi et al., 1999).

Conclusion

The significant body of research that has been developed since the term *autism* was coined in the 1940s has demonstrated that, contrary to what was previously thought, autism is not psychological in origin but has a neurobiological basis. There is not yet consensus regarding the specific site of neurodysfunction related to autism nor is there consensus regarding autism's etiology. Current views suggest that a variety of factors interplay to create the conditions necessary for the expression of autistic symptomatology. The relationships of these factors to one another and to specific symptoms that occur are not yet established. However, as technology further develops, researchers certainly will be able to take advantage of those technological advances to produce a surge of new information. Interest in this disorder is at an all-time high, and parents as well as professionals are becoming more savvy and knowledgeable as the world becomes more connected by means of the Internet. The next few years promise to be an interesting time, and occupational therapists who are working with this population need to keep current and to be aware of both the prevailing thoughts regarding etiology and the multiple options for intervention that exist. We have come a long way from Bettleheim's "refrigerator mothers" and from general practices to institutionalize those with autism, but we still have much to learn.

References

Abell, F., Krams, M., Ashburner, J., Passingham, R., Friston, K., Frackowiak, R., Happe, F., Frith, C. & Frith, U. (1999). The neuroanatomy of autism: a voxel-based whole brain analysis of structural scans. *Neuroreport, 10* (8), 1647–1651.

Al-Saleh, I., Echeverria-Quevedo, A., Al-Dgaither, S., & Faris, R. (1998). Residue levels of organochlorinated insecticides in breast milk: A preliminary report from Al-Kharj, Saudi Arabia. *Journal of Environmental Pathology, Toxicology and Oncology, 17,* 37–50.

American Psychiatric Association. (1952). *Diagnostic and statistical manual for mental disorders* (1st ed.). Washington, DC: Author.

American Psychiatric Association. (1968). *Diagnostic and statistical manual for mental disorders* (2nd ed.). Washington, DC: Author.

American Psychiatric Association. (1980). *Diagnostic and statistical manual for mental disorders* (3rd ed.). Washington, DC: Author.

American Psychiatric Association. (1987). *Diagnostic and statistical manual for mental disorders* (3rd ed., rev.). Washington, DC: Author.

American Psychiatric Association. (1994). *Diagnostic and statistical manual for mental disorders* (4th ed.). Washington, DC: Author.

American Psychiatric Association. (2000). *Diagnositc and statistical manual for mental disorders* (4th ed., TR). Washington, DC: Author.

Anderson, G. M., & Hoshino, Y. (1987). Neurochemical studies of autism. In D. J. Cohen, A. M. Donnellan, & R. Paul (Eds.), *Handbook of autism and pervasive developmental disorders* (pp. 166–191). New York: Wiley.

Aronson, M., Hagberg, B., & Gillberg, C. (1997). Attention deficits and autistic spectrum problems in children exposed to alcohol during gestation: A follow-up study. *Developmental Medicine and Child Neurology, 39,* 583–587.

Ashley-Koch, A., Wolpert, C. M., Menold, M. M., Zaeem, L., Basu, S., Donnelly, S. L., Raven, S. A., Powell, C. M., Qumsiyeh, M. B., Aylsworth, A. S., Vance, J. M., Gilbert, J. R., Wright, H. H., Abramson, R. R., DeLong, G. R., Cuccaro, M. L., & Pericak-Vance, M. A. (1999). Genetic studies of Autistic Disorder and chromosome 7. *Genomics, 61* (3), 227–236.

Aylward, E. H., Minshew, N. J., Goldstein, G., Honeycutt, N. A., Augustine, A. M., Yates, K. O., Barta, P. E., & Pearlson, G. D. (1999). MRI volumes of amygdala and hippocampus in non-mentally retarded autistic adolescents and adults. *Neurology, 53* (9), 2145–2150.

Bachevalier, J. (1996). Brief report: Medial temporal lobe and autism: A putative animal model in primates. *Journal of Autism and Developmental Disabilities, 26* (2), 217–220.

Bailey, A., Le Couteur, A., Gottesman, I., Bolton, P., Simonoff, E., Yuzda, E., & Rutter, M. (1995). Autism as a strongly genetic disorder: Evidence from a British twin study. *Psychological Medicine, 1,* 63–77.

Bailey, A., Luthert, P., Dean, A., Harding, B., Janota, I., Montgomery, M., Rutter, M., & Lantos, P. (1998). A clinicopathological study of autism. *Brain, 121,* 889–905.

Bailey, A., Phillips, W., & Rutter, M. (1996). Autism: Towards an integration of clinical, genetic, neuropsychological, and neurobiological perspectives. *Journal of Child Psychology and Psychiatry, 37* (1), 49–126.

Barak, Y., Kimhi, R., Stein, D., Gutman, J., & Weizman, A. (1999). Autistic subjects with comorbid epilepsy: A possible association with viral infections. *Child Psychiatry and Human Development, 29,* 245–251.

Bass, M. P., Menold, M. M., Wolpert, C. M., Donnnelly, S. L., Raven, S. A., Hauser, E. R., Maddox, L. O., Vance, J. M., Abramson, R. K., Wright, H. H., Gilbert, J. R., Cuccaro, M. L., DeLong, G. R., Pericak-Vance, M. A. (2000). Genetic studies in autistic disorder and chromosome 15. *Neurogenetics 2* (4), 219–226.

Bauman, M. L. (1996). Brief report: Neuroanatomic observations of the brain in pervasive developmental disorders. *Journal of Autism and Developmental Disabilities, 26* (2), 199–203.

Bauman, M. L., & Kemper, T. L. (1985). Histoanatomic observations of the brain in early infantile autism. *Neurology, 35,* 866–874.

Bauman, M. L., & Kemper, T. L. (1986). Developmental cerebellar abnormalities: A consistent finding in early infantile autism. *Neurology, 36* (Suppl. 1), 190.

Bauman, M. L., & Kemper, T. L. (1988). Limbic and cerebellar abnormalities: Consistent findings in infantile autism. *Journal of Neuropathology and Experimental Neurology, 47,* 369.

Bauman, M. L., & Kemper, T. L. (1994). Neuroanatomic observations in autism. In M. L. Bauman and T. L. Kemper (Eds.), *The neurobiology of autism* (pp. 119–145). Baltimore: Johns Hopkins University Press.

Bernard, S., Enayati, A., Roger, H., Binstock, T., Redwood, L., & McGinnis, W. (2000). *Autism: A unique type of mercury poisoning.* Retrieved from the World Wide Web: http://www.canfoundation.org

Bettelheim, B. (1967). *The empty fortress—Infantile autism and the birth of the self.* New York: Free Press.

Bird, L., & Gascon, C. G. (1988). Rett syndrome: Review and discussion of current diagnostic criteria. *Journal of Child Neurology, 3,* 263–268.

Bolte, E. R. (1998). Autism and *Clostridium tetani. Medical Hypotheses, 51,* 133–144.

Boucher, J., & Warrington, E. K. (1976). Memory deficits in early infantile autism: Some similarities to the amnestic syndrome. *British Journal of Psychology, 67,* 73–87.

Campbell, M. S., Rosenbloom, S., Perry, R., George, A. E., Kricheff, I. I., Anderson, L., Small, A. M., & Jennings, S. J. (1982). Computerized axial tomography in young autistic children. *American Journal of Psychiatry, 139,* 510–512.

Carper, R.A. & Courchesne, E. (2000). Inverse correlation between frontal lobe and cerebellum sizes in children with autism. *Brain, 124* (Pt 4), 836–844.

Chao, W. Y., Hsu, C., & Guo, Y. (1997). Middle-ear disease in children exposed prenatally to polychlorinated biphenyls and polychlorinated dibenzofurans. *Archives of Environmental Health, 52*(4), 257–262.

Chess, S., Korn, S. J., & Fernandez, P. B. (1971). *Psychiatric disorders of children with congenital rubella.* New York: Brunner/Mazel.

Chugani, D. C., Muzik, M., Behen, M., Rothermel, R., Janisse, J. J., Lee, J., & Chugani, H. T. (1999). Developmental changes in brain serotonin synthesis capacity in autistic and nonautistic children. *Annals of Neurology, 45,* 287–295.

Cohen, D. J., Caparulo, B. K., & Shaywitz, B. A. (1978). Neurochemical and developmental models of childhood autism. In G. Sherban (Ed.), *Cognitive defects in the development of mental illness* (pp. 66–100.) New York: Brunner/Mazel.

Cohen, F., & Volkmar, F. R. (1997). *Autism and pervasive developmental disorders: A handbook.* New York: Doubleday.

Colborn, T. (1995). Pesticides—how research has succeeded and failed to translate science into policy: Endocrinological effects on wildlife. *Environmental Health Perspectives, 103,* 81–86.

Colborn, T., Dumanoski, D., & Peterson Myers, J. (1996). *Our stolen future.* New York: Penguin.

Coleman, M. (1979). Studies of the autistic syndromes. In R. Katzman (Ed.), *Congenital and acquired cognitive disorders* (pp. 265–303). New York: Raven.

Comi, A., Zimmerman, A., Frye, V., Law, P., & Peeden, J. (1999). Familial clustering of autoimmune disorders and evaluation of medical risk factors in autism. *Journal of Child Neurology, 14,* 388–394.

Cook, E. H., Yeung- Courchesne, R., Cox, N. J., Lord, C., Gonen, D., Guter, S. J., Lincoln, A., Nix, K., Haas, R., Leventhal, B. L., & Courchesne, E. (1998). Linkage-disequilibrium mapping of autistic disorder, with 15q 11–13 markers. *American Journal of Human Genetics, 62*(5), 1077–1083.

Courchesne, E. (1987). A neurophysiological view of autism. In E. Schopter & G. B. Mesibov (Eds.), *Neurobiological issues in autism* (pp. 285–324.) New York: Plenum.

Courchesne, E. (1989). Neuroanatomical systems involved in infantile autism: The implications of cerebellar abnormalities. In G. Dawson (Ed.), *Autism: Nature, diagnoses & treatment* (pp. 119–143). New York: Guilford Press.

Courchesne, E., Lincoln, L. J., Kilmar, B. A., & Galambros, R. (1985). Event related potential correlates of the processing of novel visual stimuli and auditory information in autism. *Journal of Autism and Developmental Disorders, 15,* 55–76.

Courchesne, E., Lincoln, L. J., Yeung-Courchesne, R., Elmasian, R., & Grillon, C. (1989). Pathophysiologic findings in non-retarded autism and receptive developmental language disorder. *Journal of Autism and Developmental Disorders, 19,* 1–17.

Courchesne, E., Muller, R. A., & Saitoh, O. (1999). Brain weight in autism: Normal in the majority of cases, megalenciphalic in rare cases. *Neurology, 52*(5), 1057–1059.

Courchesne, E., Yeung-Courchesne, R., Press, G. A., Hesselink, J. R., & Jennigan, T. L. (1988). Hypoplasia of vermal lobules VI and VII in autism. *New England Journal of Medicine, 318,* 1349–1354.

Creasey, H., Rumsey, J. M., Schwartz, M., Duara, R., Rappaport, J. L., & Rappaport, S. I. (1986). Brain morphometry in autistic men as measured by volumetric computed tomography. *Archives of Neurology, 43*, 669–672.

Daly, H. (1992). The evaluation of behavioral changes produced by consumption of environmentally contaminated fish. In R. Isaacson & K. Jensen (Eds.), *The vulnerable brain and environmental risks* (Vol. 1, pp. 151–171). New York: Plenum.

Daly, H. (1995). Paper presented at the 38th Annual Conference of the International Association for Great Lakes Research, May 1995, East Lansing, MI.

Damasio, A. R. (1984). Autism [Editorial]. *Archives of Neurology, 41*, 481.

Damasio, A. R., & Maurer, R. G. (1978). A neurological model for childhood autism. *Archives of Neurology, 35*, 777–786.

Darby, J. H. (1976). Neuropathological aspects of psychosis in childhood. *Journal of Autism and Childhood Schizophrenia, 6*, 339–352.

Davidovitch, M., Glick, L., Holtzman, G., Tirosh, E. & Safir, M.P. (2000). Developmental regression in autism: maternal perception. *Journal of Autism and Developmental Disorders, 30* (2), 113–119.

Dawson, G. (1987). The role of abnormal hemispheric specialization in autism. In E. Schopler & G. Mesibov (Eds.), *Neurobiological issues in autism* (pp. 213–227). New York: Plenum.

Dawson, G. (1988). Cerebral lateralization in autism: Its role in language and affective disorders. In D. L. Molfese & S. J. Segalowitz (Eds.), *Brain lateralization in children: Developmental implications* (pp. 437–461). New York: Guilford.

Dawson, G., Finley, C., Phillips, S., & Galpert, L. (1986). Hemispheric specialization and the language abilities of autistic children. *Child Development, 57*, 1440–1453.

Dawson, G., Klinger, L. G., Panagiotides, H., Lewy, A., & Castelloe, P. (1995). Subgroups of autistic children based in social behavior display distinct patterns of brain activity. *Journal of Abnormal Child Psychology, 23*, 569–583.

DeLong, G. R. (1978). A neuropsychological interpretation of infantile autism. In M. Rutter & E. Schopler (Eds.), *Autism* (pp. 207–218). New York: Plenum.

DeLong, G. R. (1999). Autism: New data suggest a new hypothesis. *Neurology, 52*, 911–916.

Edelson, S. B., & Cantor, D. S. (1998). Autism: Xenobiotic influences. *Toxicological and Industrial Health, 14*, 553–563.

Egaas, B., Courchesne, E., & Saitoh, O. (1995). Reduced size of the corpus callosum in autism. *Archives of Neurology, 52*, 784–801.

Fein, D., Skoff, B., & Mirsky, A. (1981). Clinical correlates of brainstem dysfunction in autistic children. *Journal of Autism and Developmental Disorders, 11*, 303–315.

Ferguson, J. N., Young, L. J., Hearn, E. F., Matzuk, M. M., Insel, T. R., & Winslow, J. T. (2000). Social amnesia in mice lacking the oxytocyin gene. *Nature Genetics, 25*(3), 284–288.

Fidler, D.J., Bailey, J.N., & Smalley, S.L. (2000). Macrocephaly in autism and other pervasive developmental disorders. *Developmental Medicine and Child Neurology, 42*(11), 737–740.

Fisher, E., VanDyke, D. C., Sears, L., Matzen, J., Lin-Dyken, D., & McBrien, D. M. (1999). Recent research on the etiologies of autism. *Infants and Young Children, 11*(3), 1–9.

Fisher, S. E., Vargha-Khadem, F., Watkins, K. E., Monaco, A. P., & Pembrey, M. E. (1999). Localisation of a gene implicated on a severe speech & language disorder. *Natural Genetics, 18*(2), 168–170.

Folstein, S. E., & Piven, J. (1991). Etiology of autism. *Pediatrics, 87*, 767–773.

Folstein, S. E., & Rutter, M. (1977). Infantile autism: A genetic study of 21 twin pairs. *Journal of Child Psychology and Psychiatry, 18*, 297–321.

Gaffney, G. R., Kuperman, S., Tsai, L. Y., & Minchin, S. (1988). Morphological evidence for brain stem involvement in infantile autism. *Biological Psychiatry, 24*, 578–586.

Gaffney, G. R, Kuperman, S., Tsai, L. Y., & Minchin, S. (1989). Forebrain structure in infantile autism. *Journal of the American Academy of Child and Adolescent Psychiatry, 28*, 534–537.

Gaffney, G. R., Tsai, L. Y., Kuperman, S., & Minchin, S. (1987). Cerebellar structure in autism. *American Journal of Disabled Children, 141*, 1330–1332.

Gillberg, C., & Coleman, M. (1992). *The biology of the autistic syndromes*. London: Mackeith.

Gingell, K., Parmar, R., & Sungum-Paliwal, S. (1996). Autism and multiple pituitary deficiency. *Developmental Medicine and Child Neurology, 38*, 545–549.

Gladen, B. C., Rogan, W. J., Hardy, P., Thullen, J., Tingelstad, J., & Tully, M. (1988). Development after exposure to polychlorinated biphenyls and dichlorodiphenyl dichloroethene transplacentally and through human milk. *Journal of Pediatrics, 113,* 991–995.

Golden, G. S. (1987). Neurological functioning. In D. J. Cohen, A. M. Donnellan, & R. Paul (Eds.), *Handbook of autism and pervasive developmental disorders* (pp. 133–147.) New York: Wiley.

Golding, J. (1997). Unnatural constituents of breast milk-medication, lifestyle, pollutants, viruses. *Early Human Development, 49* (Suppl. 1) S29–S43.

Golub, M. S., & Jacobson, S. W. (1995). Workshop on perinatal exposure to dioxin-like compounds. Part IV. Neurobehavioral effects. *Environmental Health Perspectives, 103,* 151–155.

Guilette, E. A., Meza, M. M., Aquilar, M. G., Delia Soto, A., & Garcia, I. E. (1998). An anthropological approach to the evaluation of preschool children exposed to pesticides in Mexico. *Environmental Health Perspectives, 106,* 347–353.

Gupta, S. (2000). Immunological treatments for autism. *Journal of Autism and Developmental Disorders, 30* (5), 475–479.

Haas, R. H., Townsend, J., Courchesne, E., Lincoln, A. J., Schreibman, L., & Yeung- Courchesne, R. (1996). Neurologic abnormalities in infantile autism. *Journal of Child Neurology, 11,* 84–92.

Hardan, A. Y., Minshew, N. J., & Keshavan, M. S. (2000). Corpus callosum size in autism. *Neurology, 55* (7), 1033–1036.

Hashimoto, T., Sasaki, M., Fukumizu, M., Hanaoko, S., Sugai, K., & Matsuda, H. (2000). Single-photon emission computed tomography of the brain in autism: Effect of the developmental level. *Pediatric Neurology, 23*(5), 416–420.

Hashimoto, T., Tayama, M., & Mayao, M. (1986). Short latency somatosensory evoked potentials in children with autism. *Brain Development, 8,* 428–432.

Hashimoto, T., Tayama, M., Miyazaki, M., Sakurama, N., Yoshimoto, T., & Murakawa, K. (1992). Reduced brainstem size in children with autism. *Brain and Development, 14,* 94–97.

Hashimoto, T., Tayama, M., Miyazaki, M., Murakawa, K., Shimakawa, S., Yoneda, Y., & Kuroda, Y. (1993). Brain stem involvement in high functioning autistic children. *Acta Neurologica Scandinavica, 88,* 123–128.

Hashimoto, T., Tayama, M., Murakawa, K., Yoshimoto, T., Miyazaki, M., Harada, M., & Kuroda, Y. (1995). Development of the brainstem and cerebellum in autistic patients. *Journal of Autism and Developmental Disorders, 25,* 1–18.

Haznedar, M. M., Buchsbaum, M. S., Wei, T. C., Hof, P. R., Cartwright, C., Bienstock, C. A., & Hollander, E. (2000). Limbic circuitry in patients with autism spectrum disorders studied with positron emission tomography and magnetic resonance imaging. *American Journal of Psychiatry, 157* (12), 1994–2001.

Hillman, R.E., Kanafani, N., Takahashi, T.N., & Miles, J.H. (2000). Prevalence of autism in Missouri: Changing trends and the effect of a comprehensive state autism project. *Modern Medicine, 97* (5), 159–163.

Horwitz, B., Rumsey, J. M., Grady, C. L., & Rappaport, S. (1988). The cerebral metabolic landscape in autism: Intercorrelations of regional glucose metabolism. *Archives of Neurology, 45,* 749–755.

Hoshino, Y., Tachibana, R., Watanabe, M., Murata, S., Yokoyama, F., Kaneko, M., Yashima, Y., & Kumoshiro, H. (1984). Serotonin metabolism and hypothalamic-pituitary function in children with infantile autism and minimal brain dysfunction. *Japanese Journal of Psychiatry, 26,* 937–945.

Hoshino, Y., Watanabe, M., Tachibana, R., Murata, S., Kaneko, M., Yashimo, Y., & Kumoshiro, H. (1983). A study of the hypothalamus-pituitary function in autistic children by the loading test of 5HTP, TRH and LH-RH. *Japanese Journal of Brain Research, 9,* 94–95.

Hoshino, Y., Yamamoto, T., Kaneko, M., Tachibana, R., Watanabe, M., Ono, Y., & Kuamshiro, H. (1984). Blood serotonin and free tryptophan concentration in autistic children. *Neuropsychobiology, 11*(1), 22–27.

Howard, M.A., Cowell, P.E., Boucher, J., Broks, P., Mayes, A., Farrant, A., & Roberts, N. (2000). Convergent neuroanatomical and behavioral evidence of an amygdala hypothesis of autism. *Neuroreport, 11* (13), 2931–2935.

Hsu, M., Yeung-Courchesne, R., Courchesne, E., & Press, G. A. (1991). Absence of pontine abnormality in infantile autism. *Archives of Neurology, 48,* 1160–1163.

Hynd, G. W., & Hooper, S. (1992). *Neurological basis of childhood psychopathology* (Vol. 25). London: Sage.

Individuals with Disabilities Education Act of 1990. PL 101–476, 20 U.S.C., Ch 33.

Individuals with Disabilities Education Act Amendments of 1991. PL 102–119, 20 U.S.C. § 1400.

Ingram, J. L., Peckham, S. M., Tisdale, B., & Rodier, P. M. (2000). Prenatal exposure of rats to valproic acid reproduces the cerebellar anomalies associated with autism. *Neurotoxicology & Teratology, 22*(3), 319–324.

Insel, T. R., Obrien, D. J., & Leckman, J. F. (1999). Oxytocin, vasopressin and autism: Is there a connection? *Biological Psychiatry, 45,* 145–157.

International Molecular Genetic Study of Autism Consortium. (1998). A full genome screen for autism with evidence for linkage to a region on chromosome 7q. *Human Molecular Genetics, 7*(3), 571–578.

Jacobson, J. L., & Jacobson, S. W. (1996). Intellectual impairment in children exposed to polychloronated biphenyls in utero. *New England Journal of Medicine, 335,* 783–789.

Jacobson, R., LeCouteur, A., Howlin, P., and Rutter, M. (1988). Selective subcortical abnormalities in autism. *Psychological Medicine, 18,* 39–48.

James, A. L., & Barry, R. J. (1980). Respiratory and vascular responses to simple visual stimuli in autistics, retardates, and normals. *Psychophysiology, 17,* 541–547.

Kanner, L. (1943). Autistic disturbances of affective contact. *Nervous Child, 2,* 217–250.

Kaplan, H. I., & Sadock, B. J. (1998). *Synopsis of psychiatry.* Baltimore: Williams & Wilkins.

Kemmer, C., Verbaten, M., Cuperus, J., Cambfferman, G., & Van Engeland, H. (1995). Auditory event related brain potentials in autistic children and three different control groups. *Biological Psychiatry, 38,* 150–165.

Kemper, T. L., & Bauman, M. L. (1993). The contribution of neuropathologic studies to the understanding of autism. *Neurologic Clinics, 11,* 175–187.

Kemper, T. L., & Bauman, M. L. (1998). Neuropathology of infantile autism. *Journal of Neuropathology and Experimental Neurology, 57*(7), 645–652.

Lainhart, J. E., Piven, J., Wzorek, M., Landa, R., Santangelo, S. L., Coon, H., & Folstein, S. E. (1997). Macrocephaly in children and adults with autism. *Journal of American Academy of Child and Adolescent Psychiatry, 36*(2), 282–290.

Lamb, J. A., Moore, J., Bailey, A., & Monaco, A.P. (2000). Autism: Recent molecular genetic advces. *Human Molecular Genetics, 9* (6), 861–868.

London, E. A. (2000). The environment as an etiologic factor in autism: A new direction for research. *Environmental Health Perspectives, 108,* (Suppl. 3), 401–404.

Lotspeich, L. J., & Ciaranello, R. D. (1993). The neurobiology and genetics of infantile autism. *International Review of Neurobiology, 35,* 87–129.

Maestro, S., Casella, C., Milone, A., Muratori, F., & Palacio-Espasa, F. (1999). Study of the onset of autism through home movies. *Psychopathology, 32* (6), 292–300.

Maddox, L. O., Menold, M. M., Bass, M. P., Rogale, A. R., Pericak-Vance, J. M., & Gilbert, J. R. (1999). Autistic Disorder and chromosome 15q11–q13: Construction and analysis of BAC/PAC contig. *Genomics, 62,* 325–331.

Maurer, R. G. (undated). *Autism and the cerebellum: A neuropsychological basis for intervention.* Gainsville, FL: Center for Autism and Related Disabilities, University of Florida.

Maurer, R. G., & Damasio, A. R. (1982). Childhood autism from the point of view of behavioral neurology. *Journal of Autism and Developmental Disorders, 12,* 195–205.

Maziade, M., Merette, C., Cayer, M., Roy, M.A., Szatmari, P., Cote, R., & Thivierge, J. (2000). Prolongation of brainstem auditory-evoked responses in autistic probands and their unaffected relatives. *Archives of General Psychiatry, 57* (11), 1077–1083.

Minshew, N. J., & Dombrowski, S. M. (1994). In vivo neuroanatomy of autism: Neuroimaging studies. In M. L. Bauman and T. L. Kemper (Eds.), *The neurobiology of autism* (pp. 666–685). Baltimore: Johns Hopkins University Press.

Mouridsen, S.E., Rich, B., & Isager, T. (2000). A comparative study of genetic and neurobiological findings in disintegrative psychosis and infantile autism. *Psychiatry and Clinical Neuroscience, 54* (4), 441–445.

Murakami, J. W., Courchesne, E., Press, G. A., Yeung-Courchesne, R., & Hesselink, J. R. (1989). Reduced cerebellar hemisphere size and its relationship to vermal hypoplasia in autism. *Archives of Neurology, 46,* 689–694.

Needleman, H. L. (1995). Behavioral toxicology. *Environmental Health Perspectives,* 103, Suppl. 6, p. 77–79.

Nelson, K. B. (1991). Prenatal and perinatal factors in the etiology of autism. *Pediatrics, 87,* 761–766.

Ornitz, E. M. (1987). Neurophysiologic studies of infantile autism. In D. J. Cohen, A. M. Donnellan, & R. Paul (Eds.), *Handbook of autism and pervasive developmental disorders* (pp. 148–165). New York: Wiley.

Ornitz, E. M., & Ritvo, E. R. (1986). Neurophysiologic mechanisms underlying perceptual inconsistency in autistic and schizophrenic children. *Archives of General Psychiatry, 19,* 22–27.

Panksepp, J. (1979). A neurochemical theory of autism. *Trends in Neuroscience, 2,* 174–177.

Panksepp, J., & Sahley, T. L. (1987). Possible brain opiod involvement in disrupted social intent and language development of autism. In E. Schopler, G. B. Mesibov (Eds.), *Neurobiological issues in autism* (pp. 357–372). New York: Plenum.

Patandin, S., Lanting, C., Mulder, P. G., Boersma, E. R., Saver, P. J., & Weisglas-Kupens, N. (1999). Effects of environmental exposure to polychlorinated biphenyls and dioxins on cognitive abilities in Dutch children at 42 months of age. *The Journal of Pediatrics, 134,* 333–341.

Percey, A. (1993). Meeting report: Second International Rett Syndrome Workshop and Symposium. *Journal of Child Neurology, 8,* 97–100.

Petty, L., Ornitz, E. M., Michelman, J. D., & Zimmerman, E. G. (1984). Autistic children who become schizophrenic. *Archives of General Psychiatry, 41,* 129.

Pierce, K., & Courchesne, E. (2001). Evidence for a cerebellar role in reduced exploration and stereotyped behavior in autism. *Biological Psychiatry, 49* (8), 655–664.

Piven, J., Amdt, S., Bailey, J., & Andreasen, N. (1996). Regional brain enlargement in autism: A magnetic resonance imaging study. *Journal of the American Academy of Child and Adolescent Psychiatry, 35,* 530–533.

Piven, J., Amdt, S., Bailey, J., Haverkamp, S., Andreasen, N., & Palmer, P. (1995). An MRI study of the brain size in autism. *American Journal of Psychiatry, 152,* 1145–1149.

Piven, J., Bailey, J., Ranson, B. J., & Amdt, S. (1997). An MRI study of the corpus callosum in autism. *American Journal of Psychiatry, 154,* 1051–1056.

Piven, J., Nehme, E., Simon, J., Barta, P., Pearlson, G., & Folstein, S. (1992). Magnetic resonance imaging in autism: Measurement of the cerebellum, pons, and fourth ventricle. *Biological Psychiatry, 31,* 491–504.

Powell, J. E., Edwards, A., Edwards, M., Pandit, B. S., Sungum-Paliwal, S. R., & Whitehouse, W. (2000). Autistic Spectrum Disorders in preschool children from two areas of the West Midlands, U.K. *Developmental Medicine and Child Neurology, 42*(9), 624–628.

Prior, M. R., Tress, B., Hoffman, W. L., Boldt, D. (1984). Computed tomographic study of children with classic autism. *Archives of Neurology, 41,* 482–484.

Rapin, I. & Katzman, R. (1998). Neurobiology of autism. *Annals of Neurology, 43*(1), 7–14.

Reiss, A. L., Freund, L., Tseng, J. E., & Joshi, P. K. (1991). Neuroanatomy in Fragile X females: The posterior fossa. *American Journal of Human Genetics, 49,* 279–288.

Ritvo, E. R., Brothers, A. M., Freeman, B. J., & Pingree, C. (1988). Eleven possibly autistic parents. *Journal of Autism and Developmental Disorders, 18,* 139–144.

Ritvo, E. R., Freeman, B. J., Mason-Brothers, A., Mo, A., & Ritvo, A. M. (1985) Concordance for the syndrome of autism in 40 pairs of afflicted twins. *American Journal of Psychiatry, 142,* 74–77.

Ritvo, E. R., Freeman, B. J., Pingree, C., Mason-Brothers, A., Jorde, L., Jenson, W., McMahon, W. M., Petersen, W., Mo, A., & Ritvo, A. (1989). The UCLA–University of Utah epidemiologic survey of autism: Prevalence. *The American Journal of Psychiatry, 146,* 194–199.

Ritvo, E. R., Freeman, B. J., Scheibel, A. B., Doung, T., Robinson, H., Guthrie, D., & Ritvo, A. (1986). Lower Purkinje cell counts in the cerebella of four autistic subjects: Initial findings on the UCLA–NSAC Autopsy Research Report. *American Journal of Psychiatry, 143,* 862–866.

Ritvo, E. R., Spence, M. A., Freeman, B. J., Mason-Brothers, A., Mo, A., & Marazeta, M. L. (1985b). Evidence for autosomal recessive inheritance in 46 families with multiple incidences of autism. *American Journal of Psychiatry,142*(2), 187–192.

Rodier, P. M. (1995). Developing brain as a target of toxicity. *Environmental Health Perspectives, 103,* 73–76.

Rodier, P. M., Ingram, J. L., Tisdale, B., Nelson, S., & Romano, J. (1996). Embryological origin for autism: Developmental anomalies of the cranial nerve motor nuclei. *The Journal of Comparative Neurology, 370,* 247–261.

Rogers, S. J., & DiLalla, D. L. (1990). Age of symptom onset in young children with pervasive developmental disorders. *Journal of the American Academy of Child and Adolescent Psychiatry, 6*, 863–872.

Rutter, M. (2000). Genetic studies of autism: From the 1970's into the millenium. *Journal of Abnormal Child Psychology, 28* (1), 3–14.

Rutter, M., Bailey, A., Simonoff, E., & Pickles, A. (1997). Genetic influences and autism. In D. J. Cohen & F. R. Volkmar (Eds.), *Handbook of autism and pervasive developmental disorders* (2nd ed., pp. 370–387). New York: Wiley.

Sandler, R. H., Finegold, S. M., Bolte, E. R., Buchanan, C. P., Maxwell, A. P., Vaisanen, M. L., Nelson, M. N., & Wexler, H. M. (2000). Short-term benefit from oral vancomycin treatment of regressive-onset autism. *Journal of Child Neurology, 15*(7), 429–435.

Schain, R. J., & Freedman, D. X. (1961). Studies on 5–hydroxyindole metabolism in autism and other mentally retarded children. *Journal of Pediatrics, 59*, 315–320.

Schroer, R. J., Phelan, M. C., Michaelis, R. C., Crawford, E. C., Skinner, S. A., Cuccato, M., Simenson, R. J., Bishop, J., Skinner, C., Fender, D., & Stevenson, R. E. (1998). Autism and maternally derived aberrations of chromosome 15q. *American Journal of Medical Genetics, 76*, 327–336.

Sher, L. (1997). Autistic Disorder and the endogenous opiod system. *Medical Hypotheses, 48*, 413–414.

Shevell, M. I., & Majnemer, A. (1996). Clinical features of developmental disability associated with cerebellar hypoplasia. *Pediatric Neurology, 15*, 224–229.

Singh, V., Lin, S., & Yang, V. (1998). Serological association of measles virus and human herpes virus 6 with brain autoantibodies in autism. *Clinical Immunology and Immunopathology, 89*, 105–108.

Skuse, D.H. (2000). Imprinting, the X-chromosome, and the male brain: Explaining sex differences in the liability to autism. *Pediatric Research, 47* (1), 9–16.

Sponheim, E. (1996). Changing criteria of autistic disorders: A comparison of the ICD-10 research criteria and *DSV-IV* with *DSM-III-R*, CARS, and ABC. *Journal of Autism and Developmental Disorders, 26*(5), 513.

Steffenburg, S. Gillberg, C., & Holmgren, L. (1986). A twin study of autism in Denmark, Finland, Iceland, Norway and Sweden. *Journal of Child Psychology and Psychiatry, 30*, 405–416.

Stevens, M.C., Fein, D.H., & Waterhouse, L.H. (2000). Season of birth effects in autism. *Journal of Clinical and Experimental Neurospsychology, 22* (3), 399–407.

Sugiyama, T., Takei, Y., & Abe, T. (1992). The prevalence of autism in Nagoya, Japan. In H. Naruse & E. M. Ornitz (Eds.), *Neurobiology of infantile autism* (pp. 181–184). Amsterdam: Excerpta Medica

Tanguay, P.E. (2000). Pervasive developmental disorders: A 10-year review. *Journal of the American Academy of Child and Adolescent Psychiatry, 39* (9), 1079–1095.

Taylor, B., Miller, E., Farrington, C. P., Petropoulos, M. C., Favot-Mayaud, I., & Waight, P.A. (1999). Autism and measles, mumps, and rubella vaccine: No epidemiological evidence for a causal association. *The Lancet, 353*, 2026–2029.

Ticher, A., Ring, A., Barak, Y., Elizur, A., Weizman, A. (1996). Circannual pattern of autistic births: Reanalysis in three ethnic groups. *Human Biology, 68*(4), 585–592.

Tilson, H. (1998). Developmental neurotoxicology of endocrine disrupters and pesticides: Identification of information gaps and research needs. *Environmental Health Perspectives, 106*, 807–811.

Trottier, G., Srivastava, L., & Walker, C. D. (1999). Etiology of infantile autism: A review of recent advances in genetic and neurobiological research. *Journal of Psychiatry and Neuroscience,24*, 103–115.

Tuchman, R. F., & Rapin, I. (1997). Regression in pervasive developmental disorders: Seizures and epileptiform EEG correlates. *Pediatrics, 99*, 560–566.

Turner, M., Barnby, G., & Bailey, A. (2000). Genetic clues to the biological basis of autism. *Molecular Medicine Today, 6* (6), 238–244.

Van Gent, T., Heijen, C. J., & Treffers, P. D. A. (1997). Autism and the immune system. *Journal of Child Psychology and Psychiatry, 39*, 337–349.

Vilensky, J. A., Damasio, A. R., & Maurer, R. G. (1981). Gait disturbances in patients with autistic behavior. *Archives of Neurology, 38*, 646–649.

Volkmar, F. R., & Anderson, G. M. (1989). Neurochemical perspectives on infantile autism. In

G. Dawson (Ed.), *Autism: Nature, diagnosis and treatment* (pp. 208–224). New York: Guilford.

Volkmar, F. R., Klin, A., & Pauls, D. (1998). Nosological and genetic aspects of Asperger's Syndrome. *Journal of Autism and Developmental Disorders, 28,* 457–462.

Wakefield, A. (1998). Ileal-lymphoid-nodular hyperplasia, non-specific colitis, and pervasive developmental disorder in children. *The Lancet, 352,* 234–235.

Williams, P. G., & Hersch, J. H. (1997). A male with fetal valporate syndrome and autism. *Developmental Medicine and Child Neurology, 39,* 632–634

Wong, V., and Wong, S. N. (1991). Brainstem auditory evoked potential study in children with autistic disorder. *Journal of Autism and Developmental Disorders, 21,* 329–340.

Young, J. G., Cohen, D. J., Caparulo, B. K., Brown, H. L., & Maas, J. W. (1979). Decreased 24-hour urinary MHPG in childhood autism. *American Journal of Psychiatry, 136,* 1055–1057.

Zahn, T., Rumsey, J., & VanKammer, D. (1987). Autonomic nervous system activity in autistic, schizophrenic and normal men: Effects of stimulus significance. *Journal of Abnormal Psychology, 96,* 135–144.

Zibovicius, M., Boddaert, N., Belin, P., Poline, J.B., Remy, P., Mangin, J.F., Thivard, L., Barthelemy, C., & Samson, Y. (2000). Temporal lobe dysfunction in children autism: A PET study. *American Journal of Psychiatry, 157* (12), 1988–1993.

Zibovicius, M., & Garreau, B. (1995). Delayed maturation of the frontal cortex in childhood autism. *American Journal of Psychiatry, 152,* 248–252.

CHAPTER 2

The Nature of Pervasive Developmental Disorders: A Holistic View

Lisa R. Audet, PhD, CCC-SLP

Justin, age 3, was beginning to talk but has now stopped. His parents worry because he does not seem interested in them or in his 5-year-old sister. David, who is 4, talks incessantly but does not make sense. He seems to be reciting television jingles all the time. His parents note that he recognizes and reads logos and has done so since he was 2. Scott, who is 5 and says a few words, appears to be afraid of everything. He spends his day rocking and looking at the lines in the heat registers. Whenever his mother tries to play with him, engage him in a family activity, or transition him from the house to the van, he tantrums and bites his hand. Bobby is 6 years old and appears to be very bright. He is fascinated with the weather channel and insists on watching it up to 7 hours a day. He knows everything about tornadoes and hurricanes and will engage anyone in a conversation about these things. But Bobby does not seem to be making friends. He has great difficulty playing games. His memory for facts is wonderful, but his teacher says he seems awkward in the classroom and his penmanship is awful. Sally, a 3-year-old, was developing normally but then began to regress. Now, at the age of 5, she holds and wrings her hands at midline in front of her chest. She smiles and loves to be with people. The toileting skills she had developed have disappeared. Finally, Michael appeared to be a typical 7-year-old but then started to develop odd behaviors.

Each of these children has been diagnosed with a Pervasive Developmental Disorder (PDD). Pervasive Developmental Disorders (PDDs) is the umbrella term that includes five disorders: Autism, Asperger's Disorder, Pervasive Developmental Disorder-Not Otherwise Specified (PDD-NOS), Rett's Disorder, and Childhood Disintegrative Disorder. The severity of the particular disorder varies from child to child, as illustrated by the above examples, and the manifestation can and does change over time. Individuals with a PDD demonstrate difficulties in a number of areas of functioning such as socialization, communication, behavior, and play. Behaviors and abilities in each of these areas fall along a continuum. A compilation of multiple continuums that represent the behavioral manifestations of PDD provides a framework for discussing the effect of the disorder on any given child. See Figure 2.1.

Before discussing the symptoms and behaviors commonly seen in children who have been diagnosed with one of the disorders on the PDD spectrum, three important characteristics about PDDs must be clarified. First, PDDs range in symptoms and the severity of symptoms. Second, PDDs are considered to be neurological disorders, which means the disorders are rooted in

Figure 2.1
PDD Spectrum Continuum

SOCIALIZATION*				
	Functions	Restricted		Varied
	Frequency			
	Responder	Limited		Often
	Initiator	Limited		Often
	Readability	Unclear/Unconventional		Clear/Conventional
COMMUNICATION*				
	Receptive/Comprehension	Delayed		Developmentally Appropriate
		Routine		Novel
	Expressive			
	Means	Single		Combined
	Speech	Echolalia		Spontaneous
RESTRICTIVE-REPETITIVE ACTS*				
	Purpose	Self Regulatory		Limited Ideation
	Complexity	Multiple Components		Single/Simple Acts
	Frequency	Pervasive		Situation Specific
COGNITIVE*				
	IQ	Mental Retardation		Gifted
	Learn Style	Gestalt/Visual/Episodic		Sequential/Semantic
	Play	Restricted		Developmentally Appropriate
SENSORY				
	Stimuli Responsivity	Under	Inconsistent	Over-responsive
	Systems Impaired	Single-system	Multiple-systems	All systems
MOTOR SKILLS				
	Gross Motor	Awkward	Average	Agile
	Fine Motor	Uncoordinated	Average	Highly Dexterous
	Oral Motor	Non-Verbal	Unintelligible	Fluent

*Reflect symptomatology as defined in DSM-IV

and affect the nervous system. Although, currently, a diagnosis of a PDD is based on behavioral symptoms because of the limitations of medicine and science, a PDD is not a behavioral disorder. PDDs are neurological disorders with behavioral symptomatology. Therefore, noted behaviors may be reflections of the primary neurological disorder, or they may be aberrant behaviors that have been learned but that are not inherent to the condition. (For example, aggression is not inherent to the condition of any PDD. Living in an environment that does not support the neurological and developmental needs of the child with a PDD can create a child with a PDD who is also aggressive.) Third, a developmental perspective is critical to understanding the disorder. An interventionist must not lose sight of the fact that children with PDDs are developing human beings. Attention to the child's developmental age is critical in both assessment and intervention.

Children who are diagnosed with a PDD can and often do make positive developmental gains when they are provided with appropriate and integrated intervention. The disorder is highly individualized, however, and requires highly individualized intervention. A comprehensive understanding of PDDs is required to develop individualized intervention and to achieve gains through that intervention. The framework presented in Figure 2.1 and discussed in this chapter is intended to enhance understanding of the complex nature of PDDs.

The Spectrum of Pervasive Developmental Disorder

The framework (Figure 2.1) presented in this chapter encompasses six areas of functioning: socialization, communication, restrictive-repetitive behavior, cognition and intelligence, sensory processes, and motor skills. Children who are diagnosed with a PDD demonstrate a variety of behaviors and difficulties across each of these domains.

Socialization

Individuals with a PDD demonstrate a range of deficits related to socialization (Quill, 1995; Volkmar, Carter, Grossman, & Klin, 1997).

These deficits significantly influence the development of relationships with peers, family members, community members, and interventionists. Research has demonstrated that the development of relationships provides a foundation for other aspects of functioning such as cognition and emotional well-being (Field, 1982). Therefore, the nature of the socialization difficulties that may be encountered in individuals with a PDD is critical to understand. Socialization is intimately linked with communication (Briton & Fujiki, 1989; Lord & Paul,

1997); however, aspects of socialization and communication have been artificially abstracted here for ease of discussion.

Various authors (Prizant, 1988; Prizant & Wetherby, 1987; Stone, Ousley, Yoder, Hogan, & Hepburn, 1997; Wetherby, Cain, Yonclas, & Walker, 1988) have identified that individuals with PDD demonstrate deficits in three areas of socialization: the purpose of socialization, the frequency of socialization, and the readability of the social act. This chapter, therefore, highlights these areas. Understanding these three dimensions of socialization provides a broader understanding of the social behaviors of individuals with a PDD.

Purpose of Socialization

Human beings socialize for a variety of purposes that are referred to as "functions." These functions include requests, protests, greetings, attempts to gain attention, comments, and explanations. A person's ability to use behaviors for these functions grows and develops over time (Briton & Fujiki, 1989). Research has consistently indicated that individuals with a PDD socialize to request actions and objects but demonstrate limitations in their ability to gain attention and engage in social routines such as greeting others, and to comment on or share experiences (Lord & Paul, 1997; Stone et al., 1997).

Frequency of Socialization

Socialization requires the presence of at least two parties referred to as "the dyad" or "communicative partners." At any particular moment, communicative partners use social behaviors to initiate a communicative act or to respond to another's communicative act. Research indicates that individuals with a PDD can have difficulty with initiating, responding, or both (Bishop, Hartley, & Weir, 1994; Lord & Paul, 1997; Wetherby, Yonclas, & Bryan, 1989). Professionals may identify and describe the individual with a PDD as a person who

- Infrequently initiates social interaction
- Infrequently responds to other's initiations
- Infrequently initiates social interaction using conventional methods (verbalizations or gestures)
- Frequently initiates social interaction using unconventional behaviors (i.e., biting his or her hand or producing a specific type of imitative utterance known as echolalia)
- Responds only to the initiations of others that have been specifically taught (i.e., produces rote answers to rote questions)
- Typically has difficulty combining verbal and non-verbal (gestures, facial expressions) communicative behavior

The frequency with which an individual initiates or responds may be influenced by the individual's ability to repair or correct the social act. To repair a social act, one must have a repertoire of behaviors to choose from (gestures and words) that enhance or augment the message. The individual must also be able to interpret the communicative partner's nonverbal feedback (such as eye gaze and facial expressions) to assess whether the message needs to be repeated or clarified. Finally, the individual must be able to

tolerate remaining in the social act. This tolerance requires not only having a nervous system that can endure the frustration of not being understood but also having a history of social interactions in which communicative partners were interested and remained engaged in the interaction during attempts to clarify messages. Repairing a social act is a very complex matter that is dependent on the interrelationship of factors that are both extrinsic (relationships and the environment) and intrinsic (neurological state). An individual's ability to repair a social act, however, can directly influence the frequency of both initiated and respondent social acts that the individual displays.

Readability of Social Interaction

Various authors have identified that the communicative behaviors of individuals with a PDD are, at times, difficult to read (Burke, 1990; Durand, 1990; Lord & Paul, 1997). When an individual communicates or socializes, the partner in the dyad has a set of expectations. The partner expects certain behaviors and words within particular contexts. This predictability, or the rules of socialization, increases understanding of the other's intentions. Individuals with a PDD may use unconventional behaviors such as screams, tantrums, biting oneself or others, repetition of television jingles, or lines from videos to protest, to request actions or objects, or to express emotion. Such behaviors are difficult for the partner to read, and they also place a huge burden on the partner. This burden increases if the behaviors are used infrequently or if one unconventional behavior is used for many purposes. The partner must learn to interpret the intent of the unconventional behavior to provide the individual with alternative conventional ways of communicating the same message. The process of identifying the social intent of unconventional behaviors and teaching a conventional substitute requires careful assessment and intervention. See Table 2.1 for a summary of the socialization deficits of

Table 2.1
Behaviors That Reflect Socialization Deficits

A decrease in the frequency of attempts to initiate or respond to communication

Use of isolated means such as gestures only (i.e., leading others by the hand)

Crying that is not apparently related to obvious needs

Laughing that is not related to obvious needs

Use of unconventional behaviors such as hitting and biting oneself or others

Difficulty anticipating future events, tendency to tantrum

Problems with transitions

Difficulty being soothed by others

Problems understanding figurative language

Problems engaging in play with others (getting into play, remaining focused on play, joint attention to play)

individuals with autism and Case Study 2.1 for an illustration of the socialization abilities and inabilities of children with a PDD.

Hypotheses Regarding Deficits in Socialization in PDD

Numerous hypotheses have been generated to explain why individuals with a PDD demonstrate limitations in socialization, and although it is not possible at this time to determine which theory is correct, all of them may help us to understand some of the social deficits seen in this population. Some researchers believe socialization deficits have a sensory basis (Mundy, 1995; Ornitz, 1989). Children with a PDD may not be able to engage in social interaction because of their reactions to sensory stimulation and their inability to attend to the nonverbal and affective behaviors of others. The second major hypothesis that is used to explain the social difficulties of individuals with a PDD is referred to as theory of mind (Baron-Cohen, 1989, 1993). This theory suggests that individuals with a PDD have not developed the capacity to take the perspective of their communicative partner and are therefore limited in their ability to share events. Individuals who support the theory of mind hypothesis believe that individuals with a PDD are not aware that others may have thoughts that are different from their own. Last, some researchers believe that PDDs are neurological disorders that primarily influence the communication domain and that impaired social skills reflect the related communication deficits (Prizant & Wetherby, 1987; Rydell & Prizant, 1995).

Communication

Communication, like socialization, is very complex. Although communication and socialization deficits are essential components to the diagnosis of disorders on the PDD spectrum (APA, 2000), the manifestation of these deficits can fall within a wide range. Frequently, when

---

Case Study 2.1
Socialization Issues in PDDs

Mario, who is 4 years old, nonverbal, and diagnosed with autism, wants to participate in a tabletop activity where his peers are playing with shaving cream. He approaches the table and vocalizes. The adult interprets the vocalization as a protest and responds "Mario says, 'I'm not ready.'" Mario leaves the area, vocalizes, and shortly after, approaches once again. This interaction is repeated three times until Mario gets on a small riding toy and approaches the table. Only at this point does the adult realize that there is not an empty seat at the table and that Mario's vocalizations were possibly used to signal, "I need a seat." Fortunately, Mario was able to remain invested in the desire for social interaction and to creatively use an alternative to vocalizing when his first strategy was not effective. For other children with Pervasive Developmental Disorders, the frustration encountered in the above scenario might have resulted in a tantrum instead of a repair strategy.

Larry, who is 13, uses an augmentative communication device and some emerging words. He wants to play with his sister who is 8. He approaches her and pushes her to gain her attention. Because he is bigger than she is and because he has significant sensory-motor problems, he is not aware of how hard he is pushing her. Consequently, his sister cries, yells, and runs away from him. Larry then begins to yell and drops to the floor. Larry's sister must learn how to attend to her brother's attempts to initiate and how to respond to behaviors he engages in that may be confusing to her.

---

communication deficits in individuals with a PDD are discussed, the emphasis is on the language and speech components of communication; however, communication involves more than simply language or speech.

Language is a "socially shared code or conventional system for representing concepts through the use of arbitrary symbols and rule-governed combinations of those symbols" (Owens, 1984, p. 3). Critical concepts of the definition are that the codes are conventional, to be understood by the group using the language; that language is a symbol system in which the symbols used are abstract and arbitrarily assigned to concepts; and that the representation of those symbols is rule governed. "Speech is not an essential feature of language" (Owens, 1984, p. 3). Speech is not merely the production of words but also includes qualities of voice such as rate, intonation, volume, and rhythm. Neither speech nor language alone, however, allows for communication to occur.

Communication is "the process of exchanging information and ideas between participants" (Owens, 1984, p. 5). Communication requires the ability not only to comprehend but also to express oneself. Both comprehension and expression entail more than simply language and speech. Comprehension includes understanding both the language component and the nonverbal behaviors of others. The ability to comprehend and use nonverbal aspects of communication such as body language, facial expressions, gestures, and eye gaze support and complement the verbal component of communication. Expressive communication takes many forms other than vocalizing and verbalizing. Gestures, facial expressions, and eye gaze are also important components of expression. Table 2.2 outlines the range of receptive and expressive communication deficits that are common in the population of individuals with a PDD.

Comprehension

Comprehension of communication develops over time, with infants first beginning to comprehend the nonverbal behaviors of others. With experience, the infant associates what is heard with the behaviors that are observed and with the referent or objects. The infant begins to learn that certain words, phrases, and sentences are used in certain situations. This predictability enhances comprehension. The nonverbal components of communication further enhance the comprehension of the language used. Vocabulary knowledge grows over time and with it emerges comprehension of sentences of varying length and complexity (Owens, 1984). Three examples are provided in Case Study 2.2 that illustrate the complex nature of comprehension and the varied presentation of comprehension problems in individuals with PDD.

Individuals with a PDD can have communication delays that are developmental in nature (Tager-Flusberg, 1989). Many individuals with a PDD have cognitive delays that cause discrepancies between their chronological ages and their language ages both receptively and expressively. A very young child may initially demonstrate age-appropriate comprehension. Perhaps not until the communicative and social demands become more complex will delays be noticed. The emergence of comprehension problems in no way indicates a regression on the part of the child. Rather, it reflects the nature of PDDs and the changing social and cognitive demands of the child's environment.

Table 2.2
Receptive and Expressive Communication Deficits

Failure to vocalize, babble, or engage in jargon

The typical development of vocalizations or speech that then stops and regresses

Decreased ability to imitate

Decreased use of eye gaze shifting between people and objects (joint attention)

Oral-motor problems

Problems attending to the speech of others

Problems understanding object labels

Problems understanding directions

Infrequent use of words

No use of words

Decreased use of conventional gestures

Use of unconventional gestures

Echolalia

Unusual speech tone and speech-rhythm

Pronoun confusion

Difficulties responding to questions

A child may also have different levels of comprehension of verbal and of nonverbal information.

Many children with a PDD have a particular learning style where they rely heavily on information that is predictable. When an individual attends to the predictable and visual aspects of communication, the depth of understanding may suffer. Individuals with a PDD may therefore comprehend routine information and routine social interactions more successfully than novel ones.

Expression

Individuals with a PDD may use a variety of means to communicate. As discussed in the section on socialization, the means used may be unconventional and may confuse comprehension for the communicative partner. However, understanding the complexity of expression goes beyond identifying whether the behavior is conventional or unconventional. Typically, in individuals without a PDD, multiple behaviors are used simultaneously to express and share an idea or need (Wetherby et al., 1988). The ability to use a combination of expressive means enhances the readability of the communicative act. Therefore, the individual who can use only a gesture will have a more difficult time being understood than the one who can use a gesture, eye contact, and a word or sentence.

Figure 2.1 illustrates that an individual with a PDD may communicate using one communicative method or a combination of methods. The process is developmental in nature, and the spectrum reflects this developmental sequence. Research by Wetherby et al. (1988) indicates that individuals initially use gestures, including facial expressions, to express a need. Later, the use of gaze and vocalizations with gestures is integrated. Over time, vocalizations turn into verbalizations that are also combined with gestures and gaze. The research of this group indicates that, as an individual becomes verbal, the

---

Case Study 2.2
Comprehension

Colin, age 7, relies on gestures used by an adult and does not really understand words at all. He sees an adult point to the door, and he goes to the door but does not really understand when the adult says, "Look, Mommy's coming home" or "It's time to leave."

Paul demonstrates surface comprehension of many words. This surface comprehension means that he attaches meaning to the word based on some nonsalient feature of the object of action such as color, place, where the object is found, size, or texture. For example, he hears his mother say "cup" as she gets his plastic blue cup from the shelf. He always drinks from this blue cup. Later, Paul hears his teacher say "cup," but she is referring to a yellow paper cup. He begins to search for his plastic blue cup and tantrums when he cannot find it. To Paul, a yellow paper cup is not a cup; only plastic blue cups can be cups.

Brad is higher functioning, and his problems with comprehension are very different. Brad has difficulty integrating the nonverbal and verbal means used to communicate a message. As a result, he has difficulty comprehending abstract terms, implied messages, metaphors, analogies, humor, and sarcasm. For example, Brad's teacher gave him a worksheet and said, "This is a piece of cake." Brad did not understand what she said meant and responded, "No, I don't want any cake." This response is similar to the behavior Brad demonstrated in preschool when his teacher told the class, "If you have to use the bathroom, go by the door." She should not have been surprised when Brad stood by the door and urinated. Comprehension of figurative language and implied messages requires the ability to read tone of voice, facial expressions, and context.

---

frequency of communicative acts that are either solely gestural or solely gaze decreases (Wetherby et al., 1988). A healthy child as young as 9 months will use nonverbal means to intentionally communicate (Butterworth, 1994). For example, this child may reach for a bottle. Within weeks, the child may begin to combine an eye gaze (looking at mother) with a vocal act (crying) and a gestural act (reaching) when the bottle is withheld.

Individuals with a PDD can also demonstrate differences in expressive communication that do not follow the developmental sequence (Stone et al., 1997). Three specific areas that have been described in the literature include the use of gestures, gaze, and echolalia. Research indicates that individuals with a PDD tend to have difficulty combining gestures, gaze, and verbalizations (Stone et al., 1997; Wetherby et al., 1989). They may use only one mode of expressive communication at a time or may be able to combine only two modes.

Gestures. Gestures can be conventional or unconventional. Unconventional gestures were discussed previously in the socialization section of this chapter. Conventional gestures fall into two categories: contact and distal gestures. A contact gesture is one by which the individual touches the communicative partner. Distal gestures are those by which the individual extends an arm and hand but does not make contact with another. Distal gestures include reaching and pointing. Children with PDDs have been found to use contact gestures (taking another's hand) most frequently (Lord & Paul, 1997; Stone et al., 1997). Although contact gestures are frequently used when the individual is requesting an action, object, or assistance, distal gestures are used to comment on actions and objects. When individuals use distal gestures to comment, they are sharing their awareness of an object or action with another. This act reflects higher cognitive processes and more advanced skills in perspective taking.

Eye Contact. Eye contact is another very complex behavior. Research that is available regarding eye contact in individuals with a PDD indicates that it is an area of deficit (Phillips, Baron-Cohen, & Rutter, 1992; Sigman, Mundy, Sherman, & Ungerer, 1986). The literature refers to eye contact as "eye gaze" and "joint attention." *Eye gaze* is defined as orienting toward an object or person whereas *joint attention* occurs when an individual looks at the object and then to the communicative partner;

looks at the object, then to the communicative partner, and back to the object; looks from the communicative partner to the object; or looks from the communicative partner to the object and then back to the communicative partner (Bruner, 1982).

Researchers have identified that eye gaze progresses according to a developmental sequence with the infant first gazing solely on the face of another or gazing solely on an object. Over time, the infant develops the ability to shift gaze from the object to the adult or from the adult to the object. Researchers of eye contact believe that its early use assists the infant in regulating his or her internal state (Brazelton, 1982; Brazelton, Tronick, Adamson, Als, & Wise, 1975). That is, the infant will look away when overstimulated to regain homeostasis and will reestablish eye contact with the adult or object once calmed and ready to take in more stimuli. Mutual gaze may therefore be used as a measure of the child's readiness to interact (Miller, 1996). Eye gaze may also serve a variety of communicative functions. Eye gaze and joint attention may be used to augment a verbal message to make a request, comment, clarify, or protest. Joint attention is often combined with other facial expressions to reflect affect (Murray & Trevarthen, 1985). Individuals with a PDD have been found to have significant problems with the use of eye contact, gaze, and joint attention (Stone et al., 1997). Much more research is needed in these areas to explore why problems with gaze exist. Certainly, the complexity of both the visual system and the function of eye contact adds to the difficulty encountered when attempting to understand and intervene in this realm.

Echolalia. Many children with a PDD engage in a verbal behavior known as echolalia. Initially, echolalia was believed to be meaningless speech. The research of Prizant (1978, 1983a) and his colleagues (Rydell, 1989; Rydell & Mirenda, 1991, 1994) revealed that echolalia serves as a communicative function and may reflect the child's cognitive learning style. Environmental variables influence the frequency with which an individual engages in echolalia. That is, echolalia is responsive to the cognitive and social demands of a situation (Rydell, 1989).

Two forms of echolalia have been identified: delayed and immediate (Rydell & Prizant, 1995). Echolalia is different from imitation. When one child imitates another the imitator may change the rate and intonation of what is heard. When a child is echolalic, the imitated or echoed response sounds identical to the initial model, identical not only to the words used but also to the tone of voice and rate of speech. Delayed echolalia occurs when the utterances that the child has heard some time in the past are used in the present. For example, the child may say "Chocolate milk is good" not only as a request for chocolate milk but also as a request for anything. Immediate echolalia occurs when a child repeats what the communicative partner has just said. Frequently, immediate echolalia reflects the child's inability to comprehend what was said or to manage the social demands. Rydell and Mirenda (1991, 1994) found that when the adult used a highly directive communicative style, the child then demonstrated an increase in both delayed and immediate echolalia. However, both types of echolalia decreased when the adult used a facilitative, child-directed approach.

Restrictive-Repetitive Behaviors

The diagnostic criteria for the various disorders on the spectrum of PDDs includes the presence of restrictive and repetitive acts (APA, 2000). These behaviors can be viewed in one of four ways. First, the restrictive-repetitive behaviors can be a reflection of anxiety or, second, can indicate the presence of an Obsessive-Compulsive Disorder (OCD) (Jenike, Buttolph, Baer, Ricciardi, & Holland, 1989; McDougle, Price, & Goodman, 1990). Third, these behaviors can also reflect the individual's need to self-regulate to remain calm or alert (Dawson & Lewy, 1989;

Field, 1982; Hutt, Hutt, Lee, & Ousted, 1964) or, fourth, possibly reflect an individual's difficulties with ideation or with the ability to create and enact a plan (Ozonoff, 1997). The literature frequently refers to restrictive-repetitive behaviors as self-stimulatory (Koegel, Koegel, & Dunlap, 1996). Table 2.3 presents a range of behaviors that are seen in individuals on the PDD spectrum that could be perceived as restrictive and repetitive.

Anxiety and OCD

When restrictive-repetitive behavior reflects the presence of OCD, management of OCD behavior through medication may be warranted. When the behavior reflects anxiety, medication may still be one aspect of intervention. Management of anxiety, however, should also include (a) an assessment of the variables that trigger anxiety and (b) the systematic manipulation of variables to reduce anxiety while simultaneously providing the individual with strategies for self-management.

Table 2.3
Restrictive-Repetitive Acts

Types

Rocking

Hand flapping

Moving objects close to and away from the eyes

Spinning objects or self

Mouthing objects

Being fascinated with one's hands

Being attached to an object or part of an object

Creating very specific routines that are difficult to modify

Possible Reasons

Obsessive-Compulsive Disorder

Anxiety

Self-Regulation

Limitations with ideation. Difficulties with planning, limited cognition, motor impairments, difficulties with figure-ground discrimination

---

Self-Regulatory Functions

Individuals with a PDD may engage in repetitive acts such as rocking or finger flicking, for a variety of reasons or for a combination of reasons. The behavior may be used to help the individual maintain a state of homeostasis, calmness, or arousal. Restrictive and repetitive acts of this nature would be referred to as serving a self-regulatory function. For example, some children may begin to rock when they meet someone new. The rocking behavior helps them to calm down. Other children may hit their ears when they are sick or when the noise or light in the environment is bothersome. Still other children may bite their hands during an educational lesson or when they are touched. The biting of one's hand may reflect frustration or may be used to help calm oneself enough to attend to or to manage the offensive touch.

Ideation

Restrictive-repetitive behaviors may also reflect limited knowledge of how to interact with objects in the environment. This ability to interact with or form ideas about objects in the environment is referred to as ideation and is closely related to cognition, play development, and motor skills. A child may attend to the reflection of light on a ball but may not bounce or roll it. This child may have difficulty at a cognitive or visual level abstracting salient details of objects or events and may have difficulty with figure-ground discrimination. To this child, the reflection is more salient than the ball and the ball's function. An alternative explanation is that this child may not have a script for or knowledge of what to do with a ball, reflecting deficits in cognition and play. Another child may engage in dumping behavior or in the clearing off of shelves. This kind of behavior may reflect the child's developmental play level or fine motor problems. The child who repetitively dumps may not have the fine motor skills that are needed to hold individual objects or may not have the bimanual skills that are needed to build with objects or to carry the container that houses the objects. In addition, this child may not have the skills that are needed to discriminate figure and ground or to motor plan.

Contextual Variables

The restrictive and repetitive acts that an individual with a PDD demonstrates may occur in all contexts or be restricted to certain situations. For example, whenever in a new situation or presented with a new object, one child may move objects back and forth very close to the right side of the eye. Another may be compelled to engage in a similar behavior 24 hours per day. The individual who engages in a behavior more continuously may experience more pervasive anxiety or less comprehension of the social, cognitive, communicative, and motor demands of his or her world. The individual who engages in the act when new items or situations are presented may be using the odd behavior to help him- or herself understand the new context or object and manage any anxiety around it.

Complexity

Some children engage in acts that are very simple in nature whereas others engage in very complex behaviors. For example, one child may need to touch each corner of his or her desk every morning when entering school. Another child may need to turn the lights on and off four times, touch every person's desk, and then open all the windows. The ritual is followed in the same sequence each day. If the sequence is violated, the child must begin again. The development of simple acts into more complex acts should be carefully assessed by all members of the individual's team, including the individual's physician, psychiatrist, or neurologist. Case Study 2.3 provides an example of how a child on the PDD spectrum manifests restrictive-repetitive behavior.

Cognition and Intelligence

Individuals with a PDD can have levels of intelligence that range from profoundly mentally retarded to genius (Schuler, 1995; Volkmar, Klin, & Cohen, 1997). Frequently, it is difficult to accurately assess the intellectual ability of individuals with a PDD because their symptomatology is complex and because intellectual functioning itself is so complex. The cognitive-intellectual continuum on the spectrum of PDDs attempts to identify and describe two primary aspects of intellectual functioning that are discussed in the literature on PDDs: cognitive learning style and play. Table 2.4 presents behaviors reflecting cognitive differences that may be noted in some individuals with a PDD.

Gestalt Learning Style

Researchers (Prizant, 1983b) have noted that individuals on the spectrum of PDDs may possess a Gestalt learning style that leads them to be somewhat rigid in their thinking and to have difficulty with abstraction. This style of thinking may be related to how the individual conceptualizes events, the meaning he or she attaches to events, and the details that the individual attends to as salient or most important. The process of assimilation and accommodation, where old information is matched, modified, and integrated with new information, may not easily occur. Temple Grandin has referred to this particular learning style as "thinking in pictures" (Grandin, 1995). The degree to which a child possesses a Gestalt learning style can vary. Some individuals rely on this learning style as the primary means of making sense of experiences whereas other individuals demonstrate greater flexibility in the strategies they use to learn.

Individuals who possess a Gestalt learning style tend to learn about the world in chunks or wholes (Prizant, 1983b). They tend to take mental snapshots of events with the internal snapshot concretely representing the event.

Case Study 2.3
Restrictive-Repetitive Acts

Tim is 5 years old and is diagnosed with autism. He is verbal but has significant problems with fine motor skills. Tim also has difficulty managing the sensory load of the environment. Whenever Tim gets excited, he begins to jump up and down and, with his arms bent at the elbow, begins to pull his arms back in a jerking fashion. As he does this, he rubs his middle fingers and pointer fingers with his thumbs. Throughout this time, Tim is not engaged in the current activity.

Careful assessment of antecedents to this behavior revealed that it was not self-stimulatory but was used by Tim to help him calm himself. The repetitive act prevented Tim from exploring his world with his hands to develop fine motor and play skills. Consequently, a sensory diet protocol was designed and carried out to help Tim sustain a calm state and thus increase opportunities where adults could provide developmentally appropriate fine motor and play tasks for him.

Table 2.4
Cognition

Gestalt Learning Style	Play	
	Cognitive	Social
Desires sameness	Attachment to object	Solitary Play
Seeks repetition	Decreased imitation	Onlooker Play
Echolalic	Decreased functional object use	
Hyperlexic	Preference for construction play	
Strengths in rote memory	Preference for puzzles	
Lines up objects	Decreased pretend play	
Problems with transitions	Repetition of set pretend scripts	
Problems with change	Mouthing	

This snapshot can be referred to as the person's gestalt, schema, or script for the event. The snapshot is then applied concretely to new situations with varying degrees of success for the individual. For example, a boy who is diagnosed with a PDD may attend his own birthday party where Barney makes an appearance. There is a Barney cake and a Barney tablecloth. The child receives many gifts, which he opens. This child's schema of "birthday party" includes each of the particulars listed above, which define the event. At a later date, this child attends a birthday party for his cousin where a Power Ranger character makes an appearance and where the cake and tablecloth follow the Power Ranger motif. The child with a PDD is not allowed to open the gifts because it is not his birthday. This limitation violates his schema or gestalt, and he tantrums because, according to his conceptualization, this event is not a birthday party.

Echolalia and hyperlexia are two behaviors that may be related to a Gestalt learning style (Prizant, 1983b). Echolalia, which has previously been defined, reflects how the individual learns language, attending to the entire sentence that was used in a particular context and repeating it in a similar context. Hyperlexia reflects how the individual attends to visual stimuli, noting consistency and stability in print. Individuals who demonstrate hyperlexia are early readers. Typically, children who are hyperlexic are able to decode words but have difficulty with comprehension. The stability that print provides can become an effective teaching tool and can be used to increase comprehension of both written and oral language even in very young children (Hodgdon, 1995; Schuler, 1995).

At times, tantrum behavior may be related to the Gestalt learning style. Change is difficult to comprehend for some individuals with a PDD because the subtleties of events are not integrated into the individual's schema or gestalt. Therefore, change in the environment requires the creation of an entirely new snapshot. In addition, the individual may tantrum because he or she does not know what to expect or anticipate as new or unfamiliar events arise. Each event is discrete, and similarities between events are often not attended to by an individual who possesses a Gestalt learning style. Consequently, individuals who possess this learning style have a high preference for sameness and predictability.

Play Behavior

Deficits in play behavior are inherent to a PDD. Two aspects of play are important to the discussion of individuals with a Pervasive Developmental Spectrum Disorder: cognitive and social.

Cognitive. From a cognitive perspective, play involves three related and integrated developmental components: ideation, problem solving, and representational thought. Individuals with a PDD may demonstrate difficulties in ideation that influence play (Schuler, 1995; Wolfberg, 1995). These difficulties were discussed in the restrictive-repetitive behavior section of this chapter. The play behavior of a child with a PDD may appear to be aberrant, with the individual attending to parts of objects or playing with objects in a restrictive manner (APA, 2000). The child may develop an odd affinity for an object or part of an object, or the play may be highly repetitive in nature (APA, 2000). Research indicates that individuals with a PDD prefer to engage in construction play rather than representational or pretend play (Mundy, Sigman, Ungerer, & Sherman, 1987). Some children can create very complex objects with blocks or draw intricate pictures and detailed maps. Yet, the ability to engage in the reenactment of an event or story through pretend play may be very restricted.

The odd characteristics of play that are demonstrated by many children with PDDs are counterbalanced by behaviors that reflect developmental delays and that reflect the child's developmental age. For example, a child who is functioning at a level of 9–12 months may naturally enjoy dumping or opening and closing doors. Individuals with a PDD may also demonstrate play behaviors that reflect a developmental delay rather than an aberrant skill. Both the developmental and the atypical components of play should be noted in any individual.

Social. Individuals with a PDD may appear to prefer solitary play to the social domain of play. Social play requires the ability to manage a variety of demands, from comprehending the language used by a partner to understanding the rules of the game to knowing the rules of conversation (Wolfberg, 1995). Communicative, social, cognitive, and motor demands are integrated into social play. Nevertheless, although individuals with a PDD may appear to prefer to play alone, they may in fact desire to engage in social interaction but may have difficulty managing the complexity of the task to do so successfully (Wolfberg, 1995). To date, research that indicates ways in which individuals manage the multiple demands of play is limited. Consequently, the possibly false notion that individuals with a PDD prefer to be isolated is perpetuated. Conceivably, additional research will indicate that individuals with a PDD desire social interaction and play but are unable to manage the various demands associated with the act to be successful. Case Study 2.4 provides examples of the varied cognitive issues that individuals with a PDD may demonstrate.

Sensory Processes

The sensory issues that affect individuals with a PDD have been described in the literature since Kanner's (1943) first description of autism. However, sensory perception and integration issues have yet to be incorporated into the *Diagnostic Statistical Manual* (*DSM-IV-TR*) criteria (APA, 2000). Contemporary research on PDDs has identified sensory perception, processing, and integration issues across a number of sensory

---

Case Study 2.4
Cognitive and Intellectual Behaviors

Marty is 17 years old. He is very verbal, but people are concerned because he is quite inconsistent in his ability to follow directions. Marty can frequently be heard repeating phrases to himself such as "Don't you even think about it!" An analysis of Marty's behavior as well as receptive and expressive language skills reveals that he possesses a Gestalt learning style. A large portion of his expressive language is delayed or involves immediate echolalia, and the repeated warning is a sentence others have said to him when he attempts to engage in prohibited behavior. Apparently, he has learned to use this phrase to manage his own behavior. The analysis also reveals that although Marty uses complex sentences, his receptive language skills are significantly delayed. This delay explains the inconsistency in his ability to follow directions.

Carl, who is 6 years old and diagnosed with PDD-NOS, is in a general education first grade class. He participates in all activities, but his teacher is confused by two specific behaviors. First, Carl becomes upset whenever anyone in the class loses points on the classroom behavior chart. Second, although Carl appears to be attending to lessons, he is never able to respond to direct questions, and if he does, the answers are tangential. Assessment and dialogue with the family and educational team reveals that changing the behavior chart is what upsets Carl. Consequently, the team constructs a social story that explains the behavior chart to Carl, and they proactively support him whenever a peer loses a point. Within a couple of weeks, Carl's behavior improves. The team also realizes that Carl needs more time to process information so that he can respond when the teacher asks him a question. Consequently, the teacher changes her question-asking behavior. Instead of asking a question and expecting an immediate response, she now provides Carl with a question and tells him to raise his hand when he has the answer. Carl's participation improves as does his ability to provide topically relevant responses.

modalities from auditory (Lincoln, Courchesne, Harms, & Allen, 1995) to tactile (Baranek & Berkson, 1994; Cesaroni & Garber, 1991) to visual (Wainwright-Sharp & Bryson, 1993).

Fisher, Murray, and Bundy (1991) presented a conceptual model that described the possible relationship between sensory processing, perception, and adaptive behavior. Their model included the following sequence of sensory processes, each building on the other: arousal, perception, attention (focusing, shifting attention), modulation and regulation of sensation, and processing of input. According to the model, adaptive behavior results when a person becomes aware of sensations, attends and organizes oneself to create a plan of action, and adapts to incoming feedback. The individual's

Table 2.5
Indications of Problems With Sensory Perception and Processing

Behaviors such as rocking, flicking objects, spinning, hand flapping, fascination with hands

Sensitive startle response

Lack of response to sensory stimuli

Unusual sleep patterns

Decreased activity level or lack of response

Increased activity level

Decreased attention for that which is salient

Problems shifting attention

Problems with the texture or smells of foods

Unusual or exaggerated fears

Avoidance of eye contact

Difficulties being soothed

Acts of dropping oneself onto or into objects

Clothing sensitivities

Preference to sleep without covers

Preference to sleep between mattress and box spring

Preference to sleep in small areas such as drawers, boxes, or shelves

Lining up of objects

Periods of staring at lights or shadows

ability to self-regulate to optimize his or her state of arousal, perception, and attention appears to be fundamental to learning. Therefore, application of this model would lead interventionists to attend to the individual's state of readiness and support the individual's attempts to engage in the sequence as proposed by Fisher et al. (1991).

Impairments in the process of integrating sensation can result in possible deficits in cognition, socialization, and motor behavior. Mundy (1995) has hypothesized that sensory-based issues may be related to many of the behavioral, cognitive, emotional, and communicative difficulties that children with autism demonstrate. Lincoln, Courchesne, Harms, and Allen (1993) proposed that sensory deficits "may help explain why children with autism have rigid expectations and difficulty extracting information in a way that leads to reintegration of previously learned information" (p. 56).

Several researchers have proposed that individuals with a PDD present with a variety of sensory-processing issues. Some propose that individuals with autism demonstrate delayed or attenuated responses to stimuli and difficulties shifting attention between or within modalities (Dawson & Lewy, 1989). Others state that individuals with autism can be over- or under-aroused (Ornitz, 1989; Wainwright-Sharp & Bryson, 1993) or have sensory-regulation issues (Lincoln et al., 1993, 1995). Last, the personal accounts by individuals with autism report difficulty attending to and integrating input from more than one sensory modality at a time (Grandin, 1996; Williams, 1992). Table 2.5 provides a list of sensory-related behaviors that individuals with a PDD may demonstrate. Case Study 2.5 provides examples of the sensory issues that are manifested by individuals with a PDD.

Motor Skills

The *DSM-IV-TR* criteria that are used to diagnose a disorder on the PDD spectrum do not include problems involving motor skills (APA, 2000). However, the literature indicates that individuals who fall on the spectrum do demonstrate delays and difficulties in motor development (Atwood, 1997; Dawson & Adams, 1984; DeMeyer et al., 1972; Jones & Prior, 1985). The way in which motor difficulties are possibly related to sensory and cognitive issues is a question that remains to be answered. However, this section will describe those issues related to gross, fine, and oral motor skills that are common to individuals with a PDD. Again, the range of difficulty is quite broad. Table 2.6 provides a list of the possible motor difficulties that individuals with a PDD may encounter.

Gross Motor

Individuals with a PDD may demonstrate significant deficits in gross motor skills. One factor that is important to assess is whether gross motor difficulties are related to motor planning issues, muscular weakness, or sensory integration issues. Literature specific to Asperger's Disorder has noted that many individuals with this disorder demonstrate difficulties related to motor planning and muscle strength (Atwood, 1997). Individuals with these difficulties may shy away from group games that require gross motor skills. These individuals may fatigue easily when engaged in gross motor tasks. At times, the gross motor difficulties may be masked by the individual's level of activity. Commonly, a child with a PDD can be highly active yet have difficulty managing gravity or engaging in a variety of age-appropriate gross motor tasks.

Fine Motor

Individuals with a PDD may also demonstrate difficulties with fine motor tasks. Again, the difficulties may be related to motor planning problems, muscular weakness, or sensory issues. Fine motor problems are noted across the PDD spectrum. For example, children who are low functioning may demonstrate restricted

Case Study 2.5
Sensory Processing Behaviors

Adam is 5 years old and diagnosed with autism. He is quite large for his age. School professionals are very concerned about his behavior. He appears to be aggressive and avoids social interaction and academic tasks. He will push people down to leave an area and will push children into walls or down to the floor whenever they move. Everyone is afraid that he will hurt someone. Fewer and fewer adults are willing to work with him.

Careful assessment reveals that Adam has severe sensory processing and integration problems. His negative behaviors are his attempts to manage a world that is overwhelming and scary for him. Consequently, the team creates an integrated program that includes a sensory diet protocol to assist in integration of sensory input; use of visual supports to help him understand the structure of his day; communication training to provide him with words to use when he needs help, needs to stop, or needs time away; and a behavioral program that provides him with natural reinforcement for his accomplishments. Within 4 months, Adam is able to travel to church and to the store with his mother, who previously could not take him anywhere except the playground. Two years later, Adam is included in a general education first grade class with an educational assistant.

Table 2.6
Motor Deficits

Gross Motor	Fine Motor	Oral Motor
Delayed development	Delayed development	Mouthing
Low muscle tone	Low muscle tone	Decreased tolerance for foods
		Limited oral exploration or play
		Excessive drooling
		Prone to choking or gagging
		Apraxia

play or aberrant behaviors such as dumping containers or clearing shelves because they are unable to use their hands in more adaptive ways. Higher functioning children, however, may demonstrate fine motor problems by hav-

ing difficulties with activities of daily living and handwriting.

Oral Motor

Individuals who are diagnosed with a PDD may demonstrate oral motor deficits. Case Study 2.6 presents a sample of the oral motor skills of some children with PDDs. A large percentage of children diagnosed with disorders on the PDD spectrum are nonverbal (Lord & Paul, 1997). Research has yet to identify how many of these children are nonverbal because of oral hyper- or hyposensitivity issues or because of apraxia. A commonly held view is that if an individual with autism does not speak by the age of 6, then he or she will never speak (Rutter, 1970). However, research has neither identified the prevalence of apraxia in this population nor studied the effectiveness of treatment on the oral motor dysfunction; therefore, whether the commonly held belief is true or simply a function of the state of research and treatment is difficult to ascertain. Case Study 2.7 provides vignettes of children with a PDD who also demonstrate deficits in motor skills.

Case Study 2.6
Oral-Motor Skills and Apraxia

Kyle is 11 years old and is diagnosed with autism. He was nonverbal until the age of 9 when he began spelling words verbally instead of saying them. An assessment of Kyle's expressive language skills revealed that he attempted to use a wide range of vocabulary, some early developmental morphological markers (grammatical parts of speech), and simple sentence structures. Further assessment revealed that Kyle had severe verbal apraxia and hypersensitivity to touch around the mouth. However, Kyle really wanted to be verbal.

Kyle's therapeutic program included an oral-motor program to decrease hypersensitivity, techniques typically used with individuals who have apraxia, and use of activities that required using the visual mode to illustrate the phonetic spelling of words. Illustrating the phonetic spelling of words provided Kyle with the visual support he needed to learn that people do not say the silent e or double consonants.

Summary

A PDD is a disorder that affects abilities across multiple domains. Although common characteristics can be found within the population of individuals with a PDD, the demonstration of these characteristics in any given individual varies greatly by degree and type. In addition, the characteristics that an individual demonstrates when initially diagnosed can change dramatically over time as a result of the function of age and the appropriateness of the intervention he or she receives. The framework presented in this chapter describes the range of behaviors and symptoms typically seen in those diagnosed with disorders on the PDD spectrum and, consequently, is intended to provide a guide for understanding the variability of the disorder.

Case Study 2.7
Examples of Verbal Apraxia or Oral Apraxia and Intervention

Mark, age 5, was severely apraxic. Treatment for the apraxia resulted in an increased ability to produce speech sounds. Mitch, age 4, demonstrated oral motor delays or speech delays because of speculated auditory perceptual or processing issues. When melodic intonation was used in conjunction with techniques that are typically used with children who are apraxic, Mitch's speech began to emerge. Ryan's use of a speech output augmentative device lead to the development of speech. The device produced speech that was highly consistent, without the variability of prosodic features such as rate, intonation, volume, and stress that are found in a human voice. Interestingly, however, Ryan's speech sounded very much like the speech from his device, lacking flexibility in prosody.

References

American Psychiatric Association. (2000). *Diagnostic statistical manual of mental disorders* (4th ed., rev.). Washington, DC: Author.

Atwood, T. (1997). *Asperger's Syndrome: A guide for parents and professionals.* Philadelphia: Kingsley.

Baranek, G. T., & Berkson, G. (1994). Tactile defensiveness in child with developmental disabilities: Responsiveness and habituation. *Journal of Autism and Developmental Disorders, 24*(4), 457–471.

Baron-Cohen, S. (1989). The autistic child's theory of mind: A case of specific developmental delay. *Journal of Child Psychology and Psychiatry, 30,* 285–297.

Baron-Cohen, S. (1993). From attention-goal psychology to belief-desire psychology: The development of a theory of mind and its dysfunction. In S. Baron-Cohen, H. Tager-Flusberg, & D. Cohen (Eds.), *Understanding other's minds: Perspectives from autism* (pp. 59–82). New York: Oxford University Press.

Bishop, D., Hartley, L., and Weir, F. (1994). Why and when do some language-impaired children seem talkative? A study of initiations in conversations of children with semantic-pragmatic disorder. *Journal of Autism and Developmental Disorder, 241,* 23–37.

Brazelton, T. B. (1982). Joint regulation of neonate-parent behavior. In E. Z. Tronick (Ed.), *Social interchange in infancy: Affect, cognition and communication* (pp. 7–22). Baltimore: University Park Press.

Brazelton, T. B., Tronick, E., Adamson, L., Als, H., & Wise, S. (1975). Early mother-infant reciprocity. In M. A. Hofer (Ed.), *The parent-infant relationship* (pp. 137–155). London: Ciba.

Briton, B., & Fujiki, M. (1989). *Conversational management with language-impaired children: Pragmatic assessment and intervention.* Gaithersburg, MD: Aspen Publishers.

Bruner, J. (1982). The organization of action and the nature of the adult-infant transaction. In E. Z. Tronick (Ed.), *Social interchange in infancy: Affect, cognition and communication* (pp. 23–37). Baltimore: University Park Press.

Burke, G. (1990). Unconventional behavior: A communicative interpretation in individuals with severe disabilities. *Topics in Language Disorders, 10*(4), 75–85.

Butterworth, G. (1994). Theory of mind and the facts of embodiment. In C. Lewis & P. Mitchell (Eds.), *Children's early understanding of mind: Origins and development* (pp. 115–132). Hillsdale, NJ: Lawrence Erlbaum Associates.

Cesaroni, L., & Garber, M. (1991). Exploring the experience of autism through firsthand accounts. *Journal of Autism and Developmental Disorders, 21*(3), 303–313.

Dawson, G., & Adams, A. (1984). Imitation and social responsiveness in autistic children. *Journal of Abnormal Child Psychology, 12*(2), 209–226.

Dawson, G., & Lewy, A. (1989). Arousal, attention and the socioemotional impairments of individuals with autism. In G. Dawson (Ed.), *Autism: Nature, diagnosis and treatment* (pp. 144–173). New York: Guilford.

DeMeyer, M. K., Alpern, G. D., Barton, S., DeMeyer, W. E., Churchill, D. W., Hingtgen, J. N., Bryson, C. Q., Pontius, W., & Kimberlin, C. (1972). Imitation in autistic, early schizophrenic, and non-psychotic subnormal children. *Journal of Autism and Childhood Schizophrenia, 2*(3), 264–287.

Durand, V. M. (1990). *Severe behavior problems: A functional communication training approach.* New York: Guilford.

Field, T. (1982). Affective displays of high-risk infants during early interactions. In T. Field & A. Fogel (Eds.), *Emotion and early interaction* (pp. 101–126). Hillsdale, NJ: Erlbaum.

Fisher, A. G., Murray, E. A., & Bundy, A. C. (1991). *Sensory integration: Theory and practice.* Philadelphia: F. A. Davis.

Grandin, T. (1995). The learning style of people with autism: An autobiography. In K. Quill (Ed.), *Teaching children with autism: Strategies to enhance communication and socialization* (pp. 33–52). New York: Delmar.

Grandin, T. (1996). Brief report: Response to National Institutes of Health Report. *Journal of Autism and Developmental Disabilities, 26*(2), 185–187.

Hodgdon, L. Q. (1995). Solving social-behavioral problems through the use of visually supported communication. In K. Quill (Ed.), *Teaching children with autism: Strategies to enhance communication and socialization* (pp. 265–286). New York: Delmar.

Hutt, S.J., Hutt, C., Lee, D. & Ounsted, C. (1964). Arousal and childhood autism. *Nature, 204,* 908–909.

Jenike, M. A., Buttolph, L., Baer, L., Ricciardi, J., & Holland, A. (1989). Open trial of fluoxetine in obsessive-compulsive disorder. *American Journal of Psychiatry, 146*(7), 909–911.

Jones, V., & Prior, M. (1985). Motor imitation abilities and neurological signs in autistic children. *Journal of Autism and Developmental Disorders, 151*, 37–46.

Kanner, L. (1943). Autistic disturbance of affective contact. *Nervous Child, 2*, 217–280.

Koegel, L. K., Koegel, R. L., & Dunlap, G. (1996). *Positive behavioral support: Including people with difficult behavior in the community.* Baltimore: Brookes.

Lincoln, A. J., Courchesne, E., Harms, L., & Allen, M. (1993). Contextual probability evaluation in autistic, receptive developmental language disorder, and control children: Event-related brain potential evidence. *Journal of Autism and Developmental Disorders, 23*(1), 37–57.

Lincoln, A. J., Courchesne, E., Harms, L., & Allen, M. (1995). Sensory modulation of auditory stimuli in children with autism and receptive developmental language disorder: Event-related brain potential evidence. *Journal of Autism and Developmental Disorders, 25*(5), 521–539.

Lord, C., & Paul, R. (1997). Language and communication in autism. In D. J. Cohen & F. R. Volkmar (Eds.), *Handbook of autism and pervasive developmental disorders:* (2nd ed., pp. 195–225). New York: Wiley.

McDougle, C. J., Price, L. H., Goodman, W. K. (1990). Fluoxetine and autism. *Journal of the American Academy of Child and Adolescent Psychiatry, 29*(6), 985.

Miller, H. (1996). Eye contact and gaze aversion: Implications for persons with autism. *Sensory Integration Special Interest Section Quarterly, 19*(2), 1–4.

Mundy, P. (1995). Joint attention, social-emotional approach in children with autism. *Development and Psychopathology, 7*, 63–82.

Mundy, P., Sigman, M., Ungerer, J., & Sherman, T. (1987). Nonverbal communication and play correlates of language development in autistic children. *Journal of Child Psychology and Psychiatry, 27*, 657–669.

Murray, L., & Trevarthen, C. (1985). Emotional regulation of interactions between two-month-olds and their mothers. In T. M. Field & N. A. Fox (Eds.), *Social perception in infants* (pp. 177–198). Norwood, NJ: Ablex.

Ornitz, E. M. (1989). Autism at the interface between sensory and information processing. In G. Dawson (Ed.), *Autism: Nature, diagnosis and treatment* (pp. 174–207). New York: Guilford.

Owens, R. E. (1984). *Language development: An introduction.* Columbus, OH: Merrill.

Ozonoff, S. (1997). Causal mechanisms of autism: Unifying perspectives from and information-processing framework. In D. J. Cohen & F. R. Volkmar (Eds.), *Handbook of autism and pervasive developmental disorders* (2nd ed., pp. 868–879). New York: Wiley.

Phillips, W., Baron-Cohen, S., & Rutter, M. (1992). The role of eye contact in goal detection: Evidence for normal infants and children with autism or mental handicap. *Development and Psychopathology, 4*, 375–383.

Prizant, B. M. (1978). *The functions of immediate echolalia in autistic children.* Unpublished doctoral dissertation, State University of New York, Buffalo.

Prizant, B. M. (1983a). Echolalia in autism: Assessment and intervention. *Seminars in Speech and Language 4*(1), 63–77.

Prizant, B. M. (1983b). Language and communication in autism. Toward an understanding of the "whole" of it. *Journal of Speech and Hearing Disorders 48*, 296–307.

Prizant, B. M. (1988). Autism disorders and treatment. Paper presented at Bradley Hospital Communication Disorders Department, Providence, RI.

Prizant, B. M., & Wetherby, A. (1987). Communicative intent: A framework for understanding social-communicative behavior in autism. *Journal of the American Academy of Child and Adolescent Psychiatry, 26*, 472–479.

Quill, K. (1995). *Teaching children with autism: Strategies to enhance communication and socialization.* New York: Delmar.

Rutter, M. (1970). Autistic children: Infancy to adulthood. *Seminars in Psychiatry, 2*, 435–450.

Rydell, P. J. (1989). *Social-communicative control and its effect on echolalia in children with autism.* Unpublished doctoral dissertation, University of Nebraska, Lincoln.

Rydell, P. J., & Mirenda, P. (1991). The effects of two levels of linguistic constraint on echolalia and generative language production in children with autism. *Journal of Autism and Developmental Disorders,19*, 131–157.

Rydell, P. J., & Mirenda, P. (1994). Effects of high and low constraint utterances on the production of immediate and delayed echolalia in young children with autism. *Journal of Autism and Developmental Disorders, 24*(6), 719–735.

Rydell, P. J., & Prizant B. M. (1995). Assessment and intervention strategies for children who use echolalia. In K. Quill (Ed.), *Teaching children with autism: Strategies to enhance communication and socialization* (pp. 105–132). New York: Delmar.

Schuler, A. L. (1995). Thinking in autism: Differences in learning and development. In K. Quill (Ed.), *Teaching children with autism: Strategies to enhance communication and socialization* (pp. 11–32). New York: Delmar.

Sigman, M., Mundy, P., Sherman, T., & Ungerer, J., (1986). Social interactions of autistic, mentally retarded and normal children and their caregivers. *Journal of Child Psychology and Psychiatry, 27,* 647–656.

Stone, W. L., Ousley, O. Y., Yoder, P. J., Hogan, K. L., & Hepburn, S. L. (1997). Nonverbal communication in two-and three-year-old children with autism. *Journal of Autism and Developmental Disorders, 27*(6), 677–696.

Tager-Flusberg, H. (1989). A psycholinguistic perspective on language development in the autistic child. In G. Dawson (Ed.), *Autism: Nature, diagnosis and treatment* (pp. 92–118). New York: Delmar.

Volkmar, F. R., Carter, A., Grossman, J., & Klin, A. (1997). Social development in autism. In D. J. Cohen & F. R. Volkmar (Eds.), *Handbook of autism and pervasive developmental disorders* (2nd ed., pp. 173–194). New York: Wiley.

Volkmar, F. R., Klin, A., & Cohen, D. J. (1997). Diagnosis and classification of autism and related conditions: Consensus and issues. In D. J. Cohen & F. R. Volkmar (Eds.), *Handbook of autism and pervasive developmental disorders* (2nd ed., pp. 5–40). New York: Wiley.

Wainwright-Sharp, J. A., & Bryson, S. E. (1993). Visual orienting deficits in high-functioning people with autism. *Journal of Autism and Developmental Disorders, 23*(1), 1–13.

Wetherby, A., Yonclas, D., & Bryan, A. (1989). Communication profiles of preschool children with handicaps: Implications for early identification. *Journal of Speech and Hearing Disorders, 54,* 148–158.

Wetherby, A. M., Cain, D. H., Yonclas, D. C., & Walker, V. G. (1988). Analysis of intentional communication of normal children from the prelinguistic to the multiword stage. *Journal of Speech and Hearing Research, 31,* 240–252.

Williams, D. (1992). *Nobody nowhere.* New York: Times.

Wolfberg, P. (1995). Enhancing children's play. In K. Quill (Ed.), *Teaching children with autism: Strategies to enhance communication and socialization* (pp. 193–218). New York: Delmar.

CHAPTER 3

The Family of a Child With Autism

Debra Galvin, PhD, OTR/L

When a child is diagnosed with autism, parents' interpretation of their child's behavior and their expectations for their child in the future are altered. Parents' unique responses to the label that describes their child have been shaped by individual differences in parental thoughts and attitudes, time, and context. The overall purpose of this chapter is to expand occupational therapists' understanding of parents who have children with autism. This chapter begins with a selected review of relevant literature on parental responses to the diagnosis of autism and on the relation of those responses to the attitudes and expectations parents have regarding their children with autism. Next, the chapter discusses important issues for parents and professionals. The chapter concludes with suggested ways that professionals can apply their understanding to assist families who have a child with autism and agencies who serve individuals with autism and their families.

Influence of Time and Context on Parental Thoughts and Attitudes

Historically, parental responses toward their children with autism have shifted as the neurological origins of the disorder have become better understood and disseminated. During the Kanner era that predominated from the 1940s through the 1960s, autism was considered a form of emotional or social withdrawal by the child in response to cold, ineffectual parenting (Kanner, 1943). Research was characterized by a focus on the cause of the disorder in relation to parental characteristics, suggesting that cold, unfeeling parents who have rejected their child cause the child to retreat into his or her own world (Bettelheim, 1967). Although Kanner speculated about the role of abnormal brain function in the etiology of autism, the focus on parental blame became popularized. Bettelheim (1967) further fueled Kanner's orientation of parental self-blame by advocating that the only potential for the child's improvement was to remove the child from the family by means of a "parentectomy."

During this period, predominant research reflected a psychodynamic orientation that focused on the underlying causes of problems that arose as a result of the birth of a "defective" child (Solnit & Stark, 1961). Little research focused on the reaction of families to their child with a disability (Carr, 1985). Farber (1959) was among the first to conduct research on the effects that a child with a disability had on a family, concluding that the birth of such a child, particularly a male child, led to an adverse disruption in the family life cycle. In such early research efforts, children with autism tended to be included in samples of children with a variety of developmental disabilities. Professionals, parents, and other family members tended to accept psychogenic theory, which implied that parents were to blame for their child's autism (Ferster, 1961). Not surprisingly, parents' attitudes reflected a sense of demoralization as a result of believing that their parenting was purportedly the cause of their child's disorder and that, according to subsequent advice from professionals, they could do little to help their child (Schopler, 1971). Accordingly, most parents responded by deciding to place their child out of the home, believing that this decision was best for the child and the family (Cole, 1986).

This trend began to shift in the latter part of the 1960s and early 1970s as a result of contributions from the fields of psychology and neurology. Research findings identified neurological evidence that refuted prevailing psychogenic thought. For example, highly significant proportions of children with autism also developed epilepsy (Deykin & MacMahon, 1979; Schain & Yannet, 1960), and children tracked from a 1964 rubella epidemic were found to demonstrate a disproportionately high risk for autism (Chess, Korn, & Fernandez, 1971). Findings from such studies contributed to the transformation of social consensus that linked brain dysfunction to the symptomatology of autism and refuted prevailing psychogenic thought. Today, it is widely accepted that genetics and various brain structure deficits are strong predisposing factors in autism (Bauman, 1991; Corchesne, 1991; Piven & Folstein, 1994). Psychogenic thought was further challenged by Rimland's (1964) critical review of the literature.

Together, such investigations created a momentum that shifted how parents thought about and reacted to their child with autism. For example, the influence of this shift set the foundation for establishing the National Society for Autistic Children, an advocacy group of parents and professionals whose mission is to promote research and services for individuals with autism and their families. Correspondingly, this trend was further reflected in the growing political advocacy by parent groups, which

led to changes in public policy legislation that then contributed to the deinstitutionalization movement in the 1970s and to a more active decision-making role for parents of children with disabilities (Turnbull & Winton, 1984).

By the 1980s the self-image and, subsequently, the attitudes of parents of children with autism had undergone some significant changes. Rather than seeing themselves as primary causes of their child's autism, parents began seeing themselves as advocates for and teachers of their children (Bristol, 1984). Parents of children with autism found they had to play an active role in educating both professionals and the public about the nature and needs of their children with autism (Schopler & Mesibov, 1984). This shift in parents' roles not only influenced their own identity as parents of a child with autism but also affected the various professionals and agencies that parents encountered in the process to secure appropriate diagnostic and intervention services for their child and family. Parent advocacy at local, regional, and national levels has done much to increase public and professional understanding of the issues that are important to parents. This advocacy has influenced not only parents' perceptions but also social attitudes (Schopler & Mesibov, 1984).

Current Findings on Parental Attitudes and Expectations

By the 1980s, the theoretical orientation of research shifted from a psychogenic orientation that emphasized deficits to family systems models that emphasized complex interactions of roles, relationships, and balances of strengths and needs (Fine, 1985; Simeonsson, 1988). Research efforts emphasize that a systems approach is the most useful theoretical orientation to best expand understanding of parental attitudes and expectations because this type of focus examines the nature of family roles and relationships, needs, strengths, rules, and adjustment over time (Fine, 1985; Minuchin,

1974). Accordingly, much of what is currently known about parents' attitudes toward their child with autism is framed in literature that reports the effect of stress, depression, and the overall psychological functioning that contributes to both positive and negative adjustment.

Early research on parental reaction to the presence of a disability in their child focused on stages of response and adjustment that parents experienced. Researchers found a sequential progression of emotions that generally began with shock and confusion, which was followed by denial. Sadness, mourning, and anger emerged next and eventually progressed to adaptation and acceptance (Bicknell, 1983; Huber, 1979; Parks, 1977). Along this same theme, researchers reported the crisis that followed when a seemingly normal pregnancy resulted in the birth of a child with a disability (Drotar, Baskiwicz, Irvin, Kennell, & Klaus, 1975; Lonsdale, 1978). Often, these findings of parental reactions to their child's disability were interpreted within the framework that was proposed by Kubler-Ross (1969) to define reaction stages to death and dying. Bristol (1987) reported a developmental progression of family stress and needs similar to those reported by other researchers (DeMyer, 1979; DeMyer & Goldberg, 1983; Holroyd & McArthur, 1976). Stress proceeds from the initial negative effect on the family to parental concerns for both the well-being of the child and the family as well as the eventual integration of the child into the community.

Researchers have also focused on characteristics of the child with autism and of the child's parents that are related to negative and positive adjustment. Much of the research that is related to the effect of the child characteristics on the family reports that the needs of the child are a source of chronic stress (Milgram & Atzil, 1988). Marcus (1984) proposed that the foremost stress that families experience is the unrelieved care of rearing a chronically disabled youngster. In their review of the effects of

autism, Cutler and Kozloff (1987) noted that characteristics of autism, including communication difficulties as well as bizarre and rigid behaviors, are inherent stresses for the family. Characteristics that contribute to parents' adjustment include the severity of the handicap and the child's temperament, gender, and age. Beckman (1983) found that the amount of mother-reported stress was significantly correlated with a child's "difficult" temperament, decreased responsiveness, repetitive behavior patterns, and excessive caregiving demands. Similarly, McKinney and Peterson (1987) surveyed 67 mothers of children from ages 7 months to 3 1/2 years and found that children with moderate and severe levels of impairment presented parenting demands that accounted for significant variance in mothers' feelings of stress. With very young children who have autism, mothers are often consumed with unrelenting caregiving demands and with concern for the physical welfare of their children, who show no sense of danger and who have very limited ability to express their needs (Moes, Koegel, Schreibman, & Loos, 1992).

Moreover, parents tend to be negatively affected by the behavior and needs of their children as they grow older, bigger, and more difficult to manage (Harris, 1984; Marcus, 1984). Bristol (1979) found that older children with autism, particularly boys who were more severely impaired, were perceived as more stressful. In short, researchers have found that mothers, in particular, were most affected by the child's daily management problems, which resulted in depression that was typically not treated (Beckman, 1991; Bristol, 1979, 1987; DeMyer & Goldberg, 1983; Holroyd, Brown, Wikler, & Simmons, 1975).

Characteristics of the family also have been studied. For example, Cutler and Kozloff (1987) described the typical "career" of a family with an autistic member, characterizing the family as a closed system that revolves around the needs of the child with autism and is isolated from relatives, friends, and community activities. Lines of research investigating those characteristics of the family that seem to affect how a family will react and adjust have, in general, focused on internal coping strategies, external sources of support, and individual and family belief systems as important variables that contribute to family adjustment (McCubbin, 1989; Roberts, 1984; Winton, 1990).

The majority of research done in this area suggests that important family characteristics and factors that mitigate stress include spousal, extended family, and community support as well as perceived control over their own family's needs (Bailey, Blasco, & Simeonsson, 1992; Martin, 1986; McKinney & Peterson, 1987; Sherman & Cocozza, 1984; Vadasy, Fewell, Meyer, Schell, & Greenberg, 1984). Internal coping resources are influenced not only by stress and overall psychological functioning but also by the family's ability to draw emotional and physical support as well as to assign meaning about the effect of the disability on the family (Shapiro, 1989). External resources include social support from other parents who have a child with a disability, financial resources, and community resources that include intervention services (McCubbin, 1989).

Researchers have suggested that family characteristics that contribute to positive adjustment include flexibility; a sense of commitment and appreciation for individual family members; a common sense of purpose; a clear set of family rules, values, and beliefs; and an ability to engage in problem solving (Trivette, Dunst, Deal, Hamer, & Propst, 1990). Bristol (1984) studied 45 mothers of children with autism and found that successful adaptation for the families was most highly correlated with the degree of cohesion, expressiveness, and active recreational orientation of the families. Family adaptation can also be positively predicted by adequate social support and active coping patterns (Bristol, 1987). Researchers report poorer family adaptation tends to be pre-

dicted by other family stresses, maternal self-blame for the disability, maternal perception of the disability as catastrophic to the family, and a lack of adequate support (Akerly, 1984; Bristol, 1987; Bristol & Schopler, 1983; Rodrigue, Morgan, & Geffken, 1990).

Summary of Current Findings on Parental Attitudes

The consensus in the literature is that some families appear to adapt better to the stress of having a child with autism than do others. Morgan's (1988) review of existing research notes that a tenable conclusion could be that evidence does not clearly support a typical "parent-of-a-child-with-autism" stress syndrome or a high incidence of chronic psychological problems in the parents. Rather, parents appear to experience a variety of stressful situations associated with rearing a child with autism. The cumulative effects of such stress over the years, especially in the absence of adequate resources and support, can lead to depression and adverse family adaptation (Beckman, 1991). The process by which parents form their attitudes and expectations is influenced by how parents make sense of autism as it applies to their child (Gray, 1995). Research emphasizes that a dynamic interplay between internal and external strengths and appropriate resources all influence the attitudes and expectations that parents hold regarding their child with autism.

Parents of children with autism find that their roles change in a variety of ways that they never anticipated. They assume roles that are not normally needed in parenthood. Angell (1993), a mother of a young son with autism, offers a perspective that characterizes the numerous anecdotal accounts found in current literature in the field of autism. Angell notes that, early in their young son's life, she and her husband did not realize that they would become researchers, therapists, and advocates. Parents find themselves in the roles of case managers as they attempt to understand the characteristics of autism as it applies to their child, while also accessing community resources for intervention and support services. Accordingly, the attitude parents hold about their child with autism and how they cope may be influenced by how parents perceive the services they receive, which has obvious implications for occupational therapists and other service providers.

Important Issues for Parents and Professionals

Several important issues emerge from research findings that can inform professionals. In the previous section, important issues specifically related to family adjustment were presented. In this next section, issues experienced by families when accessing services for their child and family will be highlighted.

Process to Secure Appropriate Services

In addition to inherent characteristics of the child and family, the process by which parents come to think about their child further influences parents' attitudes and expectations, a process that typically evolves as the family seeks diagnostic and intervention services for their child. The effect on the family of having a child with autism is different for different family members and is influenced by available community supports (Galvin-Cook, 1996). Researchers have recognized that the ways in which families elicit emotional and physical support and assign meaning about the effect of the disability on the family are strongly influenced by community resources that include diagnostic and intervention services (McCubbin, 1989; Shapiro, 1989). Parents want and need competent and sensitive professionals who provide diagnostic services and intervention programs that address the unique needs of the children with autism and their families. Further, research studies report that appropriate diagnostic and intervention services are important resources that parents draw on and that

contribute to family adaptation (Bristol, 1985, 1987; Harris, 1984; Koegel, Schreibman, O'Neill, & Burke, 1983).

Parents often report that the process of obtaining an accurate diagnosis and appropriate services is difficult and stressful, and it negatively influences family adjustment (Bristol, 1985; Richman, 1988; Stone, Hoffman, Lewis, & Ousley, 1994). Parents frequently experience frustration and confusion when they attempt to secure accurate diagnostic and intervention services, and they also experience loneliness and isolation from having a child whose behaviors and demands set the family apart (Norton & Drew, 1994). Tunali and Power (1993) note that the ambiguity of the diagnosis of autism can lead to a family's difficulty in forming realistic expectations. Further, parents of young children often have difficulties finding qualified professionals who can provide accurate diagnostic, referral, and support services. Smith, Chung, and Vostanis (1994) studied 128 children with autism and found that approximately one half of the parents were initially told that there was nothing to be concerned about, initially given a misdiagnosis, and later given a diagnosis of autism.

When parents attempt to access appropriate services for their child with autism, they may find that the professionals in their community either offer few or no choices or may be confused about what kind of intervention approach is best for their child and family. Further, wide variation exists in the criteria for access to services across states and counties, which may add to the challenges that parents face when accessing services.

Discrepancies Regarding Best Practices

Central to the issue of appropriate services for children with autism and their families is the controversy that exists around what type of intervention is "best" and who is qualified to deliver those services. Family members and professionals often recognize and value similar issues but differ, or even contradict themselves, on the most effective methods to address those issues. The primary differences seem to stem from the philosophical orientations of each intervention approach and from differences in the definition of best practices for intervention services for children with autism (Galvin-Cook, 1996).

Parents are faced with decisions regarding programming that can include

- the philosophical orientation of the program,
- the projected effectiveness for their child and family,
- the appropriate number of hours per week for intervention,
- the amount of inclusion of their child with autism with children who are developing typically,
- the staff-to-child ratio.

The tremendous heterogeneity of the diagnostic category of Pervasive Developmental Disorders as well as the complex and multiple needs of children and families add to the challenge parents face when attempting to access services.

Effect on Finances

Parents identify financial concerns as a major source of fear, insecurity, and frustration (Galvin-Cook, 1996). Families may experience reduced income for a variety of reasons, one of which can be that a parent reduces or terminates employment outside the home because of unrelenting caregiving demands. Increased expenses for medical and educational expenses as well as tenuous external support from third-party payers also contribute to shifts in the financial balance of the family. Financial strains challenge day-to-day arrangements, long-term plans, and harmony in the marriage and extended family. Additionally, parents' financial concerns may stem from uncertainty about the level of independence that their child with autism might achieve, which prompts parents to begin planning for possible future living arrangements. In a qualitative investigation (Galvin-Cook, 1996), one father said, "We are coming to grips with whether our child will be living with us for the rest of our lives" (p. 3).

Suggestions for Professionals

Helping a family adjust to a child with autism is both rewarding and challenging. Occupational therapists are often uniquely qualified to address the myriad issues that parents face. This last section offers insights to support and expand the knowledge and skills of professionals who serve children with autism and their families. The following suggestions are framed in the knowledge that children with autism and their families have complex and multiple needs that are not easily met by any one program, agency, or service provider. In this context, these suggestions focus on remediating the characteristics of autism and on supporting family members. Table 3.1 provides a summary of these suggestions.

Table 3.1

Summary of Suggestions for Professionals Working With Families That Include a Child With Autism

---

- Be aware of and consider the life stage the family is in when designing intervention services.

- Be aware of differing family members' ways of coping.

- Focus on supporting all family members, not on only remediating difficulties in the child with autism.

- Use effective communication skills that are tailored for the needs of the family.

- Assist in procuring appropriate information for the family.

- Clearly identify the focus and scope of services to be provided.

- Openly discuss any issues regarding differences in theoretical orientation or any professional biases that emerge.

- Be knowledgeable of available services in the community and of any other resources that might be appropriate for families being served.

- Be knowledgeable of the range of programs and interventions available outside the immediate community.

Consider the Life Cycle of the Child and Family

Occupational therapists can help families identify what issues are most important to them in the present and consider their priorities for both the short and long term. The characteristics of the family members along with the values and beliefs the family holds are extremely important to consider when designing effective intervention strategies that best fit each member at his or her current stage in life.

For example, in early intervention programs, parents often need help assimilating the knowledge about the characteristics of autism as it applies to their child and to their roles as parents. Mothers and fathers often assimilate knowledge about autism and their own child in different ways. In one study on the effect of having a child with autism, mothers and fathers shared a myriad of experiences that represented the ways in which having a child with autism had reframed their lives (Galvin-Cook, 1996). In this study, both mothers and fathers experienced a flood of feelings such as anger, loss, and sadness when they first learned of the diagnosis. For the mothers, however, their roles focused on gathering and disseminating as much information on autism as possible and accessing services as a strategy for coping. As one mother so eloquently stated, "Attaining this knowledge was my way of getting the control back over our lives that autism had taken away" (p. 2).

Professionals can best meet the complex and changing needs of families when they consider in a sensitive and responsive way the unique needs across the life span. Parents are better equipped to cope with the many unexpected challenges faced by their families when professionals support all family members and when they consider that families are in the process of reconstructing their goals and dreams and changing their roles as parents of a child with autism. Often, professionals who provide services to children with autism take a traditional focus of remediating the characteristics of autism and do not focus on supporting the family members who are essential to that child. As a result of this focus, parents can perceive that the professionals who are supposed to be helpful to them are not helpful at all. Too often, parents' accounts of their experiences with professionals most closely resemble horror stories in which they or their child were treated in a rude, unkind, or narrow-minded way. Parents may feel pressured to follow the advice of a professional who does not consider the family as a whole, which may contribute to parents' feelings of burnout, depression, and an overall depletion of resources.

Engage in Appropriate Communication

Professionals must recognize the predictable supports and barriers that contribute to the positive and negative outcomes of families' experiences. The first barrier typically involves faulty communication, where, often, the professional does not listen to parents' attempts to express what is important to them. For example, professionals may assume that they know what is best for the family and the child with autism, and they may direct their communication style and content to whatever their priorities and values are rather than to the families' concerns.

To address the first barrier of faulty communication, professionals must be diligent about using effective communication skills that are tailored to fit the needs of the individual family. Skilled professionals typically can draw on a broad repertoire of effective communication skills, skills that provide the foundation for a positive relationship between the family and the professional. The professional rather than the parents is responsible to ensure positive communication. The parents have come to the professional for help. Parents' abilities to effectively communicate what they want and need for themselves and their child may be clouded by overwhelming emotions that challenge them to cope and by a lack of practice interacting with professionals. They may have little

Table 3.2

Summary of Program Elements and Focus of Programs

Program Elements	Focus
Curriculum content	Emphasize 5 basic skill domains: • Ability to attend to elements of the environment • Ability to imitate others • Ability to comprehend and use language • Ability to play appropriately with toys • Ability to socially interact with others
Need for highly supportive teaching environments and generalization strategies	Develop core skills in 5 basic skill domains (listed above) in highly supportive teaching environments and then systematically generalize core skills to more complex, natural environments.
Need for predictability and routine	Emphasize strategies that address arousal modulation, memory impairments, and temporal processing.
Functional approach to problem behaviors	• Prevent the development of problem behaviors by increasing the child's interest and engagement in activities using highly preferred play materials, current level of development across domains, and structured as well as unstructured environments. • When problem behaviors exist, conduct functional assessment of the target behavior and teach alternative appropriate behaviors that serve the same function for the child.
Transition from preschool	Identify and address survival skills needed to function more independently (e.g., turn taking, moving from one activity to another with minimal assistance).
Family involvement	• Program devotes time and resources to training parents and to including parents in the intervention and educational process. • Programs are sensitive and responsive to strengths, stresses, and needs of families.

Note. Adapted from "Early Intervention in Autism" by G. Dawson and J. Osterling. In M Guralnick (Ed.), *Effectiveness of Early Intervention* (pp. 307–326), 1997, New York: Brookes. Copyright 1997 by Brookes.

prior experience or may have had prior experiences that were negative. Parents want and need professionals to treat them with respect, dignity, warmth, and a desire to understand their perspective.

Clearly Identify the Focus and Scope of Services

As previously stated, parents encounter discrepancies regarding best practices for their child with autism and often experience the financial burden of services. The literature shows clear evidence that intervention is effective; however, professionals and parents frequently disagree as to how much and what kind of intervention is best. Children with autism and their families have complex and multiple needs that are not easily met by any one professional or agency. Professionals must use their knowledge of what types of services are available in their communities and must assist parents in their decision-making process, without the bias that only one type of service is best for all.

Professionals can help parents consider the various factors that influence the delivery of services for their child and family. These factors include the theoretical orientation of the agency or professionals, the role the parents play in the delivery of services, the scope and intensity of services, and finally, the financial cost of such services. Dawson and Osterling (1997) review eight examples of model early intervention programs for children with autism in the United States that have been active since the 1980s. In this review, the common elements and the focus of programs that parents should consider as "essential" are considered, regardless of the philosophical approach of the programs. These programs are summarized in Table 3.2.

Professionals can best assist parents through informed decision making that considers what the child with autism and the family needs are across the life cycle. Professionals can use the information provided in Table 3.2 to articulate to parents the scope and focus of services they provide. Evaluating such program elements and the focus of intervention assists in clear communication and allows parents to identify what focus is appropriate for their child and family. Additionally, professionals must consider how their own biases, values, and philosophical as well as theoretical orientation affect families. For example, professionals who advocate intensive services value the "more is better" belief. Additionally, some professionals value an isolated model for services whereas others value an integrated model for services. In short, there is no single, correct answer as to the method and frequency of intervention that is best. However, programs and service providers that use a family systems approach when serving children with autism and their families are best equipped to meet the individual needs of families and children.

Summary

As a mother of a child with autism, Akerley (1984) notes that family members want two things: first, for the child to be cured and, second, to be their own family. Although the first cannot yet happen, even with the recent advances in knowledge, occupational therapists can and should assist the family with the second. Each family is unique and will require an individualized approach to service delivery. Therapists must be aware of the issues that families face and the characteristics and supports that help families to cope with having a child with autism. The goal of positive family adjustment is one in which the therapist can play an important role.

References

Akerley, M. S. (1984). Developmental changes in families with autistic children. In E. Schopler & G. B. Mesibov (Eds.), *The effects of autism on the family* (pp. 85–98). New York: Plenum.

Angell, R. (1993). A parent's perspective on the preschool years. In E. Schopler, M. Van Bourgondien, & M. Bristol (Eds.), *Preschool issues in autism* (pp. 17–37). New York: Plenum.

Bailey, D. B., Blasco, P. M., & Simeonsson, R. J. (1992). Needs expressed by mothers and fathers of young children with disabilities. *American Journal of Mental Retardation, 97,* 1–10.

Bauman, M. L. (1991). Microscopic neuroanatomic abnormalities in autism. *Pediatrics, 87,* 791–796.

Beckman, P. J. (1983). Influence of selected child characteristics on stress in families of handicapped infants. *American Journal of Mental Deficiency, 88,* 150–156.

Beckman, P. J. (1991). Comparisons of mothers' and fathers' perceptions of the effect of young children with and without disabilities. *American Journal of Mental Retardation, 95*(5), 585–595.

Bettelheim, B. (1967). *The empty fortress—Infantile autism and the birth of the self.* New York: Free Press.

Bicknell, J. (1983). The psychopathology of handicap. *British Journal of Medical Psychology, 56,* 167–175.

Bristol, M. M. (1979). *Maternal coping with autistic children: The effects of child characteristics and interpersonal support.* Unpublished doctoral dissertation, University of North Carolina, Chapel Hill.

Bristol, M. M. (1984). Family resources and successful adaptation to autistic children. In E. Schopler & G. Mesibov (Eds.), *The effects of autism on the family* (pp. 289–308). New York: Plenum.

Bristol, M. M. (1985). Designing programs for young developmentally disabled children: A family systems approach to autism. *Remedial and Special Education, 6,* 46–53.

Bristol, M. M. (1987). Mothers of children with autism or communication disorders: Successful adaptation and the Double ABCX Model. *Journal of Autism and Developmental Disorders, 17*(4), 469–486.

Bristol, M. M., & Schopler, E. (1983). Stress and coping in families of autistic adolescents. In E. Schopler & G. B Mesibov (Eds.), *Autism in adolescents and adults* (pp. 251–278). New York: Plenum.

Carr, J. (1985). The effect on the family of a severely mentally handicapped child. In A. M. Clarke, A. D. B. Clarke, & J. M. Berg (Eds.), *Mental deficiency: The changing outlook* (4th ed., pp. 512–548). London: Methuen.

Chess, S., Korn, S. J., and Fernandez, P. B. (1971). *Psychiatric disorders of children with congenital rubella.* New York: Brunner/Mazel.

Cole, D. A. (1986). Out-of-home child placement and family adaptation: A theoretical framework. *American Journal of Mental Deficiency, 91,* 226–236.

Corchesne, E. (1991). Neuroanatomic imaging in autism. *Pediatrics, 87,* 781–790.

Cutler, B. C., & Kozloff, M. A. (1987). Living with autism: Effects on families and family needs. In D. J. Cohen & A. M. Donnellan (Eds.), *Handbook of autism and pervasive developmental disorders* (pp. 513–527). New York: Wiley.

Dawson, G., & Osterling, J. (1997). Early intervention in autism. In M. Guralnick (Ed.), *Effectiveness of early intervention* (pp. 307–326). Pacific Grove, CA: Brooks/Cole.

DeMyer, M. K. (1979). *Parents and children in autism.* Washington, DC: Winston.

DeMyer, M. K., & Goldberg, P. (1983). Family needs of the autistic adolescent. In E. Schopler & G. Mesibov (Eds.), *Autism in adolescents and adults* (pp. 225–250). New York: Plenum.

Deykin, E. Y., & MacMahon, B. (1979). The incidence of seizures among children with autistic symptoms. *American Journal of Psychiatry, 136,* 1310–1312.

Drotar, D., Baskiwicz, A., Irvin, N., Kennell, J., & Klaus, M. (1975). The adaptation of parents to the birth of an infant with congenital malformation: A hypothetical model. *Pediatrics, 56,* 710–717.

Farber, B. (1959). Effects of a severely mentally retarded child on family integration. *Monographs of the Society for Research in Child Development, 24*(2, Series No. 71).

Ferster, C. B. (1961). Positive reinforcement and behavioral deficits of autistic children. *Child Development, 32,* 437–456.

Fine, M. J. (1985). Intervention from a systems-ecological perspective. *Professional Psychology: Research and Practice, 16,* 262–270.

Galvin-Cook, D. (1996). The impact of having a child with autism. *Developmental Disabilities Special Interest Section Newsletter, 19*(2) 1–4.

Gray, D. E. (1995). Lay conceptions of autism: Parents' explanatory model. *Medical Anthropology, 16,* 99–118.

Harris, S. L. (1984). Intervention planning for the family of the autistic child: A multilevel assessment of the family system. *Journal of Marital and Family Therapy, 10,* 157–166.

Holroyd, J., Brown, N., Wikler, L., & Simmons, J. Q. (1975). Stress in families of institutionalized and noninstitutionalized autistic children. *Journal of Community Psychology, 2,* 26–31.

Holroyd, J., & McArthur, D. (1976). Mental retardation and stress on the parents: A contrast between Down's syndrome and childhood autism. *American Journal of Mental Deficiency, 80,* 431–436.

Huber, C. H. (1979). Parents of the handicapped child: Facilitating acceptance through group counseling. *Personnel and Guidance Journal, 57*(5), 267–269.

Kanner, L. (1943). Autistic disturbances of affective contact. *Nervous Child, 2,* 217–230.

Koegel, R. L., Schreibman, L., O'Neill, R. E., & Burke, J. C. (1983). Personality and family interaction characteristics of families with autistic children. *Journal of Consulting and Clinical Psychology, 51,* 683–692.

Kubler-Ross, E. (1969). *On death and dying.* New York: Macmillan.

Lonsdale, G. (1978). Family life with a handicapped child: The parents speak. *Child Care, Health, and Development, 4,* 99–120.

Marcus, L. M. (1984). Coping with burnout. In E. Schopler & G. B. Mesibov (Eds.), *The effects of autism on the family* (pp. 312–326). New York: Plenum.

Martin, B. (1986). Exceptional individuals and the family: Interactional processes. In R. T. Brown & C. R. Reynolds (Eds.), *Psychological perspectives on childhood exceptionality: A handbook* (pp. 274–308). New York: Wiley.

McCubbin, M. A. (1989). Family stress and family strengths: A comparison of single and two-parent families with handicapped children. *Research in Nursing and Health, 12*(2), 101–110.

McKinney, B., & Peterson, R. A. (1987). Predictors of stress in parents of developmentally disabled children. *Journal of Pediatric Psychology, 13,* 133–150.

Milgram, N. A., & Atzil, M. (1988). Parenting stress in raising autistic children. *Journal of Autism and Developmental Disorders, 18*(3), 415–424.

Minuchin, S. (1974). *Families and family therapy.* Cambridge, MA: Harvard University Press.

Moes, D., Koegel, R. L., Schreibman, L., & Loos, L. M. (1992). Stress profiles for mothers and fathers of children with autism. *Psychological Reports, 71,* 1272–1274.

Morgan, S. B. (1988). The autistic child and family functioning: A developmental family systems perspective. *Journal of Autism and Developmental Disorders, 18,* 263–280.

Norton, P., & Drew, C. (1994). Autism and potential family stressors. *American Journal of Family Therapy, 22,* 67–76.

Parks, R. (1977). Parental reactions to the birth of a handicapped child. *Health Social Work, 2,* 52–66.

Piven, J., & Folstein, S. (1994). The genetics of autism. In M. L. Bauman & T. L. Kemper (Eds.), *The neurobiology of autism* (pp. 18–44). Baltimore: Johns Hopkins University Press.

Richman, N. (1988). Autism: Making an early diagnosis. *The Practitioner, 232,* 601–605.

Rimland, B. (1964). *Infantile autism.* New York: Appleton-Century-Crofts.

Roberts, J. (1984). Families with infants and young children who have special needs. *Family Therapy Collections, 11,* 1–17

Rodrigue, J. R., Morgan, S. B., & Geffken, G. (1990). Families of autistic children: Psychological functioning of mothers. *Journal of Clinical Child Psychology, 19,* (4), 371–379.

Schain, R., & Yannet, H. (1960). Infantile autism. *Journal of Pediatrics, 57,* 560–567.

Schopler, E. (1971). Parents of psychotic children as scapegoats. *Journal of Contemporary Psychotherapy, 4,* 17–22.

Schopler, E., & Mesibov G. (1984). Professional attitudes towards parents. In E. Schopler & G. Mesibov (Eds.), *The effects of autism on the family* (pp. 3–17). New York: Plenum.

Shapiro, J. (1989). Stress, depression, and support group participation in mothers of developmentally delayed children. *Family Relations, 38,* 169–173.

Sherman, B. R., & Cocozza, J. J. (1984). Stress in families of the developmentally disabled: A literature review of factors affecting the decision to seek out-of-home placements. *Family Relations, 33,* 95–103.

Simeonsson, R. J. (1988). Unique characteristics of families with young handicapped children. In D. B. Bailey & R. J. Simeonsson (Eds.), *Family assessment in early intervention* (pp. 27–43). Columbus, OH: Merrill.

Smith, B., Chung, M. C., & Vostanis, P. (1994). The path to care in autism: Is it better now? *Journal of Autism and Developmental Disorders, 24* (5), 551–563.

Solnit, A. J., & Stark, M. H. (1961). Mourning and the birth of a defective child. *Psychoanalytic Study of the Child, 16,* 523–537.

Stone, W. L., Hoffman, E. L., Lewis, S. E., & Ousley, O. Y. (1994). Early recognition of autism: Parental reports vs. clinical observation. *Archives of Pediatric Adolescent Medicine, 148,* 174–179.

Trivette, C. M., Dunst, C. J., Deal, A. G., Hamer, A. W., & Propst, S. (1990). Assessing family strengths and family functioning style. *Topics in Early Childhood Special Education, 10*(1), 16–35.

Tunali, B., & Power, T. G. (1993). Creating satisfaction: A psychological perspective on stress and coping in families of handicapped children. *Journal of Child Psychology and Psychiatry, 34*(6), 945–957.

Turnbull, A. P., & Winton, P. J. (1984). Parent involvement policy and practice: Current research and implications for families of young, severely handicapped children. In J. Blacher (Ed.), *Severely handicapped young children and their families: Research in review* (pp. 377–397). New York: Academic Press.

Vadasy, P. F., Fewell, R. R., Meyer, D. J., Schell, G., & Greenberg, M. T. (1984). Involved parents: Characteristics and resources of fathers and mothers of young handicapped children. *Journal of the Division for Early Childhood, 8,* 3–12.

Winton, P. J. (1990). Promoting a normalizing approach to families: Integrating theory into practice. *Topics in Early Childhood Special Education, 10*(2), 90–103.

CHAPTER 4

Occupational Therapy Evaluation of the Child With Autism

**Mary Alhage Kientz, MS, OTR/L, and
Heather Miller-Kuhaneck, MS, OTR/L, BCP**

Evaluations are completed for many purposes. Occupational therapists often perform evaluations to diagnose, plan intervention, or determine the effectiveness of treatment (Meisels, 1996; Stewart, 1996; Westby, Stevens Dominquez, & Oetter, 1996). The purpose of an evaluation may differ depending on the setting where it is being completed or who the referral source is. However, an evaluation is always completed to gather information about the performance of the child who is referred. Information can be gathered in many ways, and no one approach is effective for all children or in all situations.

Children with autism demonstrate global developmental delays and behavioral challenges that necessitate a different evaluation approach than might otherwise be used. Autism affects every child differently; therefore, every child needs to be evaluated to find his or her own areas of skills and abilities. In addition, having a child with autism significantly affects the functioning of the entire family; therefore, the concerns of family and caregivers should also be considered of utmost importance when devising a plan for evaluation. An individualized and transdisciplinary approach to evaluation is imperative. The evaluation process

should begin with an emphasis on the child's functional abilities prior to the examination of component skills. The contexts in which the child performs and their influence on the child's performance must also be considered. With these ideas in mind, this chapter will present an approach for evaluating the child with autism that relies more on observations and informal tools than on standardized testing, and the chapter will suggest some specific tools and methods that may be useful when evaluating children with autism.

Focus on Function

In the past, occupational therapy evaluations have tended to use a disablement approach that focused on determining the problems a person was having in terms of component skills (Trombly, 1993). Many of the assessment tools that occupational therapists used were focused on the negative aspects of performance—the problems and the "can'ts" of the person's current level of functioning. These tools are difficult to use to create a measure of function because they primarily examine dysfunction. In the 1990s, leaders in the occupational therapy field began changing focus to reflect the basic tenets of the profession. The literature (Coster,

1998; Trombly, 1993) began presenting models for assessment that begin with social participation, roles, and task performance and then consider component skills only as they are related to limitations in participation and performance.

The "top-down" approach to evaluation focuses on a person's ability to participate in life roles before it examines specific performance components. This approach to evaluation is desirable and will help focus intervention on specific outcomes that are to be achieved. First, the therapist must assist in defining what is important for that person. What are the essential activities of his or her life, and what are the activities the person wants to perform or accomplish? For adults, the determination of a person's valued roles and the limitations to fulfilling these roles are the priority. Coster (1998) recommends that for a child, however, the top level of the top-down approach should be the examination of the child's pattern of occupational engagement in relation to the particular contexts in which they occur. For a child, the essential activities and task performances to be assessed would be centered on the contextual environments of home, school, and community. Performance components are then assessed only as a means of gathering information on the limitations to fulfilling roles and participating in valued activities.

Assessment of Context as Part of Comprehensive Evaluation

Ecological assessment is based on the belief that a child's performance is a function of the interaction between the child and the context in which he or she is performing (Lowenthal, 1991; McCormick, 1997; Welch, 1994). The ecological model assumes that the child is part of a system that includes the child, the environment (including physical, social, and cultural features), and the environmental expectations. If any part of the system is altered, the other parts of the system are also affected (Lowenthal, 1991; McCormick, 1997; Welch, 1994). Those using this model believe that if a change in the context is made, it will influence the child's performance. Therefore, ecological assessment is one method of evaluation that is compatible with a top-down evaluation approach.

Types of ecological assessments include observations, interviews, checklists, histories, and questionnaires (Crist, 1998; Dunn, 1998). Ecological assessment involves observing the performance of a child within the naturally occurring context. This process involves documenting what the child with autism does to participate in activities within the context compared to what a typical child does within the same context (Dunn, 1998). The question during the evaluation becomes how to help the child with autism function more effectively in the context in which he or she has to perform, namely, the classroom, the lunchroom, and the home (Dunn, 1998). In contrast to standardized assessment, ecological assessment examines the child's performance in relation to what the child has to do within a particular environment, not only in relation to specific test performance (McCormick, 1997). Table 4.1 describes other differences between the two assessment approaches.

Because contextual issues can significantly affect a child's functional abilities, one may choose to use a framework such as the Ecology of Human Performance (EHP) that considers context in the assessment process (Dunn, Brown, & McGuigan, 1994). The EHP helps therapists to think about performance in context by considering the child, the child's performance, and the contexts in which the child performs. Using EHP, the therapist assesses the child's performance of tasks within the naturally occurring environment and compares it to the typical performance of peers completing the same task in the same environment. Through task analysis, the therapist answers questions such as: Where does the child begin

Table 4.1
Differences Between Ecological Assessment and Traditional Assessment

	Ecological Assessment	Traditional Assessment
Reference	Compares child's performance to the demands and tasks in the child's environments	Compares child's test performance with that of a sample of similar children who were administered the same test items
Focus	Child's ability to meet setting and task expectations and participate in activities and routines in natural settings.	Language forms and structures described in the normal development research as representative of children at the child's age or stage of development
Procedures	The occupational therapist who uses the ecological assessment observes the child's behavior in daily activities and interviews persons who know the child well	Elicits the child's responses to a set of standardized tasks thought to represent major skills/abilities in the area
Assessment Context	Natural settings: Assessment team includes parents and peers	Contrived settings: Independent assessments by discipline representatives
Best Use of Results	To generate individualized goals and objectives and plan special instruction	To determine child's status relative to same-age peers; for diagnosis and determination of eligibility for special education services

Note. From: "Ecological Assessment and Planning," L. McCormick, 1997, in L. McCormick, D. Frome Loeb, & R. L. Schiefelbusch (Eds.), *Supporting Children with Communication Difficulties in Inclusive Settings: School Based Language Intervention*, pp. 223–256, Boston: Allyn & Bacon. Copyright 1997 by Allyn & Bacon. Reprinted with permission.

to experience difficulty? How much progress has the child made? and Where should intervention begin? (See Bulgren and Knackendoffel, 1986.) EHP also considers the context or environment as a factor in performance.

As Dunn (1998) states,

Many times performance takes on more meaning when it is conducted in relevant contexts; poor performance in a context not relevant for the person may only indicate lack of meaningfulness of the task in that context, not lack of skill performance. (p. 71)

The environmental aspects of contexts include physical, social, and cultural influences (AOTA, 1994).

A Transdisciplinary Approach

A transdisciplinary approach suggests that team members work together to devise an evaluation plan, decide what strategies and tools to use, and decide who will complete what part of the evaluation. This delineation is not necessarily made according to discipline but according to the individual team members' expertise, experience, and time. For example, the occupational therapist may not address fine motor skills if another team member is comfortable assessing this area. Every team member may also look at skills a little differently (Westby et al., 1996). A transdisciplinary team approach is recommended for evaluating children with autism because their needs are extremely diverse and because many areas of performance can be affected. The team approach helps everyone see the whole child instead of compartmentalizing the child into component skills.

Characteristics of Autism and Influence on Evaluation

As a label, autism does not effectively communicate the functional abilities of any particular child. The condition of autism involves limitations in a wide range of skills and behaviors.

Therefore, predetermining by only the diagnosis which areas the child will need to have evaluated is impossible. Each child will have a highly variable picture, necessitating an extremely individualized approach. However, certain issues and behaviors that can affect evaluation processes are common to this population. Children with autism exhibit difficulties with reciprocal social interaction, verbal and nonverbal communication, selective attention, imitation abilities, and sensory processing among other areas (APA, 2000; Mays & Gillon, 1993; Rapin, 1991). These specific characteristics often make evaluation challenging, particularly if standardized tests are being used.

Standardized Tests

If an evaluator wishes to use standardized tests, proper planning of the testing situation is key. A helpful approach is for the tester and the child to become familiar with each other prior to beginning any test procedure. If the examiner is prepared, he or she can adapt procedures and methods in many ways to elicit the best performance from the child (Janzen, 1996). These adaptations involve, for example, limiting eye contact during the testing situation, using gestures to help clarify instructions, giving directions nonverbally where appropriate (i.e., gesturing, modeling), omitting unnecessary words, making directions short and specific, pausing after requests to give ample time for processing, and shortening testing sessions. Enlisting parents to assist and using favorite toys or other objects to engage the child may also be helpful strategies. Findings indicate that children with autism will score higher on standardized tests if procedures are altered to increase motivation and attention (Koegel, Koegel, & Smith, 1997). However, adapting the procedures of a norm-referenced test in the ways mentioned will invalidate the scores that are generated. Therefore, interpretation of the test results must be done cautiously.

Recently, the use of standardized testing has come into question, particularly, when the use is to test children with autism (Greenspan, 1996; Greenspan & Meisels, 1996; McCormick, 1997; Spencer, Krefting, & Mattingly, 1993; Zelazo, 1997). Many believe that standardized protocols, particularly norm-referenced tests, do not allow the child with autism to demonstrate his or her best abilities in a typical environment. As Stanley Greenspan (1996) states, "We have structured tests that bear little relation to the child's everyday functional world, and that, as a result, fail to reveal most children's highest capacities" (p. 231). In addition, the contrived situations of most testing sessions do not allow generalization of performance to more typical environments and may not assist in the development of a meaningful plan with functional goals.

When evaluating a child with autism, therapists should consider how the child performs within the environments that are typical for that child and how those contexts affect the child's ability to function. The therapist needs to determine how and when the child functions most effectively and what strategies the child currently uses to improve performance. Therefore, therapists should select assessment tools and strategies that address the performance of the child within natural environments. These tools and strategies will address first the functional concerns of the family and others (i.e., child will not sit at the table for dinner). Only after the child is assessed in his or her natural environment and after overall performance is considered should component skills be addressed.

Standardized assessments typically provide information regarding component skills and not much information concerning the performance of the child in natural environments. For instance, a child with autism may perform near or above age level in motor skills on a standardized assessment, but this assessment will not allow the evaluators to see how effectively the child uses these skills in a day-to-day fashion (Mays & Gillon, 1993). Additionally, a child may use certain strategies to perform during a testing situation but may not maintain this level of skill in daily performance (Spencer, Krefting, & Mattingly, 1993).

The performance of the child at school, home, and in the community needs to be considered first when assessing children with autism. A child's abilities must be considered in relation to the environments in which the child is performing. Therefore, the strategies and methods for evaluating children with autism that are presented in this chapter will primarily focus on using an ecological approach to evaluation and will rely on the occupational therapist's skill of observation, task analysis, and problem solving.

Although a transdisciplinary team approach is ideal, certain team members commonly evaluate particular areas that fall within their expertise. Therefore, the areas that are typically included within the occupational therapist's roles and responsibilities will be presented. The following sections will discuss the possible tools and strategies that are available to evaluate the child with autism in those areas. These tools and strategies focus on the child's skills, his or her performance, or the context in which the child is performing. Table 4.2 lists specific strategies for making traditional assessment sessions as comfortable and nonthreatening as possible for the child with autism. This chapter will not include all of the specific tests to examine component skills because that information is available elsewhere; however, see Appendix 4.A for a listing of some specific assessments that examine component skills.

The Evaluation Process

A specific process is followed when an evaluation is desired. First, a referral must be made. The therapist must then define the problem to

determine the appropriate tools and methods of assessment. Last, the evaluation is completed using a variety of appropriate techniques.

Referral

Evaluation typically occurs after a referral from a parent, caregiver, physician, or another member of the child's team. A child diagnosed with autism typically has multiple team members involved in his or her life. The referral may be initiated for a variety of reasons stemming from the pervasive nature of autism and the multiple perspectives represented by members of the team. First, the therapist must determine why the evaluation is being requested. Clarifying this purpose will help determine what information is needed. The evaluation process should be driven by the wants and needs of the family and child. This person-centered approach involves selecting evaluation strategies that are related to the family and the child's reported concerns, with team members' concerns considered secondarily.

Defining the Problem

The therapist needs first to define the problem. Defining the problem as specifically as possible helps the therapist to determine the most appropriate course of action for evaluation. The therapist needs to identify not only what problem the child is having but also what behavior is expected across environments for that child. Often, this step of defining the problem is completed through interviews with significant people in the child's life. The concerns that are identified when interviewing family and team members will tend to focus on functional behaviors and difficulties that occur during participation in typical childhood roles and activities.

Choosing Specific Methods or Tools

The therapist next needs to decide the best way to gather information about the specified con-

Table 4.2
Therapeutic Use of Self Strategies for Children With a PDD

Use of self strategy	Clinical rationale for use	Target outcome	Use of strategy for assessment and treatment
Grading of proximity (manipulating your distance to facilitate the therapeutic process)	Some children with a PDD have neurological disturbances that make it difficult to process and make sense of novel stimuli, such as that associated with unfamiliar settings and people. Limiting/grading change in proximity facilitates the child's ability to predict the environment (i.e., the clinician/other team members.)	Child acclimates to the setting with minimal disorientation, discomfort, or anxiety. Child perceives clinician/team as safe and predictable. Trust/rapport is established between child and clinician/team. Trust/rapport is established between family and clinician/team.	Initial assessment: 1. Upon entering the room assume a non-threatening sitting position, for example on the floor. Maintain position and location for as long as possible. 2. If feasible only move to another location after the child orients to your presence (i.e., repeatedly eye gazes to you, walks past/behind you, or touches, sniffs you) 3. Conduct a proximity assessment, to determine the child's natural distance comfort zone for entering your space. Ongoing treatment: 1. Continually attend to child's response to your physical presence; modify proximity to ensure the child's success and comfort at all times. 2. Assist others in establishing an understanding of their own proximity-effects as they work with the child. 3. Establish adult-child proximity guidelines for the team if necessary.
Grading of pace (manipulating when you act to facilitate the therapeutic process)	Some children with a PDD experience difficulty in sustaining the proper state of readiness needed to successfully attend to, plan for, or engage in any one therapeutic activity.	Child exhibits adaptive behavior only (in lieu of maladaptive/stereotypical behaviors).	Initial assessment & ongoing treatment: 1. Before introducing objects/activity first notice what the child is attending to.

Table 4.2
Continued

Use of self strategy	Clinical rationale for use	Target outcome	Use of strategy for assessment and treatment
	Grading the introduction of novelty (i.e., a sensory, social, cognitive, or motor demand) into child-directed activity enhances the child's natural ability to sustain attention to what is familiar about the task, while shifting attention to what is novel. It is the artful introduction of novelty that supports true and conceptual motoric learning.	Child (while calm and happy) learns how to expand his play repertoire developing more age appropriate skills in the motor, social, and cognitive aspects of play. Child develops the perception that therapy is fun/non-stressful, fueling his tolerance for higher demands from clinician over time. Child's attention skills (sustaining and shifting) are enhanced.	2. Identify at least two ways to make use of that exact item/activity to facilitate the child's therapeutic process. 3. Assess the child's readiness for your intervention idea by noticing his or her: body position; arousal level; and natural eye gaze to you/the item. 4. Mentally predict how you will build on the child's success if your plan works, and how you will modify your plan if it fails, considering and securing other materials you may need. 5. When ready to begin, move, speak, and act with timing that allows the child to experience a change in only one variable at a time. Continue to manipulate only one variable at a time, until the child successfully accomplishes attending to, planning for, or engaging with the object/activity in a way that reflects progress (an improvement in the sensory, social/emotional, cognitive, or motor areas). 6. Modify your pace more dramatically (or change the target activity) if the child does not attend to, plan for, or engage in the task/play activity in the (successful) way you had predicted.

continues

Table 4.2
Continued

Use of self strategy	Clinical rationale for use	Target outcome	Use of strategy for assessment and treatment
Use of melodic intonation (manipulating your voice to facilitate the therapeutic process)	Some children with a PDD have difficulty interpreting and responding to verbal information. They often struggle to understand the semantics of speech. Children with a PDD tend to better process the para-linguistics of speech (volume, inflection, etc.). Furthermore, children with a PDD seem to have a natural affinity for music.	Child's comprehension of verbs/nouns/adjectives etc., is enhanced (receptive language). Child's ability to verbally comment, request, or protest (expressive language) is enhanced. Child experiences an effective, non-invasive (hands-off) method of being redirected. Child's attention skills (sustaining and shifting) are enhanced.	1. Before speaking to the child, discern what purpose your language will serve (i.e., to comment/label, or to request/state a directive). This helps you to predict how you will conduct yourself after speaking (i.e., repeat or modify your utterance). 2. Before speaking identify if what you plan to say matches the child's receptive language level (consult with the child's speech/language pathologist if uncertain). Determine if the word/phrase has any suggested inflection that can help the child learn about/respond to the word. For example, when assisting the child in zipping/unzipping his coat, the words "up" and "down" can be said with a rise/fall in pitch. 3. Position yourself in audible proximity of the child. 4. As you utter the word/s, use a singsong or lyrical delivery. 5. Determine child's response (eye gaze to toy/you etc.). If the desired response does not occur repeat or modify, after pausing (to avoid auditory satiation).

Table 4.2
Continued

Use of self strategy	Clinical rationale for use	Target outcome	Use of strategy for assessment and treatment
Use of self as a teaching tool (Educating family members and/or team members)	Children with a PDD demonstrate the most gains when those supporting their progress do so with consistency and continuity of care. Educating family/team members (through explanation of theory, and instruction on efficacious techniques) promotes consistency and continuity in the child's program.	Child's family learns theoretical and practical information that empowers them in understanding, caring for, and advocating for their child with a PDD. Child experiences holistic intervention featuring efficacious and consistent treatment methods. Child's therapeutic process is fully enhanced. Child requires less therapeutic/specialized intervention. Child actualizes his full potential in his childhood role as a learner, player, communicator, family member, and society/community member.	1. Allow yourself to be a vehicle through which families/other team members learn about the child from an OT perspective. Recommend helpful reading or audio/visual materials on PDD and OT. 2. Actively include family members in treatment. Invite professionals working outside your facility into your sessions (school-based or private). Use collaborative telephone conferences, round-robin letters, transdisciplinary (shared) treatment journals, or e-mailing as indicated. 3. Provide written information about the child's program, particularly sensory diet programming. Inservice others on program implementation and data collection. 4. Allow families to videotape therapy, modeling techniques appropriate to demonstrate in this way. Request that parents videotape themselves as well, thereby supporting their learning across settings.

Contributed by Lynette Scotese-Wojtila.

cerns (see Table 4.3 for questions to consider when selecting an assessment tool or strategy). Information gathering includes a review of the record, interviews, observations, and testing. Many factors need to be considered when selecting methods and specific assessment tools that are appropriate for the child being evaluated. The therapist should consider if the test or strategy addresses family and provider concerns, if it considers how a child arrived at an answer, and if it provides information that will be useful for designing intervention (Fisher, 1992; Meisels, 1996). Appendix 4.B also lists assessment tools specifically developed for use with children with autism. Although none of these tools have been developed by occupational therapists for therapy purposes, some may be of interest to the occupational therapy practitioner.

Typically, therapists will use multiple strategies or tools to gather the information they need to address the evaluation concerns. Combining the types of tools and methods that are used to gain the information needed about the child is important to do. For example, a therapist may begin the evaluation process by reviewing the child's records and history. He or she may then talk to the family and significant others in the child's life to gather pertinent information and current functional concerns. Most therapists also combine the use of formal tests with less formal testing such as observation, checklists, and rating scales. Therapists may find formal testing difficult to use because children with autism have difficulty following standardized procedures of the tests. In addition, these formal tests frequently do not address the evaluation concerns of the family because they evaluate primarily component skills. By selecting a combination of strategies and tools, the therapist can gather information from a variety of sources to create a picture of how the child is typically performing. The case study in Appendix 4.C presents an example of the evaluation process.

Evaluation of a Child With Autism

As stated earlier, autism is a pervasive disorder that has the potential to affect children's abilities to initiate and maintain relationships, to interact with their environment, and to engage in functional, daily activities. The child with autism may have difficulty engaging in activities that other children his or her age can do; thus, the child with autism may have different expectations in life roles (i.e., student, sibling, friend, child). Autism may affect every area of functioning, and it significantly affects the whole family.

Because the child's overall functioning and life roles are affected, the concerns and expectations of the child, the family, and other primary caregivers need to be considered first. These concerns are best addressed by evaluating the child in natural environments and by considering how the child's skills match the expectations and supports within the environment. Looking at the functioning of the child in different environments and considering where performance is difficult leads to functional outcomes.

Table 4.3
Questions to Consider When Selecting Assessment Tools or Strategies

1. Is the strategy relevant to reported concerns of the family and child?

2. Is the strategy completed in the child's natural environment?

3. Will the strategy show evaluators what the child can do?

4. Does the strategy use objects and tools from the child's environment during the assessment?

5. Does the strategy give information that is meaningful to the family and evaluation team?

6. Does the strategy elicit information from different sources?

7. Does the strategy use or encourage a team approach?

8. Is the information that is derived from the strategy important in relation to the child's life?

Joey has difficulty sitting at the table during mealtimes and finishing his meals. Mealtime is considered an important bonding time for the family, and the entire family is expected to eat together. The occupational therapist would first want to observe mealtime, including the activity before and after the meal, and consider the skills Joey has at meals and all aspects of the environment. Only after observing the meal would the occupational therapist consider the component skills that may be interfering with Joey's sitting at the table (i.e., he cannot calm himself, the setting is too noisy, he has difficulty maintaining his balance). By assessing Joey's performance first, the therapist develops functional goals and functional programs because the outcome will be important to Joey and his family (i.e., that Joey will sit at the table with his family for meals).

Participation

Assessment at the level of participation will be completed primarily through interviews with significant people in the child's life and, perhaps, with the child. The level of the child's current ability to participate as a family member (self-care, chores, being included in family events, mealtimes) should be discussed. In addition, the child's ability to fulfill the role of student (getting to and from school, following school routines, learning and completing academic work, interacting and communicating with peers and school staff) must be determined. Finally, if the child is expected to participate as a member of a larger community (neighborhood playmate, Cub Scout), then this area needs to be assessed also. If the child is unable to participate in community events, the specific issues that might be limiting that participation can be examined (behavior problems, sensory overload, inability to communicate).

One tool that examines participation within the school environment is the School Function Assessment (SFA) (Coster, Deeney, Haltiwanger, & Haley, 1998). The SFA is a crite-

rion-referenced assessment that can be completed by an individual or a team of individuals who are familiar with the student and the student's performance within specific environments. The SFA, though not specifically designed for students with autism, includes the domain of cognitive and behavioral activity performance and allows for scoring of the nonphysical aspects of task performance. The cognitive and behavioral areas that are assessed include communication, memory and understanding, following social conventions, task behavior and completion, compliance with adult directives, positive interaction, behavioral regulation, personal care, awareness, and safety. The child's performance is compared to peers in the same setting and is rated on a four-point scale.

Self-Care and Adaptive Behavior

The area of self-care may best be assessed through informal observation and interview. Information can be gathered about the child's ability to complete self-care tasks such as dressing, undressing, feeding, toileting, and bathing. The child's ability to participate in these tasks is compared to the expectations of the family. Certain self-care tasks may be observed to analyze the task and determine if specific performance components require further assessment.

The Vineland Adaptive Behavior Scales (VABS), although not originally developed specifically for children with autism, have recently been researched to create norms for children with autism (Carter et al., 1998). The VABS is a structured parent interview that is scored to compare the child's scores with the research sample.

The Pediatric Evaluation of Disability (PEDI) (Haley, Coster, Ludlow, Haltiwanger, & Andrellos, 1992) is another tool that examines abilities with self-care and adaptive behaviors. It may be used with children ages 6 months–7.5 years and is completed by means of a parent interview. Although it also was not developed specifically for use with children with autism, the interview process can provide much information related to functional self-care abilities.

Assessment During Play

Although play can be used as a means of observing a wide variety of component skills, occupational therapists should also assess play as an end in itself. Play is one of the occupations of a child, and the ability to be playful is an important aspect of childhood (Bundy, 1997). Playfulness is a fundamental characteristic of being a child and of maintaining peer relationships with other children.

Play is also important because it influences motor, language, cognitive, and social emotional development (Linder, 1990). Play allows a child to acquire and practice developmental skills such as manipulating, problem solving, attending to a task, and making choices (Burke, 1993; Linder, 1993). In addition, play helps develop social-emotional skills such as motivation, temperament, adult-child interactions, peer interactions, and behavior (Linder, 1993).

Play Assessments. The Test of Playfulness (ToP) assesses playfulness, which incorporates the elements of intrinsic motivation, internal control, and the freedom to suspend reality (Bundy, 1997). The ToP is a 68-item observational tool for children ages 2–10. The child is observed during play outdoors and indoors for approximately 15 minutes in an environment that is familiar to the child. Because the ToP is still in development, meaningful scores based on the assessment are not yet available. However, Bundy (1997) suggests that the ToP can help give therapists a conceptual framework to systematically assess playfulness.

Tools such as the Preschool Play Scale (Bledsoe & Shepherd, 1982; Knox, 1974) allow therapists to look at skills that are used during play. The Preschool Play Scale measures four domains in children from birth to 6 years old: space management, material management, imitation, and participation. Professionals observe

the child during play and determine a score for each domain. The results can be analyzed to allow comparisons across types of play and age ranges.

Another way to assess play skills is by using the Transdisciplinary Play Based Assessment (TPBA) (Linder, 1990). The TPBA is designed for children from 6 months to 6 years and examines the cognitive, social-emotional, communication and language, as well as sensorimotor domains. Professionals complete systematic observation within natural environments in each domain using an integrated team approach. One team member is the play facilitator, one is the parent facilitator, one is the observing team member, and another operates a video camera (Linder, 1990). The TPBA assesses all areas of development within a period of 60–90 minutes by observing structured and unstructured play, motor play, child-to-child interactions, and parent-child interactions (Linder, 1990, 1993). The assessment is flexible, allowing the child to lead; involves parents and caregivers; and is holistic in its approach because all disciplines work together (Linder, 1990; 1993). Results from the TPBA can be used to identify difficulties, plan intervention, and measure progress.

Unstructured Observation of Play. Play behavior can be assessed in numerous ways, including naturalistic observation. Observing a child at play reveals much information. The observation can include specific play activities that the team has determined to be difficult for the child, which allows the team to examine the child's ability to participate in play. Group play activities can be observed so that the child's performance can be compared to the performance of his or her peers. Social participation also can be noted by observing group play. The child can potentially be observed in all important contexts such as home, neighborhood, school, and community (playgrounds, community events). Is the child able to participate in play and be playful with his or her siblings, parents, neighborhood peers, classmates, and others within the environment?

The specific skills used during play also can be assessed through unstructured observation. Observation of play can provide information about many aspects of the performance of the child. For example, which types of toys are chosen, with what and with whom the child chooses to play, and how the child organizes play may provide information about the child's developmental levels, sensory preferences, or communication and social skills. Observation of play can also give information about the child's skill abilities in areas such as imitation and motor planning as well as fine and gross motor abilities (Schaaf & Mulrooney, 1989; Stone, Lemanek, Fishel, Fernandez, & Altemeir, 1990). Contextual observations that can be made during play include the types of toys that are available to the child, the organization of the toys, the types of play space that are available, and the kind of time (e.g., structured or free) that is available for play (Schaaf & Mulrooney, 1989). See Table 4.4 for a list of some specific play observations.

Behavioral Issues

Children with autism often display behaviors such as repetitious behavior, hitting, screaming, or self-injurious behavior that others consider challenging. Some children with autism may demonstrate no challenging behaviors, but others may have significant behavioral issues that interfere with their abilities to participate fully in a variety of settings and activities. Most of the behaviors seen in children with autism are manifestations of the disability and frequently are the only way the child has to communicate even basic things such as pleasure or anger.

These behaviors can interfere with a child's ability to participate fully in a variety of ways. For example, if a child frequently makes loud noises, the behavior may interfere with participation in some classroom settings. If a child tends to hit others as a means to request toys, a

---

Table 4.4

Specific Play Observations to Be Made for a Child With Autism

Ability to be a playmate

Ability to be playful

Ability to use toys appropriately

Ability to understand the types of play that certain objects can be used for

Joint attention with others during play

Ability to use ideation for play (what to play)

Ability to make choices for play

Ability to expand on a current play activity or alter it

Eye contact during play

Interaction during play

Arousal level during play

Ability to imitate others in play

Ability to maintain attention to play and shift attention during play

Types of activities sought out when allowed to play independently

Sensory preferences during play

Motor skills used during play

Level of play skill (functional, representational, symbolic or imaginary play, and role play)

Level of social play (onlooker, solitary, parallel, associative, cooperative)

Ability to tease or joke

Ability to understand when another is teasing or playing

Ability to handle challenge or frustration

What types of structure or assistance improve play performance

---

parent may be reluctant to bring the child to the local playgroup. Challenging behavior may also affect the child's ability to make and sustain relationships, including friendships with peers.

The occupational therapist, as a member of a transdisciplinary team, needs to be actively involved in identifying and addressing behaviors that are interfering with the child's ability to participate in typical settings and activities. The occupational therapist's understanding of contextual issues and their influence on a child's behavior is vital to a thorough assessment of the conditions surrounding the behavior. When addressing behavioral issues, occupational therapists offer a unique perspective of looking at the child and helping to determine the communicative intent of the behavior.

Functional Assessment. Professionals analyze the meaning of a behavior using functional assessment. Functional assessment is a way to understand the child's strengths, preferences, and ways of communication and it also examines the influences of the environment on the child's behavior. From the information gathered, professionals form a hypothesis regarding the function, or communicative intent, of the behavior and develop intervention strategies. Intervention focuses on teaching alternative ways to meet the communicative needs that the behavior is now serving (McCormick, 1997).

A functional assessment is composed primarily of observations across contexts and interviews with significant others in the child's life such as parents and teachers. Behaviors are considered within the typical routine of the child's day, including specific activities, diet, and types of medications. Factors such as the time of day, the setting, and the people and objects that are present are also considered and compared to the times that the behavior would most likely and least likely occur. Interviews with parents and caregivers should include asking about the child's preferred activities, the activities that are viewed positively by the child, and the circumstances that usually lead to the challenging behavior (O'Neill, Horner, Albin, Storey, & Sprague, 1990).

Within the process of functional assessment, the communicative functions of the behavior are identified. Children with autism frequently use behaviors as a means to communicate wants and needs because they do not have any other effective means to get their needs met. Important factors to consider are whether the child has an effective means of communication, how the child typically communicates wants and needs, and what method of communication the child primarily uses.

Communicative Functions of Behavior. The idea that behaviors serve a communicative function is now commonly accepted (Carr & Durand, 1985; Carr et al., 1994; Koegel, Koegel, & Dunlap, 1996). Children with autism communicate their wants, needs, and emotions by engaging in behaviors that others consider challenging. They use a certain repertoire of behaviors to functionally communicate to others because they have limited oral language skills. For instance, a child with autism may hit another child. The typical initial reaction is to correct the child by giving some sort of consequence (verbal reprimand, time-out). However, this child with autism may be trying to communicate many things by hitting the child. For example, the child could be intending to communicate any of the following types of messages:

- Request: "I want that toy" or "I need more information."
- Refusal: "I don't want to do that."
- Escape: "I can't do this anymore" or "I don't know how to do this."
- Socialization: "Hi, I want to play."
- Sensory: "You got too close to me. It didn't feel good."
- Organic: "I don't feel good, my stomach hurts."

Because the child's communication repertoire is so limited, he or she may also use the same behavior to communicate many different things (just as a baby cries for food, a diaper change, sleep, or the need for nurturing). For example, in the classroom, the child hits as a means of refusal; in the cafeteria, the child hits because of sensory overload; and at recess, the child hits to initiate an interaction with a peer. Because behaviors typically serve more than one purpose, multiple team interventions are needed.

Table 4.5, *Observation Tool for Analyzing the Communicative Functions of Behaviors* (Donnellan, Mirenda, Mesaros, & Fassbender, 1984), can be used to determine what function the behavior is serving for the child. The form considers the communicative behaviors (horizontal axis) and possible functions (vertical axis). The child would be observed to see how he or she is communicating (behaviors) and what he or she is trying communicate (functions) in a particular context. One would match possible functions and behaviors by noting the points where the horizontal and vertical axes intersect. These intersecting behaviors and functions would suggest a possible hypothesis about the communicative intent of the behavior, and a support plan then could be developed (Donnellan et al., 1984).

Another tool that assists in determining the communicative intent of behavior is the Motivation Assessment Scale (MAS) (Durand, 1988). The MAS comprises 16 statements that describe conditions during which a behavior occurs (i.e., this behavior occurs after a command to perform a difficult task). The informant (parent, teacher, caregiver) rates the statement on a scale of 0 (never) to 6 (always). The statements on the MAS reflect four possible communicative intents: sensory, escape, social attention, and tangible consequences. The area receiving the highest points is considered the possible intent of the behavior, and interventions are based on that hypothesis. The MAS is useful to examine a specific behavior in a specific setting.

Influences of Context on Behavior. The contexts in which the behavior occurs are important to examine during functional analysis. Contexts to consider include the physical setting, the social setting, the tasks, predictability, and choice making. The physical setting includes where the activity is occurring such as the classroom or lunchroom, the temperature of the room, and the lighting. The social setting includes the number of people present and who is or is not present (i.e., music teacher is now in room). The tasks context includes examining whether the activities are meaningful, interesting, and challenging to the child and whether the activities and instructions are done within the natural context. Predictability and choice making contexts include examining whether a child is aware of the schedule of activities, is able to determine when a preferred activity will end, and is able to choose activities. Table 4.6 lists other contextual features to consider when assessing behavior and performance.

Assessing the Social-Emotional Aspects of Performance

Children with autism have difficulty with social-emotional skills (APA, 2000). Yet, social-emotional skills are often overlooked when evaluating the child and developing intervention plans. The social-emotional area includes skills such as the child's ability to self-regulate, engage with others and form attachments, use intentional communication, and form a complex sense of self (Greenspan, 1996). The development of these skills begins at birth. Competence with social-emotional skills allows a child to develop relationships, learn, and meet his or her own needs (Cronin, 1996). These skills allow a child to develop satisfactory relationships with his or her caregivers and a sense of well-being and positive self-worth. In turn, these skills allow the child to accept challenges in play and other daily routines as well as develop relationships with peers.

Emotional Status. One scale to assess social-emotional skills is the Functional Emotional Assessment Scale (FEAS) (Greenspan, 1992). The FEAS examines the social, emotional, cognitive, and communicative capacities of a child by observing the interactions of the child with caregivers. The FEAS addresses six areas in children 3–48 months old: (1) primary emotional capacities; (2) emotional range: sen-

Table 4.5

Observation Tool for Analyzing the Communicative Functions of Behaviors

BEHAVIORS (columns): Aggression, Bizarre Verbalizations, Inapp. Oral/Anal Behavior, Perseverative Rituals, Self-Injurious Behavior, Self-Stimulation, Tantrum, Facial Expression, Gaze Aversion, Gazing/Staring, Gesturing/Pointing, Hugging/Kissing, Masturbation, Object Manipulation, Proximity Positioning, Pushing/Pulling, Reaching/Grabbing, Running, Touching, Delayed Echolalia, Laughing/Giggling, Scream/Yell, Swearing, Verbal/Physical Threats, Whining/Crying, Complex Sign/Approximation, Complex Speech/Approximation, One Word Sign/Approximation, Speech/Approximation, Picture/Written Word

FUNCTIONS

I. Interactive

A. Requests for
- Attention
- Play Interactions
- Affection
- Permission to Engage in an Activity
- Action by Receiver
- Assistance
- Information/Clarification
- Objects
- Food

B. Negations
- Protest
- Refusal
- Cessation

C. Declarations/Comments
- About Events/Actions
- About Objects/Persons
- About Errors/Mistakes
- Affirmation
- Greeting
- Humor

D. Declarations About Feelings
- Anticipation
- Boredom
- Confusion
- Fear
- Frustration
- Hurt Feelings
- Pain
- Pressure

II. Non-Interactive

A. Self-Regulation

B. Rehearsal

C. Habitual

D. Relaxation/Tension Release

Note. From "Analyzing the communicative functions of aberrant behavior," by A. Donnellan, P. Mirenda, R. Mesaros, and L. Fassbender, 1984, *Journal for the Association for Persons with Severe Handicaps, 9*, p. 201–212, Baltimore: TASH. Copyright 1984 by TASH. Reprinted with permission.

sorimotor; (3) emotional range: affective; (4) associated motor, sensory, language, and cognitive capacities; (5) general infant tendencies; and (6) overall caregiver tendencies. Each of these capacities is rated as not present, fleetingly present, intermittently present, present most of the time, or present consistently under all circumstances. The clinician observes the child with primary caregivers and interacts with the child on at least two occasions. The FEAS is an observational tool because the tool's author believes that children demonstrate their abilities such as intentionality and motivation through the contexts of relationships (Greenspan, 1996). Greenspan also developed the FEAS to help professionals systematically observe these developmental areas. Because it takes practice and skill to observe and make judgements using the FEAS, it is not a tool that an inexperienced clinician should use without proper training and practice.

Coping Skills. An area that occupational therapists frequently assess within the social-emotional domain is coping skills. Coping is the ability to make adaptations to meet personal needs and to respond to the demands of the environment (Williamson, Szczepanski, & Zeitlin, 1993). The child is coping when managing feelings, thoughts, and social as well as physical worlds. The outcome of adequate and effective coping is positive thoughts about self, self-esteem, and the ability to have social relationships (Williamson, Szczepanski, & Zeitlin, 1993).

Two scales are available to assess coping skills. They are the *Early Coping Inventory* (Zeitlin, Williamson, & Szczepanski, 1988) and the *Coping Inventory* (Zeitlin, 1985). The *Early Coping Inventory* is for children from 4 to 36 months and older children with special needs who are functioning within this age range. The *Coping Inventory* is for children from 3 to 16 years. Questions regarding a child's coping style and other issues are rated on a 5-point scale, from "ineffective" to "consistently effective"

Table 4.6
Contextual Features to Consider When Assessing Behavior and Performance

Number of students present

Number of adults present

Number of other students with disabilities present

Behavior of other students

Behavior of others toward the student

Time of day

Individual's expectations

Expectations of others concerning the child

Age appropriateness of materials and activity

Nature of materials

Degree to which activity occurs in natural context

Nature and type of instructions given to the individual

Environmental pollutants

Sudden change in activity or environment

Length of activity

Activity just completed

Activity to follow

Interest of activity to individual

Child's social skills (ability)

Physiological state of the individual (hunger, medications, etc.)

Individual's communicative skills and communicative system

Ability to choose activity and with whom to do it

Predictability of activities and expectations

across situations. The results yield the level of coping effectiveness and help identify a child's coping style. When assessing a child's coping skills, therapists should observe the child multiple times in a variety of environments (Williamson, Szczepanski, & Zeitlin, 1993). The parent interview is an important piece in this assessment process to determine present and past coping strategies as well as to gather information such as the child's reaction to change and what is stressful for the child (Williamson, Szczepanski, & Zeitlin, 1993).

Assessing Sensory Processing and Sensory Integration

The idea that children with autism have varying degrees of difficulty processing sensory information is commonly accepted (Ayres, 1979; Mays & Gillon, 1993; Rapin, 1991). Deficits in sensory processing skills, particularly in children ages 0–3 may be one of the greatest hindrances to relating and communicating (Greenspan, 1996; Williamson & Anzalone, 1997). Most children with autism have difficulty registering, filtering, and organizing incoming sensory input, which results in difficulty interpreting and organizing responses to people around them and the environment (Williamson & Anzalone, 1997). Typically, children with autism have difficulty modulating sensory information, which leads to inappropriate responses to sensory stimuli. They may be hyperreponsive (i.e., respond more than would be expected) in one system and hyporesponsive (i.e., respond less than would be expected) in another, or they may fluctuate between hypo- and hypersensitive responsiveness.

One can gather information about a child's sensory processing other than through standardized tests. Frequently, observation of the child during play, functional activities, and interactions with others is the most effective means of assessing sensory processing skills (Anzalone & Williamson, 1997). Observing interactions between the child and the environment as well as the challenges and supports available in the environment is important. Often, a helpful approach is to consider the sensory features of activities while observing the child at play to see how the child responds to different types of input (Williamson & Anzalone, 1997). Observations of this type will offer information about those types of stimuli that help a child function and perform most effectively and those that the child may find uncomfortable. These observations also provide information about the types of activities and toys the child prefers and the child's skill level with these different activities. See Table 4.7 for some specific observations to be made regarding sensory processing.

There are also many specific observations to be made regarding a child's abilities with praxis. The therapist may ask himself or herself the following questions as he or she observes the child.

- Can the child create ideas for sensory motor play?
- How preservative or "fixed" is the child on any given activity?
- Can the child imitate novel actions?
- Can the child create novel plans when a favorite activity is blocked?
- Can the child use verbal cues to assist with motor planning?
- Does hand-over-hand assistance to initiate an activity help motor planning?
- Does the child have the motor skills to adequately execute a motor plan?

Children with autism may also demonstrate difficulties with regulating their arousal levels because they process sensory information inefficiently. The child should be observed completing a variety of sensory motor activities and in a variety of environments to determine the effect of the sensory environment on the child's level of arousal. The child's eye contact during these observations should be noted because it may also be an indication of the child's arousal level (Miller, 1996). Observations that can be made related to arousal level include the following:

- Activity level (lethargic vs. overactive)
- Amount of body motion (sedentary vs. rapid, flighty motion)
- Attention to task
- Eye contact
- Attention to directions
- Behavior (appropriate behavior vs. extreme silliness, misbehaving, aggressive behavior, avoidant or flight behavior)

These observations should be made before and after a variety of types of motion; a variety of

Table 4.7
Observations of Sensory Processing Issues

Sensory System	Hyporesponsiveness	Hyperresponsiveness
Vestibular System	• Has poor balance • Has poor coordination • Seeks sensory stimulation such as rocking, spinning, or twirling self • Has low tone or poor endurance, is lethargic • Prefers upside down positions, jumping, bouncing • Has no nystagmus	• Fears motion • Avoids movement activities • Has behavior problems in the car or on the bus • Becomes overaroused by movement, tends to become overactive • Is very sedentary • Becomes particularly distressed with backward or upside down movement
Tactile System	• Touches everything • Has poor manipulation skills • Requires visual guiding of hands and fingers to complete tasks • Is clumsy with small objects • Mouths objects • Does not notice messy face	• Dislikes unexpected light touch, pulls away but seeks out significant amounts of very deep touch • Avoids closeness of others and retreats to own personal space • Is a very picky eater because of textures or temperatures • Seeks out being under heavy items for extreme deep pressure • Seeks out falling or crash landing • Avoids messy play • Dislikes having face washed or nose wiped • Fusses with clothing or wears only very specific clothing • Becomes extremely distressed with baths, hair cuts, and trips to dentist • Gags easily while eating
Proprioceptive System	• Seeks sensory stimulation such as chewing and biting, pushing, pulling, hitting, or kicking • Has difficulty holding positions • Has poor articulation • Plays too roughly • Seeks out pressure to top of head	• Is tense • Has rigid movements

continues

Table 4.7
Continued

Sensory System	Hyporesponsiveness	Hyperresponsiveness
Auditory System	• Enjoys and seeks out noises • Makes own loud noises • Appears not to hear or respond to noises nearby	• Covers ears, cringes, or avoids noises • Attempts to drown out noises by humming to self • Is distracted by noises • Becomes overaroused by noise such as in cafeteria • Is a very picky eater because of sounds of food inside of head (crunchy is too loud)
Visual System	• Looks at things very intensely • Seeks sensory stimulation through spinning objects, flicking fingers or objects in peripheral vision	• Covers eyes • Prefers dim lighting • Is distracted by movement in own visual field • Becomes overaroused by bright lights
Gustatory and Olfactory Systems	• Seeks out strong tastes and smells • Smells everything	• Avoids strong tastes and smells • Becomes distressed or demonstrates behavioral changes when near strong smells • Refuses to taste foods with strong odors • Gags from smells of foods

types of touch; in different environments in terms of size, number of others present, noise level, and visual stimulation; and at different times of the day.

Sensory Histories. Sensory histories are interviews or checklists that help identify behaviors that are thought to indicate sensory processing dysfunction. They are completed by interviewing a child's parents, teachers, or caregivers regarding the child's reactions to sensory input. A sensory history form typically consists of statements or questions about a child's behavior during functional tasks or activities. Sensory histories rate observed behaviors that are considered to fall within each sensory system, social-emotional behaviors, and activity level. Often, items on a sensory history form are written so the more frequently a behavior occurs, the more it is thought to indicate sensory processing dysfunction.

The process of completing sensory histories engages the family in the evaluation process, helps to begin interactions with the family in a nonthreatening manner (Nelson, 1984), and maintains a family-centered focus. A sensory history assists the therapist by describing difficulties the child may have with daily life events (e.g., cries when hearing unexpected loud noises, screams when face is washed) and allows the parents to specify issues that are difficult for the family (Dunn, 1994). For instance, a parent may report that the child takes two hours to fall asleep and wakes two times a night. The request for this information may be the first time a parent was ever asked about the child's sleeping habits and how it relates to the everyday lives of family members. The chance for parents to discuss these difficulties with the therapist provides an opportunity for parent education. Finally, a sensory history can help prioritize issues for intervention planning and can enhance discussion of the child's skills because the behaviors discussed are familiar to the parents (Dunn, 1994; Parham & Mailloux, 1996).

One sensory history form is the Sensory Profile (Dunn, 1999). Using the Sensory Profile, a parent or caregiver is asked to rate on a scale of Always to Never how often a child engages in a particular behavior. The Sensory Profile has 125 items that are grouped into three main sections: sensory processing, modulation, and behavioral and emotional responses. The items on the Sensory Profile also fit into nine factors that characterize children by their responsiveness to sensory input (Dunn, 1999). Therapists can score each section and factor of the Sensory Profile as either typical performance, probable difference, or definite difference. Although many kinds of sensory histories are available, the Sensory Profile is one of the most researched sensory history forms. A national sample of parents of typical children ages 3–10 completed the Sensory Profile to determine which items described behaviors that are uncommon for typical children (Dunn & Westman, 1996). Research was also completed using the Sensory Profile with children with various disabilities including autism and ADHD (Bennett, 1996; Ermer & Dunn, 1998; Kientz & Dunn, 1997). For example, Kientz & Dunn (1997) found that 85% of the items on the Sensory Profile differentiated between children with and without autism, revealing that it is a tool that may help distinguish children with sensory processing difficulties from those who do not.

Another sensory history form that has been researched extensively is the Evaluation of Sensory Processing (ESP) (Parham & Ecker, 2000). The ESP assesses seven sensory systems: auditory, gustatory, olfactory, proprioceptive, tactile, vestibular, and visual. The ESP also asks parents, teachers, or caregivers to rate the frequency of occurrence of behavior on a Likert scale of Always to Never. A recent study found that 84 of the items on the ESP distinguished between children with and without sensory integrative dysfunction (Johnson-Ecker & Parham, 2000). Another study comparing children with and without autism using the ESP also demonstrated differences between the groups (VerMaas-Lee, 1999).

Assessing the Sensory Qualities of an Activity. When assessing sensory processing skills in children with autism, therapists should also look at the sensory qualities of an observed activity to distinguish between sensory input that is difficult for the child to process and input that the child seeks out. *Form for Analyzing the Sensory Characteristics of Task Performance* (Dunn, 1996) allows one to examine a task and determine the sensory qualities it entails. This form guides assessment of the tasks the child is completing as well as the environment the child is performing in and assists the therapist in determining where a child might be challenged during the completion of an activity. It is helpful in determining the sensory qualities of the task, the environment, and the child's interactions with objects and others (Dunn, 1996).

Assessing the Movement Aspects of Performance

Many children with autism will have some degree of difficulty with motor planning (Donnellan & Leary, 1995; Greenspan & Wieder, 1997; Leary & Hill, 1996). A review of 200 cases of children with autism found that all children had some degree of difficulty with motor planning, and severe problems were seen in 48% of the children (Greenspan & Wieder, 1997). Many professionals have described differences in movement patterns and the term *movement differences* is frequently used in the field of autism to describe difficulties with motor planning and other motor disturbances (Donnellan & Leary, 1995; Leary & Hill, 1996). For this discussion, the term *movement differences* will be used.

Table 4.8
Observations to Assess Movement Differences

Motor Function

- odd hand and body postures
- facial expression and gesture absent or socially inappropriate
- involuntary motor tics
- lack of eye contact
- motor stereotypes (i.e., rocking, spinning, swaying whole body)
- vocal and verbal tics

Volitional Movements

- slowness of spontaneous movements
- motor planning difficulties
- repetitious spontaneous movements (i.e., lining up objects, hand flapping)
- gait disturbances (i.e., reduced arm swing, slow shuffling walk, toe walking)
- speech-language disturbances (i.e., poor speech volume control, jargon, perseverative speech, atypical rate and rhythm)

Disturbances of Overall Behavior or Activity

- extreme response to minor environmental changes
- constant movement (hyperkinesis)
- aggressive behavior
- excessively slow execution of movement (bradykinesis)
- impaired or no imitation
- lack of initiation
- follows routines in repetitive way

Note. From M. Leary & D. A. Hill, "Moving on: Autism and movement disturbance," 1996, *Mental Retardation, 34* (1), pp. 39–53. Copyright 1996 by the American Association on Mental Retardation. Reprinted with permission.

Leary and Hill (1996) describe movement differences as a disruption in the regulation of movement and a disruption in acts such as starting, executing, stopping, combining, and switching movements. The types of symptoms seen can be grouped into three areas: (1) those affecting motor function, (2) those affecting volitional movements, and (3) those affecting overall behavior and activity (Leary & Hill, 1996). Table 4.8 lists behaviors observed within these three areas. For example, stopping one activity to start another (switching), difficulty maintaining a rate or rhythm with movements (executing), and not being able to get a tune out of one's mind (stopping) are all considered to be movement differences common to those with autism. These difficulties in movement interfere with one's posture, actions, speech, thoughts, perceptions, emotions, and memories (Donnellan & Leary, 1995). For example, if a child with autism is constantly in motion, that child may also experience thoughts and emotions that are racing or quickly fleeting. Individuals with autism have reported that getting their bodies to move or stop routinely is difficult (Donnellan & Leary, 1995). They have also reported difficulty maintaining or stopping a topic of conversation, stopping a repetitive thought, and demonstrating the appropriate emotions. All of these are examples of how movement differences can affect thoughts, emotions, and perceptions (Donnellan & Leary, 1995). Movement differences can also affect social interactions and cognitive performance.

Effect of Movement Differences on Social Interaction. Difficulty creating sequences of motor or behavioral patterns hinders engagement in complex social interactions. Children with autism may also have difficulty connecting intent or affect to their actions to provide a purpose or goal (Greenspan & Wieder, 1997). Difficulty with sensory regulation may affect the production and coordination of movements that are critical in communication and social situations (Autism National Committee,

1996). Many nonverbal behaviors and gestures used in communicating are influenced by movement differences. For instance, if a child with autism smiles at an inappropriate time or takes too long to respond, the effect can be enormous.

Effect of Movement Differences on Cognitive Performance. Typically, the child with some movement differences can complete activities that are automatic more easily than those that are volitional (Donnellan & Leary, 1995). For example, the child may be able to blow out a candle when presented with a birthday cake but may not be able to purse his or her lips to throw a kiss when asked. The behaviors or actions that require thought can be difficult if not impossible to complete.

A child's difficulty with movement differences may suggest cognitive deficits or noncompliance. In fact, a child may understand a concept that is being asked of him or her, but cannot demonstrate his or her knowledge. For example, 10-year-old Danny was still being taught his colors. His teacher insisted that, because Danny could not touch the correct colored block when requested, he still did not know his colors despite years of teaching him. However, Danny had significant movement differences such as pointing, that impeded his ability to do motor tasks quickly and effortlessly. When Danny was asked to identify colors by clicking a mouse instead of pointing, he identified his colors with 100% accuracy.

Assessment Strategies for Movement Differences. Because no particular test has been developed to assess movement differences, the therapist must observe task performance and the contextual influences on performance. One needs to consider the performance of the child on a variety of tasks in a variety of contexts. Considering the motor function, volitional movements, and overall behavior of the child is important. These observations may include looking for repetitious movements (lining up objects, motor perseveration), gait disturbances

(slow shuffling walk, lunging), and speech and language disturbances (perseverative speech, use of jargon, atypical speech rate and rhythm) (Leary & Hill, 1996). The professional should make observations of the materials and equipment used, the presentation of the activity, the rules, and the interaction styles that are used with the child to help determine the conditions with which the child performs best (Donnellan & Leary, 1995).

Conclusion

The evaluation of children with autism is often challenging for professionals because of the unique characteristics of children with autism. However, using a child- and family-centered approach with assessment strategies that evaluate performance in natural contexts can produce vital and relevant information to assist with program planning and intervention. This approach also makes the evaluation process meaningful to the child, the family, and the team of professionals. Although evaluation is best done by a transdisciplinary team, certain areas tend to fall within the occupational therapist's expertise, areas which are highlighted in this chapter with descriptions of specific tools and strategies.

References

American Occupational Therapy Association. (1994). Uniform terminology for occupational therapy (3rd ed.). *American Journal of Occupational Therapy, 48,* 1047–1054.

American Psychiatric Association. (2000). *Diagnostic and statistical manual of mental disorders* (4th ed., rev.). Washington, DC: Author.

Anzalone, M. E., & Williamson, G. G. (1997). *Strategies to improve sensory integration and regulation in young children.* Paper presented at the Zero to Three 12th National Training Institute, Nashville, Tennessee.

Autism National Committee. (1996). *Seeing movement: How our perception of movement and sensory differences can change our perceptions of people diagnosed with autism/PDD, mental retardation, & related disabilities* [Pamphlet]. Ardmore, PA: Author.

Ayres, A. J. (1979). *Sensory integration and the child.* Los Angeles: Western Psychological Association.

Bennett, D. (1996). Comparison of sensory characteristics: Chil̶ ̶ ̶ ̶ ̶ ̶ attention deficit ̶ ̶ ̶ ̶ ̶ Unpublished Maste̶ ̶ ̶ ̶ ̶ Kansas, Lawrence, Kansas.

Bledsoe, M. P., & Shepherd, J. T. (1982). A study of reliability and validity of a preschool scale. *American Journal of Occupational Therapy, 36,* 783–788.

Bulgren, J. A., & Knackendoffel, A. (1986). Ecological assessment: An overview. *The Pointer, 30*(2), 23–30.

Bundy, A. C. (1997). Play and playfulness: What to look for. In L. D. Parham & L.S. Fazio, *Play in occupational therapy for children* (pp. 52–66). St. Louis, MO: Mosby.

Burke, J. (1993). Play: The life role of the infant and young child. In J. Case-Smith (Ed.), *Pediatric occupational therapy and early intervention* (pp. 198–224). Boston: Andover Medical Publishers.

Carr, E. G., & Durand, V. M. (1985). Reducing behavior problems through functional communication training. *Journal of Applied Behavior Analysis, 18,* 111–126.

Carr, E. G., Levin, L., McConnachie, G., Carlson, J. I., Kemp, D. C., & Smith, L. E. (1994). *Communication based intervention for problem behavior.* Baltimore: Brookes.

Carter, A. S., Volkmar, F. R., Sparrow, S. S., Wang, J. J., Lord, C., Dawson, G., Fombonne, E., Loveland, K., Mesibov, G., & Schopler, E. (1998). The Vineland Adaptive Behavior Scales: Supplemental norms for individuals with autism. *Journal of Autism and Developmental Disorders, 28*(4), 287–302.

Coster, W. (1998). Occupation-centered assessment of children. *American Journal of Occupational Therapy, 52,* 337–344.

Coster, W., Deeney, T., Haltiwanger, J., & Haley, S. (1998). *The school function assessment.* San Antonio, TX: Psychological Corporation and Therapy Skill Builders.

Crist, P. (1998). Standardized assessments: Psychometric measurement and testing procedures. In J. Hinojosa & P. Kramer (Eds.), *Evaluation: Obtaining and interpreting data* (pp. 77–106). Bethesda, MD: American Occupational Therapy Association.

Cronin, A. F. (1996). Psychosocial and emotional domains of behavior. In J. Case-Smith, A. S. Allen, & P. Nuse Pratt (Eds.), *Occupational therapy for children* (3rd ed., pp. 387–429). St. Louis, MO: Mosby.

Donnellan, A. M., & Leary, M. R. (1995). *Movement differences and diversity in autism/mental retardation: Appreciating and accommodating people with communication and behavior challenges.* Madison, WI: DRI Press.

Donnellan, A., Mirenda, P., Mesaros, R., & Fassbender, L. (1984). Analyzing the communicative functions of aberrant behavior. *Journal of the Association for Persons with Severe Handicaps, 9,* 201–212.

Dunn, W. (1994). Performance of typical children on the sensory profile: An item analysis. *American Journal of Occupational Therapy, 48,* 1047–1054.

Dunn, W. (1996). The sensorimotor systems: A framework for assessment and intervention. In F. P. Orelove & D. Sobsey (Eds.), *Educating children with multiple disabilities: A transdisciplinary approach* (3rd ed., pp. 35–78). Baltimore: Brookes.

Dunn, W. (1998). Person-centered and contextually relevant evaluation. In J. Hinojosa & P. Kramer (Eds.), *Evaluation: Obtaining and interpreting data* (pp. 47–76). Bethesda, MD: American Occupational Therapy Association.

Dunn, W. (1999). *Sensory Profile: User's manual.* San Antonio, TX: Psychological Corporation.

Dunn, W., Brown, C., & McGuigan, A. (1994). The ecology of human performance: A framework for considering the effect of context. *American Journal of Occupational Therapy, 48*(7), 595–607.

Dunn, W., & Westman, K. (1996). The Sensory Profile: The performance of a national sample of children without disabilities. *American Journal of Occupational Therapy, 51*(1), 29–34.

Durand, V. M. (1988). Motivation assessment scale. In M. Herson & A. Bellack (Eds.), *Dictionary of Behavioral Assessment Techniques* (pp. 309–310). New York: Pergamon.

Ermer, J., & Dunn, W. (1998). The Sensory Profile: A discriminant analysis of children with and without disabilities. *American Journal of Occupational Therapy, 52*(4), 283–290.

Fisher, A.G. (1992). Functional measure, part 1: What is function, what should we measure and how should we measure it? *American Journal of Occupational Therapy, 46*(2), 183–185.

Greenspan, S. I. (1992). *Infancy and early childhood: The practice of clinical ~~assessment and interven~~ tion with emotional ~~chal~~ lenges.* Madison, CT ~~: International Universi~~ ties Press.

Greenspan, S. I. (1996). Assessing the emotional and social functioning of infants and young children. In S. J. Meisels & E. Fenichel (Eds.), *New visions for the developmental assessment of infants and young children* (pp. 27–52). Washington, DC: National Center for Infants, Toddlers, & Families.

Greenspan, S. I., & Meisels, S. J. (1996). Toward a new vision for the developmental assessment of infants and young children. In S. J. Meisels & E. Fenichel (Eds.), *New visions for the developmental assessment of infants and young children* (pp. 11–26). Washington, DC: National Center for Infants, Toddlers, & Families.

Greenspan, S. I., & Wieder, S. (1997). Developmental patterns and outcomes in infants and children with disorders in relating and communicating: A chart review of 200 cases of children with autistic spectrum diagnoses. *Journal of Developmental & Learning Disorders, 1,* 87–141.

Haley, S. M., Coster, W., Ludlow, L. H., Haltiwanger, J., & Andrellos, P. (1992). *Administration manual for the Pediatric Evaluation of Disability Inventory.* San Antonio, TX: Psychological Corporation.

Janzen, J. E. (1996). *Understanding the nature of autism: A practical guide.* San Antonio, TX: Therapy Skill Builders.

Johnson-Ecker, C. L., & Parham, L. D. (2000). Evaluation of sensory processing: A validity study using contrasting groups. *American Journal of Occupational Therapy, 54,* 494–503.

Kientz, M., & Dunn, W. (1997). A comparison of the performance of children with and without autism on the Sensory Profile. *American Journal of Occupational Therapy, 51*(7), 530–537.

Knox, S. (1974). A play scale. In M. Reilly (Ed.), *Play as exploratory learning* (pp. 247–266). Beverly Hills, CA: Sage.

Koegel, L. K., Koegel, R. L., & Dunlap, G. (1996). *Positive behavioral support: Including people with difficult behavior in the community.* Baltimore: Brookes.

Koegel, L. K., Koegel, R. L., Smith, A. (1997). Variables related to differences in standardized test outcomes for children with autism. *Journal of Autism & Developmental Disorders, 27*(3), 233–243.

Leary, M., & Hill, D. A. (1996). Moving on: Autism and movement disturbance. *Mental Retardation, 34*(1), 39–53.

Linder, T. W. (1990). *Transdisciplinary play-based assessment. A functional approach to working with young children.* Baltimore: Brookes.

Linder, T. W. (1993). *Transdisciplinary play-based intervention: Guidelines for developing a meaningful curriculum for young children.* Baltimore: Brookes.

Lowenthal, B. (1991). Ecological assessment: Adding a new dimension for preschool children. *Intervention in School and Clinic, 26*(3), 148–151.

Mays, R. M., & Gillon, J. E. (1993). Autism in young children: An update. *Journal of Pediatric Health Care, 7,* 17–23.

McCormick, L. (1997). Ecological assessment and planning. In L. McCormick, D. Frome Loeb, & R. L. Schiefelbusch (Eds.), *Supporting children with communication difficulties in inclusive settings: School based language intervention* (pp. 223–256). Boston: Allyn and Bacon.

Meisels, S. J. (1996). Charting the continuum of assessment and intervention. In S. J. Meisels & E. Fenichel (Eds.), *New visions for the developmental assessment of infants and young children* (pp. 27–52). Washington, DC: National Center for Infants, Toddlers, & Families.

Miller, H. (1996). Eye contact and gaze aversion: Implications for persons with autism. *Sensory Integration Special Interest Section Newslette, 19*(2), 1–4.

Nelson, D. L. (1984). *Children with autism and other pervasive disorders of development and behavior: Therapy through activities.* Thorofare, NJ: Slack.

O'Neill, R. E., Horner, R. H., Albin, R. W., Storey, K., & Sprague, J. R. (1990). *Functional analysis of problem behavior: A practical assessment guide.* Sycamore, IL: Sycamore Press.

Parham, D., & Ecker, C. (2000). *Evaluation of sensory processing.* Unpublished test, University of Southern California, Los Angeles.

Parham, L. D., & Mailloux, Z. (1996). Sensory integration. In J. Case-Smith, A. S. Allen, & P. Nuse Pratt (Eds.), *Occupational therapy for children* (3rd ed., pp. 307–356). St. Louis, MO: Mosby.

Rapin, I. (1991). Autistic children: Diagnosis and clinical features. *Pediatrics,* (Suppl.) 751–760.

Schaaf, R. C., & Mulrooney, L. L. (1989). Occupational therapy in early intervention: A family centered approach. *American Journal of Occupational Therapy, 43*(11), 745–754.

Spencer, J., Krefting, L., & Mattingly, C. (1993). Incorporation of ethnographic methods in occupational therapy assessment. *American Journal of Occupat_____ _____ 47*(4), 303–309.

Stewart, K. B. (1996). Occ_____ _____ment in pediatrics. Purposes, proce__ __methods of evaluation. In J. Case-Smith, A. S. Allen, & P. Nuse Pratt (Eds.), *Occupational therapy for children* (3rd ed., pp. 165–199). St. Louis, MO: Mosby.

Stone, W. L., Lemanek, K. L., Fishel, P. T., Fernandez, M. C., & Altemeir, W. A. (1990). Play and imitation skills in the diagnosis of autism in young children. *Pediatrics, 86,* 267–272.

Trombly, C. (1993). The issue is—anticipating the future: Assessment of occupational function. *American Journal of Occupational Therapy, 47,* 253–257.

Vermaas-Lee, J. R. (1999). *Parent ratings of children with autism on* The Evaluation of Sensory Processing (ESP). Unpublished Master's thesis, University of Southern California, Los Angeles.

Welch, M. (1994). Ecological assessment: A collaborative approach to planning instructional interventions. *Intervention in School and Clinic, 29,* 160–164, 183.

Westby, C. E., Stevens, Dominquez, M., & Oetter, P. (1996). A performance/competence model of observational assessment. *Language, Speech, & Hearing Services in Schools, 27,* 144–156.

Williamson, G. G., & Anzalone, M. (1997). Sensory integration: A key component of the evaluation and treatment of young children with severe difficulties in relating and communicating. *Bulletin of Zero to Three, 17,* 29–36.

Williamson, G. G., Szczepanski, M., & Zeitlin, S. (1993). Coping frame of reference. In P. Kramer & J. Hinojosa (Eds.), *Frames of reference for pediatric occupational therapy* (pp. 395–436). Baltimore: Williams & Wilkins.

Zeitlin, S. (1985). *Coping inventory.* Bensenville, IL: Scholastic Testing Service.

Zeitlin, S., Williamson, G. G., & Szczepanski, M. (1988). *Early coping inventory.* Bensenville, IL: Scholastic Testing Service.

Zelazo, P. R. (1997). Infant-toddler information processing assessment for children with pervasive developmental disorder and autism: Part 1. *Infants & Young Children, 10*(1), 1–14.

Appendix 4.A
A Sample of Specific Assessment Tools for Examining Component Skills

Name of Tool	Age Range	Component Skills Tested	Type of Test
Peabody Developmental Motor Scales	Birth–7 years old	Gross and fine motor skills	Norm referenced
Brunicks-Oseretsky Test of Motor Proficiency	Age 4.5–14.5 years old	Gross and fine motor skills	Norm referenced
Miller Assessment of Preschoolers	3–6 years old	Screen for sensory, motor, cognitive, and combined abilities	Norm referenced
DeGangi-Berk Test of Sensory Integration	3–5 years old	Bilateral integration, postural control, reflex maturation	Criterion referenced
Sensory Integration and Praxis tests	4–8.11 years old	Sensory integration	Norm referenced
Beery Developmental Test of Visual Motor Integration	3 years to adult	Visual motor integration by having child copy designs	Norm referenced
Motor Free Visual Perception Test-Revised	4–11 years old	Visual perceptual skills	Norm referenced

Appendix 4.B
Assessments Developed Specifically for Use With Children With Autism

Tool	Use	Information
Communication and Symbolic Behavior Scale	Children 9 months to 6 years; Early identification of communication delays or disorders	Wetherby & Prizant (1993)
Psychoeducational Profile, Revised	Children up to age 12; Diagnostic and developmental assessment	Schopler, Reichler, Bashford, Lansing, & Marcus (1990)
Adolescent and Adult Psychoeducational Profile	Adolescents and adults; Functional developmental level	Mesibov, Schopler, Schaffer, & Landrus (1988)
Miller Umwelt Assessment Scale	Children 18 months to 8 years; Body scheme, contact with environment and social contact, play, problem solving, motor coordination and communication.	Miller & Miller (1989)
Assessment of Information Processing	Infants and toddlers; Examines cognitive processing via measurement of heart rate recorded while a child observes sequential visual and auditory events.	Zelazo (1997)

Appendix 4.C
Case Study: The Evaluation Process

Referral

Joey was 12 years old and in the sixth grade when he was referred by his family for an occupational therapy evaluation. The occupational therapy practitioner worked for an organization that provided services in the home and community for individuals with autism and collaborated with school personnel to help guide appropriate intervention in all settings.

Defining the Problem

Joey had been diagnosed with autism, and he spent most of his school day in a classroom for learning disabled students. He was mainstreamed for math, science, lunch, art, music, and physical education. The referral was requested by the family because they were concerned about how Joey was functioning with everyday activities at home and school. They also were concerned because Joey was going to the middle school next year.

The therapist first gathered a history from Joey's mother over the telephone. The mother reported that he was a full-term baby and had normal development until he began to lose speech at the age of 2. He was diagnosed with autism at the age of 4. His mother reported that Joey was verbal but still had difficulty communicating at times. He had occupational therapy intervention in the past to help with sensory processing and fine motor issues, but the intervention had been educationally related and she was concerned about his performance at home. For example, Joey only takes baths; he cannot ride a bike, which limits his ability to go places with his younger brother and friends in the neighborhood; and he is frightened to go to places with open staircases or escalators. In addition, she felt that he was not performing activities at home as well as other children his age. He was having difficulty completing his chores and occasionally refused. She was also concerned with his ability to engage in appropriate leisure activities with his peers.

After getting the brief history from Joey's mother, the therapist decided that it would be helpful to interview the teacher for any additional concerns at school. The teacher reported that they had been having problems with Joey during classroom transition times. At times, he became aggressive by kicking. The teacher also reported that he was primarily a nonreader, and although typically he could speak well, he could not verbalize when he was upset.

Joey's mother and teacher identified the following main issues:

1. Difficulty engaging in age-appropriate life roles at home and school such as doing chores, completing class work, riding a bike with friends
2. Difficulty with open spaces, which limits where he goes in the community and may cause possible difficulty negotiating stairwells at middle school
3. Challenging behavior during classroom transitions in the hallway and occasional aggression

Selecting Assessment Methods and Strategies

The therapist developed her evaluation plan based on the information she received from the interviews. The therapist believed that observation of Joey both at home and at school was imperative to evaluate his ability to participate in the roles that were important to him and his family such as student, friend, and son. The therapist also believed it was important to observe Joey while he was playing with neighborhood peers after school (attempting to ride a bike), at home during the completion of one of his chores, and at school during a transition time that was typically difficult. She would pay careful attention to contextual issues that might be affecting his performance and to what might be supporting or impeding his performance at home and school.

In addition to the observations, the therapist decided to complete a sensory history with Joey's mother because many of her concerns during the interview process seemed possibly related to sensory processing issues. The sensory history would give the therapist possible additional functional concerns and a history of past and current issues. While doing the observations at school and home, the therapist would also make observations of Joey's reactions to various sensory information presented to him during the day.

The teacher and therapist also decided to have the teacher document on a chart when Joey was becoming aggressive and what was happening in the class at that time. The purpose of this chart was to document any trends in the behavior (e.g., it happened every time the class got very noisy, or it was always right after lunch).

Completing the Evaluation

The therapist completed the sensory history with Joey's mother and scheduled times to complete her observations. During the observation process, the therapist generated hypotheses regarding the causes of his difficulties. She then systematically went about determining which of the hypotheses might be correct. For example, while observing Joey in the hallway at school, she noted that he walked with his hand brushing the wall until he came to an obstacle or another person. If he bumped into the other person or had difficulty negotiating around the other person, he tended to erupt in an aggressive episode (pushing, kicking). The therapist hypothesized that the aggressive behavior may have occurred for the following reasons:

- Tactile defensiveness (he reacted to the unexpected touch)
- Difficulty because of rigidity and a need for predictability (his routine was disrupted)
- An attempt at communication that he was unable to verbalize

She then compared these observations with others to look for similarities. She went to the other sources of information (interviews, questionnaires) to determine whether or not there were other issues potentially related to tactile defensiveness, rigidity, or communication difficulties. She interviewed Joey's mother again to gather more information about those three specific areas.

The information that had been gathered during the evaluation process then was shared at a team meeting that included the family and the school personnel, including his school therapists, to help develop appropriate intervention strategies for Joey.

CHAPTER 5

Transdisciplinary Intervention for Children With a Pervasive Developmental Disorder

Lynette Scotese-Wojtila, OTR/L, and Lisa R. Audet, PhD, CCC-SLP

Children who are diagnosed with one of the Pervasive Developmental Disorders (PDDs) often present complex behaviors that are perplexing to family members, community members, and professionals. The emotional and behavioral needs of individuals with a PDD often span a number of domains that require the perspective and training of multiple professionals. Families frequently seek services from a variety of professionals who may each create a separate intervention plan designed to address the needs of the child within a particular discipline. The involvement of so many professionals who are potentially operating from different theoretical backgrounds may make parents feel overwhelmed, confused, and exhausted in their attempt to coordinate and participate in their child's treatment. Furthermore, the child may experience inconsistencies in his or her care.

The complex nature of a PDD requires integrated intervention, a team approach, where every professional is aware of the goals and methods that are used across disciplines. A team approach has numerous benefits. It can lead to an increase in the frequency with which goals for the child are addressed. The potential for progress can be dramatically enhanced through

its use. In addition, through a team approach, professionals and parents can learn practical ways to address goals within both therapeutic and natural contexts.

Transdisciplinary Intervention

An integrated team approach is referred to as *transdisciplinary intervention*. This chapter describes not only transdisciplinary intervention but also the skills that are necessary to successfully carry out such an approach. The chapter also discusses the contributions of professionals such as occupational therapists, speech-language pathologists, psychologists, and special educators who are commonly involved in the treatment of children with PDDs.

Transdisciplinary Intervention Versus Multidisciplinary Intervention

Multidisciplinary and transdisciplinary intervention constitute two of the models commonly used by professionals who serve children with PDDs. Both approaches share common processes: evaluation, the assessment of needs, the design of strategies, and intervention. However, the two interventions also differ significantly in the way these four processes are completed.

These differences can influence the effectiveness of intervention.

Team members, using a multidisciplinary approach, operate from their particular discipline-specific perspectives. Each individual is responsible for his or her own domain throughout each of the four processes. In a multidisciplinary model, clinical experience indicates that discipline-specific information about any of the four processes is often made available to the team through team meetings. During these meetings, a team member may present information about the child based on a perspective that is unique to that member's domain. However, synthesis of this information does not necessarily occur. For example, the occupational therapist on the team may not integrate and apply the information presented by the speech-language pathologist in his or her treatment of the child. Working together to achieve common goals does not necessarily or intentionally occur within a multidisciplinary team.

In contrast to the multidisciplinary team, members of a transdisciplinary team demonstrate clinical reasoning that goes beyond the constraints of the individual members' domains. Professionals on a transdisciplinary team value and respect the information that team members share, and they use this information in their treatment. They also intentionally provide information to others in an effort to ensure cohesive programming. Members of a transdisciplinary team intentionally support the synthesis of discipline-specific theory, goals, and methods. For example, a speech-language pathologist serving a child with delays in play, discusses the implications of fine motor deficits on play with the occupational therapist to collorborate around the creation of an intervention plan that strategically and simultaneously addresses fine motor skills and play development. Similarly, the physical therapist, whose treatment plan addresses the child's low muscle tone, determines, through collaboration with the special educator, which type of seating support the child requires and during which classroom activities the device should be used. Successfully realizing transdisciplinary intervention requires that each professional demonstrate specific collaborative skills.

Collaboration and Transdisciplinary Intervention

Successful collaboration within a transdisciplinary team requires effective communication skills, well-established knowledge of one's own discipline, and the carrying out of specific practices that support shared learning. Effective communication skills include the abilities to listen actively, to request and provide clarity, and to describe aspects of one's own field with simplicity. As effective communicators, team members gain valuable information that, when applied, has a positive and pervasive influence on the child's treatment. For example, a team who serves a child with tactile defensiveness is able to attain a deeper understanding of the child's avoidance behaviors by synthesizing the information shared by the occupational therapist, special educator, and psychologist. This deeper understanding then supports the team in designing a more efficacious intervention plan when addressing avoidance behaviors. Effective team communication leads to enhanced understanding of the nature of the child's disability and its influence on his or her functioning.

Successful collaboration within a transdisciplinary team requires that all professionals possess knowledge and mastery of concepts and theories within their professions. Deep knowledge of theory allows the professional to apply theory to practice. For example, the special educator draws on his or her knowledge of cognitive development theories when identifying that a child has deficits in sequencing. As a result of the special educator's ability to apply these theories to practice, he or she recognizes that this deficit has the potential to influence a wide range of functional skills from self-care (i.e., shoe tying) to academics (i.e., reading comprehension).

The application of knowledge guides the clinical reasoning of the team. Clinical reasoning is the therapeutic thought process that supports the professional's rationale for applying a particular theory or for using a particular method in the child's care. Clinical reasoning results from the active synthesis of theoretical knowledge and clinical observations. In the preceding example, the clinical reasoning of the special educator supports his or her decision to use a particular intervention strategy (e.g., visual supports for the child with sequencing deficits). Through the collaborative process, the team refines the strategy so it can be applied across contexts throughout the child's day.

Cross training and role releasing are two specific practices that support the success of a transdisciplinary team. Cross training occurs when professionals teach methods specific to their own discipline that others then apply in their work with the child. Cross training allows consistent application of intervention, thus, enhancing the child's progress. Role releasing occurs as a professional empowers fellow team members to address goals that have not traditionally been considered part of the other team members' responsibilities. For example, a role releasing occurs when a speech-language pathologist empowers the occupational therapist to use language development techniques during sensory-integration treatment sessions. The occupational therapist is therefore afforded the opportunity to help the child attain goals while the child is outside of the speech pathologist's immediate scope of care. Consequently, in a transdisciplinary model, traditional discipline-specific boundaries are expanded as professionals trust fellow team members to work on all aspects of the child's intervention plan, using consistent methods across disciplines.

Through each team member's continuous display of collaborative skills, an integrated understanding of the child emerges. This common conceptualization of the child results from the merging of perspectives through the transdisciplinary approach. A transdisciplinary program is not field or discipline specific; rather, the program is child specific. Parents, as team members who participate in this process, witness a model of collaboration where individuals listen to one another, all members are respected and valued for their perspectives, and problem solving occurs naturally. Carryover and consistency in the child's care are inherent to the transdisciplinary model. Table 5.1 provides a summary of skills and strategies that support successful collaboration.

The following sections describe the theoretical backgrounds and the roles of the various professional members of a transdisciplinary team. These members typically include the occupational therapist, the speech-language pathologist, the psychologist, and the special educator. The parents' role on these teams is

Table 5.1
Successful Collaboration

Interpersonal Skills	Professional Skills	Strategies
Effective communication	Knowledge of	Cross training
• Listening actively	• Professional field	
• Requesting clarification	• Theories	
• Providing clarification	• Informal assessment methods	
• Expressing knowledge simply	• Therapeutic methods	
Respect for others	Clinical reasoning	Role releasing
	• Problem solving	
	• Influence of one area of functioning on another	
	• Application of theory to practice	
Holistic or Humanistic perspective		

also critical and valuable; however, their backgrounds and roles vary and are not described in this chapter.

Occupational Therapist

Pediatric occupational therapists are trained to develop a holistic and comprehensive view of a child's strengths and difficulties. In addition to the areas that are traditionally assessed in occupational therapy (i.e., fine motor, play, cognition, self-care, and psychosocial-emotional development), an occupational therapist who is assessing a child with a PDD should assess specific areas that are of particular importance given the child's neurological condition. These areas include sensory processing, attention and arousal, and sensorimotor development.

Figure 5.1
The open system representing human occupation.

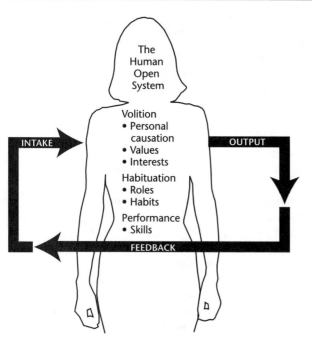

Note. From *Willard and Spackman's Occupational Therapy* (8th ed., p.77) by Gary Kielhofner, 1998, Philadelphia: Lippincott Williams & Wilkins. Copyright 1998 by Lippincott Williams & Wilkins. Reprinted with permission.

Occupational therapists contribute knowledge to the transdisciplinary team regarding two specific theories in particular. One theory is the Model of Human Occupation (Kielhofner & Burke, 1980), described in the remainder of this section. Sensory integration (Ayres, 1968/1974) is the second theory and is described in chapter 6.

Model of Human Occupation

The frame of reference, the Model of Human Occupation, was derived from earlier theories of occupational behavior which were developed in large part by Reilly in the late 1960s (Levy, 1993). The Model of Human Occupation, first introduced by Kielhofner and Burke (1980), is commonly referred to as MOHO. In MOHO, an individual is conceptualized as a complex open system that, according to Levy (1993), "evolves and undergoes different forms of growth, development, and change through an ongoing interaction with the external environment" (p. 77). In MOHO, the human as an open system comprises three subsystems. As shown in Figure 5.1, the three subsystems, Volition, Habituation, and Performance are hierarchical. Subsystems interrelate, thus influencing the complexity and effectiveness with which the system (i.e., the child) functions in the environment (Bruce & Borg, 1993). Each subsystem will be briefly described. The descriptions are intended to highlight those aspects of each subsystem that are especially relevant to the assessment and the treatment of children with a PDD. For a comprehensive review of MOHO and the interrelated subsystems, see *A Model of Human Occupation* (Kielhofner, 1985).

Volition Subsystem. The volition subsystem is the highest and ruling subsystem. The volition system is responsible for motivating behavior and for motivating the decisions a person makes regarding which behavior to pursue at any moment (Bruce & Borg, 1993). The volition system includes three components: values, personal causation, and interests.

According to Kielhofner and Burke (1985), values can be defined as images of what is good, right, or important. The child with a disorder on the PDD spectrum may have difficulty comprehending and developing values. Little research is available on the development of value systems in individuals with a PDD. However, the known abstract-thinking difficulties that are common in children with a PDD (Baron-Cohen, 1989, 1993; Baron-Cohen & Ring 1994) suggest that these children may have difficulties with the development of values.

Personal causation is defined as one's belief that he or she has skills that can be used effectively. In addition, personal causation is a sense of self-influence on achieving success or experiencing failure in future outcomes (Bruce & Borg, 1993). Personal causation involves a number of cognitive functions. The ability to predict success or failure, to recall past events, and to make associations between past and future events are three such skills. An understanding of the passage of time, or temporal awareness, is also needed. Children diagnosed with a PDD often have difficulties in these cognitive areas (Minshew & Wiznitzer, 1999). Subsequently, children with a PDD may experience difficulty developing a sense of personal causation.

Interests, according to Bruce and Borg (1993), are defined in MOHO as "the individual's propensity to enjoy specific occupations" (p. 152). In this context, the term *occupations* can be used synonymously with the term *roles*. Interests also help one to establish priorities for activity participation. For instance, a person who enjoys growing roses may choose to join a gardening club. Clinical experience suggests that professionals struggle in assessing the interests of children with a PDD. Specifically, the child's tendencies are frequently misinterpreted as interests. For example, in noting a child's repetitive behavior (e.g., string twirling), an interventionist may incorrectly deduce that the child's perseverance in twirling is indicative of his or her interests. In doing so, the professional equates interests to tendencies (or perseverative acts) instead of adhering to the definition of interests as one's propensity to enjoy a particular role or occupation.

Habituation Subsystem. The habits and roles of a person's daily routine constitute the habituation subsystem. The energy that one possesses and expends when engaging in habits and routines stems from this subsystem. In MOHO, theorists hypothesize that the presence of a disability limits a person's energy, which makes performing routines difficult. Consequently, adaptive or maladaptive habits may be created to assist the individual in conserving energy or in refueling.

Roles influence and shape a person's identity. Opportunities to develop new roles and identities emerge for individuals throughout the life span. According to Bruce and Borg (1993), roles have "a set of expectations, responsibilities, and privileges" (p. 153) associated with them. Childhood roles include that of a learner, player, communicator, socializer, family member, and community member. The development of roles results from a person's ability to engage in purposeful behavior. Children with a PDD experience neurological difficulties that influence their ability to develop and engage in purposeful or adaptive behaviors. Rather, they may develop particular maladaptive habits that consequently limit their ability to develop conventional habits. The absence of conventional habits in children with one of the PDDs directly impedes the success they may have at living out a particular childhood role.

Performance Subsystem. The performance subsystem is at the bottom of the hierarchy. It includes the skills necessary for producing purposeful behavior (Bruce & Borg, 1993). The performance subsystem encompasses three skill areas: perceptual motor skills, process skills (e.g., planning and problem solving), and communication skills. The criteria for disorders on the PDD spectrum in the *Diagnostic and Statistical Manual of Mental Disorders, Fourth Edition,* or the *DSM-IV-TR* (APA, 2000), identifies deficits in communication as characteristic of the disorder. The *DSM-IV-TR* also indirectly implies deficits in perceptual motor functioning, planning, and problem solving as illustrated by deficits in play. Furthermore, the works of Attwood (1998), Ayres (1979), Donnellan and Leary (1997), and R. G. Maurer (personal communication, March 1, 1996) suggest that individuals with PDDs often present with characteristic disturbances in motor performance. In short, the literature indicates and clinical experience suggests that children who experience the symptoms of PDDs have problems in one or more performance areas.

Sensory Integration

The second theory that supports the clinical reasoning of occupational therapists as they assess and treat children with a PDD is sensory integration. Sensory integration was initially described by Sherrington (1906/1961) as a neurological process that is fundamental to human development. Later, Ayres (1968/1974) elaborated on the idea of sensory integration as a neurological process by creating the sensory-integration theory of practice. The work of Fisher, Murray, and Bundy (1991), which was based on the work of Ayres (1968/1974), depicts sensory integration as a dynamic process represented by a circular schematic that illustrates the movement of sensory stimuli in this sequence: intake, neurological processing of the stimuli, planning and organizing behavior, adaptive behavior and learning, and feedback. Occupational therapists apply this schemata to better understand the behaviors of children with a PDD, which allows the clinicians to identify appropriate methods for treatment. The process of sensory integration is thoroughly discussed in chapter 6 of this volume.

Speech-Language Pathologist

Pediatric speech-language pathologists are trained to develop a holistic and comprehensive view of communication and apply this view to the development of children with a PDD. The role of the speech-language pathologist is to provide the team with information and strategies regarding communication development. To fulfill this role, the speech-language pathologist must have a well-grounded knowledge of communication development in typical children and in children with disabilities. The speech-language pathologist must also possess comprehensive knowledge of how communication develops from infancy to adulthood, namely, from nonverbal communication to gestures combined with speech and symbolic language.

Knowledge of the role that social interaction, play, and cognition have on the development of language and communication is critical to being an effective therapist. Speech-language therapists' knowledge of these areas is typically rooted in one of four theoretical frameworks: sociolinguistic theory, developmental theory, behavioral theory, or information processing. Table 5.2 provides a summary of these four theories.

Sociolinguistic Theory

A sociolinguistic perspective incorporates two main aspects: mutual regulation and pragmatics (Duchan, 1995; Tronick, 1980, 1982). According to Tronick (1980), mutual regulation involves one's capacity to effectively regulate one's external environment using verbal and nonverbal behaviors. Pragmatics is the use of multiple methods for the purpose of expressing wants, needs, desires, and observations (Briton & Fujuki, 1989). Application of sociolinguistic theory is especially important to the assessment and treatment of children with a PDD because researchers indicate that this population has difficulty integrating the means of conventional communication for a variety of pragmatic purposes (Audet, 2000).

Developmental Theory

The second perspective of speech-language pathology, also used by other disciplines, is developmental theory (Berk & Winsler, 1995; Piaget & Inhelder, 1969). Drawing on their knowledge of developmental theory, speech-language therapists evaluate the sequential progression of both receptive and expressive communication skills in children with a PDD. Receptive communication skills include those that reflect the child's comprehension of gestures, words, and sentences. Expressive communication skills include a range of both verbal and nonverbal behaviors. These behaviors can be unconventional and intentional (i.e., head banging to protest), conventional and intentional (i.e., guiding someone's hand to a door knob to request "open"), or symbolic (i.e., use of the word, sign, or picture of "no" to reject an object). Field (1982), Tronick (1980, 1982), and Brazelton (1982) identify that gaze (to either an object or a person) is one of the first communicative behaviors observed in infant development, which is followed by the pairing of gaze with gesture within the first year of life. Shortly thereafter, the child begins to combine gaze with gesture and vocalization, followed by the combining of gaze, gesture, and verbalizations. Wetherby and colleagues (Wetherby, Cain, Yonclas, & Walker, 1988; Audet, in press) have identified that individuals with autism demonstrate differences in this developmental sequence.

Behavioral Theory:
The Speech-Language Perspective

The third perspective that is fundamental to speech-language therapy is behavioral. This perspective, which originates in the field of psychology, is widely used by a variety professionals. The field of Applied Behavior Analysis

Table 5.2
Speech-Language Theories

Sociolinguistic
  Self-Regulation
  Mutual Regulation
Developmental
  Sequential Progression of
    Receptive language (comprehension)
    Expressive language (production)
    Nonverbal communication skills
    Social skills
    Play skills
Behavioral
  Communicative Intent
  Systematic Manipulation of Antecedents
    Control of the rate, volume, complexity,
      frequency of output, and purpose of adult language and
      speech
    Strategic and supportive withholding
    Placement of items out of reach
    Systematic sabotage of environment
    Functional Communication Training
Information Processing
  Concept Formation
  Schema Development
  Individual Learning Style

(ABA), formerly called behavioralism, is vast and includes multiple techniques. Using an ABA approach, speech-language therapists who are working with children with a PDD assess the communicative intent of the child's behavior (Carr & Durand, 1985). This functional assessment leads to functional communication training (Durand, 1990). Clinicians strategically attempt to evoke receptive and expressive communication behavior. Evoking communication behavior is accomplished by systematically manipulating or influencing the events and objects referred to as antecedents. Some helpful behavioral strategies that are used in the field of speech-language pathology include controlling the rate, volume, complexity, and frequency of adult language; manipulating environmental variables; and manipulating the timing of interactions.

Information Processing

The fourth perspective adopted by speech-language therapists is information processing. Information processing offers a conceptual model as to how individuals process information from sensory experiences into thought, memory, and behavior (Wallach & Butler, 1984). Schema development is the primary focus in this model. Schema development refers to the sequence and manner in which ideas (schemas) are generated. The information processing model suggests that schemas provide a framework through which objects and experiences are conceptualized. This conceptualization serves as the foundation from which associations and predictions are made. Using this model in assessment and treatment of children with a PDD allows clinicians to become aware of a child's individual thinking and learning style. Many children with autism possess a unique learning style (Prizant, 1982), which results in a strong need for sameness and predictability.

Table 5.3
Psychological Theories

Psychodynamic Theory
  Development of emotion and attachment
    Stages
      Self-regulation
      Intimacy
      Two-way communication
      Complex communication
      Emotional ideas
      Emotional thinking
Transactional Theory
  Dynamic interrelationship between
    internal system (self)
    intimate system (caregivers)
    environment (people or events)
  Relationship as context for change
Behavioral Theory
  Analysis of
    behavior
    antecedents to behavior
    consequences of behavior

Psychologist

Pediatric psychologists are trained in the comprehensive assessment of cognitive, developmental, social-emotional, and behavioral functioning. Psychologists incorporate three theoretical models: psychodynamic theory, transactional theory, and behavioral theory. In this section, various components of each model are identified and applied to children with a PDD. Table 5.3 presents an overview of these three models.

Psychodynamic Theory

Components of the psychodynamic theory include emotional development and attachment. Greenspan and Wieder (1998) used the theories and the research of many scholars (Brazelton, 1982; Bruner, 1982; Dunham & Moore, 1995; Field & Fogel, 1982; Tronick, 1980) to create their popular model of emotional development that categorizes emotional milestones. Categories are developmentally sequenced and include six stages: self-regulation and interest in the world, intimacy, two-way communication, complex communication, emotional ideas, and emotional thinking (Greenspan & Wieder, 1998).

Self-Regulation and Interest in the World. In infancy, a newborn is challenged to take in novel sensory stimuli while balancing this novelty with his or her need to remain calm. The infant expends much energy actively regulating his or her own state while simultaneously attempting to establish and sustain interest in the world.

Intimacy. Greenspan and Wieder (1998) hypothesize that, in the intimacy stage, the baby's interests become specialized, resulting in the emergence of an associated value for the primary caregiver (i.e., mom equals comfort). In healthy child development, the baby's value for these familiar individuals begins to manifest through the establishment of eye contact and other social-communicative behaviors such as smiling at his or her parents. Intimacy emerges as the parent reciprocates the behavior, reinforcing bonding and attachment.

Two-Way Communication and Complex Communication. Two-way communication and complex communication are referred to by Greenspan and Wieder (1998) as circles of communication. Circles of communication are verbal or nonverbal dialogues of interaction such as a baby looking at mother and mother reciprocating, thus closing the circle. As the child develops, he or she learns to engage in multiple circles. The child experiments with opening and closing circles with increased frequency and complexity. For instance, the child calls out to the mother by vocalizing or gesturing to re-elicit her attention after she looks away. The child's intent is to initiate or expand contact. The theorists propose that, over time, the child engages in more complex circles with a wider range of people, moving from a two-way communication stage into the complex communication stage. The development of more language competency continues to fuel the child's growth in the complex communication stage.

Emotional Idea. In the fifth category, the emotional idea stage, children learn both isolated emotional concepts and relational concepts. These concepts are observed in play. For example, a 3-year-old girl might conceptualize that "baby dolls are fed by Mommy dolls" (Greenspan & Wieder, 1998, p. 82). This statement is an example of a simple, isolated emotional concept. The child does not necessarily connect or associate this idea with any other emotional concept.

Emotional Thinking. In this final category, the emotional thinking stage, the child continues to experiment with emotional concepts but in a more complex and predictive way. This progression occurs naturally as the child becomes more skilled in comprehension and expressive language. A child in this emotional thinking stage begins to predict that "if I get angry and hit, Daddy will get mad" (Greenspan

& Wieder, 1998, p. 86). Children in this stage are more adept in modifying their behavior based on past experiences as well as verbal and nonverbal feedback from others.

A psychologist who applies psychodynamic theory to the case of a particular child with a PDD may incorporate this proposed model of emotional development. In the process, the psychologist might then hypothesize that the child's absence of direct eye gaze with mother reflects the child's value for her. Clinical experience suggests that, through a transdisciplinary approach, a fuller interpretation of the child's absent eye gaze could be attained. For example, from occupational therapy and speech-language pathology perspectives, assessment of the absent eye gaze would yield information about the child's underlying self-regulatory and mutual regulatory state. As a result, the team could then assist the family in understanding that their child's absence of eye gaze is not necessarily synonymous with an absence of value for caregivers but, rather, is more likely related to the child's inability to endure the sensory and social demands associated with attaining direct eye gaze.

Transactional Model

The second model discussed from the perspective of psychology is the transactional model. Sameroff (1987) proposed a model for conceptualizing the dynamic interrelationship between the child, the caregiver, and the environment. One basic premise to this model, supported by theorists (Andrews & Andrews, 1986; Audet & Ripich, 1994; Prizant et al.; 1990; Rollins, 1987; Sameroff, 1987), is that change does not occur in isolation but in the context of relationships. In a transactional approach, attention is paid to the dynamic role of the family and to the external influences on the family that potentially influence the development of the child. Clinicians who apply this model value the role of family members as fellow interventionists, recognizing that "if generalization is to occur, therapy must consider the dynamics of the child's relationships" (Audet & Ripich, 1994, p. 200).

Behavioral Theory: The Psychology Perspective

The field of psychology also draws from a behavioral perspective. Behavioralists observe human behavior while considering three inter-related components that are based on the work of Skinner (1953): antecedents, behaviors, and consequences. *Applied Behavior Analysis* (*ABA*) is the term commonly used to describe a behavioralist orientation and the many behavioral intervention methods available.

Within an ABA model, clinicians systematically manipulate antecedents and consequences. Antecedents include all events that occur before a behavior manifests and those events that can foster the occurrence of the behavior. Behavior is defined as an individual's response to a stimuli or antecedent. Consequences include all events that happen immediately after the behavior. When analyzing a child's behavior, clinicians look at all three

components using an ABA model. Thorough analysis of behavior is critical prior to the design of a behavioral intervention plan. After a thorough analysis of all three factors, clinicians next determine to what extent the plan will manipulate antecedents and to what extent consequences will be manipulated. Behavioralists influence what the child experiences as a consequence using three different methods: positive reinforcement, negative reinforcement, and punishment (Alberto & Troutman, 1995).

Special Educator

Special educators are trained to assess cognitive and functional skill development. Educators also attend to the child's role within a group context and his or her future role within the work force. Special educators also possess skills that can enhance the success of inclusion within the general education curriculum. In this role, the educator may operate as a consultant to those who do not have backgrounds in the methods of teaching children with special needs. Special educators operate from two theoretical models that allow them to effectively perform the duties of educator and consultant: behavioral theory and constructivist theory. Table 5.4 provides an overview of these theories.

Behavioral Theory: The Special Education Perspective

Like psychologists, speech-language pathologists, and other team members, special educators use a variety of behavioral intervention strategies to teach specific and discrete skills or to reinforce desired behavior. Special educators who use behavior strategies also have knowledge of a variety of ABA techniques including the use of a token economy, positive and negative reinforcement, and time-out or punishment (Alberto & Troutman, 1995). Strategies are used to prompt or evoke behaviors. Prompting strategies include the use of visual cues, ver-

---

Table 5.4
Special Education Theories

Behavioral
  Prompts behaviors
    Visual cues
    Verbal cues
    Modeling
    Graduated guidance
    Strategic withholding
  Reinforces behaviors
    Token economy
    Positive reinforcement
    Negative reinforcement
Constructivist
  Developmental sequence
  Scaffolding
  Encouragement of active participation
  Support for assimilation and accommodation

bal cues, modeling, graduated guidance, and strategic withholding.

Constructivist Theory

Professionals in special education also function from a constructivist perspective. Constructivists acknowledge a developmental sequence of skills and provide the child with an environment that systematically supports the development of skills according to that developmental sequence. Theorists who described a constructivist approach include Berk and Winsler (1995), Dewey (1938), Piaget and Inhelder (1969), and Vygotsky (1962). Each theorist addressed ways in which children construct meaning or make meaning of their experiences through support from the environment. Furthermore, Vygotsky (1962) believed that adults engage in "scaffolding" where they provide the child with challenges that are equally matched to the child's ability level. As a result of this relationship matching optimal learning can occur (Berk & Winsler, 1995). Dewey (1938) believed that children learn from active participation and engagement in the environment. He hypothesized that, through active engagement, the child constructs principles of understanding that he or she applies to new situations. Piaget discussed the importance of assimilation and accommodation where the child observes similarities and differences between events and objects that he or she encounters. Piaget hypothesized that, through this process, learning occurs (Piaget & Inhelder, 1969).

A constructivist model is especially relevant to intervention for children with a PDD. Researchers indicate that children with a PDD have difficulty understanding the relationship between actions and objects in their worlds. Providing a child with experiences that match his or her skill level while simultaneously providing him or her with the necessary supports can enhance learning. The perspectives of different professionals on the transdisciplinary team can enrich this process.

Conclusion

Children with PDDs demonstrate complex behaviors that require the integration of theories and methods from a variety of perspectives. The transdisciplinary approach is designed to support professionals and families in the process of understanding these complex behaviors and, consequently, to develop a cohesive and integrated intervention program. See Case Study 5.1 for an example of the use of transdisciplinary approaches for a child with autism. This chapter described the fundamentals to successful transdisciplinary intervention and the collaborative skills that team members must develop to ensure success. In addition, the chapter elucidated the roles of the team members and reviewed the theoretical foundations that guide clinical reasoning within each discipline.

Three basic concepts were emphasized in this chapter. First, transdisciplinary intervention requires effective communication between team members. Second, transdisciplinary intervention requires that methods be carried out consistently across disciplines. Third, transdisciplinary intervention is effective because it integrates shared theoretical perspectives.

Critical elements of collaboration also have been illustrated in this chapter. These elements include the professional's ability (1) to listen to the perspectives of other disciplines and (2) to ask questions of team members to gain their perspectives. Team members must also be willing to experiment with cross training and role releasing. The participation of each member of the team must be respected as essential and critical. Last, team members must view the child as a dynamic, complex, developing, and individual human being.

Application of the information in this chapter may increase professionals' awareness of the perspective of fellow team members. The active collaboration of a transdisciplinary team ultimately leads to a greater understanding of the whole child. When the team understands

Case Study 5.1

Ron was diagnosed with autism at the age of 30 months. He tantrummed almost continuously, and the tantrums worsened whenever a transition occurred. He appeared to be calm whenever he was allowed to watch sand flow through his fingers. He did not explore his environment. Ron was also nonverbal and seldom made sounds or indicated needs other than by screaming.

Following the diagnosis, Ron was evaluated by a speech-language pathologist, occupational therapist, and music therapist who operated from a transdisciplinary approach. His parents were integrated into the evaluation process and were asked to identify the areas that were of greatest concern to them. A treatment plan was created and carried out in a manner in which every therapist was responsible for addressing every goal within the context of his or her session. This approach required that each therapist learn methods recommended by other team members and provide information to team members that would help problem solving and assist in the assessment of progress.

Three areas of concern were identified by the parents: (1) Ron's tantrumming behavior, (2) Ron's fascina-

tion with watching sand fall, and (3) Ron's limited communication skills. The transdisciplinary approach allowed the team to address these concerns in the following manner.

Tantrumming Behavior

The team identified that Ron's tantrumming occurred at the onset of any type of transition, ranging from getting dressed before leaving the house to seeing that a favorite television show had ended. The first task the team faced was to target specific transitions that, according to the family, occurred with a high degree of regularity and most influenced family functioning. Once these priority transition times were identified, the team began to explore the nature of the tantrums.

The team identified two major factors that influenced Ron's ability to transition. One factor was best understood within a sensory integration model. The occupational therapist determined that Ron had great difficulty sustaining a homeostatic state and, consequently, designed for him a sensory diet protocol to assist with self-regulation. She trained the team in related therapy techniques and identified behaviors the team could attend to

that would indicate the program's effectiveness.

Ron also appeared to possess a Gestalt learning style, a particular learning style that does not easily accommodate modifications to previously learned information and that is common in children with autism. The speech-language pathologist, operating from an information processing model, provided information to the team about how this particular learning style influences the ability to transition and to learn. Consequently, the team brainstormed possible strategies that might support a child's Gestalt learning style and assist with learning. The strategies included creating simple songs that would be sung at every particular transition such as dressing, going to bed, taking a bath, toileting, and leaving the house. The music therapist was responsible for creating these songs and teaching them to the team. The team then identified objects that could serve as supports during these transitions. For example, a diaper was used to signal toileting, a water toy signaled bath time, and car keys signaled leaving the house. The objects were used in conjunction with the songs. Picture supports were also integrated into this program and affixed to a board

that was kept in a standard location within the child's home. The caregiver would present the picture that corresponded to the event, provide the child with the object, and begin to sing the song, whenever a transition occurred.

The execution of both the sensory diet protocol and the information processing strategies proved to be highly effective. Within 3 months, the frequency of tantrumming behavior had decreased from 30 instances per day to approximately 1 instance per day. The family was very relieved and, for the first time, expressed optimism regarding their ability to parent their son.

Preoccupation With Watching Falling Sand

To address the behavior of watching sand fall, the team used three theories, two of which stem from the field of occupational therapy (sensory integration and the Model of Human Occupation) and one that is commonly used in the field of speech-language pathology (developmental). The occupational therapist identified that Ron engaged in watching sand fall as a self-regulating strategy. The sensory diet protocol that she designed provided Ron with alternative strategies he could

Case Study 5.1   *Continued*

use to assist with self-regulation. Using the Model of Human Occupation, the occupational therapist identified that Ron needed support to develop play routines aside from engaging with sand. She provided the team with strategies designed to increase Ron's awareness of and performance in alternative play routines. These strategies were integrated with the developmental theory within which the speech-language pathologist operated.

Routines were created that matched the team's assessment of Ron's developmental level. For example, many gross motor and cause-effect routines were integrated into his day. The speech-language pathologist instructed the adults who interacted regularly with Ron about the appropriate language to use when engaging in these routines. The adults were also given information regarding the developmental communicative behaviors that Ron could possibly use when engaged in these routines. The speech-language pathologist also provided strategies to support Ron's use of adaptive communicative behaviors.

Ron made considerable progress in this area. Parents identified that Ron enjoyed using alternative sensory diet selections such as the thera-

py ball and the bean bag. They noted that Ron's requests for sand diminished when these two therapeutic tools were provided. They also noted that Ron enjoyed self-directed use of the net swing. They reported that bedtime routines were easier and that Ron was beginning to sleep for 5-hour intervals. They were delighted with this change because, prior to intervention, Ron was unable to sleep for more than 2 hours at a time. In addition, the parents were amazed to identify the connection between sleep and self-regulation. They were surprised that strategies designed to address the sand-watching behavior had a positive influence on other behaviors of concern to them.

Limited Communication Skills

To develop a treatment plan that addressed communication skills, the team videotaped Ron at home and in the therapeutic environment. Together, the team viewed the videotape and identified specific behaviors that Ron engaged in for communicative purposes. For example, they found that Ron would consistently whine and walk away from an area when presented

with an object or event that he disliked. Ron also jumped up and down and whined whenever he was excited by an event. The team also noted that Ron seemed to engage in throwing behavior as a way to request that an event occur again.

The speech-language pathologist, operating from both behavioral and sociolinguistic theories, assisted the team in interpreting these communicative behaviors. The team decided to select signs that would enhance the readability of Ron's nonverbal behavior, thus increasing the likelihood that adults would successfully interpret and respond to his intent. The occupational therapist contributed by suggesting that Ron's difficulties with body awareness and motor planning be considered when selecting which expressions in sign language the team would help Ron learn. Consequently, three signs (STOP, MORE, and HAPPY) were chosen. The chosen signs were contact signs, which produce tactile input in their execution and, thus, encourage body awareness.

The speech-language pathologist trained the team in the use of methods that would increase the frequency with which Ron needed to convey protest, express

pleasure, and request recurrence. She used methods, developed using a behavioralist theory, that encouraged adults who worked with Ron to systematically manipulate the environment to evoke the desired communicative behavior from the child. She further encouraged the team to develop these communicative behaviors within a naturalistic context, thus increasing Ron's ability to successfully regulate his environment by using adaptive communicative behaviors. Application of sociolinguistic theory supported the speech-language pathologist in developing these strategies.

Ron's parents reported that Ron began to spontaneously use the sign STOP at home within 2 weeks of intervention. They also noted that, during certain routines such as eating and watching television, Ron would sign MORE. They were delighted with his progress and expressed the many ways they now felt more connected to their son.

In fact, they began to identify for the team other nonverbal behaviors that Ron appeared to be using for communicative purposes. They were eager to collaborate with the team to identify new strategies and signs to teach their son.

the theoretical foundations that guide each team member, the team can discover the natural interconnections of theories among the various disciplines. These interconnections provide the exact foundation necessary to support the specialized collaborative process that is unique to a transdisciplinary approach. In the context of this support, individual professionals are afforded the opportunity to operate collectively rather than individually. Those responsible for the child's care are then equipped to respond holistically to the changing nature of child's needs. As a result, the child progresses with greater success and at a faster rate toward goals that are designed to promote his or her independence in any one life role.

References

Alberto, P. A., & Troutman, A. C. (1995). *Applied behavior analysis for teachers* (2nd ed.). Columbus, OH: Merrill.

American Psychiatric Association (2000). *Diagnostic and statistical manual of mental disorders* (4th ed., rev.). Washington, DC: Author.

Andrews, J., & Andrews, M. (1986). The family as the context for change: Language habilitation. *Seminars in Speech and Language, 7(4),* 359–365.

Attwood, T. (1998). *Asperger's syndrome: A guide for parents and professionals.* Philadelphia: Kingsley.

Audet, L. (2000). *Commenting in children with autism.* Unpublished doctoral dissertation, Kent State University, Kent, Ohio.

Audet, L. (2001). The nature of pervasive developmental disorders: A holistic view. In H. Miller-Kuhaneck (Ed.), *Autism: A comprehensive occupational therapy approach* (pp. 23–41). Bethesda, MD: American Occupational Therapy Association.

Audet, L., & Ripich, D. (1994). Psychiatric disorders and discourse problems. In D. Ripich & A. Creaghead (Eds.), *School discourse problems* (2nd ed., pp. 191–228). San Diego, CA: Singular.

Ayres, A. J. (1968/1974). Sensory integrative processes in neuropsychological learning disability. In A. Henderson, L. Llorens, E. Gilfoyle, C. Myers, & S. Prevel (Eds.), *The development of sensory integrative theory and practice: A collection of the work of A. Jean Ayres* (pp. 96–113). Dubuque, IA: Kendall/Hunt. (Original work published 1968).

Ayres, A. J. (1979). *Sensory integration and the child.* Los Angeles: Western Psychological Services.

Baron-Cohen, S. (1989). The autistic child's theory of mind: A case of specific developmental delay. *Journal of Child Psychology and Psychiatry, 30,* 285–297.

Baron-Cohen, S. (1993). From attention-goal psychology to belief-desire psychology: The development of a theory of mind and its dysfunction. In S. Baron-Cohen, H. Tager-Flusberg, & D. Cohen (Eds.), *Understanding other minds: Perspectives from autism* (pp. 59–82). New York: Oxford University Press.

Baron-Cohen, S., & Ring, H. (1994). A model of mind reading system: Neuropsychological and neurobiological perspectives. In C. Lewis, & P. Mitchell (Eds.), *Children's early understanding of mind: Origins and development* (pp. 183–210). Hove, East Sussex: Lawrence Erlbaum.

Berk, L., & Winsler, A. (1995). *Scaffolding children's learning: Vygotsky and early childhood education.* Washington, DC: National Association for the Education of Young Children.

Brazelton, T. B. (1982). Joint regulation of neonate-parent behavior. In E. Z. Tronick (Ed.), *Social interchange in infancy: Affect, cognition and communication* (pp. 7–22). Baltimore: University Park Press.

Briton, B., & Fujuki, M. (1989). *Conversational management with language-impaired children: Pragmatic assessment and intervention.* Gaithersburg, MD: Aspen.

Bruce, M. A., & Borg, B. (1993). *Psychosocial occupational therapy: Frames of reference for intervention* (2nd ed.), Thorofare, NJ: Slack.

Bruner, J. (1982). The organization of action and the nature of the adult-infant transaction. In E. Z. Tronick (Ed.), *Social interchange in infancy: Affect, cognition and communication* (pp. 23–37). Baltimore: University Park Press.

Carr, E. G., & Durand, B. M. (1985). Reducing behavior problems through functional communication training. *Journal of Applied Behavior Analysis, 18(2),* 111–126.

Dewey, J. (1938). *Experience and education.* New York: Macmillan.

Donnellan, A. M., & Leary, M. R. (1997). *Movement differences and diversity in autism/mental retardation: Appreciating and accommodating people* with communication and behavior challenges. Madison, WI: DRI Press.

Duchan, J. F. (1995). *Supporting language learning in everyday life*. San Diego, CA: Singular.

Dunham, P. J., & Moore, C. (1995). Current themes in research on joint attention. In C. Moore & P. J. Dunham (Eds.), *Joint attention: Its origins and role in development* (pp. 15–28). Hillsdale, NJ: Erlbaum.

Durand, V. M. (1990). *Severe behavior problems: A functional communication training approach*. New York: Guilford.

Field, T. (1982). Affective displays of high-risk infants during early interactions. In T. Field & A. Fogel (Eds.), *Emotions and early interaction* (pp. 101–126). Hillsdale, NJ: Erlbaum.

Field, T., & Fogel, A. (Eds.). (1982). *Emotion and early interaction*. Hillsdale, NJ: Erlbaum.

Fisher, A. G., Murray, E. A., & Bundy, A. C. (1991). *Sensory integration: Theory and practice*. Philadelphia: F. A. Davis.

Greenspan, S. I., & Wieder, S. (1998). *The child with special needs: Encouraging intellectual and emotional growth*. Reading, MA: Addison-Wesley.

Kielhofner, G. (Ed.). (1985). *A model of human occupation*. Baltimore: Williams & Wilkins.

Kielhofner, G., & Burke, J. P. (1980). A model of human occupation. Part 1: Conceptual framework and content. *American Journal of Occupational Therapy, 34*, 572–581.

Kielhofner, G., & Burke, J. P. (1985). Components and determinants of human occupation. In G. Kielhofner (Ed.), *A model of human occupation*. Baltimore: Williams & Wilkins.

Levy, L. L. (1993). Model of human occupation frame of reference. In H. L. Hopkins & H. D. Smith (Eds.), *Willard and Spackman's occupational therapy* (8th ed., pp. 76–79). Philadelphia: Lippincott.

Minshew, N., & Wiznitzer, M. (1999). *Update on high-functioning autism research*. Paper presented at the meeting of the Autism Society of Ohio, Cleveland, OH.

Piaget, J., & Inhelder, B. (1969). *The psychology of the child*. New York: Basic.

Prizant, B. M. (1982). Gestalt processing and gestalt language in autism. *Topics in Language Disorders, 3*, 16–23.

Prizant, B. M., Audet, L., Burke, G., Hummel, L., Maher, S., & Theodore, G. (1990). Communication disorders and emotional/behavioral disorders in children. *Journal of Speech and Hearing Disorders, 55*, 179–192.

Rollins, W. (1987). *The psychology of communication disorders in individuals and their families*. Englewood Cliffs, NJ: Prentice Hall.

Sameroff, A. (1987). The social context of development. In N. Eisenburg (Ed.), *Contemporary topics in development* (pp. 273–291). New York: Wiley.

Sherrington, C. S. (1961). *The integrative action of the nervous system*. New Haven, CT: Yale University Press. (Original work published 1906).

Skinner, B. F. (1953). *Science of human behavior*. New York: Free Press.

Tronick, E. Z. (1980). Emotions and communicative intent. In A. Reilly (Ed.), *The communication game: Perspectives on the development of speech, language and nonverbal communication skills* (pp. 4–9). Baltimore: Johnson & Johnson

Tronick, E. Z. (1982). Affectivity and sharing. In E. Z. Tronick (Ed.), *Social interchange in infancy: Affect, cognition, and communication* (pp. 1–6). Baltimore: University Park Press.

Vygotsky, L. S., (1962). *Thought and language* (E. Kaugmann & G. Voltar, Trans.). New York: Wiley.

Wallach, G., & Butler, K. (1984). *Language learning disabilities in school-age children*. Baltimore: Williams & Wilkins.

Wetherby, A. M., Cain, D. H., Yonclas, D. C., & Walker, V. G. (1988). Analysis of intentional communication of normal children from the prelinguistic to the multiword stage. *Journal of Speech and Hearing Research, 31*, 240–252.

CHAPTER 6

Sensory Integration

Zoe Mailloux, MA, OTR, FAOTA, and Susanne Smith Roley, MS, OTR

Even though sensory disorders are not yet part of the diagnostic criteria for autism (APA, 2000), descriptions of the way in which sensory integration issues prevail in autism are common in the literature (Dawson & Lewy, 1989b; Grandin, 1995; Ornitz, 1974; Ornitz, Guthrie, & Farley, 1977; Stehli, 1991; Williams, 1994). Grandin (1995) describes in detail the way in which she and others with autism process sensory experiences differently from people without autism. Williams (1994) also reports the effects of sensory differences in her experiences as an individual with autism. Personal accounts such as these suggest that the sensory-integration frame of reference will be increasingly relevant to occupational therapists working with individuals who are diagnosed with autism. An increasing body of research is exploring the way in which sensory processing plays a role in autism (Dawson & Lewy, 1989b; Miller, Reisman, McIntosh, & Simon, in press; Ornitz, 1974). The purpose of this chapter, therefore, is to present the relevance of sensory integration in occupational therapy for individuals with autism.

To illustrate concepts related to sensory integration and its relevance to occupational therapy interventions, several short vignettes about Jared and Quinn, two boys with autism are included. Although Jared and Quinn, introduced in Case Study 6.1, are quite different in terms of their functional abilities, they both have significant sensory-integration problems.

Sensory Integration Overview

Sensory integration is a term that is used to describe both the basic and essential neurological function that involves organizing sensory information for use (Ayres, 1979) and a specific theory and intervention approach that emerged from within the field of occupational therapy. Sensory-integration theory, originally developed by Dr. A. Jean Ayres, is a commonly used frame of reference within occupational therapy. When occupational therapists working with children within the autistic spectrum were surveyed, 95% to 99% reported using a sensory-integration frame of reference (Case-Smith & Miller, 1999; Watling, Deitz, Kanny & McLaughlin, 1999). In addition, Case-Smith and Bryan (1999) reported that five children diagnosed with autism showed gains in mastery, play and engagement following intervention using a sensory integration approach. Primarily applied to pediatrics, sensory integration encompasses theory, assessment, and intervention strategies. Therapists who use sensory-integration theories subscribe to the investigation and remediation of possible "hidden disorders" in what Dr. Ayres identified as sensory-integration disorders and developmental dyspraxia. Dr. Ayres discovered that these hidden processes contribute substan-

Case Study 6.1

Jared bounds off the school bus and runs toward his classroom. He drops his backpack in the doorway and rushes to the corner of the room where the small cars and airplanes are kept on shelves. Jared searches for a blue airplane, and when he finds it, he brings it close to his face and twirls it with glee. As more children enter the classroom and the noise level increases, Jared covers his ears, and when the school bell rings, he begins to shout and rock. When led back to put away his backpack, Jared allows the classroom aide to guide his hands to pick up the pack and put it in a cubby, but he does not actively participate in the action. He is brought to circle time and sits down but continues to rock and occasionally stands and jumps during the morning routine.

Quinn gets up about an hour earlier than is necessary to get ready for his day at middle school. He follows exactly the same routine each morning: He gets dressed in clothes he has picked out the night before; he eats two pancakes and drinks a glass of juice; he brushes his front teeth 20 strokes and does the same to his bottom and side teeth; he watches the morning stock report and makes a list of the performance of five specific companies, and then he goes outside to wait for the bus about 20 minutes before it will pick him up at his house.

tially to the development of perception and organization of behavior.

Sensory integration theory takes into account the individual's neurobiological ability to process and integrate information and also considers how that ability either helps or inhibits participation in a wide array of environments. Praxis encompasses the individual's ability to originate novel ways of interacting in the environment, to plan and sequence the activity, and to execute it. See Figure 6.1.

Many researchers, theorists, and clinicians have explored sensory integration since Dr. Ayres's time. Most recently, Spitzer (1999) described sensory integration as a dynamic process of interactions, suggesting that the ramifications of disorders in sensory integration and the effects of the intervention are often nonlinear and unpredictable. Typical behavior and abilities are affected by the qualities and types of sensations, the individual's existing capacity to process and interpret stimuli, and the complexity of social and physical environmental factors that either support or detract from the individual's ability to participate meaningfully.

An ecological framework for sensory integration begins to explain this complexity by considering both internal dimensions and external dimensions of interactions (Miller, Reisman et al., in press). External dimensions are those aspects outside of the individual that include the barriers and supports in the physical and social environment that limit or enable engaging in activity and participating in society (World Health Organization, 1999, 2000). Internal dimensions of concern are those aspects of body structure and function that include sensory registration, modulation, discrimination, and praxis (Ayres, 1972).

Qualities and Types of Sensation

Sensory integration highlights sensory processing of information that goes beyond the five senses (sight, hearing, taste, touch, and smell). Notably, it additionally considers vestibular and proprioceptive information as key sensations in development and function. Information from each of the sensory arenas is processed and integrated to form multidimensional perceptions of the world. For example, as a result of experience, a mature individual's single sensory system such as vision can provide information about not only color and distance but also weight and texture. This capacity to "see weight," is built on a multitude of multisensory experiences early in life. It is, in effect, a result of the correlation of information embedded in memory that has converged to form perception (Sacks, 1985).

Location of Sensation

Sensations occur both inside and outside of an individual. Perceptual development requires that a person distinguish types, quality, duration, and intensity from three distinct locations:

- From inside the body (interoception)
- From the head and the musculoskeletal system (proprioception)
- From outside of the body (exteroception)

Interoception. Information from inside of the body is used primarily for survival. Hunger, visceral pain, body temperature, and bowel and bladder distention are all perceived through interoception. Typically, this information is not conscious, but it does drive behaviors such as eating, toileting, and choice of appropriate clothing. Disorders in eating, toileting, and inaccurate interpretation of painful experiences are all typical of children with autism. Porges (1993) reported that poor interoceptive processing could alter stress reactivity and inhibit appropriate social behavior in infants. It is possible that some individuals with autism do not accurately perceive sleepiness, hunger, internal pain, or the need to eliminate. The ability to differentiate these sensations is an essential prerequisite to choosing appropriate activities, for example, eating when hungry and not eating when full. Inappropriate differentiation may result in behaviors or perceptions that are quite abnormal such as inflicting pain on oneself when sleepy, perceiving hunger as nausea, or interpreting anxiety as pain.

Proprioception. Proprioception is used to describe sensations that are received from the tendons, muscles, and joints. The proprioceptive system carries information about joint position and movement (Herdman, 1994). The vestibular system detects position and movement of the head relative to gravity. Together, the vestibular and proprioceptive systems provide information about the body's position in space, the body's parts relative to each other, and the dynamic movement of the body through space. This information is used to support postural control; balance; and coordinated movement of the eyes, head, neck, and body.

Figure 6.1

For the child with autism, the capacity to process and interpret sensory information either supports or detracts from the individual's ability to participate meaningfully.

Copyright 2001 Shay McAtee. Reprinted with permission of photographer.

Someone who has good vestibular and proprioceptive perception is likely to move gracefully, keeping their balance while moving with skill and precision. When the vestibular or proprioceptive system is not working well, individuals have difficulty developing a good body scheme. They will have poor balance, poor postural control, difficulty forming good laterality, and poorly coordinated movements of the body and limbs, both separately and together. Individuals with autism have been noted to have difficulty integrating vestibular and proprioceptive information (Ayres, 1979). The vestibular system provides information necessary to support the most primal of relationships, that of the self to the earth. When the vestibular system is not working properly, other relationships also may suffer (Schilder, 1964).

Exteroception. Exteroception encompasses several different kinds of stimuli that detect information located outside of the body. Touch, smell, and taste are all designed to detect whatever the individual comes into contact with from the environment and differentiate that from parts of the self. Vision and hearing are the only sensations that are not perceived through contact receptors. Vision and hearing allow the individual to perceive information that is both close to the body and at a distance. Visual perception is generally considered an area of strength in many individuals with autism; however, auditory processing is more likely to be problematic (Grandin, 1995).

Multimodal Processing

Early in development, babies begin to associate sensory experiences. As these memories are recorded, the sensory systems increasingly differentiate so that an adult no longer has to put things into his or her mouth to understand their texture or shape. Experience provides the basis for interpreting all interactions. In a well-developed system, this differentiation allows a person to infer qualities of the environment from a single data source such as feeling the cold hard metal of a key and knowing its shape, weight, and function (Streri, 1993).

The interrelationship of sensations is apparent in any functional activity (Turkewitz, 1994). Typically, the interoceptive, proprioceptive, and exteroceptive sensations are integrated so that an individual can pay attention to relevant aspects of the environment while the body operates unconsciously. For example, the vestibular and proprioceptive systems work together, supporting an upright posture against gravity and making subtle postural adjustments when moving (Baloh & Honrubia, 1979; Cohen, 1999; Herdman, 1994). The tactile and proprioceptive systems work together to initiate and guide movement through space. Internal perceptual maps are formed from sensory data from the visual and auditory systems along with these other sensations. The visual and auditory systems can provide feedback on the accuracy of perception of the other senses, and as development then progresses, they can be free to gather data on a wide external environment (Tsurumi & Todd, 1997). The complexity of this process cannot be overstated.

Figure 6.2
Sensory integration is necessary to accurately perceive the body's relationship to gravity and other objects.

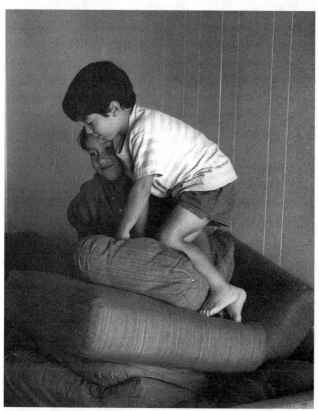

Copyright 2001 Shay McAtee. Reprinted with permission of photographer.

Organization of Behavior

The integration of sensory information is necessary to provide an individual with a reference for the body's relationship to gravity, the body's relationship to itself, the body's relationship to people and other things in the environment, and for the relationship of people and things in the environment to each other. See Figure 6.2. These are, in essence, different levels of temporal-spatial relationships. Interoceptors provide information about where and how things are happening inside the body. The proprioceptors provide temporal and spatial information about the body relative to gravity and itself, and the exteroceptors provide spatial information about the external environment. Although the visual and auditory systems are primary distance receptors, they build their spatial perceptions on the experiences that are typically obtained in early childhood (Gilfoyle, Grady, & Moore, 1990).

The vestibular and proprioceptive systems are the bridge between the body and any action in a gravity environment. Primarily acting unconsciously to provide position and joint sense, these sensory systems provide the background data for all action. Knowing where the head and body are located and are moving in space (including the speed, direction, and relationship between parts of the body and other people or objects) is critical when interacting skillfully. This background information is essential to process rapid accommodations for balance, to maintain stability of the visual field during moving, and to perform skilled action. When these sensory systems do not provide precise and immediate feedback about position and movement, individuals may show an over-reliance on vision. When vision is not available, postural control may be compromised (Shumway-Cook, & Woolacott, 1995).

Application of Sensory Integration Concepts to the Diagnosis of Autism

Current neurophysiological research (that is referred to by Miller-Kuhaneck, Glennon, and Case-Smith in this book) provides insight to the sensory-integration disorders that are present in many individuals with autism. These disorders have been clinically observed and documented through research (Parham, Mailloux, & Smith Roley, 2000). Case Study 6.2 describes behaviors of Jared and Quinn that suggest inadequate sensory perception and integration.

The following sections will discuss the relevance of the major aspects of sensory-integration disorders to autism. These include dis-

---

Case Study 6.2

Jared is often seen jumping and twirling on the playground. Further observation reveals that Jared does not engage in most of the typical playground activities, including going on the swings or slides, climbing on the gym apparatus, or running and jumping during the common playground games. Because these are ways that most children receive the basic sensory input they need for normal development, Jared's lack of engagement leaves his nervous system craving sensory experiences and puts him at risk for the complications that lack of these experiences will bring. Although his sensory-seeking behavior (seen in jumping and twirling) is not considered purposeful activity in the usual sense, it does suggest an attempt to engage in sensory-based actions that address a primal need. These actions may help Jared to stay alert, to be more organized, and to have a better sense of where his body is in relation to the world around him.

Quinn, in contrast to Jared's behavior, does not show many of the behaviors that might be called self-stimulatory. However, he does show signs of inadequate sensory perception. When Quinn writes, he often presses so hard that he breaks the pencil lead. Unless he concentrates on the pressure he exerts on the pencil, he is not aware of how hard he is pressing. Apparently, unless he presses firmly when writing, Quinn loses track of his fingers and hand, and soon his letters and words wander off the page. Quinn struggles with tactile and proprioceptive feedback in a similar fashion when he attempts to fasten small buttons, snaps, or buckles. He must rely on his vision to complete these simple everyday tasks.

---

orders related to sensory registration, sensory modulation, sensory perception, and praxis.

Sensory Registration

Ayres used the term "registration of sensation" (Ayres, 1979) to refer to the way that a child's awareness of sensory stimuli is associated with attaching meaning to situations. Occupational therapists have used the term "poor sensory registration" to mean a failure to notice, record, and respond to relevant information from the environment (Miller & Lane, 2000). Ayres hypothesized that some children with autism have deficits in sensory registration (Ayres, 1979; Ayres & Tickle, 1980). Poor registration may account for some of the behaviors observed in individuals with autism. Lack of regis-

tration may be the result of having unusually high thresholds for receiving sensory information (Miller, Reisman, et al., in press). This lack of registration sometimes causes problems related to attention. A child may pay attention to only part of the visual or auditory field, and events that are significant to others may go unnoticed by the child with autism. Case Study 6.3 describes behaviors of Jared and Quinn that demonstrate possible problems in sensory registration.

Sensory Modulation

Recent research has greatly refined our understanding of sensory modulation in relation to autism (Baranek, 1998, 1999; Miller, Reisman, et al., in press). A critical factor in sensory modulation is the interaction between internal processing and the external environment. More specifically, the interaction between the physiologic stability, the perceived challenge imposed by the environment, and environmental supports affects a person's ability to tolerate stress and find adaptive coping and interaction strategies (Kraemer, in press). Physiological data are beginning to allow comparisons of different diagnostic groups (Miller et al., 1999) and are beginning to make distinctions between physiological and behavioral modulation processes. Preliminary research involving children with autism suggests that, as a group, children with autism demonstrate underresponsivity to sensation as measured by electrodermal reactivity but hyperreactivity to all sensory stimuli in behavioral measures. In contrast, children with Fragile X Syndrome exhibit similar behaviors that are suggestive of modulation deficits and, as a group, tend to demonstrate overresponsivity to sensation.

Individual behavioral differences vary widely between extreme hyporesponsivity and extreme hyperresponsivity, sensory seeking and sensory avoiding, and unusual patterns of sensory play. Ayres and Tickle (1980) identified children who were hyporesponsive or hyper-

---

Case Study 6.3

Jared does not seem to pay attention to toys in a typical way. In an environment with a variety of toys or equipment, he is likely to run from one thing to the next. Although he does not pay attention to playthings that would be appealing to most children, he often gives excessive attention to some aspect of an object such as a string on a pull toy or the shadow of light coming through a blind. One of his favorite toys is a doll that has a striped body. He likes to hold it close to his face and twirl it back and forth.

As a young child, Quinn did not seem to notice many things that would have caught the attention of other children. For example, he often did not seem to notice that toys or objects were in his hand if he got distracted by something else. His mother reported that the whole house could be burning down and he would not notice. This lack of attention to certain things was confusing because at other times he noticed the smallest noise or scrap of paper on the floor. Sometimes, when Quinn's mother talks to him, he seems to look right through her. Quinn also often seems oblivious to the feelings of others. He does not seem to be aware when someone is angry, irritated, or sad. This apparent lack of empathy creates difficulty for him in social situations.

responsive. The children who were hyporesponsive tended to respond less well to sensory-integration procedures than children who were hyperresponsive. Baranek (1999) suggests that an aversion threshold alters arousal so the children's arousal level may fluctuate between over- and under-reactivity to sensory stimuli and environmental events.

Common patterns of hypersensitivity are auditory and tactile defensiveness (Keintz & Dunn, 1997), and visual fixations. Unusual patterns of sensory responsiveness affect activities of daily living such as dressing and eating. For example, the diets of children with heightened sensitivities may be extremely restricted, including avoidance of foods with certain textures. A common indicator of hyporesponsiveness is a high pain tolerance. Children who are hyporesponsive show behavior that may include seeking extremely intense movement such as spinning and twirling, inflicting injuries on themselves, and throwing themselves into things and people for deep pressure and proprioceptive sensation.

The learning and behavior of a child with autism may be hindered by inadequate sensory modulation, as this condition is associated with negative emotions. Sensory modulation is addressed through varying the type, intensity, and duration of different sensory stimuli so the child with autism can maintain a calm, alert state. An analysis of the environmental aspects that most disturb the child is essential, and environmental modifications are often necessary to accommodate the child's peculiar sensory needs and sensitivities. For example, a child with autism may enjoy tight-fitted exercise clothing rather than loose clothing or a quiet atmosphere rather than one where the television is playing. A child may be able to focus only if he or she can hear white noise in the background such as the hum of a ceiling fan. A variety of different intensities and combinations of sensations must be explored to find the child's comfort level. Jared and Quinn display

---

Case Study 6.4

Jared demonstrates heightened sensitivity to a variety of sensory experiences. At home and school, he demonstrates classic signs of tactile defensiveness in his intolerance of substances such as glue, paint, sand, or soap on his hands. He is also extremely sensitive on his face and feet. Jared also overreacts to certain sounds, smells, and visual stimuli. His typical responses to sensory experiences that irritate him include withdrawing from the activity, squealing, or striking out at other children who are nearby.

Quinn shows more subtle signs of a sensory modulation disorder. He does not usually show overt reactions, except to certain sounds. He reacts as if he is in pain at times when he hears loud noises. He usually covers his ears or tries to leave the area in which the sounds are occurring. The sounds in crowded areas such as the cafeteria or the mall are especially disturbing to Quinn. He is also a very picky eater, which appears to be at least partially related to sensory reactions. Quinn usually eats only plain pasta, cheese sandwiches, and pancakes.

---

varying indications of inadequate sensory modulation. Case Study 6.4 describes the signs of this disorder in their behavior.

Sensory Perception

Although sensory responsiveness in children with autism has been studied (Ayres & Tickle, 1980; Baranek & Berkson, 1997a, 1997b; Miller, Reisman, et al., in press; Ornitz, 1974; Ornitz et al., 1977), little has been documented concerning sensory discrimination. The following sections consider, in particular, the issues related to the visual, auditory, and vestibular-somatosensory perception of children with autism.

Visual. A recent study by Parham, et al. (2000) suggests that visual perception is a relative strength in children with autism. This finding is verified by personal reports from individuals who have autism (Grandin, 1995; Williams, 1992, 1994). Grandin (1995) states, "One of the most profound mysteries of autism has been the remarkable ability of most autistic people to excel at visual spatial skills, while performing so poorly at verbal skills" (p. 20). Understanding the visual perception strengths of many individuals with autism is an important consideration in educational and therapeutic programs because the visual sensory system offers a means to compensate for other areas of difficulty. For example, relative skills in visual perception often make activities (such as puzzles) and mechanical tasks (such as constructing) attractive and organizing for the individual with autism. These kinds of tasks may be helpful to provide support for other areas that are more likely to be difficult such as social play and language skills. However, an excessive preference for visual tasks can preclude engagement in active play. Children with high-functioning autism, in particular, may prefer to work on puzzles and computer games or to look at books instead of play at a playground or interact with peers.

Nevertheless, the fact that children with autism often prefer visual activities must not lead to the assumption that a task with a visual component will be easy for a person with autism. Very young children with autism are sometimes misidentified as having a visual impairment because they demonstrate poor ocular motor control, do not establish meaningful eye contact, and have poor registration of the total visual field. Functions such as reading that involve visual perception but also rely on the ability to process language can be difficult despite good visual perception skills. Visual motor skills or functional hand skills in these children are often quite impaired, affecting, especially, two-dimensional and three-dimensional construction, which requires praxis in addition to visual perception. In addition, tasks that require cooperative use of the two hands together such as opening a bag of chips or a container are often compromised.

Auditory. Auditory perception is an area more frequently suspected as being inefficient in many individuals with autism. Grandin (1995) describes specific auditory tests that suggest areas of difficulty in auditory perception that individuals with autism experience. These include auditory functions of processing complex sounds such as those in spoken words and in dichotomous listening as well as the timing of sound input. Identifying possible auditory perception difficulties is essential when planning educational programs for individuals with autism. Noisy classrooms can further interfere with auditory processing. Placing the child at the most appropriate location in the classroom, using other supplemental sensory information such as visual cues, and limiting extraneous stimuli are all strategies that might enhance auditory processing. The transient nature of auditory stimuli is often difficult for individuals with autism, who tend to process concrete images better than those that are implied (Grandin, 1995).

Vestibular-Somatosensory. Tactile, proprioceptive, and vestibular perception appears to be more varied in individuals with autism. Parham, et al. (2000) found that children with autism had significantly lower scores than a matched pairs control group on tests measuring tactile discrimination. Because sensory modulation disorders often accompany sensory perception difficulties, these kinds of problems can be difficult to differentiate. This difficulty is especially true in relation to these basic somatosensory systems. In general, however, children with autism often show clear signs of poor tactile, proprioceptive, and vestibular sensory perception. Poor sensory feedback can be seen in functional problems such as poor fine motor skills, limited utensil use, difficulties in positioning, and poor balance. When children have inefficient sensory perception, they will tend to seek additional sensation in that area, often relying on additional feedback to guide their interactions (Ayres, 1979).

Children with autism are commonly seen searching for ways to receive additional sensory input that is tactile, proprioceptive, or vestibular in nature. Examples of sensory-seeking actions include twirling or spinning, jumping, rubbing or squeezing, biting, head banging, and rocking. How these behaviors are viewed from different perspectives on autism will be explored in this chapter. In terms of sensory perception, these kinds of sensory-seeking actions often suggest that an individual may need additional information from various sensory channels to feel calm, to feel organized, or to have a better sense of position and orientation in space.

Praxis as it Relates to the Diagnosis of Autism

Although the sensory disorders associated with autism have become more acknowledged and are commonly included in descriptions of the major symptoms of this condition (Baranek, 2000; Grandin, 1995; Greenspan & Weider, 1997; Miller, Reisman et al. in press), difficulties in praxis are not yet routinely acknowledged as part of the diagnosis of autism. However, dyspraxia is becoming more widely recognized as a critical aspect of the functional deficits associated with this disorder.

Praxis is the ability to have an idea and plan about a future novel activity that involves deciding what to do and how to do it. Although routine and stereotyped motor activities that do not require praxis such as walking, running, or climbing are typically easy for individuals diagnosed with autism, motor activities that require adaptation such as building models or using tools appear to be very difficult for them (Ayres, 1979). Motor execution is frequently intact, meaning that once children with autism learn a motor skill, their actions can look exquisitely smooth and coordinated. However, specific aspects of praxis such as timing, sequencing, initiating, and transitioning are commonly difficult for these children. See Figure 6.3.

Ayres (1979) suspected that, among individuals with autism, abnormalities in the lim-

Figure 6.3
Praxis is typically difficult for children with autism.

Copyright 2001 Shay McAtee. Reprinted with permission of photographer.

bic system contributed to this group's typical lack of drive to engage in activities usually thought of as meaningful or purposeful in our culture. Neurobiological studies conducted by researchers such as Baumann and Kemper (1994) and Courchesne (1989a, 1989b; Courchesne, Hesselink, Jernigan, & Yeung-Courchesne, 1987) have supported Ayres's early hypotheses. Other research has demonstrated poor imitative abilities in many individuals with autism (Baranek, 1999; Dawson & Lewy 1989a; Dawson & Adams, 1984; Smith & Bryson, 1994). A disorder in the drive to engage coupled with poor imitation and deficits in sensory processing create a high likelihood of poor praxis abilities. Parham, et al. (2000) demonstrated that praxis scores were consistently and significantly low in children with autism compared to a matched sample of typically developing children. In particular, the Oral Praxis Test, a test of the ability to imitate mouth, lip, and tongue movements, significantly discriminated between typical children and those identified with autism. This finding is consistent with others that have found deficits in the ability to make and imitate facial gestures (Dawson & Lewy 1989a; Smith & Bryson, 1994).

Case Study 6.5

When Jared enters the playroom of his after-school day care, he usually goes to a corner of the room where the carpet is frayed. If left unattended, Jared can wind and twirl the frayed carpet threads for long periods of time. Although a variety of toys are placed around the room within easy access, Jared does not appear to know what to do with the toys. New toys that quickly capture the interest of the other children do not appear to hold Jared's attention or interest. During outdoor play periods, Jared spends most of his time on the swings, often lying across a swing on his stomach. Although other children experiment wildly with placing their bodies in ever changing positions on the monkey and parallel bars, Jared never ventures far from the swings.

Quinn dreads the physical education class he attends each day at middle school. He feels inept during all of the team sport activities, never quite able to keep up with the pace of the other children. Although he watches their motions and positions intently, he cannot seem to imitate their actions. Fast-paced games such as basketball, soccer, and handball are the most frustrating for Quinn. Recently, he has discovered that he is rather good at running. Quinn finds that by thinking about the things that interest him, he can run fast and for long distances. He is hopeful that his success in this area will offer him some acceptance by the other boys in the physical education classes.

Observations of children with autism often reveal a paucity of abilities in the aspect of praxis called "ideation." One of the diagnostic features of autism is resistance to change and avoidance of novelty (APA, 2000). Poor ideation is likely associated with this feature of autism because an individual would be threatened when encountering unfamiliar situations if he or she did not have the ability to form an idea or plan for how to interact with something new. Poor ideation is probably a key aspect of the limited play skills observed in children with autism (Mailloux & Burke, 1997; May-Benson, in press). The ritualistic and repetitive use of toys often replaces imaginary and exploratory play for children with this disorder. Obsession and routine may replace the more creative ways that individuals interact when they have good praxis and a well-developed sense of themselves. In Case Study 6.5, Jared and Quinn demonstrate behaviors and reactions that indicate problems with praxis.

Individuals who are diagnosed with autism have difficulty figuring out how to interact adaptively with objects and with people in the environment. Sensory information from the somatosensory and vestibular systems is used to provide information about where the body is in space and how it is moving. Basic information regarding the body is then used in conjunction with information about the environment within which an individual is moving and with information about the motion of other people and objects in the environment relative to the individual's movements. The complex interplay between the interpretation of movement, prediction of the outcome of the movement, and the planning and organizing of one's response appears to be quite difficult for individuals with autism.

Praxis is essential in planning interactions with the physical environment, and it is potentially even more important when interacting with the social environment. Objects are typically more predictable than people. People move in unpredictable patterns and react in unpredictable ways. When interacting with people who are moving, therefore, one must attempt to anticipate the speed and direction of their movements. People also frequently interpret the meaning of other's movements, for example, by predicting that a person is going to get a drink of water. Interpreting the trajectory of movement of people in space is superimposed on the ability to interpret and direct one's own position and movement in space. All of these skills may be extremely difficult for a child with autism.

Much of the difficulty with sensory registration and praxis may be linked to the inability to comprehend the intangible. For example, the vestibular system detects the pull of the unseen force of gravity. The auditory system detects sound waves that do not have a constant source. Praxis requires planning actions prior to their taking place. Human interactions require the anticipation of future trajectories and the reading of nonverbal gestures and verbal cues. Transitions require leaving a known, stable activity to move toward an anticipated future goal. Predicting the future and modifying behavior in response to the actual reality involves a considerable amount of problem solving. Individuals with autism tend to have difficulty identifying and planning their interactions with these intangible factors such as anticipation of the future and predicting trajectories. Case Study 6.6 shares an example of Quinn's difficulties in responding to variations.

Assessment

Because of the common incidence of sensory-integration dysfunction present in children with autism, assessment of underlying sensory integration and praxis abilities is generally a critical aspect of an occupational therapy assessment for these children. An occupation-centered assessment considers the effect that engaging in daily activities has on the well-being of these individuals and on the systems

---

Case Study 6.6

Quinn has difficulty following verbal directions. He becomes very distressed if someone tells him to do something that disrupts his current activity. He has developed rituals around starting and stopping his play and around how the sequence unfolds during his play. He cannot tolerate a situation in which the entire sequence is not played out thoroughly. His mother is concerned about his perseveration and obsessive rituals. She would like for him to be able to vary things a little to fit in better with his friends. She told him that he could not cry when his rituals are disrupted, or the older children will not play with him. Quinn understands and tries to correct his behavior, especially if his mother can be very concrete about what he is supposed to do and how it will be accepted.

---

that surround them. Sensory integration and praxis are fundamental components that are essential to an individual's ability to use information and participate adaptively within an ever changing environment. The evaluation uncovers the "hidden processes" that contribute to adaptive or maladaptive interactions (Ayres, 1972).

Behavioral manifestations of underlying sensory issues are often viewed in isolation from the antecedent sensory incidents that evoke reactions from the child, a practice that potentially leads to misunderstanding the child. Responding adaptively to the changing sensory qualities of the environment may present an overwhelming level of challenge to children with autism and may result in responses that are maladaptive. Analysis of engagement and participation in everyday activities from a sensory-integration perspective takes into consideration an individual's ability to process sensory information and form novel ways of interacting with the environment. The results of the sensory-integration evaluation provide an understanding of the sensory and motor underpinnings of the child's choices and capabilities while participating in daily life. The analysis often reframes the interpretation of problematic behaviors and mannerisms and allows an intervention plan to be generated.

Evaluating children with autism presents many varied challenges. For children with autism who are able to respond reliably in a standardized test situation, the Sensory Integration and Praxis Tests (Ayres, 1989) offer the most comprehensive measures of sensory-integration functions. More frequently, however, children with autism have difficulties with cognition, language, attention, transitions, and social reciprocity that rule out the use of standardized tests.

Many aspects of sensory-integration functions can be assessed through structured and unstructured observations of the child. The parents' and caregivers' narratives are an essential part of the assessment of a child with autism. During interviews, significant individuals in the child's life are asked to describe what the child can and cannot do in everyday life and to describe the context in which the child is performing. Structured observations are conducted in both typical and clinical settings by the therapist. The STEP-SI (sensations, task, environment, predictability, self-monitoring, and interactions) clinical reasoning model has been proposed as a method to structure ongoing observation and decision making, (Miller, Wilbarger, Stackhouse, & Trunnell, in press). Each of these elements can be analyzed to determine if these aspects of the child's life either support or hinder the ability to cope and participate.

Whether standardized or nonstandardized assessments are feasible for the child, the following types of information will be helpful in attaining a more complete understanding of the child with autism:

- Does the child show patterns of under- or over-responsivity to certain types of sensory experiences? What behaviors generally signal that the child is reacting to sensory experiences? In relation to what conditions (e.g., sleep-wake cycles, hunger, illness, time of day, environmental setting) does the child tend to show what types of reactions?
- Does the child have functional perception and discrimination of specific information from various sensory systems? Do test scores or functional performance indicate signs of poor discriminative ability?
- What does the child do in unfamiliar or novel environments? Does the child show curiosity and exploratory play? Does the child demonstrate ideation about how to use novel toys or objects? Is the child generally purposeful in activities? Does the child show self-initiation in play?
- Does the child demonstrate adequate skills for play and work? How does the child use utensils and materials? Do any strength or muscle-tone issues interfere with performance? Is the child able to coordinate both sides of his or her body in activities such as cutting, writing, pedaling, and swimming?
- Can the child imitate actions? Does the child follow directions that are given verbally? Can the child complete sequences of actions?
- How does the child relate to other people in the environment? Does the child appear to regard others? Does the child show interest in watching peers? Does the child show interest in interacting with peers? Does the child initiate interaction with others?
- How does the environment help or hinder the child's level of comfort, organization, attention, and learning? Are the child's caregivers informed about the child's abilities, level of responsivity, and areas of challenge? What compensatory strategies and environmental accommodations are available for the child?

Case Study 6.7 provides observations of Jared and of Quinn that answer the questions on the above list.

Intervention

Because disorders of sensory integration are prevalent among individuals with autism, it is

Case Study 6.7

Jared, at age 5, is not yet toilet trained. He seems not to notice if he is wet and does not seem to be bothered by soiled pants. At times, he plays with his feces. He no longer wears diapers, but he has difficulty keeping his hands out of his pants now that his diapers are off. His family no longer goes on outings that are longer than one hour because of these embarrassing incidents.

Jared cannot cope with more than two visitors at a time in his home, especially if people are talking loudly and laughing. At first, he runs up and down the hallway, but then his behavior escalates to screaming, arm biting, and head banging. To calm him down requires an adult to provide one-on-one attention and to remove him to a quiet area.

Jared has a functional pencil grasp, but he is unable to use his hands together for functional tasks such as securing fasteners and opening food containers. All of his pants have elastic waistbands. His mother has given up hope that he will ever tie his shoes.

His mother reported that she would really like the following for her family:
• Jared could play by himself for at least 20 minutes.
• She could go grocery shopping with her son.

• The family could enjoy a holiday such as Christmas without Jared becoming disruptive.
• Jared would someday play quietly with a friend.

Jared was unable to complete a standardized assessment to test his sensory-integration abilities. His mother answered questions on the Sensory Profile (Dunn, 2000), and he was observed in both a therapeutic clinic setting as well as in his home and school environments. The therapist determined Jared's general developmental level through observation and comparison to developmental norms because standardized testing was not possible. The responses that Jared's mother provided on the Sensory Profile suggested many signs of sensory defensiveness. These findings were verified by observations of Jared in a variety of sensory experiences such as movement activities in the clinical setting, craft and sandbox activities at school, and grooming and feeding tasks at home. Signs of hyperresponsivity were evident and consistent with his mother's report. Jared demonstrated developmental skills in a range that was below his chronological age. Jared's teacher and mother were well informed about autism and had already begun to make accommodations in

his environment to help him be more comfortable and organized. Table 6.1 details Jared's evaluation.

When he was very young, Quinn's parents thought he was gifted. He had precocious language, and he knew every make and model of car on the road by age 4. In fact, his grandfather who is an automobile engineer brought home a marketing video for specially designed cars that he watched over and over.

Quinn's mother began to be concerned in preschool when he was not developing friends. He has required a regimented routine so much that his family has since realized how uneventful and monotonous their lives have become. They are rarely spontaneous and have stopped participating in outdoor sports and activities.

His mother's hopes for her family are
• That the family would be able to do more hiking and camping activities like they did in the past
• That Quinn can eventually be more like other children
• That she can cook gourmet meals again and that Quinn might actually enjoy them
• That Quinn will one day have a lot of friends

Quinn, at age 11, was older than the age norms for the Sensory Integration

and Praxis Tests. However, he had not been given these standardized tests previously, and his therapist felt that it would be helpful to administer them at this time to have the opportunity to systematically observe Quinn's performance on measures of sensory perception and praxis. The therapist felt that the SIPT might help to explain some of the discrepancies between Quinn's academic performance and his organizational skills. Quinn scored in the above-average range on the tests measuring motor-free visual perception whereas his responses on the tests of tactile perception were mixed. He demonstrated significant difficulty with the measures of proprioceptive and vestibular sensory processing and showed several very low scores on the measures of praxis. The Evaluation of Sensory Processing (ESP) (Johnson-Ecker & Parham, 2000) revealed uneven responsivity to sensory experiences. At school, Quinn was observed to do well academically with concepts, but his grades suffered because he had problems with organizing the work he produced, writing quickly, and managing his papers and assignments. Social skills were noted to be a significant area of concern for Quinn. Table 6.2 details Quinn's evaluation.

Table 6.1

Jared's Sensory Integrative Evaluation: Observations and Goals

	Presenting Problems	Assessment Data	Goals
Sensory Registration	• High pain threshold • Speech and language delays • Cognitive delays	• Did not register relevant voice sounds, human touch, or the visual image of the cat in front of him, even though he was looking for the cat • Had selective attention to penlight and refused to give it back to the examiner • Fixated on fear of the toilet flushing and refused to leave bathroom area following toileting	• Increase awareness of total sensory field from multiple sensory channels (i.e., verbal cues, visual cues, tactile cues, and movement)
Sensory Modulation	• Difficulty tolerating high stimulus environments • Anxiety • Self-stimulatory behaviors • Constant eating • Sensitivity to noise (becomes disturbed)	• Screamed when asked to relinquish penlight • Wanted clothes off and light massage • Became distressed when mother stopped the massage • Had difficulty tolerating the examiner and mother talking during the evaluation • Rocked self and flapped hands vigorously when agitated • According to mother, does not tolerate the sound of the toilet flushing but insists on loud music when he wants to dance	• Improve his ability to participate in family events such as going to a restaurant, birthday parties, and his siblings' sports and drama events without screaming or tantrumming. • Decrease self-stimulatory behaviors when in public. • Improve his ability to tolerate typical noise and activity during the day such as flushed toilets, the garbage disposal, and dishwasher.
Sensory Perception	• Difficulty engaging in conversation • Poor fine motor control • Jumps and twirls instead of playing	• Could not understand verbal directions • Had difficulty localizing where he was touched and with what object • Seems disoriented when provided rotation on postrotary nystagmus board • Lost balance when he turned his head to look to the side • Broke the crayon from the use of too much force when drawing	• Improve ability to process language when there is background noise. • Improve ability to stabilize his posture when moving his head in space. • Increase awareness of where and how he is touching other people and objects. • Increase awareness of the force and intensity with which he is holding objects and pets.

continues

Table 6.1
Continued

	Presenting Problems	Assessment Data	Goals
Praxis	• Difficulty opening containers • Runs away when asked to do something • Does not know what to do with toys	• Could not open a box of raisins • Could not unfasten pants for toileting • Refused to copy block designs • Could not imitate facial gestures or body movements	• Improve self-care skills such as independent dressing, playing with toys, participating in play with other children, and copying designs and structures such as puzzles.
Organization of Behavior	• Strikes out at other children; squeals • Dependent on others for completing all aspects of daily routines such as eating, dressing, bathing, and playing	• Repeatedly asked for food • Whined when he was denied his request • Threw toys out of the room when they were presented to him • Could not sequence bathroom routine without specific step-by-step verbal instructions • Became overwhelmed when asked to interact in a play activity • Could not tolerate activities for more than one minute except for water play and eating	• Improve ability to participate in familiar routines and structures without distress. • Improve ability to carry out a five-step sequence such as preparing to go to bed. • Improve ability to structure 1/2 hour of playtime productively. • Increase ability to transition from one activity to the next with ease.

difficult to imagine a comprehensive therapy program that would not include at least some components of the sensory-integration framework. A sensory-integration approach uses a variety of strategies to address the range of disorders in sensory integration and praxis that is common in individuals with autism. When using the sensory-integration frame of reference alone or in combination with other methods of intervention used in occupational therapy, the overarching goal of the occupational therapist is to establish or restore a healthy lifestyle for the child and the child's family by engaging the child in meaningful occupations (Parham & Primeau, 1997).

Sensory-integration intervention has many unique features. More than just a technique, it is a philosophy of practice (Spitzer & Roley, in press). This philosophy is based on Dr. Ayres's style and her belief that human beings have an innate drive to learn, grow, and interact adaptively (Ayres, 1972). She applied her theories and developed strategies for intervention that supported growth and development with respect for the child.

Ayres declared the use of this intervention to be both an art and a science (Ayres, 1972). The artistry emerges with the therapist and the child creating a new scenario each time they play. This scenario unfolds as a consequence of the existing state of the child, his or her ability to handle novelty and challenge that day, and the skillfulness of the therapist to guide and support the child's emerging competencies (Ayres, 1972; Koomar & Bundy, 1991).

Key constructs guide the therapist in the delivery of therapeutic interactions when using sensory-integration principles. The following

Table 6.2

Quinn's Sensory Integrative Evaluation: Observations and Goals

	Presenting Problems	Assessment Data	Goals
Sensory Registration	• Parents wondered about hearing loss when he was younger • Seems not to notice many things	• Difficulty detecting changes in facial expressions and tone of voice when asked to signal when he noticed a change	• Develop and utilize strategies to detect cues needed for appropriate social interactions.
Sensory Modulation	• Anxiety and immobilization during loud, busy situations or environments such as parties, shopping malls, and the cafeteria • Heightened sensitivity to being close to people, to certain tones of voice, and to heights, especially during times of stress	• According to mother, has extreme reactions to sensory input on the ESP, demonstrating both hypo- and hypersensitivity • During the evaluation, appeared easily startled by unexpected sounds and by being touched when his vision was occluded during the tests	• Develop and use strategies for managing sensory modulation issues to maintain an optimal level of attention and organization. • Increase tolerance for trying a greater variety of foods. • Improve tolerance for outdoor activities with the family such as camping and hiking.
Sensory Perception	• Always seemed "mechanically inclined" and is good at putting things together • Has always been considered a visual versus an auditory learner	• Scored well above average in motor free visual perception, but had scores below average in some tests of tactile perception • His scores on the tests of Kinesthesia, Postrotary Nystagmus, and Standing and Walking Balance were all below average	• Increase body awareness and balance for improved finesse in physical and social activities. • Enhance tactile perception, compensate with visual strategies, or both for improved fine motor skills dependent on tactile feedback.
Praxis	• Was never skilled at sports • Had difficulty learning new physical tasks as a younger child, and now avoids new challenges	• Had very low scores on the tests of Praxis on Verbal Command and on Oral and Postural Praxis • Had slightly low scores on Design Copying and Motor Accuracy but scored well on Constructional Praxis • Appeared coordinated while running and climbing but seemed hesitant when asked to try something unfamiliar	• Develop and use strategies for learning new tasks, highlighting strengths in visual and cognitive skills. • Increase repertoire of familiar physical skills to enhance social participation.
Organization of Behavior	• Does well academically at school but struggles with basic functional skills such as organization of his materials • Likes to keep his desk neat but has difficulty keeping track of things when routines change	• Appeared to respond well to the structure of the standardized tests but became anxious when he felt he was not doing well • Seemed more uncomfortable when observed in unstructured situations in a therapy clinic or when expected to transition between classes at school	• Develop and use strategies for enhanced management of time and materials. • Increase comfort level with novel and unpredictable situations. • Increase initiation of social events with peers.

characteristic hallmarks are present when the sensory-integration frame of reference is being used:

- Use of a structured sensory environment that highlights the proprioceptive, vestibular, and tactile systems
- A focus on tapping the inner drive of the child
- Delivery of intervention in the context of play
- "Artful vigilance" on the part of the therapist
- Child-directed sessions
- Elicitation of adaptive responses
- Delivery of the "just-right level of challenge"
- Emphasis on active versus passive participation where the engagement in the activity is its own reward (Ayres, 1972; Clark, Parham, & Mailloux, 1989; Koomar & Bundy, 1991; Parham & Mailloux, 1996)

Structured Sensory Environment

Ayres identified the environment as a key element in sensory-integration intervention. She discussed a classic clinical setting as having characteristics of a "naturalistic" environment (Ayres, 1972). She was referring to natural environments "in the wild" as opposed to the understanding of "natural environment" as used in current legislation. These more primal environments have naturally occurring rhythms, cycles, quiet space, and distance, and they allow physical activities such as running, jumping, swinging, and climbing. With the advent of early childhood programs for typical children, sensory-integration clinic-style settings are becoming more typical environments in which interventions for gross motor play occur.

In developing this therapeutic approach, Ayres tried to provide children with opportunities to participate in multisensory activities that had the effect of being calming, alerting, challenging, organizing, and fun. See Figure 6.4. Therefore, intervention requires therapists to create, modify, and adapt the sensory environment. The environment provides opportunities to improve body-centered perceptions through touch, proprioception, and vestibular sensations. Additionally, the environment provides challenges for the child to develop praxis skills by creating, adapting, and manipulating objects and interactions. Although the perception of visual and auditory sensations is often enhanced through sensory-integration intervention, Ayres (1972) considered visual and auditory perception to be end products of a more fundamental sensory-integration process. In fact, it is often beneficial to reduce visual and auditory sensations that might be distracting while the child processes more foundational body-related sensations such as proprioception.

The sensory environment used in therapy is structured in a way that enhances the child's possibilities to achieve praxis and organization of behavior through proprioceptive, vestibular, and tactile sensations. The following sections demonstrate how these sensations are essential to interventions in a structured sensory environment.

Proprioceptive Sensations. Proprioception has been described as the cornerstone of sensory-integration intervention (Blanche & Schaaf, in press). Proprioception is both alerting and calming, and, therefore, it is a key sensation that alters levels of arousal and enhances self-regulation. Proprioception is also the gateway to functional movement. Proprioceptive sensations are achieved through traction, compression, movement of the joints and muscles, or use of the muscles against resistance. Jumping, climbing, hanging, pushing, and pulling activities all provide proprioception. Common equipment that is used to provide these sensations includes mats, mattresses, trampolines, tires, bungee cords attached to swings, trapeze bars, chin-up bars, and climbing structures. In addition, children can receive joint traction through use of a trapeze or by hanging on a climbing structure. Although some children may show sensitivities to proprioception, this occurence is uncommon in children with autism.

Figure 6.4
Sensory integrative approach provides for multisensory experiences.

Copyright 2001 Shay McAtee. Reprinted with permission of photographer.

Vestibular Sensations. Vestibular sensations can be both organizing and disorganizing. The environment is structured to provide opportunities for movement through space. A variety of swinging equipment is used so that children have choices about the type of movement they can experience. Possibilities for rotary, linear, or orbital movements or combinations of these movements are made available for sensory play, often in conjunction with proprioception. Common equipment that is used to provide these sensations includes single suspension swings, dual suspension swings, gliders, rockers, rolling objects, and spinning seats. The therapist should use care, however, because some individuals have extreme sensitivity to rotation or linear movement; are extremely fearful of moving their head in space; or may experience a loss of control over posture, equilibrium or visual stability during rotation of the head.

Tactile Sensations. Tactile experiences are an essential component to sensory-integration intervention. Deep pressure contact is a prime organizing sensation. Activities and equipment that provide deep pressure are made available often in conjunction with proprioception. Heavy pillows, large bolsters, mats, beanbag chairs, and cushions may be used to provide deep pressure. Often, the equipment is structured so that the child encounters different textures in context, for example, a carpeted barrel or flannel sheets. Additionally, items with varying textures are available for play such as soap foam, clay, beans, rice, or water. Common equipment that is used to provide tactile sensations includes carpet; ball baths; Theraputty™; Playdoh™; beans, rice, popcorn, and other foods; brushes; vibrators; cloth samples; water; and items that are hot or cold. The therapist should be cautious, however, because some individuals are extremely sensitive to certain textures, and some have extreme hyporesponsiveness and may not experience appropriate levels of pain.

Tapping the Inner Drive

Ayres (1972) held that every human being has an innate drive to learn and grow. In fact, Dunn (1994) found that typical children often engage in sensory-seeking behaviors. Observations of typically developing children in play settings support the idea that children naturally seek a great variety of sensory-based activities (Chew, 1985). Ayres felt that the natural inner drive toward purposeful, often sensory-based activity among children would lead most children with deficits to seek the types of experiences that would ultimately be both satisfying and growth promoting. This concept of inner drive poses a major challenge in applying the sensory-integration approach with children with autism.

As mentioned earlier, neurobiological research suggests that the limbic structures in the brain that normally orchestrate motivation and drive are impaired in individuals with autism (Bauman & Kemper, 1994; Courchesne, 1989a, 1989b; Courchesne et al. 1987, 1993). Because the limbic structures are critical to initiation, motivation and drive are not optimally developed in the child with autism (Bauman & Kemper, 1994; Courchesne, 1989a, 1989b). Therefore, an important focus of therapeutic intervention is to help the child acquire these

abilities or to compensate for deficiencies in this area. Using carefully selected sensory-based activities can be helpful in enhancing abilities such as initiating action, transitioning from one activity to the next, sustaining participation, and finding meaning and purpose in tasks and activities. Consequently, occupational therapists will often need to find creative ways to engage the child with autism.

The inner drive operating in many children with autism may provide imperatives to engage in unhealthy occupations that are counterproductive such as obsessive, ritualistic, or repetitive behaviors; self-injurious actions; or socially inappropriate habits or patterns. In these cases, the therapist must disrupt these engagement patterns and provide healthy occupational choices.

In contrast, for some children, any inner drive toward productive participation may be impaired by inadequate skills or limited ideation. The child with inadequate skills may seek sensation with a maladaptive activity. For example, a child may repeatedly throw him or herself into another person or wall. The child may desire interaction, but a negative behavior might be demonstrated because the child has a limited repetoire of ideas about what to do. The therapist can provide alternative activities that will approriately provide the sought after sensation. Broadening the child's repertoire of learned interactions is a way to intervene. Often, carefully chosen sensory-based activities in a playful context can replace more stereotypical behaviors that occur when the child is seeking specific sensations or when the child becomes bored or overstimulated. Therefore, an important aspect of intervention using a sensory-integration approach for the child with autism is the process to understand what motivates the child.

Context of Play

Skillful therapists can tap the inner drive of the child through play (Mailloux & Burke, 1997;

Parham & Primeau, 1997). When observing a session where sensory-integration principles are being used, families and children perceive that the therapist and the child have the intent to play together and that the child is a well-respected playmate. The child's current capabilities guide the play. As the child's joy of interaction emerges, the therapist and child enter into challenges that they perceive as pleasurable, purposeful, and meaningful. The rewards are not provided at the end of an activity but, rather, are intrinsic in the activity and in the social sharing. Using behavioral reinforcers out of context (such as providing a reward if the child does an action a specified number of times) is not done. Instead, the child often repeats the activity spontaneously in an effort to gain mastery.

Social play is often problematic for children with autism. Consequently, engaging the child in playful interactions may take skill on the part of the therapist. Often, the therapist must interpret the child's behaviors to know that the child is enjoying the activity. For example, the child might pull the hand of the therapist to indicate his or her desire for the therapist to stay in the activity. In a qualitative analysis of play in children with autism, Spitzer (2000) described an interaction where the child pulled the adult to seemingly unrelated areas that, in fact, ultimately led to a meaningful outcome for the child. She suggests that successful interpretation of occupational choices by individuals with autism may require suspension of bias or judgment about those activities.

Artful Vigilance

The therapist must maintain "artful vigilance" as he or she watches for opportunities to engage the child adaptively while altering the sensory and motor challenges (Clark, Parham, & Mailloux, 1989). Vigilance is required to ensure the child's successful engagement. Often, the child with autism has a narrow range of comfort with

stimuli. He or she can shift from sensory-seeking during an activity, to a disorganized state, to sensory avoiding behavior in a short period of time. The therapist must be alert to signs that the child is becoming over-or under-responsive to the various qualities of sensation and alert to the potential disorganizing or aversive effects of an activity. Through this level of vigilance, the therapist can determine what is needed for optimal self-regulation and for helping the child to make an adaptive response.

The observations made by the therapist can involve reading very subtle cues from the child such as body language, eye gaze, or minor gestures. Although the therapy session will often look like a fun, playful exchange, the vigilance required on the part of the therapist demands constant observation, interpretation, and adjustments. For example, a child with autism may appear to want to swing. If the child approaches a swing that is somewhat unstable and therefore perceives it as possibly threatening, the therapist may have only a moment to adjust the activity to the child's capabilities. Quickly adding a stabilizing element (such as an inner tube that is placed on a platform swing) may be the needed adjustment that allows the child to engage. Watching the child's reactions, determining what is "just right" for the child, and anticipating what should come next are all important elements of using artful vigilance within the sensory-integration framework.

Child-Centered Approach

The philosophy of sensory-integration theory and practice maintains the belief that children will generally seek the types of experiences they need to grow and develop, even if they do not have the skills to go about engaging in activities in an appropriate way. For children with autism, a child-centered approach is often challenging because they may likely have difficulty with organization of their behavior. When using a sensory-integration approach, clinicians follow the lead of the child while providing the activities and structure that are necessary for him or her to make appropriate responses to people and things in the environment. However, taking the child's lead does not mean following the child around. Ayres (1980) believed that if the children who came for therapy could organize their own interactions, they would not need therapy. The approach to the child is to allow his or her responses to guide the intervention, but the therapist must provide an adequate balance of freedom and structure so the child benefits from the therapeutic interaction.

Grandin (1995) describes important teachers in her life who took her interests into account to help her learn concepts that were difficult for her. In much the same way, the sensory-integration framework encourages the therapist to watch carefully for those things that interest a child and that draw him or her toward participation. For the child with autism, the initial lead from the child might appear nonpurposeful or stereotypical. The skillful clinician can take cues from the child to understand the underlying characteristics of an activity or situation that appeal to him or her. With this knowledge, the therapist can then orchestrate opportunities for productive interaction that are initiated by the child's interest.

The Adaptive Response

The concept of the adaptive response is especially important for the child with autism. Ayres (1979) defines an adaptive response as "an appropriate action in which the individual responds successfully to some environmental demand" (p. 181). The adaptive response is the single most essential feature that guides the direction of the therapy. Adaptive responses are unique to an individual child depending on the circumstances. Climbing high on equipment may not indicate an adaptive response for some children whereas taking turns climbing down a ladder might. Adaptive responses are identified when the child interacts in a slightly new and more complex way to a challenge.

Ayres identified one of the most basic adaptive responses as holding on and staying put (Ayres, 1972). For many children with autism, therapy programs will begin by encouraging very simple adaptive responses. Because the child with autism may have problems in sensory registration and ideation, he or she will often need help to make very simple adaptive responses such as sitting on a swing and holding onto the ropes or chains that suspend it.

As the child begins to be more adaptive socially, emotionally, motorically, or through self-regulation, the therapist knows that the conditions are good for this child to be more adaptive if additional challenges are posed. The child often shows focused and intent immersion in the activity and, usually, a great deal of satisfaction at its accomplishment.

The Just-Right Challenge

Therapists who use a sensory-integration approach constantly seek the "just-right level of challenge." It may be compared to "flow" as proposed by Csikszentmihalyi (1990). The just-right challenge is a point in therapy where the conditions are right for the child to make an adaptive response. The child and the therapist work together until the appropriate level of challenge is reached.

The just-right challenge is often most apparent when fostering the somatomotor adaptive response. When performing a skilled action, the task can be altered so the child can meet the task demand. An activity that provides a just-right challenge will keep the child's interest and will encourage further growth and development. To create this condition, the therapist must make continual adjustments in the environment so the challenges in processing sensory data, making motor responses, or preparing for future action are neither too great nor too little. The perfect challenge is difficult to anticipate because each child varies from day to day and with each activity.

Emphasis on Active Versus Passive Participation

Building on the neuroscience research that has been done on the effect of enriched environments on brain development and function, Ayres (1979) states, "The child must participate actively with the environment to improve the organization of his nervous system" (p. 142). Ayres's emphasis on the importance of active versus passive participation was influenced by studies such as those by Walsh and Cummins (1976). These authors found that active physical interaction with sensory experiences was an important factor in brain recovery, and that, in comparison, patients who received passive sensory stimulation did not show the same level of recovery. Thus, the sensory-integration approach is a natural framework for occupational therapy, which has always stressed the importance of active, purposeful, and meaningful participation.

The importance of this principle of sensory-integration intervention holds true for the child with autism. Certain passive sensory experiences such as swinging the child in a slow, rhythmic manner, providing deep pressure by pressing the child between cushions, or rubbing the child's skin with lotion or various textures of fabric might be calming, alerting, or organizing to the child. These kinds of passive activities might be used to help get a child ready for participation in more challenging tasks. Teachers, parents, and other caregivers can also use sensory experiences to help the child throughout the day. Ideally, the child can begin to actively seek and engage in activities that increase his or her ability to be attentive and purposeful.

The discovery of calming, alerting, or organizing techniques such as the ones noted

previously can be made available to the child in ways that can be self-administered. In some ways, the emphasis on active participation holds special importance for the child with autism, who, because of the nature of this brain disorder, may have significant difficulty with initiation and self-direction. Encouraging active participation will more likely help the child develop these abilities than merely administering passive sensory stimulation. Finally, striving for active participation also promotes the individual nature of an occupational therapy program that uses a sensory-integration framework. Active engagement on the part of the individual enhances the individuality of a therapy program because personal preferences and familial and cultural values are more likely to emerge.

Case Study 6.8 describes a therapy session in which Jared participates both passively and actively. In the case study, note the adaptations that the therapist and the mother make during the session to keep Jared engaged.

Application of Sensory Integration Intervention Principles for the Child With Autism

No prescriptions are used for the application of sensory-integration techniques. The analysis and application of intervention is a complex and dynamic process that involves coordinating the interactive nature of the child with the people and things in the environment as well as with the spatial and temporal aspects of organizing what is done in that environment. During direct intervention, the therapist applies sensory-integration techniques while also managing a dynamic evaluation of the process. Within the therapeutic interaction, the therapist guides, alters, and adapts the interaction to ensure success as the child, therapist, and environment changes.

Through clinical reasoning, the therapist uncovers the optimal structure for the child

Case Study 6.8

Jared and his mother, Mrs. R., join Chris, Jared's occupational therapist, in the waiting room of the therapy clinic. Chris asks Mrs. R. how things have been going since Jared's last therapy session. Jared is eager to play in the therapy room, so Mrs. R. and Chris discontinue their conversation and follow Jared into the large, colorful playroom. Jared immediately runs to a large, foam-filled pillow and throws himself onto it. Mrs. R. says, "Looks like Jared wants to play "Mountain Climber."" Chris looks to Mrs. R. for more of a clue, and Mrs. R. explains that Jared likes having pressure on his body when he lies prone on a pillow or cushion. She explains that she tells him he is like a mountain climber with lots of supplies on his back. Chris quickly gathers smaller cushions, bolsters, and beanbags and places or rolls them across Jared's back. As she places or rolls each object over Jared, Chris says, "Here is your sleeping bag and here is your food pack and here are your climbing ropes." Jared emits one-word responses such as "mo" for "more" and "gen" for "again."

After a while, Jared lifts his head and looks around the room. Chris recognizes that Jared has become calmed and organized by the heavy-pressure activity and that he is ready to move on to something else. "Are you ready to climb now Mr. Mountain Climber?" says Chris. "Mommy will help you get your supplies ready while I clear the way to the mountain." Mrs. R. helps Jared up from under the pillows, cushions and bolsters while Chris makes a path over various pieces of equipment to a climbing structure.

Jared looks as though he may lose his interest and become distracted by the activity in a nearby room. "Oh, we need your backpack, don't we?" Chris says and hands Mrs. R. a weighted vest. Mrs. R. helps Jared to don the vest and he becomes redirected to the activity. However, Jared appears to have neither the ideation nor the skills for imaginary play that are needed to begin the activity.

Mrs. R says, "I will put Ruffy at the top of the mountain, Jared." She takes out a dinosaur figure and puts it atop the climbing structure. Jared becomes animated and makes it clear that he wants to get to Ruffy. Chris says, "This way, Jared" and helps Jared to get started on the path, encouraging him to maneuver independently by offering support only when it is needed to maintain balance or keep on track. Jared laughs and smiles when his mother or therapist comments on his strength and bravery as he climbs the mountain. "You must save Ruffy, Jared! He is on the edge of the cliff!" exclaims Mrs. R. Once at the top of the mountain, Jared grabs Ruffy and looks across the therapy gym to a suspended Lycra™ swing. Chris says, "Is it time for you and Ruffy to rest, Jared? Mountain climbers sometimes like to rest in a hammock." Chris opens the Lycra™ swing and offers her knee as a step for Jared to climb inside. Jared lies inside the swing with Ruffy and pulls on a rope suspended nearby to make the swing move side to side. Mrs. R and Jared sing one of his favorite songs about dinosaurs.

Chris brings over some soap foam and asks if Jared wants to give Ruffy a bath before they get into their sleeping bags for the night. Jared takes the soap foam and rubs it on his own arms, legs, hands, and feet as well as on Ruffy. While Jared and his mother continue to sing, Chris readies a nearby tent that is filled with beans and rice. She places a cloth tunnel inside. Jared jumps out of the Lycra™ swing and runs over to the tent to see what Chris has prepared for him. Chris opens the tunnel, and Jared crawls inside the cloth tunnel that is tight against his body.

During this segment of the therapy session, Jared was invested in the activity and engaged in movements that were quite challenging for him with respect to his awareness of body position, balance, ideation, sequencing, timing of movements, and awareness of his environment. He is not yet able to develop his own imaginary play scenarios; thus his mother and therapist use his interests and read his cues to help Jared make adaptive responses. Although sometimes the therapist provides sensations somewhat passively for Jared during the session to help calm and organize him (such as the initial use of deep pressure), the activity is still individualized. During other portions of the session, active participation is encouraged whenever possible. For example, a suspended rope near the Lycra swing gives Jared the ability to swing himself rather than to receive passive swinging. An attempt is made to engage Jared by making the activity playful and by building a theme that has some familiarity that is likely to interest him. Jared's inner drive is tapped by incorporating a favorite object and by keeping the activities at a "just-right" level of challenge. Throughout, Jared's mother and therapist work together to help Jared remain organized and in an optimal state for purposeful participation. The therapist learns from the mother how to engage and interest the child, and the mother gains new insights to both the difficulties her son has and to the gains he is making.

to perform adaptively. These discoveries can be made and operationalized in a variety of settings. This clinical reasoning process encompasses all hallmarks of sensory integration principles simultaneously. Although the assessment process separates components of strengths and weaknesses, the intervention process uses a child's strengths to build competencies in weaker areas of processing and in the resulting capabilities for planning and executing action.

The therapist assists in "scaffolding," or providing the supports necessary for the child to be a competent participant during the interaction. Scaffolding is a term used in education to describe the process of providing supporting elements for the child or to the environment to ensure success in the learning process (Dunkerly, Tickle-Degnen, & Coster, 1997; Tickle-Degnen & Coster, 1995). As competence emerges, the scaffold is removed piece by piece or, in other words, faded until, ultimately, the child is successful with as few supports as possible.

The following clinical reasoning sequence is typically used by therapists using a sensory-integration approach for children with autism: registration, arousal level and modulation, perception and discrimination, motor skills, and praxis. Although it is broken down for the purposes of description in the following sections, it is not uncommon for a child and therapist to work on several parts of this continuum within the same activity.

Registration

Fundamental to therapeutic interaction is mutual attention. Given that mutual attention is difficult for the child with autism, the therapist approaches registration by observing what the child is attending to and joining the child in his or her interests even when these interests would not be considered as typical. The therapist then works to broaden the child's field of attention to include the therapist as well as interesting and meaningful activities.

Arousal Level and Modulation

Arousal levels and the ability to modulate sensory information is an area of particular importance with children with autism because of their narrow band of comfort in engagement (Baranek, 2000). Awareness of the child's level of arousal requires constant vigilance by the therapist as challenges and changes are introduced. Depending on the level of alertness and attention, the therapist will either follow or initiate interactions, finding ways to engage the child socially. If the child seems to be over- or under-responding, the environment is adjusted appropriately so the child can perceive and cope with the demands of the sensory environment. Inhibitory and excitatory techniques are included and removed as needed. Knowledge of the specific sensory experiences that typically are calming and organizing, arousing, or disorganizing for the specific child assists the therapist in creating the appropriate level of arousal during the therapy session. For example, when a therapy session is focusing on attention and arousal levels, smell and taste can often enrich the process and can allow for active participation as the child reaches for, holds onto, and perhaps chews or sucks on appropriate food substances.

Perception and Discrimination

The ability to discriminate aspects of the sensory environment is a prerequisite to forming perception and other developmental skills. Depending on the child's abilities, the various qualities of sensory stimuli can be a focus during therapy. For example, tactile discrimination can be advanced through the use of various textures, vibration, and pressure to the skin. Tactile media may be used to refine skills such as picking up a dime. Body awareness can be increased through a variety of movement activities that provide multisensory inputs to the somatosensory and vestibular systems. When the child seeks out vestibular sensations, equipment that provides movement can be supplied. Children may seek movement while in unusual positions such as hanging upside down or reclining on one side. Visual and auditory input also can be used but, often, are used as a supplement to more body-centered sensory activities.

When a child is not processing a specific type of sensation well, the therapist must consider the relationships between the sensations. Vibration is carried along multiple sensory channels and may assist in the processing and tolerance of other types of sensory data. The proprioceptive system is intimately linked to both the vestibular system and the tactile system. Therefore, if the child has extreme sensitivities to touch or movement, proprioceptive activities may provide a more acceptable means by which to approach him or her. If the child is avoiding touch and sound, visual and proprioceptive activities may be more acceptable. If the child is avoiding vestibular sensations, proprioceptive and tactile activities may be more comfortable. In therapy, one must find a way to connect with each child, often through awareness of the child's unique sensory preferences.

Motor Skills

When an acceptable level of arousal and sufficient sensory perception has been reached, the therapist can begin to promote development of specific motor skills. Activities that build muscle tone, promote postural control, and develop strength can also help the child to challenge gravity and refine skilled motor interactions. Bilateral motor control is also essential for coordinated motion through the environment.

Motor skills that are executed in isolation or out of context are less likely to be meaningful. For example, a child may be able to stand on one foot, but he or she may not be able to stand on one foot long enough to kick a ball or put on pants. A child may show adequate hand strength and grasping patterns; however, he or she may not have any idea how to interact functionally with objects such as clothing fasteners, food containers, or doorknobs. Working on skills in the context of meaningful activity is critical to learning and may help the child to generalize learned skills to other environments.

Practice is necessary before any new skill can become automatic. However, the therapist must be a careful observer to ensure that the child remains within an appropriate range of arousal as motor skills are being learned and practiced. A challenge that is too hard or a skill that is too easy will usually lead to inattention. During periods of activity that are challenging, the therapist may need to periodically allow the child to "regroup" by means of specific sensory activities. This regrouping can sometimes be accomplished by having one step of a multistep activity be a preferred sensory experience. This preferred experience should come prior to or immediately after a motor challenge.

Intervention for Problems Related to Praxis

Praxis is difficult for the child with autism. If the child is in a reasonable zone of arousal, then challenges to develop skills and praxis can be approached. Language is typically an important feature in planning, sequencing, and remembering steps of an activity, and language is an area of difficulty for most children with autism.

Visual cues can often help immensely. These cues can include, for example, putting the plan on paper so it is made concrete and can be referred to as many times as necessary or providing a visual stimulus to encourage the completion of the next step. In addition, visual cues can aid the process of ideation, which is often difficult for a child with autism. Forming an initial idea of what to do is often the first step in facilitating praxis. Visual aids to initiation include certain equipment, objects, or toys that are placed within the child's visual environment and demonstration by the therapist or a peer so the child can see what to do with the specific equipment. The initial action plan is graded relative to the abilities and interest of the child. However, the activity must also be broken down into manageable components, and continual modifications for increased success may become necessary.

Beyond praxis is the organization of behavior in time and space (Blanche & Parham, in press). Because comprehending increasingly more abstract temporal spatial relationships involves cognitive elements, this organization of behavior may be a very difficult aspect of remediation for individuals with autism. The child may enhance capacities for self-organization and the organization of relevant aspects of his or her environment by engaging in increasingly more complex series of activities and tasks.

Direct and Consultative Service Delivery

Although classic sensory integration intervention is provided in a structured clinical environment, therapy is often administered in a variety of settings. By translating what is observed in the structured therapy setting and applying it to the environments in which the child plays, learns, and develops on a daily basis, these other environments can be modified more effectively. The therapist can provide information regarding sensory conditions that may be agitating, conditions that are calming and organizing for the child, or both. This interpretation is often helpful for other significant people interacting with the child.

Most successful intervention programs will include a combination of direct therapy and consultations with families, educational staff members, and others who are working closely with the child. Direct services are designed not only to address the specific areas of sensory-integration deficits that create challenges for the child but also to identify individual strengths. It is also important to tap other available resources to promote success for the child in the environments and situations in which he or she participates such as school, neighborhood play groups, and religious activities. Optimal intervention programs not only address sensory integration concerns directly but also compile strategies, activities, and adaptations that can be incorporated into daily life in an ongoing way.

Providing consultative service is especially important in working with children with autism because these individuals have lifelong needs that will require collaboration among all those who live and work with them. The occupational therapist may find that she is reframing ideas for families or teachers who have previously viewed the child from primarily a behavioral viewpoint. Education, therefore, is often a key component in the therapy program that uses a sensory-integration framework. Helping the adults to identify and anticipate the child's responses to various sensory experiences can be one of the most important roles the occupational therapist can play in the intervention with the child with autism.

Home and Community Integration

Most parents naturally identify the things that help to comfort, organize, and bring pleasure to their children. Similarly, children and adults generally seek experiences and activities that provide a good fit with their own level of skill and with their individual temperaments and personalities. Parents of children with autism and these children themselves face a much greater challenge to find routines, experiences, and activities that will lead to satisfaction and success in daily life. Managing sensory processing and praxis challenges throughout the life span is an important component of life at home and in the community for the individual with autism.

Once a parent understands the way in which a child processes sensory information, then anticipating responses, avoiding distress, and supporting organization at home becomes much more likely. Although most parents cannot feasibly replicate all of the sensory-integration activities that might be available in a fully equipped therapy environment, many parents will be able to translate appropriate sensory-based activities and activities involving motor planning into daily life routines.

Community integration presents the greatest challenge with respect to sensory-integration issues for the child with autism because the arena becomes so much less predictable and controllable. A combination of finding ways to select the most desirable activities and environments and developing strategies to cope with the inevitable situations that will cause discomfort and confusion is an important part of the lifelong intervention plan for individuals with autism. Case Study 6.9 illustrates how this combination of selecting and strategizing supports Quinn in the school environment.

Conclusion

The recognition of the relevance of the sensory-integration framework for children with autism continues to expand both within the field of occupational therapy and beyond its borders. The germinal work of Ayres (1972, 1979) that forecasted many of the recent discoveries about autism continues to evolve and develop in ways that heightens its importance in relation to this diagnosis. Sensory integration theory as well as the evaluation and intervention strategies that emanate from this approach provide a unique avenue for enhancing the understanding of and, therefore, compassionate intervention for individuals who experience this condition. Autism is a lifelong condition for which no intervention approach currently offers a cure. However, the sensory-integration framework does offers supportive, pertinent guidance and the hope of improved quality of life for the people who are diagnosed with autism as well as for the families and significant others who care for them.

References

American Psychiatric Association (APA). (2000). *Diagnostic and statistical manual of mental disorders* (4th ed., rev.). Washington, DC: Author.

Ayres, A. J. (1972). *Sensory integration and learning disabilities.* Los Angeles: Western Psychological Services.

Ayres, A. J. (1979). *Sensory integration and the child.* Los Angeles: Western Psychological Services.

Ayres, A. J. (1980) *The adaptive response* [Videotape]. Torrance, CA: Sensory Integration International.

Ayres, A. J. (1989). *Sensory integration and praxis tests.* Los Angeles: Western Psychological Services.

Ayres, A. J., & Tickle, L. (1980). Hyperresponsivity to touch and vestibular stimuli as a predictor of positive response to sensory integration procedures by autistic children. *American Journal of Occupational Therapy, 34,* 375–381.

Baloh, R. W., & Honrubia, V. (1979). *Clinical neurophysiology of the vestibular system.* Philadelphia: F. A. Davis.

Baranek, G. T. (1998). Sensory processing in persons with developmental disabilties: Considerations for research and clinical practice. *Sensory Integration Special Interest Section Quarterly, 21*(2), 1–4.

Baranek, G. T. (1999). Autism during infancy: A retrospective video analysis of sensory-motor and social behaviors at 9–12 months of age. *Journal of Autism and Developmental Disorders, 29*(3), 213–224.

Baranek, G. T. (2000, February). *Early symptoms of autism.* Paper presented at Research 2000, Redondo Beach, CA.

Baranek, G. T., & Berkson, G. (1997a). Sensory defensiveness in persons with developmental disabilities. *Occupational Therapy Journal of Research, 17*(3), 173–185.

Baranek, G. T., & Berkson, G. (1997b). Tactile defensiveness and stereotyped behavior. *Occupational Therapy Journal of Research, 51*(2), 91–95.

Bauman, M. L., & Kemper, T. L. (1994). Neuroanatomic observation of the brain in autism. In M. L. Bauman & T. L. Kemper (Eds.), *The neurology of autism* (pp. 119–145). Baltimore: Johns Hopkins University Press.

Blanche, E. I., & Parham, L. D. (in press). Praxis and organization of behavior in space and time. In S. Smith Roley, E. I. Blanche, & R. C.

Case Study 6.9

Quinn is often anxious when he gets off the bus for his day at middle school. His occupational therapist, Donna, has found that she can help Quinn most by scheduling his occupational therapy session at the beginning of the day on Mondays. Quinn has received occupational therapy in a variety of forms and settings over the last several years. His initial occupational therapy program addressed his significant sensory integration issues in a therapeutic clinic setting that afforded him the opportunity to develop many foundational skills. Quinn then transitioned into a group program that helped him to maintain and continue to develop his capabilities. When Quinn's need for specialized therapy equipment decreased, and he was able to access the sensory experiences he needed at home and at school, Quinn began to receive a combination of direct and consultative occupational therapy at school. Currently, Quinn meets with Donna every Monday morning for about 20 minutes to prepare for the week ahead. Donna also collaborates with the rest of the educational team through both informal and formal communication. At the end of the week, the entire educational team meets for about an hour to address any changes that might need to be made in any of the student's programs during the following week.

On this Monday morning, Quinn shows his usual anxiety about the upcoming week. Donna and Quinn, together with Quinn's parents and teachers, have developed daily routines and activities that help Quinn to stay calm and organized. When Quinn can achieve this state, he is better able to interact appropriately with his peers. Quinn reports to Donna that he was not able to complete his home-based program of physical activities such as jumping on a trampoline, lifting weights, and running around the block because there had been a family wedding and accompanying activities over the weekend. The extra strain of being in noisy, crowded situations, staying up late, interacting with unfamiliar people, and having his normal routine disrupted had added extra stress to Quinn's weekend. These experiences, in combination with his inability to participate in the types of activities that help him to stay calm, had significantly increased his level of anxiety at the beginning of this new school week.

Recognizing this circumstance, Donna said "Quinn, I need your help with a special project today. The school just purchased a lot of new therapy equipment, and I need your help unloading it from my van." Donna explained that the boxes in her van would need to be carried to the supply room, opened, and the contents placed on the top shelves. Quinn knew that he usually needed to have a written reminder for this kind of task (something he learned through his work with Donna and with the resource specialist at school who helps him with his study habits). Donna and Quinn made a checklist for the task, and then Donna helped Quinn get started.

While Quinn began unloading the boxes, Donna went and talked to Quinn's homeroom and physical education teachers. She alerted the homeroom teacher about Quinn's weekend and suggested that the sensory-based activities they had previously identified as useful to Quinn be carried out fully today and as needed throughout the week. These activities included the use of an inflated cushion for Quinn to sit on while at his desk, a sports water-bottle with a thick plastic straw, and a "stress ball" for Quinn to squeeze while reading and doing his worksheets. The homeroom teacher would be able to communicate with the other teachers about Quinn's needs for the day.

Donna then found the physical education teacher and asked if Quinn could be given some extra physical activities that day. The physical education teacher reported that she had planned to start the group on racquetball that day. Because racquetball would involve noise, timing, speed, and coordination that would be extremely challenging for Quinn, the teacher said she would give the kids the option of racquetball or physical conditioning that would involve running, weightlifting, push-ups, and chin-ups. She was certain that some of the boys would choose this option and that Quinn would not be left out during the physical education session.

This form of direct and consultative occupational therapy, heavily guided by the sensory-integration frame of reference places emphasis on putting mechanisms in place throughout the child's day to help regulate his level of alertness and attention and to manage the challenges that arise. The time and effort needed on the part of the therapist and teachers are manageable because the necessary communication, training, and planning has already been put in place. Quinn will probably always face greater difficulties than most in dealing with the unpredictable nature of daily life. However, by receiving early therapy, which helped to enhance many of his capabilities, and by continuing to receive ongoing analysis and monitoring of his state, Quinn has a good chance of coping with his autism in a way that will allow satisfying and productive participation in life.

Schaaf (Eds.), *Understanding the nature of sensory integration with diverse populations*. Tucson, AZ: Therapy Skill Builders.

Blanche, E. I., & Schaaf, R. C. (in press). Proprioception, the cornerstone of sensory integrative intervention. In S. Smith Roley, E. I. Blanche, & R. C. Schaaf (Eds.), *Understanding the nature of sensory integration with diverse populations*. Tucson, AZ: Therapy Skill Builders.

Case-Smith, J., & Bryan, T. (1999). The effects of occupational therapy with sensory integration emphasis on preschool-age children with autism. *American Journal of Occupational Therapy, 53,* 489–497.

Case-Smith, J. & Miller, H. (1999). Occupational therapy with children with pervasive developmental disorders. *American Journal of Occupational Therapy, 53,* (5), 506–513.

Chew, T. (1985). *The developmental progression of vestibular based playground play of preschool children.* Unpublished Master's thesis, University of Southern California

Clark, F. A., Parham, P., & Mailloux, Z. (1989). Sensory integration and learning disabilities. In P. N. Clark & A. Allen (Eds.), *Occupational therapy for children* (pp. 457–509). St. Louis, MO: Mosby.

Cohen, H. (1999). *Neuroscience for rehabilitation.* (2nd ed.).Philadelphia: Lippincott

Courchesne, E. (1989a). A neurophysiological view of autism. In E. Shopler & G. Mesibov (Eds.), *Neurobiological issues in autism* (pp. 285–324). New York: Plenum.

Courchesne, E. (1989b). Neuroanatomical systems involved in infantile autism: The implications of cerebellar abnormalities. In G. Dawson (Ed.), *Autism: Nature, diagnosis and treatment* (pp. 119–143). New York: Guilford.

Courchesne, E., Hesselink, J. R., Jernigan, T. L., & Yeung-Courchesne, R. (1987). Abnormal neuroanatomy in a nonretarded person with autism. *Archives of Neurology, 44,* 335–341.

Courchesne, E., Townsend, J. P., Akshoomoff, N. A., Yeung-Courchesne, R., Press, G. A., Murakami, J. W., Lincoln, A. J., James, H. E., Saitoh, O., Egaas, B., Haas, R. H., & Schreibman, L. (1993). A new finding: Impairment in shifting attention in autistic and cerebellar patients. In S. H. Broman & J. Grafman (Eds.), *Atypical cognitive deficits in developmental disorder: Implications for brain functions* (pp. 101–137). Hillsdale, NJ: Erlbaum.

Csikszentmihalyi, M. (1990). *Flow: The psychology of optimal experience.* New York: Harper & Row.

Dawson, G., & Adams, A. (1984). Imitation and social responsiveness in autistic children. *Journal of Abnormal Child Psychology, 12,* 209–226.

Dawson, G., & Lewy, A. (1989a). Arousal, attention, and the socioemotional impairments of individuals with autism. In G. Dawson (Ed.), *Autism: Nature, diagnosis and treatment* (pp. 49–74). New York: Guilford.

Dawson, G., & Lewy, A. (1989b). Reciprocal subcortical influences in autism: The role of attentional mechanisms. In G. Dawson (Ed.), *Autism: Nature, diagnosis and treatment* (pp. 144–173). New York: Guilford.

Dunkerly, E., Tickle-Degnen, L., & Coster, W. J. (1997). Therapist-child interaction in the middle minutes of sensory integration treatment. *American Journal of Occupational Therapy, 51,* 799–805.

Dunn, W. (1994). Performance of typical children on the sensory profile: An item analysis. *American Journal of Occupational Therapy, 48,* 967–974.

Gilfoyle, E. M., Grady, A. P., & Moore, J. C. (1990). *Children adapt* (2nd ed.).Thorofare, NJ: Slack.

Grandin, T. (1995). *Thinking in pictures.* New York: Doubleday.

Greenspan, S., & Weider, S. (1997). Developmental patterns and outcomes in infants and children with disorders in relating and communicating. A chart review of 200 cases of children with autistic spectrum diagnoses. *Journal of Developmental and Learning Disorders, 1*(1), 87–141.

Herdman, S. J. (1994). *Vestibular rehabilitation.* Philadelphia: F.A. Davis.

Keintz, M. A., & Dunn, W. (1997). A comparison of the performance of children with and without autism on the Sensory Profile. *American Journal of Occupational Therapy, 51,* 530–537.

Koomar, J., & Bundy, A. (1991). The art and science of creating direct intervention from theory. In A. G. Fisher, E. A. Murray, & A. C. Bundy (Eds.), *Sensory integration: Theory and practice* (pp. 251–315). Philadelphia: F.A. Davis.

Kraemer, G. (in press). The dynamics of attachment. In S. Smith Roley, E. I. Blanche, & R. Schaaf (Eds.), *Understanding the nature of sensory integration with diverse populations*. Tucson, AZ: Therapy Skill Builders.

Mailloux, Z., & Burke, J. P. (1997). Play and the sensory integrative approach. In L. Parham & L. Fazio (Eds.), *Play in occupational therapy for children* (pp. 112–125). St. Louis: Mosby.

May-Benson, T. (in press). A theoretical model of ideation in praxis. In S. Smith Roley, E. I. Blanche, & R. Schaaf (Eds.), *Understanding the nature of sensory integration with diverse populations* Tucson, AZ: Therapy Skill Builders.

Miller, L. J., & Lane, S. (2000). Toward a consensus in terminology in sensory integration, Theory and practice: Part 1. Taxonomy of neurophysiological processes. *Sensory Integration Special Interest Section Quarterly, 23,* (1) 1–4.

Miller, L. J., McIntosh, D. N., McGrath, J., Shyu, V., Lampe, M., Taylor, A. K., Tassone, F., Neitzel, K., Stackhouse, T., & Hagerman, R. (1999). Electrodermal responses to sensory stimuli in individuals with Fragile X Syndrome: A preliminary report. *American Journal of Medical Genetics, 83*(4), 268–279.

Miller, L. J., Reisman, J., McIntosh, D. N., & Simon, J. (in press). An ecological model of sensory modulation: Performance of children with Fragile X Syndrome, autism, attention deficit with hyperactivity, and sensory modulation disorder. In S. Smith Roley, E. I. Blanche, & R. Schaaf (Eds.), *Understanding the nature of sensory integration with diverse populations.* Tucson, AZ: Therapy Skill Builders.

Miller, L. J., Wilbarger, J. L., Stackhouse, T. M., & Trunnell, S. L. (in press). Use of clinical reasoning in occupational therapy: The STEP-SI Model of sensory modulation dysfunction. In A. C. Bundy, S. J. Lane, & E. A. Murray (Eds.), *Sensory integration: Theory and practice* (2nd ed.). Philadelphia: F. A. Davis.

Ornitz, E. M. (1974). The modulation of sensory input and motor output in autistic children. *Journal of Autism and Childhood Schizophrenia, 4,* 197–205.

Ornitz, E. M., Guthrie, D., & Farley, A. H. (1977). The early development of autistic children. *Journal of Autism and Childhood Schizophrenia, 7,* 207–229.

Parham, L. D., & Mailloux, Z. (1996). Sensory integration. In J. Case-Smith, A. Allen, & P. N. Clark (Eds.), *Occupational therapy for children* (pp. 307–352). St. Louis: Mosby.

Parham, L.D., Mailloux, Z., & Smith Roley, S. (2000, February). *Sensory processing and praxis in high functioning children with autism.* Paper presented at Research 2000, Redondo Beach, CA.

Parham, L. D., & Primeau, L. A. (1997). Play and occupational therapy. In L. Parham & L. Fazio (Eds.), *Play in occupational therapy for children* (pp. 2–21). St. Louis: Mosby.

Porges, S. (1993). The infant's sixth sense: Awareness and regulation of bodily processes. *Zero to Three, 14*(2), 12–16.

Sacks, O. (1985). *The man who mistook his wife for a hat and other clinical tales.* New York: Summit Books

Schilder, P. (1964). *Contributions to developmental neuropsychiatry.* New York: International Universities Press.

Shumway-Cook, A. S., & Woolacott, M. (1995). *Motor control: Theory and practical applications.* Baltimore: Williams and Wilkins.

Smith, I. M., & Bryson, S. E. (1994). Imitation and action in autism: A critical review, *Psychological Bulletin, 116*(2), 259–273.

Spitzer, S. (1999). Dynamic systems theory: Relevance to the theory of sensory integration and the study of occupation. *Sensory Integration Special Interest Section Quarterly, 22* (6), 1–4.

Spitzer, S. (2000, February). *Playing without words.* Paper presented at Research 2000, Redondo Beach, CA.

Spitzer, S., & Roley, S. S. (in press). Sensory integration revisited: A philosophy of practice. In S. Smith Roley, E. I. Blanche, & R. Schaaf (Eds.), *Understanding the nature of sensory integration with diverse populations.* Tucson, AZ: Therapy Skill Builders.

Stehli, A. (1991). *The sound of a miracle: A child's triumph over autism.* New York: Bantam Doubleday Dell Publishing Group.

Streri, A. (1993). *Seeing, reaching, touching: The relations between vision and touch in infancy.* Cambridge, MA: MIT Press.

Tickle-Degnen, L., & Coster, W. J. (1995). Therapeutic interaction and the management of challenge during the beginning minutes of sensory integration treatment. *Occupational Therapy Journal of Research, 15,* 122–141.

Tsurumi, K., & Todd, V. (1997). Theory and guidelines for visual tasks analysis and synthesis. In M. Scheiman (Ed.), *Understanding and managing vision deficits: A guide for occupational therapists* (pp. 376–394). Thorofare, NJ: Slack.

Turkewitz, G. (1994). Sources of order for intersensory functioning. In D. Lewkowicz & R. Lickliter (Eds.), *The development of intersensory perception: Comparative perspectives* (pp. 3–17). Hillsdale, NJ: Erlbaum.

Walsh, R. N., & Cummins, R. A. (1976). Neural responses to therapeutic environments. In R. N. Walsh & W. T. Greenough (Eds.), *Environment as therapy for brain dysfunctions*. New York: Plenum Press.

Watling, R., Deitz, J., Kanny, E. & McLaughlin, J. (1999). *Current practice of occupational therapy for children with autism.*

Williams, D. (1992). *Nobody nowhere: The extraordinary autobiography of an autistic.* New York: Times Books.

Williams, D. (1994). *Somebody somewhere: Breaking free from the world of autism.* New York: Time Books.

World Health Organization. (1999). *ICIDH-2: International classification of functioning and disability. Beta-2 draft, full version.* Geneva, Switzerland: Author.

World Health Organization. (2000). *ICIDH-2: International classification of disability and health. Prefinal draft.* Geneva, Switzerland: Author.

Play and Praxis in Children With Autism: Observations and Intervention Strategies

Anne Trecker, MS, OTR/L

Play is a primary occupation of childhood. Through play, children achieve developmental milestones and learn skills that are needed to successfully interact with the environment. Children with developmental disabilities depending on the nature of their disability, may demonstrate atypical play skills. Because engaging in play activities is such an integral part of childhood, improving play skills is often earmarked as an intervention goal for these children. In addition, because play itself involves a wide range of developmental skills, it is frequently used as a modality for intervention. Descriptions of the play behavior of children with autism have pointed out stereotypical features, a lack of symbolic qualities, and limited flexibility (Lifter, 1996). Many children with autism exhibit difficulties with praxis or motor planning. Effective play requires effective praxis. Therefore, play is an ideal intervention tool to promote motor planning in children with developmental disabilities.

What Is Play?

Imagine this scene. Three 10-year-old girls come running in the door from school. They drop their backpacks, announce that they have already done their homework, and head upstairs to Sarah's bedroom.

Excited voices drift out of the closed door. One girl makes a suggestion, which is debated by the other two. Voices grow louder, more tense, and then settle into the language of compromise. Finally, the three girls emerge from the bedroom in a procession that seems to have been designed around one of Sarah's new stuffed animals, a large sand-filled frog covered with purple, gilt-edged material. Jane leads the procession. She is wearing several books on her head that are tied on with old leggings. She carries a book. Sarah is next, wearing a similar headpiece and carrying the frog. Emily, who also wears a book "hat" and carries several fake flowers, a wooden spoon, and a small umbrella, follows her. The girls sit in a circle in the living room, with the frog in the center. Each takes turns reading from a book, while the others perform "rituals" with the spoon, flowers, and umbrella. The game, which has a definite resemblance to a social studies unit on ancient Egypt, continues for several hours. The location changes from the living room to the bedroom to the kitchen where snacks are incorporated into the ritual. Several tense moments occur when it is necessary to make a decision about the course of action, but the general demeanor is one of cooperation and fun. At the end of the afternoon, all

133

three girls are surprised and upset that it is time to clean up and go home.

Reading the previous description, we clearly understand that these three girls are playing. They are enjoying interacting with one another and are taking pleasure in a situation that they have created. The conceptualization of the idea for this game demands their abilities to integrate information from past experience with what is available in the immediate environment. As they play, they are communicating verbally and through body language. Each girl not only is communicating her own ideas but also is called on to quickly comprehend and respond to the ideas of others through her ability to perceive and understand sensory information. Motor skills are also needed to imitate one another's actions and to carry out the plans of the game.

Describing play by identifying its characteristics (e.g., fun, spontaneous, voluntary, creative) is a task that we can easily accomplish by observing children at play. Precisely defining play, however, is more complicated. In her book, *Play as Exploratory Learning*, Mary Reilly (1974) wrote that defining play was like "defining a cobweb" (p. 59). She states that play is a "multidimensional phenomenon" (p. 122) requiring several theories from several disciplines to create a precise definition.

Although cultural and historical perspectives differ, play has been consistently viewed as an essential aspect of childhood. To understand the true value of play and its contributions to human development, researchers have observed and documented the act of play and have introduced many theories (Hughes, 1995). Early biogenetic theorists viewed play as instinctual. They believed that the purpose of play was to promote biological, cultural, and evolutionary development. Play has been described as a means of reducing the inevitable anxieties faced during childhood and a means of strengthening the child's ego (Erickson,

1963; Freud, 1933/1974). Play also has been viewed as an essential component in the development of cognitive skills (Piaget, 1962).

Despite the differences in theoretical orientation of these authors, several common characteristics that define the construct of play emerge from their work (Rubin, Fein, & Vanderberg, 1983). The concept of intrinsic motivation refers to the idea that play is an activity governed by the players, who are not concerned with complying with social demands or external influences. Attention to means rather than ends describes the idea that the players have a greater interest in the process than in the end result. Because the goals of play are self-imposed, the players may vary, revise, or alter these goals as they see fit. A means-end activity such as walking to the corner store to buy candy can be transformed into play when a child experiments with unusual ways of walking or adds an imaginative scenario that results in a few detours along the way. This characteristic separates play from pleasurable work, which is always goal directed.

Unlike exploratory behavior, play is organism rather than stimulus dominated. Instead of being driven by a need to identify and understand the intended purpose of objects, children who are playing often use objects to fit the intended purpose of their games. In addition, play is a nonliteral behavior. It is symbolic and often involves pretending and incorporating imaginative ideas into activities. Children who are playing are involved in transforming a familiar environment into a representational setting that supports their play.

Freedom from externally imposed rules is an aspect of play that distinguishes play from games with rules. The participants themselves control play activity, and they set parameters as the situation develops. Knowing the rules of the game, however, is critical for participants in group activities, and therefore, cooperative play cannot ever be completely free from imposed rules. In fact, at some ages, children develop a strong interest in play that involves games with rules. This interest, however, is initiated and guided by the participants and not by an outside authority.

Finally, play requires the active participation of the player. Active participation can occur only when play activities are neither too hard nor too easy. Similarly, activities cannot produce anxiety or be boring. When the challenge is appropriate, the player experiences what Csikszentmihalyi describes as "flow." "An activity that produces such experiences is so gratifying that people are willing to do it for its own sake, with little concern for what they will get out of it, even when it is difficult, or dangerous" (Csikszentmihalyi, 1990, p. 71).

Bundy (1991) likens defining play to defining a color. "Although the distinction between red-orange and orange-red is of little concern to most people, it may be of great concern to the artist whose livelihood may require using the precise colors needed to recreate a sunset" (Bundy, 1991, p. 48). Occupational therapists, who, by the nature of their profession, enable others to play, are like artists and, therefore, need to be precise about defining their tools. Bundy has drawn from the work of Rubin, Fein, and Vanderberg (1983) and Neumann (1971) to develop a definition of play that is clear, concise, and easily usable when determining the presence of play during therapeutic activities. "Play is a transaction between an individual and the environment that is intrinsically motivated, internally controlled, and free of many of the constraints of objective reality" (Bundy, 1991, p. 59).

Bundy goes on to explain that complete intrinsic motivation, internal control, and freedom from constraints of reality may not always be the most desirable or most possible experience. Therefore, she states that "play transactions are considered to represent a continuum of behaviors that are more or less playful, depending on the degree to which the criteria are present" (p. 59). In the description of play at

the beginning of this section, the three girls are motivated by their own play creation rather than by any influences from adults or other peers. They are in control of this situation and have determined the representational qualities of the objects, the order of events, and the roles of the players. They are removed from reality in that they are operating completely within their own definition of the play scenario.

The Role of Praxis in Play

Praxis, simply defined, is the ability to do. It has been described as a "uniquely human skill requiring conscious thought and enabling the brain to conceptualize, organize, and direct purposeful interaction with the environment" (Ayres, Mailloux, & Wendler, 1987, p. 94). This definition goes beyond motor skill development in that praxis involves the act of thinking about doing rather than the act of doing. Ayres (1985) uses the example of her cat, who despite having extraordinary motor abilities was not able to adapt or vary his actions to fit unusual situations. Her cat reacted to situations with movement but did not motor plan or use praxis. These ideas broaden the definition of praxis to include not only purposeful interaction with the environment but also the planning of new and unfamiliar motor tasks.

Other researchers have discussed the importance of environmental interaction in descriptions of praxis. Paillard (1982) defines praxis as "the operations that intervene between the mental representation that a subject has of his body and the physical world that surrounds it, and the intentional triggering of an appropriate act as directed within the framework of that reality" (p. 112). Accurate mental representation of both the person and the physical world is a cognitive process that is heavily dependent on the effective integration of sensory input. The physical environment, then, elicits and determines both the idea and the motor plan (Ayres, 1985). Gibson (1977) has further discussed this relationship between ideas, motor plans, and objects that are available in the environment. He feels that all objects have affordances, or particular qualities that can be recognized within an environmental context and that invite interaction. For example, a low bench, when encountered by an adult, may offer a seat or be used as a platform to stand on to reach a high object. The same bench, when encountered by a child, may suggest a place under which to hide. The conceptualizations of the ideas for motor plans are, therefore, dependent on the ability to recognize the affordances of objects.

Incoming sensations—tactile, visual, auditory, olfactory, gustatory, proprioceptive, and vestibular—provide information about the environment. This information is needed to understand environmental possibilities and to generate ideas. Sensory information also contributes to the development of a body map—the location of the body in space and the relation of body parts to one another. Body-spatial information is essential for generating motor ideas, planning specific actions, and executing movements. Body scheme is a crucial component of motor planning (Ayres, 1972, 1975, 1979, 1985), and research has indicated that the integration of tactile, visual, proprioceptive, and vestibular information contributes to the development of body-spatial awareness (Cermak, 1991).

Children who are dyspraxic have been described as being clumsy and disorganized as well as having difficulty across many areas of occupational performance (Ayres, 1972, 1985; Cermak, 1985, 1991; Gubbay, 1975, 1979; Walton, Ellis, & Court, 1963). Children with dyspraxia may have problems in the areas of motor development, social interaction, play skills, classroom performance, and self-care activities (Cermak, 1991). When faced with these difficulties on a day-to-day basis, these children may experience anxiety, frustration, anger, avoidance, and eventually, poor self-esteem.

The nature of play, as described previously, requires participants to actively engage in the play activity of the moment. Intrinsic motivation and internal control are dependent on some level of mastery of the specific activity. These characteristics are also dependent on some level of ability to interact with the environment, to recognize the affordances of objects, and to generate ideas. When the activities that are needed to participate in play are forever overchallenging, Csikszentmihalyi's (1990) state of "flow" can never be attained. The child's lack of expertise or difficulties with praxis often will not allow experience that is truly free from the constraints of reality.

Components of Praxis

The process of praxis is hypothesized to include several defined steps (Ayres, 1972). The first of these is ideation, or the ability to grasp the idea or concept that will allow purposeful interaction with the environment. Ideation involves visualizing, imagining, and creating ideas. From the idea, a plan is formulated that is meant to lead to an adaptive response. The planning of a response involves deciding how to react, how to organize behavior, and how to sequence ideas in space and time. During the formulation of the plan, a process called "feedforward" sends a copy of the plan forward to compare it to sensory information and to detect motor errors. Through this process, the plan can be corrected before the action is completed. Finally, the plan is executed, or carried out. Throughout the ideation, planning, and execution steps of the praxis process, internal and external feedback loops compare actual performance with the initial plan to determine the extent of success or failure of the plan. Feedback information is then used to formulate future plans of action. The integration of information from all sensory systems is a critical component of all steps of this process (Szklut & Trecker, 1996). See Figure 7.1 for the role of comparator structures and sensory input in praxis. Although these individual steps are useful in conceptualizing this process, it is important to understand that the nervous system instantaneously consolidates all of this external and internal information that allows praxis to emerge as a functional response to environmental demands.

In relation to play, all components of the praxis process are important. The three girls in the previous example are formulating complex ideas. These ideas are expressed verbally, refined by the group, and acted on. Each child is conceptualizing, creating, and executing motor plans individually and as a member of the group. The desire of these girls to continue playing together is dependent on the effectiveness of these motor plans. Play and praxis are inextricably linked. Intervention that is intended to improve praxis should, theoretically, improve play skills, and using play as an intervention modality should, theoretically, improve praxis.

Dyspraxia in Autism and Effect on Play Skills

Difficulty interacting appropriately with individuals and the environment is one of the hallmarks of the diagnosis of autism. The American Psychiatric Association's *Diagnostic and Statistical Manual of Mental Disorders*, 4th edition, revised (APA, 2000), lists qualitative impairment in reciprocal social interaction, impairment in communication, and a markedly restricted repertoire of activities and interests as major criteria of the disorder. Descriptive criteria under these headings include several difficulties that can be related to deficits in praxis and that can also severely affect the ability of children with autism to engage in productive play activities. Socially, these children may exhibit impaired or inappropriate nonverbal interaction, lack of spontaneous interaction, and diminished social-emotional reciprocity. These problems make forming peer relationships very difficult. In addition, delayed or inappropriate speech and

Figure 7.1

The role of comparator structures and sensory input in praxis.

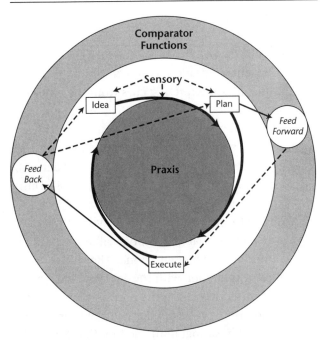

impaired imaginative play skills affects the ability of these children to develop peer relationships through play. Finally, preoccupation with objects and specific interests, engagement in stereotypical activities, and general lack of flexibility present distinct barriers to the reciprocal interaction that is essential in group play.

Several studies have examined the play of children with autism in an effort to further delineate areas of difficulty. Children with autism have been found to engage more often in solitary play (Restall & Magill-Evans, 1994), to have diminished empathic reactions to others, to lack interest in social interaction, and to have difficulties with joint attention (Charman et al., 1997). Several studies have shown that children with autism have problems imitating expressions, gestures, and actions (Charman et al., 1997; DeMyer et al., 1972; DeRenne-Stephan, 1980; Huebner, 1992). Particular problems have been observed when children with autism attempt to imitate tasks that have several parts such as dressing and feeding a doll

(Libby, Powell, Messer, & Jordan, 1997). Examining the theorized components of praxis in relation to the play skills of these children shows evidence that deficits can exist throughout the process.

Ideation

Frequently, ideation is a significant problem. Difficulties interpreting cues from the environment limit the possibilities to initiate motor plans. Many children with autism are attracted to objects by their particular qualities and not by their affordances for action (T. May-Benson, personal communication, June 22, 1998). Difficulty forming a visual percept of an object and abstracting its potential uses (Ayres, 1979) can lead to play that is stereotypical and repetitive rather than representational. Repetitive play limits exploration with the environment, thereby further decreasing the possibilities for ideas. In addition, preoccupation with objects severely limits meaningful interaction. Case Study 7.1 illustrates this point.

Difficulties with social interaction may impede ideation for some children with autism. Sharing ideas and, hence, learning from people and the environment is very difficult to do without the ability to understand other people's perspectives and to interact effectively. The interaction needed to exchange ideas is affected by problems with expressive speech; difficulties with pragmatic language as well as with unusual rhythms and tones of speech; and inappropriate use of facial expressions and gestures (Rapin, 1991). Finally, children with autism may have difficulties with ideation because their lack of nonverbal communication hinders imitation. Early cooperative play is built on the imitation of actions, and through this imitation, children develop their own play schemes and ideas (Piaget, 1962; Whaley & Rubinstein, 1994).

Children with autism who have ideational difficulties also may have problems with transitions. A child who does not easily generate ideas may not be able to visualize the next activity in his or her mind. He or she may become anxious and insist on remaining with the current, familiar activity. The ability to understand temporal concepts may be diminished, which can further compound the situation. Resistance to change in routines is strong and, often, results in major temper tantrums (Rapin, 1991). Even when motor skills have reached a level of proficiency, children who have problems with ideation may become anxious at the prospect of moving from one motor challenge to the next, and they may be unable to do so without assistance. David, who is described in Case Study 7.2, exhibits reactions to transitions that can be attributed to problems with ideation.

Ideation can be hindered by difficulties with sensory processing. Children with autism frequently have significant problems modulating sensory information. Modulation refers to the nervous system's ability to regulate sensory input to maintain homeostasis. A difficulty in this area may "manifest itself as either lack of responsiveness or an exaggerated reaction to sensory stimuli" (Ornitz, 1974, p. 198). Modu-

Case Study 7.1

Emily ran into the large occupational therapy room that was filled with interesting and unusual objects. She moved directly to a crate on the floor and began rummaging through the collection of balls. After a few minutes, she chose a small ball covered with tiny pink, yellow, and green suction cups. This kind of ball is designed to be thrown against the wall where, if it is hurled with enough force, it will stick. She held the ball up to her eyes, and standing in front of the window, she turned it so the light would catch the colored tips. Although her occupational therapist attempted to talk to her about the ball, she turned her head and moved to another patch of light in the treatment room. Emily resisted interaction and play with both the object and the therapist in favor of the visual stimulation she was receiving from the colored ball.

lation directly affects arousal level. To attend, concentrate, and perform tasks in a manner suitable to the situational demands, one's nervous system must be in an optimal state of arousal (Williams & Shellenberger, 1995). Children with autism, then, may have difficulty accessing ideas because they may experience major fluctuations in arousal level that are brought on by an over- or undersensitivity to sensory input. Case Study 7.3 provides an example in which sensory overload hinders performance.

In addition, difficulties with sensory discrimination, or the ability to use sensory information for skilled activity, can affect ideation. Creating an effective course of action depends on the ability to integrate sensory information (Paillard, 1982). A child may have a general idea in mind, but a limited understanding of the body's relative position in the environment may impede the creation of a specific plan for the desired actions. Ayres related problems in ideation to poor sensory discrimination stating that "children lacking adequate ideation do not recognize the potential play possibilities of therapeutic equipment, or lacking concepts for complex body-environment interaction, they tend to use equipment in a simplified way" (Ayres, 1985, p. 12). Sensory discrimination problems have been described in children with autism (Damasio & Maurer, 1978; Grandin, 1995; Huebner, 1992). The possibility has been suggested that these children receive limited amounts of sensory information because their nervous systems have reacted to the environment by shutting out sensations (Ornitz, 1974). Sensations that are not fully registered by the nervous system cannot be discriminated or used for the performance of motor skills. Play, therefore, may be less developed because of these problems in sensory discrimination and body spatial awareness.

Planning and Sequencing Tasks

Effective processing of sensory information, in addition to being critical for ideation, is critical

---

Case Study 7.2

David, an 8-year-old boy diagnosed with a Pervasive Developmental Disorder, had made significant improvements in motor skills. He was able to use balls effectively in a variety of situations, perform tricks on the trapeze, and move through complex obstacle courses. He was motivated and satisfied, engaging in activities during occupational therapy sessions that challenged his skill. He continued, however, to have difficulty with ideation. When he had mastered an activity, he would become grumpy, saying that the game was boring or stupid. He did not have ideas for the next activity, and he was not able to make alterations that would increase the challenge. Instead, he depended on his occupational therapist to generate plans. When she did not immediately suggest an idea, David's irritation progressed quickly to anger.

Case Study 7.3

Julia, a 3-year-old-girl diagnosed with autism, was placed in a public school integrated preschool program that was housed in the high school in her community. The special needs children in this classroom attended a separate gym class that was led by a physical education teacher with support from the school occupational and physical therapists. This special class took place in the high school gymnasium, a gigantic room with two-story ceilings and fluorescent lights that hummed. Although, instructionally, this was an excellent model for providing physical education for these children, it was a disaster for Julia as a sensory environment. The moment she walked into the room, Julia began to scream and cry. She was momentarily comforted when one of the staff people picked her up, but when she was asked to engage in a familiar activity, she responded with a temper tantrum. Although Julia clearly possessed the skills needed to engage in this task, she was able to access neither the idea nor the plan for this activity because she was experiencing significant sensory overload.

for planning. Difficulties in both sensory modulation and sensory discrimination can severely affect the formulation of effective motor plans. Ayres (1979) explains that during normal development, humans build an immense library of neural memories that contribute to the formation of body percept.

Our body percept consists of "maps" of every body part, somewhat like a world atlas. As a child moves and does things, he or she stores countless bits of sensory information, just as world explorers map the lands they discover. The more variations of movement the child performs, the more accurate his or her body maps will be. The brain can refer to its body percept to plan movements in much the same way as we use maps to navigate a journey. The more accurate the maps, the more able one is to navigate unfamiliar body movements (Ayres, 1979, p. 95).

Ayres (1965, 1966, 1969, 1977, 1979, 1985) has discussed the role of tactile, proprioceptive, and vestibular input in formulating body scheme, or body maps, and, hence, in effectively planning motor actions. Other researchers (Cermak, 1991; Goldberg, 1985; Hecaen & Albert, 1978) have written about the contributions of sensory information to motor planning. Learning a new task may significantly challenge a child who does not have a clear body percept. One has difficulty moving with accuracy if the relationship of body parts is not clearly understood. The left foot may not step out at the command of the gym teacher, the ball may not reach its intended target, puzzle pieces may not arrive in the correct holes, and fingers may not be able to work together to tie shoes. A child who lacks an understanding of his or her body position in relation to the surrounding environment cannot plan or move effectively in that environment. This child may miss bars on the jungle gym while climbing, fall and stumble on stairs, bump into people and objects, or not be able to judge the distance needed to jump over a mud puddle. In these cases, inadequate body percept has affected the ability to plan motor actions and has resulted in movements that appear clumsy, unskilled, and unsafe. Case Study 7.4 describes a situation in which this inadequate body percept may be affecting a child's motor skills.

The social difficulties seen in children with autistic symptoms also affect the ability to formulate motor plans. Problems with joint attention or sharing time with others have a considerable negative effect on motor planning (Charman et al., 1997). The rigidity, lack of flexibility, and intense desire for sameness (Damasio & Maurer, 1978) that are often seen in children with autism also affect the ability to easily interact with a group of peers. Young children change their play ideas frequently. On the playground, they may be horses one minute, then Power Rangers™, then a family at home. When a child has difficulty quickly planning responses, "keeping up" may be impossible to do. These children may become angry

---

Case Study 7.4

Janet, who was not able to speak, enjoyed gentle swinging in the tire swing. During one treatment session, she had been smiling, vocalizing, and looking at her mother who was pushing the swing. Suddenly, her expression changed. She looked away and stopped smiling. Her mother stopped the swing and asked Janet if she wanted to get out. Janet sat up and peered over the edge of the swing, indicating that, yes, she would like to get out. She spent several minutes standing up, attempting to move her body over the tire and then sat down again. With each attempt, she looked over the edge of the tire and then at her mother, asking for help. Finally, her mother lifted her down from the swing, and Janet ran off, finally appearing satisfied. At this time, Janet's motor skill level was such that she should have been able to climb out of the swing once it was still. She also appeared to have an idea of what she wanted to accomplish. She was not, however, able to plan and execute her descent from the swing, perhaps because she was not able to accurately perceive her body position in relation to the swing and the floor.

and frustrated and, eventually, avoid group activities, opting instead for solitary play of their own choosing. In Case Study 7.5, Rachel's behavior demonstrates the affect that social difficulties have on her play.

Imitation and Planning

Play at an early age may use imitation as the language of friendships (Whaley & Rubenstein, 1994). When the play interactions of toddlers were observed in a child-care setting, observers found that the toddler friends were able to share with each other and that they exhibited helpfulness, loyalty, and intimacy. The dimension of friendship noted most frequently in these children, however, was nonverbal similarity or precise imitation of one another's actions. The toddlers imitated one another's play activities, eating styles, and even ways of taking naps. Through this imitation, the toddlers created routines that were repeated from day to day, solidifying their relationships. Acting in similar ways or doing things together appeared to be the essential element in forming these early friendships. Imitation is one way that children learn to play. To learn, children imitate simple and then more complex actions. Eventually, they combine these actions to develop their own, meaningful play scenarios.

Children with autism may have difficulty either with the ability to visually remember motor actions or with the ability to transfer information from a visual stimulus to the motor system (DeMyer et al., 1972). An examination of play skills in young children (Charman et al., 1997) found that 18-month-old children with autism were not able to imitate as capably as a control group of age-matched children who were developmentally delayed. These researchers also found that children with autism in this age group did not engage in any pretend play during their study. These children did, however, engage in play that represented functional activities, indicating a relative difficulty with abstraction and the expansion of ideas.

Case Study 7.5

Rachel was a 5-year-old girl who had many ideas for play. She was shy and exhibited some of the deficits in social skills that are seen in children diagnosed on the autism spectrum. At her preschool, Rachel preferred to play in the dress up area. She dressed herself as Cinderella® and began playing a game based on a video of the Cinderella® story that she had seen many times. Rachel did not welcome other children into her pretend play scheme. She preferred to be alone and in control of the situation. When another child or a teacher approached her and tried to join the game, Rachel turned away. If they called her by her name, she often cried and angrily told them that she was Cinderella®. Several times during the school day, Rachel's teacher asked her to join her classmates in an activity. When pressed, Rachel would spend 5 to 10 minutes with the other children. She fatigued quickly, however, and returned to her dress up corner and Cinderella®.

Imitation is a building block for conceptualizing ideas and for formulating effective motor plans. A child may be able to perceive an action but may be unable to plan effective movements to actually accomplish the action. Imitation is often the bridge between perception and action. Children who have difficulties in planning and whose imitation is also impaired may not be able to make this connection. When children with autism were compared to matched groups of children with Down's syndrome and of typical children, the study showed that the children with autism were able to imitate some types of symbolic play tasks as capably as the other groups (Libby et al., 1997). The children with autism were able to imitate single-scheme tasks such as using a wooden cube as a cup, but they were not able to imitate multischeme tasks such as giving a doll a bath. The term *echopraxia* (similar to the echolalia found in the speech of some children with autism) was used to describe the quality of this imitation, which may have been a result of copying actions rather than understanding the meaning of the activity. This research also noted that few children with autism commented on the inappropriateness of using a wooden cube for a cup, again pointing to rote imitation rather than to comprehension. The research findings suggested that the multischeme tasks were more difficult for the children with autism. These tasks not only were more complex but also required remembering the actions as part of a contextual, coherent script. The concept of echopraxia and related inabilities to handle multischeme activities are shown in Case Study 7.6.

Imitation appears to be a building block of both early friendships and early pretend play. Children who have difficulties with imitation and motor planning may, therefore, be hampered in their social development. When children are unable to follow the play scenarios of their peers, they become less desirable playmates. Friendships develop through play, and success in future social interaction can be dependent on childhood relationships. Some of the social difficulties seen in children with autism may, in part, be caused by deficits in imitation and motor planning.

Feedback

Throughout the praxis process, the nervous system uses internal and external feedback to correct and refine motor plans both during the action and after it has occurred. Again, efficient processing of sensory information is critical to the effective use of various forms of feedback. Internal feedback is important in correcting a motor plan before the action occurs. Ayres (1979) believes that active, self-directed movement produces strong signals in the brain, increasing the amount of internal feedback. When children with autism avoid movement because of an overloaded nervous system or when they spend much of their time engaging in repetitive activities, they may be losing opportunities to develop internal feedback mechanisms. Without these mechanisms, effective motor planning may be compromised. In addition, the difficulties in sensory perception that have been documented in children with autism (Grandin, 1995; Huebner, 1992; Ornitz, 1974; Siegal, 1998) may result in misinterpretations of external or production feedback that compromise future motor planning. For example, Zachary's behavior in Case Study 7.7 suggests that he may have problems processing external sensory feedback.

Execution

Ayres (1985) believes that execution is not the primary area of difficulty for children with dyspraxia. However, through observations of execution, deficits in ideation, planning, and feedback become evident. Although qualities that interfere with execution such as reduced muscle tone, postural instability, as well as poor

---

Case Study 7.6

Joe was a 5-year-old boy with autism who, much to the delight of his parents, was beginning to independently put his stuffed animals to bed. He pretended that they were sleepy, kissed them good night, and tucked them into pretend beds. His parents learned that Joe's teachers were modeling this activity at school, and they were pleased with the carryover of this new skill to home. During one of his occupational therapy sessions, Joe took a stuffed "Big Bird"® toy from a box and began to pretend to put it to bed. Joe's therapist was excited by this new development and proceeded to join Joe in his play scenario. She found, however, that she was not able to move Joe from pretending bedtime to pretending a meal or a trip in the car. In addition, Joe was not willing to put any other animals in the therapy room to bed. During one session, Joe became quite upset because Big Bird® was being repaired and was not available. Joe was adamantly stuck on the idea of bedtime with Big Bird®. He apparently was imitating a specific play action that he had learned and, at this time, was not able to internalize and generalize this skill into broader pretend play.

hand strength and dexterity are often seen in children with developmental dyspraxia, most of these children have "close to normal neuromotor skill" (Ayres, 1985, p. 33). Children with autism are similar. Once a motor act is conceived and planned, the execution of the motion may be normal or close to normal. Some children with autism do, however, demonstrate differences in movement that can compromise execution (Damasio & Maurer, 1978; Huebner, 1992; Ornitz, 1974; Rapin, 1991).

These movement differences appear to be strongly related to the symptoms of autism and cannot be attributed to pathological muscular conditions. Individuals with autism often have difficulty initiating and sustaining movements. The abilities to smoothly combine different actions and to quickly change a motion to accommodate to a new situation may be problematic. The ramifications of these difficulties are seen in simple movements such as facial expressions, hand gestures, and motions that are necessary for appropriate communication within environmental contexts. Abnormal postures, delayed motor responses, stereotypical and repetitive movements, facial grimacing, unusual gait patterns, under- and overactivity, and other movement differences appear to interfere not only with execution but also with the broader definition of praxis (Leary & Hill, 1996).

Play as an Intervention Tool for Children With Autism

Play is an area of occupational performance that demands well-developed abilities in praxis. Children who engage in solitary play must conceptualize ideas, create effective plans, and carry out their strategies successfully to remain productively engaged. During group play, children not only must be able to successfully generate their own ideas and plans but also must be flexible to incorporate their ideas with the ideas of others. Flexibility, as we have seen, requires an ability to correct, alter, and accept variation

---

Case Study 7.7

Zachary, a 6-year-old boy diagnosed with Asperger's Disorder, was constantly on the go. He loved climbing, jumping, and running, but his difficulties with body scheme and motor planning had created severe safety issues. His teacher reported that she had to continually monitor his playground activity because he so often was unsafe. In fact, she described one difficult recess when Zachary jumped from the top of the playground jungle gym three times. The first time, he skinned his knee and appeared to hear his teacher's warning to not jump from the top again. After 10 minutes of relatively safe play, he again jumped from a high place on the jungle gym and fell into a classmate who delivered a loud protest. Still, Zachary found himself on the top of the jungle gym at the end of recess when his teacher signaled for all of the children to come inside. Without considering his height from the ground or the feedback he had received from previous jumps, his teachers, and his classmate, Zachary, again, jumped off the climbing structure.

---

in planning. Many difficulties described in children with autism affect praxis and, hence, the ability to engage in productive, meaningful play. To help these children function optimally in their environment, a useful strategy is to expand their play abilities. Because play is an area that is an essential component of childhood development and because, through play, important skills can be taught, intervention goals for children with developmental disabilities may focus both on learning to play and on learning other skills through play (Lifter, 1996). Through play, a child can be led into a motivating activity that encourages active movement and, eventually, self-direction. These kinds of activities become sensory building blocks for developing body scheme and are a key component of intervention for children with dyspraxia (Ayres, 1985).

Child psychiatrist Dr. Stanley Greenspan trains parents and caregivers to work with their children using child-directed play that he refers to as "Floor Time." The goals of this play are to improve attention and intimacy, to promote two-way communication, to encourage the expression and use of feelings and ideas, and to develop logical thought (Greenspan, Wieder, & Simons, 1998). During Floor Time, parents do not impose their ideas on the child. They do not try to teach skills or force their child to engage in activities that the adult sees as useful. Instead, parents are taught to view every action as purposeful, whether it is pretend play with dolls, lining up objects, or running around the room. Parents encourage children to complete "circles of communication" by engaging in the child's chosen activity and then expanding that activity by responding to the child in ways that will elicit interaction and communication. "Insist on a response . . . do whatever it takes to keep the interaction going . . . do not interrupt or change the subject as long as your child is interacting" (Greenspan, Wieder, & Simons, 1998, p. 440) are some of the suggestions Greenspan provides to parents who are working with their children in this way.

Lifter, Edwards, Avery, Anderson, & Sulzer-Azaroff (1988) have developed Project Play, an ongoing research study that includes assessment and intervention strategies for children with developmental disabilities, particularly autism. Recognizing that these children do not readily initiate play activities, these researchers have designed an intervention strategy that directly teaches play skills. Objectives for each child are established using the Developmental Play Assessment (Lifter et al., 1988). Developmentally appropriate play activities are taught to children, both individually and in groups, in natural settings (home and classroom). Preliminary findings indicate that children are able to learn play tasks in these settings and generalize these skills to other play situations. These tasks are more easily learned and generalized when they are developmentally appropriate rather than age appropriate. Lifter's method has some

similarities to a Floor Time approach in that she begins at the child's developmental level and demands interaction during the teaching process. Her method is more directive, however, in that specific skills are directly taught.

"Play is a secret that occupational therapists have danced around for years" (Parham & Fazio, 1997, p. xi). Pediatric occupational therapists recognize that play is the primary occupation of childhood and thus promoting play skills can be a major goal of their intervention. Those therapists who regularly "play" with their clients recognize the power of play as an intervention modality. Within an occupational therapy session, play can be used to develop skills that are needed for functional performance in daily life. If therapists are able to create an atmosphere where their clients are, according to Bundy's (1991) definition of play, intrinsically motivated, internally controlled, and free from the constraints of reality, they have created a truly supportive environment that will foster the development of a variety of functional skills. Effective intervention for children with dyspraxia requires eliciting active movement, and therefore, play is the natural intervention modality to develop praxis. Table 7.1 lists specific strategies to enhance play and praxis in children with autism.

Using Play to Develop Praxis

Developing both ideation and planning involves providing controlled amounts of sensory information to help develop body scheme while challenging the child to begin creating ideas and formulating new plans. Therapists who address dyspraxia in children at all levels have a goal to create an environment or set up a challenge that will elicit an adaptive response (Ayres, 1972). To foster a child's adaptive response, the therapist must devise a challenge that is neither too hard nor too easy but that is just right for the child (Ayres, 1975). The challenge must be motivating and must tap into the

Table 7.1
Strategies for Enhancing Play in Children With Autism/PDD

- Provide a safe environment, allowing for exploration.
- Provide an optimal sensory environment and level of stimulation.
- Be an astute observer of behavior and indications of the child's wants, desires, and attempts at subtle communication.
- Observe and respond appropriately to the child's comfort level with your physical proximity during play.
- Be aware of your level of eye contact with the child as you play and modify accordingly.
- Be appropriately playful and animated.
- Be interested in what the child is doing; if necessary, "get into their world."
- Attempt to motivate the child to engage or interact at some level.
- Set up environments that are attractive and that invite interaction.
- Set up for play activities that are developmentally appropriate.
- Allow the child to have control in initiating and ending activity, follow the child's lead whenever possible, and allow choices.
- Respond to all the child's attempts to communicate.
- Provide appropriate verbalizations during play; talk about what you are doing.
- Sing and use music, exaggerate vocalizations, and use silly talk or sounds.
- Provide appropriate assistance to allow success, perhaps using nonverbal hand-over-hand guiding.
- Provide opportunities for turn taking.
- Imitate the child and allow opportunities for the child to imitate you; expand on what the child is doing.
- Playfully block repetitive play to create new play (e.g., add obstacles to negotiate for a child who is running or walking in circles around an area or put something in the way of a child who is repetitively pushing blocks like a train).
- Provide appropriate levels of predictability and novelty.
- Use familiar play themes to begin pretending (for example, favorite movie or cartoon characters).

child's inner drive at that moment in time, whether that inner drive is to run in circles, ride a swing, or hang from a trapeze and kick a ball. When working with children with autism, the therapist should begin at their developmental level, no matter how basic, and slowly elaborate on the children's themes until engagement, interaction, and praxis emerge.

Children who are nonverbal can be encouraged to create new ideas when the environment is arranged to necessitate invention. For example, limiting the choices in a room may lead to a new motor plan. The child who prefers to run in circles may create new motor plans when the floor is covered with obstacles that must be negotiated. This kind of environment can also provide an opportunity for interaction. A simple game format such as hide, chase, or keep-away involves both motor planning and interaction with another individual. Many children who are nonverbal find these games to be moti-

vating and are able, through the structure of the game, to move away from pure sensory-seeking activity into ideation, planning, and interaction. Children who are "stuck" on objects can often be encouraged to formulate new motor plans when the object itself is used in this process. The therapist in Case Study 7.8 uses this technique with her client.

At some points in the intervention process, the therapist will need to encourage children to enlarge their repertoires of activities. Just as Lifter (1996) found that children with developmental disabilities need to learn specific play skills, occupational therapists may find that children need to learn specific motor skills. The child may benefit if the therapist or teacher models a new activity. Peer modeling, however, can be more motivating than adult modeling and may help some children with autism to engage in highly skilled, unfamiliar activities. Hand-over-hand assistance may be useful when

Case Study 7.8

One of Emily's occupational therapy goals was to increase the amount of time she spent actively engaged with objects or people. For her play to be considered productive, Emily needed to develop her own ideas for activities so she could vary her play. In addition to other sensory integration techniques, Susan, Emily's occupational therapist, decided to use a Floor Time approach to encourage Emily to interact. When Emily picked up her favorite ball, her therapist took it away. Emily looked at Susan, reached for the ball, and took it back again. After a few minutes, Susan, again, took the ball from Emily and placed it on top of a climbing structure. This time, Emily looked towards Susan who suggested, "Climb up!" Emily climbed the structure, re-trieved her ball, and made her way down to the floor where she sat laughing and holding the ball. Susan approached Emily and said in a playful voice, "I'm going to take the ball." Emily looked at her and smiled as Susan reached for the ball. Susan kept smiling and held the ball just out of Emily's reach. Emily followed Susan (and the ball) over crash pads, in and out of tires, and, finally, onto the platform swing. As Emily reached for the ball again, Susan decided to challenge her further. She held the ball out of Emily's reach and said, "I want . . .," pausing for a moment. Emily looked at Susan and repeated, "I want ball!" Susan quickly gave her the ball. Emily smiled at Susan and took the ball back up the climbing structure.

---

the child is not overly bothered by touch. For some children with autism, however, these techniques are unsuccessful because the activity being taught is too different from their usual routines. In these cases, gradual exposure to the activity without demands of performance may be helpful. Hanging a new piece of equipment in the treatment room for several sessions without actively encouraging the child to use it, for example, can increase familiarity. Once the child feels comfortable, trying the new task may be easier and more successful.

Children who are able to engage in interactive play can continue to have difficulties with ideation that compromise the generalization of play skills. Despite age-appropriate motor skills, their lack of flexibility and need for sameness can restrict ideas. In Case Study 7.9, the therapist expands Josh's ability to create his own ideas by building on a favorite activity.

Some children with well-developed verbal skills are often able to make use of cognitive approaches. Starting each treatment session by creating a list of activities can alleviate the burden of having to come up with an idea in a difficult moment of transition. Verbal cues such as "You seem to be finished with this game" or "What do you want to do next" may be enough to help the child generate a new idea. Suggesting that the child move to another area of the room or use a new piece of equipment but not suggesting the specific activity may be another way to encourage ideation without producing anxiety. At times, the therapist may need to provide the beginning of an idea and allow the child to complete the plan. For example, by setting up the first step of an obstacle course and playfully challenging the child to devise the next step, the therapist might provide the incentive to complete the plan. When a therapist uses this kind of strategy, playfulness is often the element that sustains the child's motivation during the difficult process of formulating a plan. Case Study 7.10 describes how a therapist, during an activity, provides an idea that gives David a support on which to build and transition to something new.

Similarly, to encourage the formulation of novel motor plans in children who are functioning on a variety of levels, the therapist may often need to begin with an activity that is completely motivating to the child. Case Study 7.11 describes Martin's progress with motor skill development and planning, which resulted from therapy that was designed around his favorite activity.

Motor planning is often compromised by an inability to imitate the actions of others. Through imitation, children learn and actively engage in motor skills, which, as we have seen, contributes to the formation of body percept and, hence, improved motor planning. Early imitation can often be encouraged by using simple imitative games such as patty-cake or peekaboo. The therapist can precisely imitate the child and then give the child the opportunity to repeat the imitation. As this game develops, the therapist can elaborate on the child's theme. For example, Greenspan (1995) suggests that parents join their children in perseverative play and expand their children's ideas. For example, the child rips a piece of paper, the parent rips a piece of paper, the child repeats the action, and the parent rips the paper and throws it into the air. Gradually, this kind of activity can develop into interactive play that elicits more complex motor plans. Case Study 7.12 describes a therapy session in which the therapist follows Greenspan's suggestion.

To address timing and sequencing of movements as well as execution, children need to be led into activities that involve more challenges. Jumping and landing in specific places, throwing balls at still and moving targets, and moving between pieces of equipment are appropriate activities for children who are working on motor planning refinements. Some children find these activities intrinsically motivating whereas others do not. One very important strategy is for the therapist to find a "hook," or a particular interest of the child, to encourage the child to willingly engage. Playing basketball or baseball or some derivation of any sport can often be the key that sparks engagement. Those children who feel insecure with their sports skills may feel more comfortable playing a game of "silly baseball" in which the child must climb over obstacles or jump into suspended equipment serving as bases.

For children without athletic interest, games such as delivering packages from a mail truck, throwing trash in a trash can, or shooting at asteroids while riding a spaceship may encourage active participation. Emily, whose Cinderella game was discussed earlier, was not interested in participating in ball games. During

---

Case Study 7.9

Josh was a 5-year-old hyperlexic boy with some autistic symptoms. He was extremely talkative, and he loved to read, write, and solve math problems in his head. Although he enjoyed movement and had developed many age-appropriate motor skills, his repertoire of ideas for activities was limited to familiar, well-rehearsed games. One of his favorite occupational therapy activities was setting up and moving through obstacle courses. He often numbered the steps and enjoyed moving forward and then backward through his courses, directing himself with commands such as "Do step one, two, and three, then go back and repeat step one, then go on to step four!" Josh's therapist, wanting to use an activity that was motivating to Josh while working on expanding ideas, created a game called "Detour." Josh would move through his obstacle course, and, at an undisclosed time, his therapist would shout, "Detour! Move to the ladder!" Josh would then have to abandon his course and climb the ladder. Josh's therapist also took her turn moving through the obstacle course with Josh indicating the time for detours. This game evolved to the point where the therapist said, "detour," and Josh himself conceived of the detour step. By beginning with a game that was already highly motivating and continuing to use the game format, the therapist was able to challenge Josh to create his own ideas while maintaining his high degree of motivation.

Case Study 7.10

David loved sports and often selected activities during occupational therapy sessions that involved elements of basketball, baseball, or football. Once he had selected his initial activity, his therapist often attempted to expand the activity using the same sports theme. For example, at the beginning of one session, David decided to stage a Final Four basketball game, with himself as the players and his therapist as the sports announcer. Before they began playing, his therapist suggested that, following the game, they have a victory parade for the winning team. With this thread of an idea, David was able to feel less anxious as the basketball game came to a close. He was able to create a parade float out of a swing and devise a way for the team and the sports announcer to participate in the parade.

Case Study 7.11

Martin was a 10-year-old boy who had significant difficulties with sensory processing and motor planning as well as cognitive and language delays. His postural control was poor, and he was not motivated to engage in gross motor activities. Martin was quite socially interactive, and he loved to play with adults. He also became ecstatic whenever he watched professional wrestling on television. During occupational therapy sessions, Martin craved heavy work activity that involved pushing, pulling, and falling and that provided strong input to his muscles and joints. After some consideration, his therapist decided that the use of play wrestling during occupational therapy sessions could address many of Martin's goals. A safe environment was arranged, and the rules were carefully discussed (i.e., no hitting, no pulling clothes). Martin thoroughly enjoyed this game, which involved both him overpowering the therapist and the therapist, at times, overpowering him. As therapy continued, his therapist devised ways to encourage Martin to plan new motor actions. For example, she would not allow herself to be knocked off a small platform until Martin had tried several different ways to push her over. Martin's planning improved, as did his repertoire of movements. In pursuit of the therapist, he climbed structures that had been impossible for him to navigate previously. He also was able to select equipment and help set up the room before wrestling. The positive energy fostered by this activity helped motivate Martin to engage in other, more challenging treatment activities.

one treatment session, her therapist suggested that Emily pretend to be a princess riding in a royal carriage. During the royal trip, the princess encountered a witch who put her under a spell. To break the spell, the princess was commanded to throw and catch the ball five times. Using this play scenario, Emily happily engaged in a throwing and catching activity.

Younger children or those having more difficulty with engagement in productive activities may need a different kind of hook. Placing a favorite object on a windowsill with a ladder leading up to it may encourage climbing. Singing a familiar song while swinging or jumping often promotes interaction and prolongs attention to that activity. Using simple games (i.e., hide or chase) as discussed earlier also can elicit novel motor plans.

To encourage pretend play in children with autism, some bridges may have to be built between reality and fantasy. One therapist was attempting to persuade a 5-year-old boy with autism to eat lunch (a beanbag) and then throw the trash (the same beanbag) into a trash can (an inner tube lying on the ground). He refused, saying that the inner tube was definitely not a trashcan. To move toward representational play, the therapist brought a wastepaper basket into the treatment room and suggested that the boy throw his beanbag (trash) directly into it. With one piece of reality intact, the boy was able to play the game while working on targeting skills.

Games that use targets provide an ideal vehicle to improve the mechanism of production feedback. Without perceiving and understanding the results of even simple actions, one cannot correct mistakes and create effective motor plans in the future. Whether the ball reaches the target or it does not, the result provides clear visual feedback about the outcome of the motor action. For example, Peter loved to play grocery store. He would sit in a swing, which represented his car, and would catch food thrown by his therapist, who played the grocery store clerk. Peter was motivated by his goal of quickly acquiring all the food in the grocery store and storing it in his car. He was able to control the timing of the game by requesting specific food at specific moments. When he reached but missed, Peter received immediate visual feedback, which helped him to correct the extent of his arm movement when he reached for the next item.

The development of skills is often clearly seen in the controlled environment of therapy sessions. But what happens in other environments that may not be as controlled or supportive? Playgrounds are noisy and visually stimulating. The school experience includes both academic and social demands. Adults and peers are not always attuned to the nuances that help children with developmental disabilities demonstrate their abilities.

Carefully designed support systems at school are essential. The use of a sensory diet, a selection of planned sensory activities that help to maintain optimal arousal, can be extremely important for children with autism. As discussed earlier in this chapter, these children experience great difficulty accessing ideas or motor plans when they are pushed to a state of overarousal by bothersome sensory information. Accommodations or adaptations in the classroom are also important. A visual schedule of daily routines reduces anxiety during transitions. Providing step-by-step directions for classroom activities using the child's most effective means of processing (i.e., visual, verbal, written) can help with task sequencing and completion.

Although the push to improve academic skills may seem to overshadow play goals once a child enters elementary school, the critical role of play in a child's development must not be forgotten. Many children with autism find success within the structure of academic tasks and have significant difficulty during unstructured playground time. Often, a one-on-one aid is more critical to the child in these situations than during classroom instruction. An adult can ease peer interaction; however, using a peer as a buddy or model is one of the most effective means of fostering play in a school environment. An understanding peer who can model play activities and elicit interaction can become an informal coach for the child with motor planning difficulties. Case Study 7.13 describes a situation in which the teacher built on a natural friendship to help a child with a Pervasive Developmental Disorder improve play skills.

Case Study 7.12

Dan, a 6-year-old hyperlexic boy with autistic symptoms, found it challenging to imitate the actions of others. He was cautious during occupational therapy sessions and did not often seek out strong movement. He did, however, love words, and he enjoyed imitating unusual sounds. One of Dan's favorite games was to make up silly rhyming songs, which he usually sang while sitting in a swing. His therapist began adding movements to Dan's silly songs to help him develop more gross motor skills and improve motor imitation. She sang and moved, and Dan followed her singing and moving. They spent entire treatment sessions jumping, climbing, and hanging as they sang about their movements. Their songs began simply with lines such as "Dan is jumping in purple, in purple, in purple." As the game continued, Dan was able not only to imitate his therapist but also to add verses and movements of his own.

Summary

Play, the primary occupation of childhood, is an important goal in itself for occupational therapy intervention for children with autism. By engaging in play, children learn to play. In addition, social-emotional well being, cognitive processes, motor skills, communication, and interaction with the environment are developed through play. Effective praxis is essential to play. To fully engage in play, a child must be

---

Case Study 7.13

William, a 5-year-old boy diagnosed with a Pervasive Developmental Disorder, befriended another boy in his kindergarten class. William's teacher allowed the boys to sit beside each other during snack time and line up next to each other when getting ready for recess. On the playground, William stayed close to his friend, who led him to climb the jungle gym, walk around the edge of the sandbox, and finally, engage in a game of tag. Through peer modeling that was encouraged by his teacher, William was able to engage in age-appropriate play.

able to create ideas as well as to formulate and execute motor plans. Play, then, can be an effective modality for occupational therapy intervention to address difficulties in praxis. For adults, this use of play can be hard work. They must be able to follow the child's lead while constantly creating ideas that can stimulate expanded play skills. However, when the therapist and the client experience intrinsic motivation, internal control, and freedom from the constraints of reality (Bundy, 1991), then that therapist has truly blended his or her skills as a playmate and a professional. "Such competence represents more than technical proficiency [in both therapists and their clients]; it approaches an art" (Ayres, 1972, p. 256).

References

American Psychiatric Association. (2000). *Diagnostic and statistical manual of mental disorders* (4th ed., rev.). Washington: American Psychiatric Association.

Ayres, A. J. (1965). Pattern of perceptual-motor dysfunction in children: A factor analysis study. *Perceptual and Motor Skills, 20,* 335–368.

Ayres, A. J. (1966). Interrelationships among perceptual-motor functions in children. *American Journal of Occupational Therapy, 20,* 68–71.

Ayres, A. J. (1969). Deficits in sensory integration and handicapped children. *Journal of Learning Disabilities, 2,* 160–168.

Ayres, A. J. (1972). *Sensory integration and learning disorders.* Los Angeles: Western Psychological Services.

Ayres, A. J. (1975). Sensorimotor foundations of academic ability. In W. M. Cruickshank & D. P. Hallahan (Eds.), *Perceptual and learning disabilities in children: Vol. 2. Research and theory* (pp. 301–358). New York: Syracuse University.

Ayres, A. J. (1977). Cluster analysis of measures of sensory integration. *American Journal of Occupational Therapy, 31,* 362–366.

Ayres, A. J. (1979). *Sensory integration and the child.* Los Angeles: Western Psychological Services.

Ayres, A. J. (1985). *Developmental dyspraxia and adult onset apraxia.* Torrance, CA: Sensory Integration International.

Ayres, A. J., Mailloux, Z., & Wendler, C. L. (1987). Developmental dyspraxia: Is it a unitary function? *Occupational Therapy Journal of Research, 7,* 93–110.

Bundy, A. (1991). Play theory and sensory integration. In A. Fischer, E. Murray, & A. Bundy (Eds.), *Sensory integration theory and practice* (pp. 46–68). Philadelphia: F. A. Davis.

Cermak, S. (1985). Developmental dyspraxia. In E. A. Roy (Ed.), *Neuropsychological studies of apraxia and related disorders* (pp. 225–248). New York: North Holland.

Cermak, S. (1991). Somatodyspraxia. In A. Fischer, E. Murray, & A. Bundy (Eds.), *Sensory integration theory and practice* (pp.137–165). Philadelphia: F. A. Davis.

Charman, T., Baron-Cohen, S., Swettenham, J., Coc, A., Baird, G., & Drew, A. (1997). Infants with autism: An investigation of empathy, pretend play, joint attention, and imitation. *Developmental Psychology, 33,* 781–789.

Csikszentmihalyi, M. (1990). *Flow.* New York: Harper & Row.

Damasio, A., & Maurer, R. (1978). A neurological model for childhood autism. *Archives of Neurology, 35,* 777–786.

DeMyer, M., Alpern, G., Barton, S., DeMyer, W., Churchill, D., Hingtgen, J., Bryson, C., Pontius, W., & Kimberlin, C. (1972). Imitation in autism, early schizophrenic, and non-psychotic subnormal children. *Journal of Autism and Childhood Schizophrenia, 2,* 264–287.

DeRenne-Stephan, C. (1980). Imitation: A mechanism of play behavior. *The American Journal of Occupational Therapy, 34,* 95–102.

Erickson, E. (1963). *Childhood and society* (2nd ed.). New York: Norton.

Freud, S. (1974). *A general introduction to psychoanalysis* (J. Rioviare, Trans.). New York: Washington Square Press. (Original work published 1933)

Gibson, J. J. (1977). The theory of affordances. In R. Shaw & J. Bransford (Eds.), *Perceiving, acting, and knowing* (pp. 67–82). Hillsdale, NJ: Erlbaum.

Goldberg, G. (1985). Response and projection: A reinterpretation of the premotor concept. In E. A. Roy (Ed.), *Neuropsychological studies of apraxia and related disorders* (pp. 251–266). New York: North Holland.

Grandin, T. (1995, November). *A personal look at sensory problems, visual thinking, and communication of the autisic individual.* Lecture presented at the Current Trends in Autism conference, Boston, MA.

Greenspan, S. (1995). *The challenging child.* Cambridge, MA: Perseus.

Greenspan, S., Wieder, S., & Simons, R. (1998). *The child with special needs.* Reading, MA: Addison Wesley.

Gubbay, S. S. (1975). *The clumsy child.* Philadelphia: Saunders.

Gubbay, S. S. (1979). *The clumsy child.* In F. C. Rose (Ed.), *Pediatric neurology* (pp. 145–160). London: Blackwell.

Hecaen, H., & Albert, M. L. (1978). *Human neuropsychology.* New York: Wiley.

Huebner, R. (1992). Autistic disorder: A neuropsychological enigma. *American Journal of Occupational Therapy, 46,* 487–500.

Hughes, F. (1995). *Children, play and development.* Boston: Allyn & Bacon.

Leary, M., & Hill, D. (1996). Moving on: Autism and movement disturbances. *Mental Retardation, 34,* 39–52.

Libby, S., Powell, S., Messer, D., & Jordan, R. (1997). Imitation of pretend play acts by children with autism and Down Syndrome. *Journal of Autism and Developmental Disorders, 27,* 365–383.

Lifter, K. (1996). Assessing Play Skills. In D. B. McLean, P. Bailey, & M. Wolery (Eds.), *Assessing infants and preschoolers with special needs* (pp. 435–461). Englewood Cliffs, NJ: Merrill.

Lifter, K., Edwards, G., Avery, D., Anderson, S. R., & Sulzer-Azaroff, B. (1988, November). *Developmental assessment of children's play: Implications for intervention.* Paper presented at the annual convention of the American Speech-Language-Hearing Association, Boston, MA.

Neumann, E. A. (1971). *The elements of play.* New York: MSS Information.

Ornitz, E. (1974). The modulation of sensory input and motor output in autistic children. *Journal of Autism and Childhood Schizophrenia, 4,* 197–215.

Paillard, J. (1982). Apraxia and the neurophysiology of motor control. *Philosophical Transactions of the Royal Society of London,* (Series B: Biological Sciences, B298), 111–134.

Parham, D., & Fazio, L. (Eds.). (1997). *Play in occupational therapy for children.* St. Louis, MO: Mosby.

Piaget, J. (1962). *Play, dreams and imitation in childhood.* New York: Norton.

Rapin, I. (1991). Autistic children: Diagnosis and clinical features. *Pediatrics, 87,* 751–760.

Reilly, M. (1974). *Play as exploratory learning.* Newbury Park, CA: Sage.

Restall, G., & Magill-Evans, J. (1994). Play and preschool children with autism. *The American Journal of Occupational Therapy, 48,* 113–120.

Rubin, K., Fein, G. G., & Vanderberg, B. (1983). Play. In P. H. Mussen (Ed.), *Handbook of child psychology: Vol. 4* (4th ed.). *Socialization, personality and social development* (pp. 693–774). New York: Wiley.

Siegal, B. (1998, December). *Learning styles of children with autism and their relation to educational planning.* Lecture presented at the Current Trends in Autism conference, Boston, MA.

Szklut, S., & Trecker, A. (1996, November). *When you can't do what you want: Bottom up and top down treatment strategies for dyspraxia.* Lecture presented at "Praxis: Strategies for Success," course sponsored by Occupational Therapy Associates-Watertown, Boston, MA.

Walton, J. N., Ellis, E., & Court, S. D. M. (1963). Clumsy children: A study of developmental apraxia and agnosia. *Brain, 85,* 603–613.

Whaley, K., & Rubenstein, T. (1994). How toddlers "do" friendship: A descriptive analysis of friendships in a group child care setting. *Journal of Social and Personal Relationships, 11,* 383–400.

Williams, M. S., Shellenberger, S. (1995). *How does your engine run? A leader's guide to the alert program for self-regulation.* Albuquerque, NM: Therapy Works.

CHAPTER 8

Social Skills Intervention for Children With Autism and Asperger's Disorder

Sandra Greene, MA, OTR

Everyone has experienced awkward social moments. Embarrassing and memorable as they may be, most people have the social, coping, and adaptive skills to mask their discomfort and survive these uncomfortable situations. Imagine a child's level of distress if he or she did not have these skills and, instead, had difficulty picking up the social nuances of interactions and was not able to grasp the informal rules and ways of being with other people. This experience is a common one for children with autism and Asperger's Disorder. Social interactions can be mysterious in meaning. Genuine attempts to interact with other children can be met with indifference, teasing, or bullying. In spite of their best and most persistent efforts, many of these children experience devastating results when trying to make friends. Some social interactions are overstimulating and confusing, leaving the child unsure about how to respond.

The social domain, a skill area that influences a child's ability to successfully function in almost every daily situation, is just one of the many areas typically affected by autism. The clinician who provides therapeutic services for children with autism and Asperger's Disorder must have a grasp of the unique pattern of social problems that these children experience. This chapter focuses on typical interactional difficulties and includes information on social skill development, the consequences of social limitations, as well as evaluation and intervention models.

Diagnostic Criteria and Social Deficits

The fourth edition of the *Diagnostic and Statistical Manual of Mental Disorders,* or *DSM-IV-TR* (American Psychiatric Association [APA], 2000), lists qualitative observations of social interactions as part of the diagnostic criteria for autism. These include impairment in the use of nonverbal behaviors such as eye-to-eye gaze, facial expression, body postures, and gestures to regulate social interaction; failure to develop peer relationships appropriate to developmental level; a lack of spontaneous seeking to share enjoyment, interests, or achievements with other people; and a lack of social or emotional reciprocity. In addition, delays or abnormal functioning in symbolic or imaginative play are also identified as part of the diagnostic criteria. Asperger's Disorder is diagnosed with similar criteria; however, children with Asperger's tend to use language in a formal, pedantic manner, and the child's cognitive abilities are often in the above average to superior range (APA, 2000).

Wing and Gould (1979) identified four general patterns of social interaction in children with autism. Those children who function according to the first pattern tend to be aloof and indifferent toward others, seeking others only as providers of physical comfort or stimulation. This pattern of interaction is more common among lower functioning children. A second group of children demonstrates a pattern of social passivity, rarely making social bids but responding by imitating others' actions. These children will take a passive role in games devised by sociable children. Copying other people's actions without real understanding is common behavior in this group. The third group demonstrates a pattern that is described as "active but odd." These children approach both peers and adults in a repetitive, one-sided fashion, generally perseverating on circumscribed interests. Their behavior is not modified by the reactions of people they approach. The fourth group includes children who tend to be polite, are apparently aware of other people, and are able to initiate and take part in the "give and take" in conversational exchanges. However, they tend to have a stilted, mechanical quality to their social behavior and seem to have learned the rules of social interaction by intellect rather than by instinct (Wing & Gould, 1979). In addition to these groups, some children may be identified as having a "shadow" of the characteristics of either autism or Asperger's Disorder. These children exhibit mild characteristics of the conditions, but the symptoms are not evidenced to the degree that a diagnosis would be made (Ratey & Johnson, 1997).

A number of published research studies explore the biological basis for the manifestations of social deficits in children with autism and Asperger's Disorder (Bailey, Phillips, & Rutler, 1996; Seri, Cerquiglini, Pisani, & Curatolo, 1999; Waterhouse, Fein, & Modahl, 1996). Although a review of this research is beyond the scope of this chapter, clinicians should be aware of the existence of this work. Other researchers are engaged in examining the extent of social deficits in children with autism and the effects of these deficits on a child's ability to function. These include theories involving sensory-arous-

al states (Lincoln, Courchesne, Harms, & Allen, 1995), the ability to shift attention (Courchesne et al., 1994; Pascualvaca, Fantie, Papageorgiou, & Mirsky, 1998; Swettenham et al., 1998), complex information processing (Minshew, Goldstein, & Siegel, 1997), weak central coherence (Happe, 1996; Jarrold & Russell, 1997; Shapiro & Hertzig, 1991), executive dysfunction (Griffith, Pennington, Wehner, & Rogers, 1999; Hughes, Russell, & Robbins, 1994), and theory of mind (Baron-Cohen, O'Riordan, Stone, Jones, & Plaisted, 1999; Jarrold, Butler, Cottington, & Jimenez, 2000). The theories of executive dysfunction and theory of mind will be reviewed in this chapter.

Theory of Mind

One model that is useful in conceptualizing the particular social deficits evidenced by children with autism is the theory of mind (Baron-Cohen, Leslie, & Frith, 1985; Baron-Cohen et al., 1999; Jarrold et al., 2000). Theory of mind refers to the ability of a person to understand that other people have thoughts, beliefs, and feelings separate from their own. Typically developing children acquire this type of understanding by approximately age 4. In a study of children with Asperger's Disorder, however, the children did not develop any basic understanding of another person's ability to have his or her own perspective until between ages 9 and 14 (Happe & Frith, 1995). The children with Asperger's Disorder also seemed to lack the ability to use this information in more sophisticated ways, namely, that not only did other people have their own thoughts but also they were able to compare, analyze, and reflect on their own and other people's ideas and emotions. In a study by Baron-Cohen et al. (1999), the abilities of typically developing children to recognize social faux pas was compared to those of high-functioning children with autism and children with Asperger's Disorder. The typically developing children, ages 9–11 years, were quite capable in recognizing social missteps whereas the children with autism and Asperger's Disorder, who were matched for age, demonstrated impairment in the same situations.

The lack of ability to take the perspective of another person may lead to behaviors that appear odd or insensitive to others. Jordan and Powell (1995) provide a review of areas of concern, including the following:

- Limited ability to predict what another person will do next or to understand another person's intentions and motives; problems understanding that other people might deceive or try to fool someone
- Limited ability to explain one's behavior as it relates to a social situation as well as difficulty understanding and predicting how another person might react to one's own behaviors in that situation
- Limited ability to understand that one's behavior influences how one is treated or viewed by other people
- Limited ability to understand and label emotions in oneself and others as well as poor ability to understand social "signals" that are sent in facial expression or body language
- Limited use of facial expressions and body language to convey feelings to others
- Limited ability to comprehend what information a person is likely already to be familiar with, which leads either to providing no supporting information or to providing background information in exacting detail
- Difficulty with perceiving and monitoring a person's level of interest in what one has to say
- Focus on one area of particular interest to the exclusion of all other interactions or available information
- Difficulty with taking turns in conversation and poor social use of eye contact
- Problems with understanding pretend play or abstract references (Jordan & Powell, 1995)

A child may exhibit these interactional characteristics to a greater or lesser degree. It is crucial for the therapist to understand that the child is not intentionally behaving in socially inappropriate ways but, rather, does not understand the basic manner of interacting in a socially effective way.

Executive Functioning

Another model that is useful when looking at the functional difficulties of people with autism is that of executive functioning. Executive functioning refers to higher level, goal-directed abilities related to frontal-lobe functions such as planning, sequencing, cognitive flexibility, working memory, and the monitoring and cessation of inappropriate behaviors. A person with executive functioning deficits may do extremely well on familiar tasks performed in familiar surroundings but would have great difficulty with combinations of activities that might be new, abstract, or take place in unfamiliar surroundings. Social situations are particularly difficult for a person with executive functioning deficits. This person would not have the ability to flexibly and intuitively interpret, predict, and form a response to the range of facial expressions, body language, and conversation that might occur during the interaction (Hughes, Russell, & Robbins, 1994; Ozonoff, Pennington, & Rogers, 1991; Ozonoff, Strayer, McMahon, & Filloux, 1994).

The Developmental Importance of Social Abilities and the Effects of Autism and Asperger's Disorder

As children enter school, they begin to engage in more complex types of play, develop and maintain friendships, and begin to learn the importance of fitting in with peers. They move away from the sole social support of their families and begin to develop their self-concept based largely on how they compare with other children (Havinghurst, 1973; Mussen, Conger, & Kagen, 1963). More and more time is spent with their peer group. Children are judged and judge themselves on their success as group members. For children with autism, significant difficulties in acquiring these skills may occur during this developmental period.

Restall and Magill-Evans (1994) examined the relationship of play and adaptive abilities among children with autism.

> Children with autism may frequently receive feedback that their social participation does not meet the expectations of their environment or the standards of their peers. This may lead to a decreased desire to engage in play activities that require social participation. The result is a negative cycle in which the children do not avail themselves of opportunities to practice the skills they need. Play provides a medium through which children develop skills, experiment with roles, and interact with others. Differences between the play of children with autism and children who are developing normally suggest that children with autism are disadvantaged in their use of play for these purposes. (p. 118)

Stone and Lemanck (1990) presented the results of a research study identifying a pattern of play skill deficits that are unique to children with autism. When compared to children of similar developmental levels who were either developmentally disabled or typically developing, children with autism were less likely to show interest in other children, to imitate the movements of other children, to play cooperatively for lengths of time between 2 and 10 minutes, to engage in simple make-believe activities, to play simple group games, to join in play with other children, and to follow rules in simple games. The study's results suggest that these play patterns are specific to autism and "reveal circumscribed areas of difficulty for children with autism relative to other children at comparable developmental levels" (p. 520). Many of the children with autism want friends but do not have the ability to initiate and sustain friendships. They may actively alienate

other children and not understand why. As one child poignantly states "people give each other messages with their eyes, but I do not know what they are saying" (Schopler & Mesibov, 1992, p. 8).

Verbal and nonverbal communication, interest in a range of activities, and interest as well as skill in social interactions are major developmental areas that allow and motivate children to engage with others. The majority of children with autism and Asperger's Disorder also experience difficulties in other major developmental areas, including sensory processing, perceptual, and motor skills, although they are not addressed in this chapter. These skills are also critical to full and successful participation in play and social activities. Because children with autism interact oddly, have difficulty communicating effectively, or seem to ignore others, some may assume that they have no awareness of being left out of social interactions. Although a lack of awareness is possible, many higher functioning children are actually acutely aware of social rejection, difficulties, and differences, although they lack the ability to change the situation. Certainly, social difficulties become more complicated with odd or inappropriate behaviors such as preoccupations, inflexibility in routines, stereotyped or repetitive mannerisms, or persistent preoccupations with parts of objects (APA, 2000), behaviors that may also increase social isolation and rejection from peers. For example, consider the following observation of a preschool child's experience.

During recess, a preschool boy with high-functioning autism isolated himself in the repetitive activity of smearing mud on a rock. Peers initially attempted to join the child in the activity, even ignoring the oddness of it. When the child did not recognize or respond to their attempts to join in, the peer group quickly found other interests that drew them away from him. They called to him to join them, but this invitation, too, was ignored. Finally, the group moved away from this child who was still completely absorbed in the mud and the rocks. About 20 minutes later, the child suddenly looked toward the group of children, now engaged in climbing a small hill and jumping down. Instead of running and joining the children in the activity, this child attempted to enter the group by tackling one of the boys, knocking the boy down, and starting an altercation. While the teacher reprimanded the child with autism for knocking the other child down, he repeatedly cried, "I just wanted to play."

The abilities to be social, to be accepted, and to fit in weave through almost everything a person does in life. The psychosocial consequences of not fitting in can be potentially devastating to children with autism or Asperger's Disorder. Some of these children are quite skilled academically and are often expected by adults to perform at the same level socially. Although all children have to cope with conflicts and teasing, the level of teasing and bullying that children with autism or Asperger's Disorder experience may be well beyond what would be considered an acceptable childhood experience. Playgrounds may be particularly troublesome. They are generally undersupervised, and many children are left to fend for themselves.

One boy with autism, a third grader, reported over and over that he was being bullied on the playground. During an observation of him at recess, the observer noticed that a group of boys in his class waited until it was almost time for the end of recess bell to ring and then gathered around him in a circle to taunt and shout at him. The boy started to run around wildly within the circle, becoming more and more upset until he finally started crying, which brought another round of teasing. The bell rang and the boys in the group ran to get in line to go back to class. The boy with autism, now extremely upset and disorganized, did not line up promptly. He received a warning from the

playground aid for not lining up. The boy, who had been teased, now was crying and received another reprimand from the adult in front of his entire class who were all lined up to go in. Although the teasing and bullying had gone on for about 5 minutes prior to the recess bell, no one stepped in to help this child. As he returned to class, the teasing continued in a subtle way. By the time he arrived back in his classroom, he was so upset that he was sent out in the hall to "calm down," which took about 30 minutes.

Another child, an 8-year-old boy, wanted to play basketball at school but said that the boys were mean, made fun of him, and would not let him play. An occupational therapist visited the school to observe. This child did want to play and was able to get into the game. Physically, he was able to play on a level with most of the boys in the group. However, just as the game got started and everything was going along well, he began to lecture his fellow players on the minute points of what he perceived to be rule transgressions. At first, the boys tried to ignore him, and then they began to tease him. He would not stop his lecture. The boys took the ball and walked away to another court. The boy giving the lecture fled the court in tears. He was unaware of the facial, emotional, and verbal cues that the other boys were giving him. He never realized how his actions had irritated the other boys. Even when the incident was later reviewed with him, the boy had no idea of the effect that his behavior had on the situation. His interpretation was that no one liked him and that the boys were mean.

These childhood experiences can have devastating effects in later years. During adolescence or young adulthood, many children enter the at-risk group for developing clinical depression and some may become suicidal. The primary cause of psychiatric hospitalization for people with autism in adolescence and adulthood is depression, being suicidal, or both because they have difficulty coping with the social abilities needed to hold a job, have a group of friends, or marry (Wing, 1981). In addition, evidence may suggest that some members of this population have a predisposition toward affective disorder (Attwood, 1998). Therefore, these difficulties must not be ignored. Intervention to address social abilities must be an integral part of any therapeutic plan.

In addition to reducing the psychological effect of social deficits, the development of greater social skills may also enhance employability and independence for the transition out of school. A study by Freeman et al. (1991) discusses the long-term importance of social skill intervention for children with autism. They report the findings of a 12-year prospective study of children with autism, ages 2 to 5. In looking at the maladaptive behavior of the children with autism in the study and the subsequent planning of educational placements for children with autism, the researchers found that

> more emphasis should be placed on long-term social skills and vocational training than on special education programs designed to improve cognitive functioning. Indeed, it appears that social deficits, more than cognitive limitations, handicap autistic teenagers during the transition from home/school childhood to residential/vocational adulthood (Freeman et al., 1991, p. 482).

Expanding Occupational Therapy's Role

Unfortunately, considering how a child functions behaviorally and socially in school, home, and community environments is not a routine part of every occupational therapy evaluation and intervention process. No matter how expert children become in certain skill areas, if their social behaviors are too odd or unacceptable to the people around them or if the skills they have been taught have little vocational use, they have little chance to be independent

or to succeed in getting and keeping a job as they enter adulthood.

In just one of many similar situations that occur regularly, a school-based occupational therapist expressed frustration regarding one of her clients because she could not get him to sit down to do handwriting, the only occupational therapy service noted on that child's Individualized Education Plan (IEP). Her frustration stemmed from the fact that, although this child was certainly in need of school-based occupational therapy services, his problematic social behaviors, his inability to merely move around the classroom without irritating the other children, and his difficulty engaging on some level in playground games took precedence over working with him solely on handwriting. The function of the therapist in this case was limited by the assumed scope of her practice.

Occupational therapy interventions in the schools could and should address social skills as a core functional and adaptive skill. Although this type of functional intervention is one of the founding principles of occupational therapy, the profession has moved away from this core area over the years, leaning more toward individual treatment of discrete skills. The proposition that school-based occupational therapists be involved in social skill intervention may therefore be initially unfamiliar to other professionals on the educational team. Questions of professional boundaries may arise. Therapists must redefine their roles in the educational setting and regain the ability and the authority to prioritize what constitutes and encompasses functionally based intervention.

The role of consultant to the educational team has been underexplored by occupational therapists. Specific recommendations regarding the adaptation of the social and physical environments are important contributions in planning academic interventions. This role as a consultant should be combined with a clinical role in the school system to allow clinicians to provide occupational therapy interventions in which children with autism and Asperger's Disorder can focus on enhancing social abilities.

Why is intervention often limited to specific skills and not expanded to a more contextual level? If a higher functioning child with autism is referred for handwriting, is it possible to see him with another child in a small group, focusing not only on handwriting but also on interactional skills such as sharing materials, working together on a handwriting project, or participating in a game requiring practice of writing skills? Is it possible for one specialist to see the child in a joint session with a specialist from another discipline such as a speech and language pathology to address common goals such as the child's organizational and pragmatic skills? Would the child's parents or guardians and the school district agree to combine the occupational therapy and the speech times in a co-treatment session with another child so each child would effectively receive more time from each service? Going beyond individual treatment, when appropriate for the child, capitalizes on the availability of peers in the child's natural environment and is more cost effective to the school district. If this approach is not appropriate at first (i.e., the child needs one-to-one intervention because of his or her level of skill), could the child eventually be moved into small group intervention? What about those children who have made gains in individual treatment but no longer need that level of service? In the real world of the classroom, almost everything a child does—including handwriting—is a group experience that requires skills to get along with others.

The transition to a more contextual model of practice requires the therapist to redefine the areas that require and demand intervention as well as to consider that the development of social and behavioral skills is equally important to a child's life experience as the development of other academic and functional skills. The

appropriate assessment process, the principles used in intervention, and the actual interventions are keys to this contextual model of practice to address social deficits.

Assessment

Prior to the creation of an effective intervention plan to address social deficits, a thorough assessment is required. Although assessment is discussed more specifically elsewhere in this book, specific tools and techniques for examining the social realm will be presented here. Many tools are available that range from observational checklists to standardized instruments (Cartledge & Milburn, 1986). Standardized assessments that focus on adaptive and functional abilities but that are not specifically developed for those with autism include the Vineland Adaptive Behavior Scales (Sparrow, Bolla, & Chichetti, 1984) and the Social Skills Rating System (Gresham & Elliott, 1990). These assessments establish a baseline of the child's adaptive behavior and substantiate the functional difficulties the child is experiencing in the areas of social behavior and daily living skills. These tools are particularly useful as the basis for developing intervention plans for school districts when the child is doing well academically but is functioning poorly with peers (Siegel, 1996).

Often, a clinically useful and relevant assessment approach is to rely on both an interview with the child's parents or guardians and a structured observation of the child in a play environment. The interview with the child's parent or guardian is most beneficial if conducted prior to seeing the child for assessment. During this interview, the clinician can acquire background information on the child, summarize a developmental history, allow the parent or guardian to describe the child's history of peer relationships, and solicit the parent's concerns and priorities for intervention. The clinician should then observe the child in his or her natural environment. If the child is assessed while out of the usual environment and away from other children, any social difficulties may not be as evident. An observation should provide an accurate qualitative view of how the child is functioning in a typical social context. An informal rating scale may be used to guide the observation (see Appendix 8.A for an example). The areas to address during the assessment process include social initiations and responses; eye contact; play skills; the offering, requesting, and providing of assistance; sharing; tone of voice; appropriate gestures; imitation; greeting behavior; general conversational skills; the ending of social exchanges; the making of requests; recruitment of praise; expressions of affection; appropriate avoidance of social interaction; appropriate affect; and appropriate distance from others while interacting (Newsom, Hovanitz, & Rincover, 1988; Schreibman, 1988).

Principles and Goals for Social Skill Intervention

Intervention to address social skill deficits in children with autism and Asperger's Disorder generally can be based on the following principles. These principles were originally described by Lord (1992) in a discussion about providing treatment to young children with autism; however, the list is appropriate for many children who are beginning social skill intervention. This intervention should provide the following:

- Structure and predictability—routines that allow a child to foresee beginnings and ends of social activities, timing of demands, breaks and rewards, and likely behaviors of other people
- Active engagement of the therapist and opportunities for the active engagement of the child—during developmentally appropriate tasks, therapist is actively engaged and child is socially responsive; during activity that is too difficult, child remains passive and has to be prompted frequently
- Involvement of parents—parents engage in

consultation with the therapist so they can carry on the intervention at home; clinician helps parent interact with the child in a positive way, which may entail helping the parent come to terms with past negative social interactions they may have had with their child
- Inseparability of cognition, affect, and social development
- Individualization of goals and techniques—treatment goals take into account the child's level of cognitive, affective, and social development
- Work within a natural environment—natural aspects of social situations used as much as possible

Children with autism have difficulty generalizing information. As much as possible, intervention should take place in their natural physical and social environments. A school setting would be an ideal environment for social skill intervention to occur; however, school settings are rarely put to use in this way. Social interactions are not routinely identified as an area for educational intervention. For children whose social and adaptive behaviors are affecting their ability to take part in their educational program, social interactions may be an important and educationally relevant area of intervention.

Social interventions should maximize the abilities of the child with autism to do the following:
- Spontaneously and comfortably maintain proximity to other children
- Imitate and be socially responsive
- Engage in functional and beginning symbolic play
- Share activities and cooperate at a simple level
- Use adaptive skills such as turn taking, initiating, requesting help and information, and negotiating for space and activities
- Be alert to social contexts and appropriate behaviors
- Understand and appropriately express affect (Schopler, Van Bourgondien, & Bristol, 1993)

Any of the above areas are educationally relevant and could be included within an education plan such as an IEP. Goals for social interaction are often neglected when a child's educational goals are formulated, but social interaction is an area in which the child spends a great deal of time during his or her school day.

Social Skills Intervention

Children with autism have social skill deficits that are pervasive, and often, these children need help with basic skills before they can go on to more complex social interactions (Newsom, Hovanitz, & Rincover, 1988). Social skills intervention can start as early as age 2 1/2 to 3 years in many cases, soon after a diagnosis is made or after social difficulties are suspected. Because many higher functioning children with autism are often either not diagnosed or misdiagnosed in early childhood, some parents may not seek social skills intervention until the child is in middle childhood or adolescence. Learning new ways to interact is more difficult after a child has been using ineffective or odd social techniques for a long period of time, especially when that child may be inflexible about changing his or her patterns and routines. In addition, an older child may hold accumulated memories of miserable social experiences and, initially, may be inclined to avoid social interactions in general. However, intervention can still be quite effective with older children.

Higher functioning children can be taught rules of social interaction. With many children, although these rules may be incorporated into practice on an intellectual rather than an instinctual basis through teaching, the repetition and use of these skills will result in more positive social interactions with peers. Social skills groups and activity groups are safe environments that allow children with autism to learn and practice new skills within a normal social context of a small peer group.

Many well-researched social skills programs such as Social Skills Lessons and Activities (Begun, 1995), Jump Starters (McElherne, 1999), Social Skills Activities for Special Children (Mannix, 1993), and the Walker Social Skills Curriculum: The Accepts Program (Walker et al., 1983) are available on a commercial basis. Most of the available programs were not developed specifically for children with autism, and they base the progression of social skill lessons on assumptions that the child is able to understand social inferences and has developed a theory of mind—the ability to take the perspective of another person. This progression may be difficult for children with autism (Ozonoff & Miller, 1995). Clinically, these programs can still be quite useful to guide a social skills program but must be adapted for children with autism. (See Appendix 8.B)

One social skills program, Social Stories (Gray, 1986), is developed specifically for children with autism. This program has a variety of stories related to everyday life activities, for example, riding a school bus or going out to recess. The story sequentially describes a situation and the appropriate responses to social cues within the situation. The stories are written from the perspective of high-functioning children with autism and Asperger's Disorder. Another useful tool is that of "social autopsies" (Bieber, 1994). This technique was first developed for children with learning disabilities to examine and analyze social mistakes. With a trusted adult, a child is helped to identify the social error, explore a more appropriate response, discuss who was affected by the mistake, and develop a plan to avoid making the same mistake. Peers can also take part.

Most programs that are commercially available are based on verbal interactions and are not activity based. This format presents a basic problem to a child with autism because it requires the child to actually generalize the information he or she has learned in a typical social skills program. Many of the children have excellent rote memory skills, and they are able to repeat many social rules. More importantly, however, they have great difficulty performing these same skills in the context of a social interaction. Thus, when an everyday childhood activity is used as the format for teaching social skills, the occupational therapist usually has to creatively adapt it. Ideally, the therapist will sustain a natural progression, first helping children gain basic social skills and then gradually increasing the complexity of the social demands and the activity. When these considerations and modifications are made by the therapist, the social skills group can be an ideal way for occupational therapy intervention to occur.

The social skills group operates on several levels: (1) teaching social skills, (2) giving the child a chance to practice the skills and successfully engage in group activities with other children, and (3) giving the child a chance to gain experience with a wider variety of activities than he or she would usually choose. In addition, while engaged in the activity, other occupational therapy services such as intervention for motor skills, planning, and sequencing can also be provided. Education and support for the child's family is an important aspect of the group interventions. Parents often become quite devastated when their child experiences painful social interactions. The parent should be aware of what is going on within the group sessions so skills can be carried over to the home. In addition to social skills training and practice during a group session, children with autism or Asperger's and their families often benefit from supplemental written or visual information that is provided (Myles & Simpson, 1998).

Planning for Social Skills Activity Groups

A social skills activity group can occur in any setting that is available, but it has to be carried out in a way that addresses the social challenges the child actually faces on a daily basis. In the group setting, the child is receiving social skills training in the context of normal play activities with peers. Social skills groups can be conducted in class as part of regular activities, at lunch, after school, or on the weekends with activities and expectations that would normally be found at other social activities such as the "Y" and Scouts. This training gives the child with autism or Asperger's Disorder practice and familiarity with activities to transition into community groups.

Clinically and practically, to participate in a group session, a child should have the ability to learn and retain simple concepts from session to session. Interest in participating in activities is helpful. A child's behavior should be carefully assessed to ensure appropriate placement in a social skills and activities group. If the child is having behavioral problems, the problems should not be so severe that the child could not be safely managed by the therapist in a group situation. This assessment is an essential area of clinical judgement to maintain the safety of the child, the other participants, and the therapist. The child could have one-to-one supervision and still be part of the group, or if the child is very aggressive, avoidant, or inattentive, he or she might initially need individual intervention to develop more adaptive behaviors and skills before joining a group.

Safety concerns and the amount of direct intervention each child requires guide decisions about the number of children in a group. Three to four children creates a peer group but is also small enough to provide a level of individual attention for each child. Children with verbal abilities tend to make faster gains in a group, although nonverbal children also have shown increased social and play abilities as a result of behavioral intervention and group participation.

The group is composed of children with similar cognitive and task abilities who, ideally, differ in age by no more than one year. Children tend to not consider the other children as peers if age differs by more than one year. The children's diagnoses do not need to be the same. Grouping the children with respect to their abilities is more important, and selecting children with a variety of strengths and problem areas is advantageous. Group sessions range from 30 to 60 minutes for younger children and from 60 to 90 minutes for older children.

As an alternative for children who do not need the level of intervention a small group affords or as a way of integrating the social skills teaching more directly into the classroom, the social skill sessions can be conducted with the entire class. One boy who had been in a small, private social skills group began to have increased difficulties with friendships at school. The problems occurred at the beginning of the fall school semester, about six months after being discharged from his group. His social difficulties began to affect his behavior and his ability to complete his academic work. Instead of having him come back for more small-group sessions, intervention was provided to his entire class in three, 60-minute social play activities over a 3-week time frame. The sessions were presented with the themes of friendship, inclusion of children with different abilities in play, and cooperation. By conducting sessions within the classroom, the child was not singled out as the one who needed help, the entire class benefited from the intervention, and the intervention directly addressed the difficulties this boy was having. In addition, before and after these sessions, the boy's teacher had the opportunity to ask questions about how she could maximize this child's success in her classroom and what adaptations might be successful for him. Over the course of the sessions, these adaptations were carried out, reviewed, and modified. Although the child continued to struggle in some areas, overall, his interactions with other children and schoolwork improved (see Appendix 8.C).

One commonly used method of carrying out the social skill portion of the activity groups is social modeling, a form of direct teaching. Social modeling is a cognitive behavioral approach and involves the process of presenting a model of social behavior that enables another to learn by observation and imitation. Social modeling most typically consists of instruction, skill performance, and practice.

The instructions for social modeling encompass both verbal directions as well as modeling and include a social skill rationale, the identification of specific skill components, and information on skill performance. It is important to present these instructions on a level at which the child with autism or Asperger's Disorder can understand, taking into account that these children usually have difficulty understanding what other people may be thinking and anticipating what others may do next, even in the presence of strong social cues. Interestingly, many children respond very positively to the exaggerated use of affect and facial expression to demonstrate how other people may feel and react.

Skill performance in social modeling involves having the children reproduce the target skill after which they receive feedback on their performance and positive social reinforcement. The practice component emphasizes production of the target behavior at future times and under a variety of conditions and activities. This component is extremely important. Children with autism and Asperger's Disorder may overgeneralize and use an inappropriate, rote response to the situation. Children should not learn to use the same strategy every time a certain social situation comes up. They should learn that social situations are not always the same.

An example of the social modeling approach is to read a short story about a child who does not know what to do at a birthday party and then talk about this situation, with the therapist acting out what he or she would do at a party, paying particular attention to all of the social pitfalls that a child might experience. The children in the group can practice by having a pretend birthday party or, better yet, a real party for a group member. If problems arise during the interaction, the therapist can model a more appropriate response or give the children options for how they might react and respond to a situation. After a child has participated in a group for a period of time, they often begin to ask for help with specific problems that they have encountered and start to recognize difficulties in social situations.

Adult-mediated and peer-mediated activities are another method of social skill instruction. Both of these approaches involve directly prompting the child to initiate and sustain interactions in social situations. In peer-mediated intervention, typically developing children are taught how to help a child with a disability initiate interactions with other children and how to "coach" the child with the disability in social situations to help him or her maintain the interaction once it is started. Although research results for this type of intervention are varied, in general, when a child with disabilities is paired with a peer "coach," his or her rate of social interactions is increased (Goldstein, Kaczmarek, Pennington, & Shafer, 1992). Peer-mediated strategies are seen as more normal and less disruptive than adult-mediated strategies because adult intervention has the potential to disrupt normal social interactions within a group of children. Peer-mediated interventions are quite useful in school environments because many children are available to take part in them (Myles & Simpson, 1998).

Types of Activities

Just as with other activities in occupational therapy, group activities have elements of cognitive, motor, and social complexity and must be adapted for the children in the group. For example, although the long-term goal for group members might be associative play with consistent conversation and limited sharing of toys, the reality of the situation may be that, at the first group session, each child chooses a corner of the room and isolates him- or herself. Thus, one short-term goal for the group would be to have the children engage in an individual activity and tolerate staying at the same table in proximity to one another for 5 to 10 minutes at a time. As the children become more comfortable with being near one another at the table, more complex interactions such as sharing, making eye contact, and waiting to talk while others are talking are taught and encouraged.

Children with autism and Asperger's Disorder tend to learn social skills in a cognitive manner because they have difficulty intuitively deciphering the meaning of everyday social exchanges. To learn and retain a skill, they must consistently practice that skill after it has been taught and modeled. Skills that are linked only with verbal exchanges and that are not tied to an activity are very difficult to retain, integrate, and use.

For example, a child may not recognize facial expressions. Although, with assistance, some children can identify emotional feelings such as anger or happiness within themselves, they have extreme difficulty recognizing the meaning of facial expressions or the tones of voice that signify emotional states in other people. One example of an activity that could be used to help the children learn to recognize the meaning of facial expressions is a game in which pictures of people with different expressions are passed around the group. Each child takes a turn imitating the face in the picture he or she has chosen, and the other group members, with help from the therapist, try to recognize what face the person is making and what it means. Is the person happy, sad, or surprised? Why? What happened to them to make them respond that way? By introducing and repeating the concepts in activities such as this one, many of the children learn to recognize and respond in a more adaptive way to the social and emotional signals that people around them are sending. In addition, by putting this activity in game form, the children are practicing turn taking, following rules, and making eye contact with peers as they look to see what face each child is making.

Behavioral intervention is carried out to help the children function together as a group, experience positive reactions as a response to positive behavior, and develop more self-control over their behavior. Generally, groups are highly structured initially, with structure decreasing as the children's skills improve. Without this initial structure and the insistence from the therapist that the children become more social beings, most children with autism or Asperger's Disorder would isolate themselves, continue to engage in social interactions that are not adaptive, or continue to pursue their areas of extreme interest to the exclusion of participating with others. Some rules and expectations must be a part of participation in the group, but the children find it extremely helpful to learn that rules and expectations can also be flexible. Children can participate in making up their own rules such as "don't get too rowdy—no hitting" and "try and listen when someone is speaking." The therapist can supplement these with well-placed suggestions such as "use your words" and "play together."

Providing structure for children encompasses several areas (Florey & Greene, 1997), namely, the physical, social, and activity environments. The therapist structures the physical environment by ensuring that interesting toys and materials are available to the children. Too many choices can be overwhelming to children with autism or Asperger's Disorder. Remember that these children prefer to play in a repetitive manner with favorite toys and often need assistance to move on to unfamiliar play activities and materials. The social environment is also structured. Rules help children to negotiate the boundaries of a situation and to gain independence by thinking of more prosocial ways to interact and get along with one another. Rules and consequences for transgressing those

rules should be consistent. Each child should have a very good understanding of what the rules of the setting are. Finally, the therapist structures the activity environment by analyzing the level of skill that is needed to participate. The therapist and the children have more freedom to work on the social aspects of the activity when that activity is slightly below the children's intellectual abilities. Participating in an easier activity decreases each child's anxiety about social performance. As the children in the group begin to gain social skills, less structure is provided, and they have more freedom of choice in activities with peers. The goal of intervention is for the child to improve interaction skills and experience greater acceptance by peers and adults.

Monitoring Outcomes From Intervention

Whether a social skill group is well planned or expertly carried out does not matter if learned skills are not being used outside of the group. The best outcomes from group involvement are improvements in specific social skills that the child then generalizes to more complex social situations at home, at school, and in the community. Frequent communication on an ongoing basis with the people in the child's life, including parents, teachers, after-school staff, and sports coaches, is extremely important as the child begins to participate in the social skills group. This communication assists in determining if the intervention is helping the child and also allows the therapist to be informed as difficult social situations come up so they can be addressed in a timely manner in the group.

In addition to verbal reports of improvements, more quantifiable measurement of outcomes must somehow be incorporated into the plan to determine if generalization is occurring. Outcome measures should be individualized for each child. In a review of social skills research, Hughes and Sullivan (1988) suggest that both target behaviors (specifying measures) and social outcomes (effect measures) be considered. An example of a target behavior might be that the child with autism will approach another child and ask a question. An example of the social outcome is how that child responded to the question. Did the question start a conversation, or did the child ignore the question?

Researchers suggest caution, however, when interpreting measures of target behaviors with instruments that do not take into account the specific cognitive difficulties of people with autism, for example, the difficulty that the child with autism has in taking the perspective of others. Outcome measures should be adapted or formulated for the specific needs of children with autism or Asperger's Disorder (Ozonoff & Miller, 1995). Outcome measures may be tracked at intervals by re-administering standardized evaluations or by comparing informal rating scales.

Conclusion

This chapter has presented the pattern of social difficulties that children with autism and Asperger's Disorder have in the context of the social demands of daily life, a review of the relevant literature, and methods for assessment and intervention. Children with autism or Asperger's Disorder and their families are a group in need of realistic, practical, and useful help in the area of social skills and social functioning. Although demand for these services is growing, the resources for this kind of assistance are few, and these are overwhelmed by the numbers of children needing help. Those who are providing social skills assessment and intervention for this group are pioneering in an area of practice that is particularly rich and rewarding, one that offers meaningful professional and personal rewards: the satisfaction of helping a child to get along in class, have friends, and be an accepted member of a group.

References

American Psychiatric Association. (2000). *Diagnostic and statistical manual of mental disorders* (4th ed., rev.). Washington, DC: American Psychiatric Association.

Attwood, T. (1998). *Asperger's syndrome.* London: Kingsley.

Bailey, A., Phillips, W., & Rutler, M. (1996). Autism: Towards an integration of clinical, genetic, neuropsychological and neurobiological perspectives. *Journal of Child Psychology and Psychiatry, 37,* 89–126.

Baron-Cohen, S., Leslie, A. M., & Frith, U. (1985). Does the autistic child have a theory of mind? *Cognition, 21,* 37–46.

Baron-Cohen, S., O'Riordan, M., Stone, V., Jones, R., & Plaisted, K. (1999). Recognition of faux pas by normally developing children and children with Asperger syndrome or high-functioning autism. *Journal of Autism and Developmental Disorders, 5,* 407–418.

Begun, R. W. (Ed.). (1995). *Social skills lessons and activities.* West Nyack, NY: The Center for Applied Research in Education.

Bieber, J. (Producer). (1994). *Learning disabilities and social skills with Richard LaVoie: Last one picked, first one picked on* [Videotape]. Washington, DC: Public Broadcasting Service.

Cartledge, G., & Milburn, J. (1986). *Teaching social skills to children: Innovative approaches.* Newton, MA: Allyn & Bacon.

Courchesne, E., Townsend, J., Akshoomoff, N. A., Saitoh, O., Yeung-Courchesne, R., Lincoln, A. J., James, H. E., Haas, R. H., Schreibman, L., & Lau, L. (1994). Impairment in shifting attention in autistic and cerebellar patients. *Behavioral Neuroscience, 5,* 848–865.

Florey, L., & Greene, S. (1997). Play in middle childhood: A focus on children with behavior and emotional disorders. In L. D. Parham & L. S. Fazio (Eds.), *Play in occupational therapy for children* (pp. 126–143). St. Louis, MO: Mosby.

Freeman, B. J., Rahbar, B., Ritvo, E., Bice, T. L., Yokota, A., & Ritvo, R. (1991). The stability of cognitive and behavioral parameters in autism: A twelve-year prospective study. *Journal of the American Academy of Child and Adolescent Psychiatry, 30,* 479–482.

Goldstein, H. Kaczmarek, L,. Pennington, R., & Shafer, K. (1992). Peer-mediated intervention: Attending to, commenting on, and acknowledging the behavior of preschoolers with autism. *Journal of Applied Behavior Analysis, 25,* 289–305.

Gray, C. (1986). *The original social story book.* Arlington, VA: Future Horizons.

Gresham, F. M., & Elliott, S. N. (1990). *Social skills rating system.* Circle Pines, MN: American Guidance Service.

Griffith, E. M., Pennington, B. F., Wehner, E. A., & Rogers, S. J. (1999). Executive functions in young children with autism. *Child Development, 4,* 817–832.

Happe, F. (1996). Studying weak central coherence at low levels: Children with autism do not succumb to visual illusions. A research note. *Journal of Child Psychology and Psychiatry, 7,* 873–877.

Happe, F., & Frith, U. (1995). Theory and mind in autism. In E. Schopler & G. B. Mesibov (Eds.), *Learning and cognition in autism* (pp. 1377–1400). New York: Plenum.

Havinghurst, R. (1973). *Developmental tasks and education.* New York: David McKay.

Hughes, C., Russell, J., & Robbins, T. W. (1994). Evidence for central executive dysfunction in autism. *Neuropsychologist, 32,* 477–492.

Hughes, J. N., & Sullivan, K. A. (1988). Outcome assessment in social skills training with children. *Journal of School Psychology, 26,* 167–183.

Jarrold, C., Butler, D. W., Cottington, E. M., & Jimenez, F. (2000). Linking theory of mind and central coherence bias in autism and in the general population. *Developmental Psychology, 1,* 126–138.

Jarrold, C., & Russell, J. (1997). Counting abilities in autism: Possible implications for central coherence theory. *Journal of Autism and Developmental Disorders, 1,* 25–37.

Jordan, R., & Powell, S. (1995). *Understanding and teaching children with autism.* New York: Wiley.

Lincoln, A. J., Courchesne, E., Harms, L., & Allen, M. (1995). Sensory modulation of auditory stimuli in children with autism and receptive developmental language disorder: Event related brain potential evidence. *Journal of Autism and Developmental Disorders, 5,* 521–539.

Lord, L. C. (1992). Early social development in autism. In E. Schopler, M. E. Van Bourgondian, & M. M. Briston (Eds.). *Preschool issues in autism* (pp. 61–94). New York: Plenum Press.

Mannix, D. (1993). *Social skills activities for special children.* West Nyack, NY: The Center for Applied Research in Education.

McElherne, L. N. (1999). *Jump starters: Quick classroom activities that develop self-esteem, creativity and cooperation.* Minneapolis, MN: Free Spirit Publishing.

Minshew, N. J., Goldstein, G., & Siegel, D. J. (1997). Neuropsychologic functioning in autism: Profile of a complex information processing disorder. *Journal of the International Neuropsychological Society, 3,* 303–316.

Mussen, P., Conger, J., & Kagen, J. (1963). *Child development and personality.* New York: Harper & Row.

Myles, B. S., & Simpson, R. L. (1998). *Asperger syndrome: A guide for educators and parents.* Austin, TX: PRO-ED.

Newsom, C., Hovanitz, C., & Rincover, A. (1988). Autism. In E. Marsh & L. G. Terdal (Eds.), *Behavioral assessment of childhood disorders* (pp. 355–401). New York: Guilford.

Ozonoff, S., & Miller, J. (1995). Teaching theory of mind: A new approach to social skills training for individuals with autism. *Journal of Autism and Developmental Disorders, 4,* 411–434.

Ozonoff, S., Pennington, B. F., & Rogers, S. J. (1991). Executive function deficits in high functioning autistic children: Relationship to theory of mind. *Journal of Child Psychology and Psychiatry, 35,* 1015–1032.

Ozonoff, S., Strayer, D., McMahon, W. M., & Filloux, F. (1994). Executive function abilities in autism and Tourette syndrome: An information processing approach. *Journal of Child Psychology and Psychiatry, 6,* 1015–1032.

Pascualvaca, D. M., Fantie, B. D., Papageorgiou, M., & Mirsky, A. F. (1998). Attentional capacities in children with autism: Is there a general deficit in shifting focus? *Journal of Autism and Developmental Disorders, 6,* 467–478.

Ratey, J. J., & Johnson, C. (1997). *Shadow syndromes.* New York: Pantheon Books.

Restall, G., & Magill-Evans, J. (1994). Play and preschool children with autism. *American Journal of Occupational Therapy, 48,* 113–120.

Schopler, E., & Mesibov, G. (1992). *High functioning individuals with autism.* New York: Plenum.

Schopler, E., Van Bourgondien, M. E., & Bristol, M. (1993). *Preschool issues in autism.* New York: Plenum.

Schreibman, L. (1988). *Autism.* Newbury Park, CA: Sage.

Seri, S., Cerquiglini, A., Pisani, F., & Curatolo, P. (1999). Autism in tuberous sclerosis: Evoked potential evidence for a deficit in auditory sensory processing. *Clinical Neurophysiology, 10,* 1825–1830.

Shapiro, T., & Hertzig, M. E. (1991). Social deviance in autism: A central integrative failure as a model for social nonengagement. *Psychiatric Clinics of North America, 1,* 19–32.

Siegel, B. (1996). *The world of the autistic child.* New York: Oxford University Press.

Sparrow, S., Bolla, D., & Chichetti, D. (1984). *Vineland adaptive behavior scales manual.* Circle Pines, MN: American Guidance Service.

Stone, W. L., & Lemanck, K. L. (1990). Parental reports of social behaviors in autistic preschoolers. *Journal of Autism and Related Disorders, 20,* 513–521.

Swettenham, J., Baron-Cohen, S., Charman, T., Cox, A., Baird, G., Drew, A., Rees, L., & Wheelwright, S. (1998). The frequency and distribution of spontaneous attention shifts between social and nonsocial stimuli in autistic, typically developing, and nonautistic developmentally delayed infants. *Journal of Child Psychology and Psychiatry, 5,* 747–753.

Walker, H. M., McConnell, S., Holmes, D., Todis, B., Walker, J., & Goldern, N. (1983). *The Walker social skills curriculum: The accepts program.* Austin, TX: PRO-ED.

Waterhouse, L., Fein, D., & Modahl, C. (1996). Neurofunctional mechanisms in autism. *Psychological Review, 3,* 457–489.

Wing, L. (1981). Asperger's syndrome: A clinical account. *Psychological Medicine, 11,* 115–129.

Wing, L., & Gould, J. (1979). Severe impairments of social interaction and associated abnormalities in children: Epidemiology and classification. *Journal of Autism and Developmental Disorders, 9,* 11–29.

Appendix 8.A
Example of an Informal Rating Scale

Social Skills Rating Scale

Name:

Date:

For each of the listed behaviors, rate the child according to the following scale.

1 = No Skill   2 = Little Skill   3 = Adequate Skill   4 = Good Skill   5 = Considerable Skill

Sociability

1. Makes eye contact appropriately   1 2 3 4 5

2. Smiles in response to others   1 2 3 4 5

3. Responds when others ask questions or make statements   1 2 3 4 5

4. Says thank you   1 2 3 4 5

5. Says please   1 2 3 4 5

6. Offers to assist others   1 2 3 4 5

7. Aware of social situations   1 2 3 4 5

8. Apologizes appropriately   1 2 3 4 5

9. Speaks to others appropriately   1 2 3 4 5

10. Able to gauge the amount of information another person needs or is interested in   1 2 3 4 5

11. Makes positive comments to others   1 2 3 4 5

12. Listens to others   1 2 3 4 5

Cooperation

1. Follows group rules   1 2 3 4 5

2. Complies with requests   1 2 3 4 5

3. Takes turns   1 2 3 4 5

4. Shares   1 2 3 4 5

5. Participates in group activities   1 2 3 4 5

6. Able to stay with group activities   1 2 3 4 5

7. Understands the feeling of others   1 2 3 4 5

8. Tries to dominate other children   1 2 3 4 5

Assertiveness

1. Speaks up for self, expresses feelings appropriately   1 2 3 4 5

2. Asks for help appropriately   1 2 3 4 5

3. Able to enter conversations with others   1 2 3 4 5

Note. Adapted from "Assessment and Evaluation of Social Skills," G. Cartledge & J. Milburn, 1986, in G. Cartledge & J. Milburn (Eds)., *Teaching Social Skills to Children* (p. 37), 1986, New York: Pergamon. Copyright 1986 by Allyn & Bacon. Adapted by permission.

Appendix 8.B
Resources

Animal Town

P.O. Box 485
Healdsburg, CA 95448
Phone: 1 (800) 445-8642
Cooperative and noncompetitive games; books
on cooperation and family activities; catalog

Childswork/Childsplay

P.O. Box 1586
King of Prussia, PA 19406
Phone: 1 (800) 962-1141
Cooperative and noncompetitive games; books
on self-esteem, cooperation; catalog

Free Spirit Publishing Inc.

400 First Ave North, Suite 616
Minneapolis, MN 55401-1724
Phone: 1 (800) 735-7323
Books and materials on social skills; catalog

PRO-ED

8700 Shoal Creek Blvd.
Austin, TX 78757-9965
Phone: 1 (800) 897-3202
Books on autism and Asperger's Disorder;
catalog

Special Needs Project

3463 State Street #282
Santa Barbara, CA 93105
Phone: 1 (800) 333-6867
Extensive selection of books for parents and
children; catalog

Woodbine House

5615 Fishers Lane
Rockville, MD 20852
1-800-843-7323
Small but good selection of books for parents
and children with special needs; good parent
guides; books on special education; catalog

Appendix 8.C
Suggestions for Schoolroom Adaptations

MEMO

Re: M.C.

Suggestions/School Observation on 10/1/98

1. M. tends to follow rules very closely. For circumstances that are concrete and occur daily, M. would be helped by having a rule made for that situation. For example, the children are expected to place personal belongings in their "cubbies" in the morning and leave them there except for recess and lunch time. M. has had difficulty with repetitive questioning to his teacher regarding bringing toys from his backpack to his desk. I think it would be helpful to tell him that having no toys or personal belongings is a class rule, and he is only allowed to play with the toys at recess and lunch.

2. Continue to have a playground buddy for M. I think that this continues to benefit him. Check in with the buddy and M. on a regular basis to see if there are any new problems developing or problems that you may anticipate developing. Continue to monitor that M. is not on the periphery of the playground or in the classroom.

3. Warn M. if there are going to be any new changes or transitions for the day. He would benefit from having a daily schedule taped to the corner of his desk that he could refer to. If he becomes "stuck" in a transition, state what you expect of him, and reassure him that you will help him through this. If he is still having a hard time, tell him that you expect him to move ahead by the time you count to three. Sometimes this structure is enough, and sometimes, you actually have to count to three.

4. If he cries, encourage him to use words. Try to identify situations when he might be overwhelmed and preempt this state by encouraging him to speak up about why he is upset before he becomes overwhelmed and starts crying. Remember that it is difficult for M. to monitor his feelings beforehand, he may not be able to predict situations that will be hard for him, and he may not recognize difficulty until he is in the middle of those situations.

5. If it is not disruptive to the class, allow him to stand up, pace, or both when he needs to. Sometimes his attention improves if he can hold a small ball or object in his hands while seated. There are also special seat cushions that are very helpful for children who tend to move a lot at their desks, which we might consider for M. if this activity continues to be an issue for him.

6. Monitor any odd or inappropriate social behaviors. For example, if M. starts to talk at length about airplanes when the group is discussing animals, firmly redirect him to the subject at hand. Remember that it is difficult for M. to monitor himself and to anticipate how the children in the class will respond to him. It will help him a great deal if you can provide this type of structure.

It was a pleasure meeting you and observing M. Please don't hesitate at all to phone me if anything comes up that you would like advice on.

Behavioral and Educational Intervention Approaches for Children With Autism

Renee Watling, MS, OTR/L

When working with children who have disorders within the autism spectrum, an occupational therapist will likely be exposed to at least one of several behavioral and educational interventions. Although occupational therapists typically do not develop or carry out these programs alone, they should be knowledgeable about the interventions their clients are receiving and about the techniques that characterize them. The more knowledge occupational therapists have with respect to the methods used by other professionals, the better they are able to assist with program planning and decision making for the children they serve.

Behavioral approaches use strategies to systematically change behavior, to teach new skills, and to use rewards to reinforce behavior change. These programs may include intensive one-to-one services provided in a highly structured environment. Although educational approaches may be systematic in nature, they are designed to be carried out readily within a dynamic classroom environment and to emphasize integration of the child with autism into typical school activities. Many educational programs, however, also use behavioral techniques within the classroom environment.

In practice, the overlap of techniques is common, and the strategies described may be present to some degree in either behavioral or educational programs. Therefore, rather than classify techniques into behavioral or educational categories, common strategies used in either type of program will be discussed, and specific programs will be presented according to the degree of adult involvement or external structure they involve. The specific approaches that are included in this chapter are not intended to serve as an exhaustive list but, instead, are representative of the many programs available.

Behavioral Strategies

Behavioral methods of intervention are derived from the idea that behaviors can be changed through carefully programmed, systematic interactions with the environment. In a behavioral approach, various stimuli called antecedents can influence the occurrence of a behavior. Behavioral techniques recognize that human behavior is subject to modification through operant and respondent methods. In operant conditioning, a response or behavior is changed by manipulating the consequences that the child receives after the response. In respondent conditioning, a previously neutral stimulus, or cue, begins to elicit a desired behavior by being paired with a stimulus that already elicits the desired behavior. Behavioral interventions manipulate antecedents and consequences to effect change in an individual's behavior. When carried out effectively, behavioral interventions are powerful teaching tools.

The behavioral process of systematically applying consequences to bring about change is governed by principles of reinforcement. Reinforcement is a process in which a behavior is strengthened with respect to frequency, rate, duration, or intensity because of a consequence (stimulus, event, or condition) of that response (Sulzer-Azaroff & Mayer, 1991). Reinforcement can be either positive or negative. Reinforcement is positive when a consequence that immediately follows a behavior increases the future likelihood that the behavior will occur. In contrast, reinforcement is negative when a person performs a behavior to avoid a consequence. To be a reinforcer, the consequence must strengthen the behavior. The effectiveness of a reinforcer is dependent on the child being in a state of deprivation for that object or activity. Common reinforcers are foods, objects, or activities that the child enjoys and experiences in a positive manner; however, whether something is a reinforcer is determined exclusively by examining the effect of the consequence on the behavior. In behavioral programs, the application of a positive reinforcer that follows a learner's correct response is guided by systematic procedures that are designed to increase the possibility of the response occurring again. For example, if after putting away his or her toys, a child receives a cookie, and this act results in an increase in toy-putting-away behavior, then the cookie is a consequence that positively reinforces the behavior of putting toys away. Reinforcement is applied deliberately and systematically. During training, it is applied immediately after the desired behavior so the reinforcer is received by the child in conjunction with production of the desired response rather than with production of an intervening behavior.

Reinforcement also can be applied in a systematic manner for increasingly accurate approximations of the desired behavior. In this process, called shaping, initial attempts at a task are gradually molded into the desired behavior (Billingsley, Liberty, & White, 1994). For example, if a child is learning to throw a ball, he or she is reinforced for first reaching out and touching the ball. The child is then reinforced for each successive approximation of the skill. Successive approximations are intermediate behaviors that are prerequisite components of the final behavior. For ball throwing, approximations may include picking up the ball, dropping it, flinging it with extensor thrust, and finally, throwing it. The child is reinforced at each level of skill approximation. Once the child's performance at each level is consistent, reinforcement is withheld until the child performs the next level of approximation. Over time, the child learns to perform the entire skill before receiving the reinforcer.

Sometimes providing prompts is necessary to elicit the desired behavior. Prompting strategies include providing additional stimuli or exaggerating the aspects of items or objects in a task to help learning (Billingsley, Liberty, & White, 1994). In essence, the teacher is adding to the natural cues for the behavior to increase the child's chance of success. For example, the therapist may provide additional stimuli such as gestures, verbal cues, pictures, lists, or a touch to the child's arm or hand to elicit a response to the instruction. Other prompts may include stimulus manipulation such as altering the configuration or appearance of a stimulus by varying the size, color, shape, position, texture, or another characteristic. In all cases, the therapist should use the lowest level of prompting necessary to produce the correct response and should decrease prompts as soon as possible so the child does not become dependent on the prompt.

The teaching of complex skills often includes chaining the steps of the task in a forward or backward direction (Walls, Zane, &

Ellis, 1981) although whole-task teaching also is used. When an adult uses a forward chain of teaching, the child first learns to perform Step A to a preestablished criterion level after which the adult completes the remaining steps of the task. The child is then taught to perform Steps A and B to the criterion level. Each time the child performs the combination of steps to the appropriate criterion level, subsequent steps are added to the chain until the child is able to perform the entire chain. For example, when a child is learning to clear the table after a meal, he or she is initially reinforced for placing his or her own plate in the sink. When performance for this step becomes consistent, the additional task of placing his or her mother's plate in the sink is added. Achieving mastery of this step, the child is expected to add an additional step to the process. The child is systematically reinforced for the performance of each step until he or she has mastered the entire task of clearing the table. Backward chaining uses the same methods but in the reverse direction. The adult completes all but the last step of the task, which the child learns. When the child performs the last step to the criterion level, he or she learns to perform the next to last and last steps of the chain. In whole-task teaching, the child actively participates in all steps of the task each time it is performed. Appropriate assistance is provided initially and is gradually faded as the child gains fluency with each step.

The techniques described in this section strive for errorless learning. This concept is based on the ideas that unsuccessful performance interferes with learning, errors impair motivation, and repeated errors develop into patterns that are learned and become hard to change. Shaping and prompting techniques decrease errors. When teaching new tasks, it is crucial to ensure success by conscientiously presenting the task and by carefully selecting and applying supporting strategies. In addition, gradually increasing the complexity of the task

by fading or delaying prompts or by adding competing stimuli is important.

Educational Strategies

Naturalistic educational techniques in which learning occurs during natural events are commonly used with children with autism. Although naturalistic strategies typically place less emphasis on deliberate manipulation of antecedents, stimuli, and consequences than behavioral methods, instruction is carefully planned and intentional. Some hallmarks of naturalistic teaching include (a) instruction in the natural environment, (b) brief individual teaching interactions distributed throughout the day, (c) child-initiated instructional interactions, and (d) use of natural consequences (Noonan & McCormick, 1993). Naturalistic teaching procedures include children with disabilities in typical instructional activities and routines.

Incidental teaching, a primary component of naturalistic methods, includes a variety of techniques in which opportunities for instruction are determined by observing the child's behavior. The adult watches for opportunities in the child's natural activities to then encourage more developmentally appropriate or sophisticated behavior. Incidental teaching includes arranging the environment to increase the child's participation in activities that present opportunities for instruction, responding to and helping to expand the child's initiations, reinforcing the child's efforts through attention and assistance, and placing an emphasis on the development of conventional behavior. Incidental teaching also incorporates the deliberate use of modeling, the mand-model procedure, and time-delay procedures (Hart & Risley, 1968, 1974).

Mand-model procedures refer to verbal prompting strategies that are used as part of incidental teaching (Noonan & McCormick, 1993; Rogers-Warren & Warren, 1980). The teacher introduces verbal prompts without waiting for the child to initiate an interaction. The teacher may prompt the child with a direction, question, or request to perform a behavior such as saying to the child, "Tell me what you want." Mand-model procedures also include feedback or expansion of the child's verbalization. For example, giving the response "Here's your favorite game" to a child who just requested "play," gives the child feedback that his or her request was understood and provides the child with additional information to use the next time he or she makes the same request. Finally, these verbal prompts may serve as models of the desired response. For example, the therapist may use the prompt, "Say book" when he or she wants the child to verbalize the word *book*. The type of verbal prompt used varies with the child's ability level, the given situation, and the content of the learning experience.

Time-delay procedures are designed to reduce the opportunity for error while teaching new skills. Initially, an instructional cue is presented simultaneously with the natural cue that indicates the child should perform the skill. An interval is then introduced between the natural cue and presentation of the instructional cue. For example, if the task is sorting by color, the teacher may say the instructional cue "sort" while placing the initial objects into the correct containers. This cue would be given simultaneously with the natural cue, which is the presentation of the sorting containers and materials. Later, the containers and materials would be presented first, and a delay would occur before the instructional cue was given. Eventually, the complexity of the instructional cue would be gradually faded so the demonstration was no longer a part of the instruction. The length of the interval between the presentation of the natural and instructional cues is held constant while the child is learning the task. Once the task has been learned, the interval is progressively increased over time (Noonan &

McCormick, 1993; Schuster & Griffen, 1990). Gradually, the child learns to perform the skill in response to the natural cue without a need for the instructional cue.

The interruption of routines and behavior chains also can be very effective in teaching children new skills. Once a routine has been established and the child anticipates the events in the routine, deliberate interruption can encourage child participation in the behavior. Three procedures guide routine and behavior-chain interruption (Noonan & McCormick, 1993):

- Withhold or delay expected objects or events to create opportunities for the child to gain attention, make a request, or indicate his or her desire.
- Provide an incomplete set of materials for a routine that is inherently reinforcing, allowing an opportunity for the child to gain the adult's attention and request the missing materials.
- Make "silly" mistakes that are related to what an object is used for or to whom it belongs, which create opportunities for the child to correct the adult.

The interruption of routines or behavior chains creates an instructional opportunity in the middle of a sequence of events. The child anticipates the next step of the sequence and acts to complete it.

In addition to the strategies that have been discussed, many behavioral strategies may be applied within the naturalistic teaching paradigm. Reinforcement, prompting, and shaping may all take place within a classroom using a naturalistic approach. For example, when conducting an art lesson, the teacher places the glue out of reach. The target child is reinforced for obtaining the teacher's attention and requesting the glue. If the child does not attempt to obtain the glue, a prompt may be introduced. If the child has difficulty manipulating the glue, his or her attempts may be shaped to increase success. However, rather than create teaching opportunities and apply these techniques when systematically teaching the steps of a task, naturalistic teaching takes advantage of naturally occurring opportunities to teach and practice skills. Naturalistic teaching typically uses instructional strategies that maintain the natural flow of classroom activities and includes children with disabilities in inclusive instructional situations. As a whole, naturalistic teaching methods are child-centered, child-directed, and teacher-guided.

Direct Instruction Methods

Direct instruction approaches include those methods in which adults are directly involved in teaching situations. The adult maintains control of most aspects of the program. Areas targeted for development often include academic, motor, and communication skills. Varied methods may be used to help the child acquire the skill being taught.

Direct instruction methods are relatively easy to learn, and they provide a high degree of structure for families and teachers. Many have been shown through research (Koegel & Frea, 1993; Rogers, 1996) to be especially effective at teaching basic skills such as attention and compliance, receptive language skills to comprehend simple instructions, and hard-to-establish skills. However, determining exactly what sort of outcome families can expect or what intensity of intervention is needed is extremely difficult to do. Most direct instruction methods place little emphasis on child initiation, intrinsic motivation, and naturally occurring social skills. Subsequently, children may have difficulty generalizing skills that are learned through direct instruction. To be successful, programs, therefore, must plan for generalization to occur.

Discrete Trial Training

Discrete trial methods are behavioral in nature. In discrete trial teaching, a child is engaged in repeated teaching trials in which he or she has multiple opportunities to learn the correct response to a given stimulus. Discrete trial teaching typically applies the behavioral methods defined above in a systematic manner as part of an intensive and highly structured teaching situation. The teacher determines which skills to teach according to the child's areas of deficit, breaks down the individual skills and goals into small parts, and then teaches each part using a fixed stimulus. When the child has learned an individual part, the teacher chains together the other parts to produce the whole. When needed, the child receives a prompt to encourage an appropriate response. After the teacher rewards each correct response with positive reinforcement, the next cue or instruction is given. Multiple teaching trials are often repeated in succession within a short period of time. The child's performance is analyzed to identify those variables that were effective in changing the behavior so they may be systematically applied to additional behaviors.

Many discrete trial programs are guided by curricula of predesigned drills that have been created to help the child learn a range of cognitive, play, and language skills. The goal of these programs is to increase and maintain socially significant, appropriate, and adaptive behaviors. The effectiveness of discrete trial methods for teaching new skills to a particular child is determined through continuous data collection, including documentation of the child's success, the level of prompting necessary, the type and frequency of reinforcers being used, the format of teaching, and demonstration of significant behavioral responses.

Research on Discrete Trial Training. A large body of research provides experimental evidence that supports discrete trial techniques for children with autism (Anderson, Avery, DiPietro, Edwards, & Christian, 1987; Lovaas, 1987; Lovaas & Smith, 1988; Rogers, 1996; McEachin, Smith, & Lovaas, 1993). In one study (Lovaas, 1987), 19 children received more than 40 hours per week of discrete trial teaching for a minimum of 2 years. Of the children in this group, 47% achieved normal intellectual and educational functioning compared to 2% of the similarly achieving children who received 10 or fewer hours per week of the same techniques. Other programs across the United States (Fenske, Zalenski, Krantz, & McClannahan, 1985; Harris & Handleman, 1994; Hoyson, Jamieson, & Strain, 1984; Rogers & DiLalla, 1991; Rogers & Lewis, 1989; Zelazo, 1997) have also published work that supports the use of discrete trial techniques with children with autism in both individual and group situations.

Although many reports that favor discrete trial methods have been published, the research methods that were used in some of the studies have been criticized in peer reviewed journals. Critiques of the Lovaas (1987) study argue that the lack of rigorous experimental designs, failure to use evaluators who were blind to all aspects of the studies, and failure to randomly assign study participants compromised the study results (Baer, 1993; Gresham & MacMillan, 1997a, 1997b; Kazdin, 1993; Mesibov, 1993). Despite these and a host of other criticisms, the popularity of behavioral methods and discrete trial teaching continues to increase. In addition to empirical research, a multitude of anecdotal reports and testimonials of parents of children with autism provide further support for the effectiveness of discrete trial teaching. Appendix 9.A provides selected references regarding the use of discrete trial methods with children with autism.

Application of Discrete Trial Methods.
Children with autism who are participating in home-based discrete trial programs may benefit from the carryover of these behavioral techniques into occupational therapy sessions. In particular, the therapist may find it helpful to use commands the child has learned to increase compliance with requests. Many behavioral programs use simple commands such as "Come here," "Sit down," "Hands down," or "Stop" during the everyday routine of the program.

Occupational therapists who are having difficulty engaging the child in fine motor or tabletop tasks may realize increased success and compliance when using the terminology with which the child is familiar. In this situation, the therapist can increase the benefits of the occupational therapy services because he or she is not spending time trying to gain the child's compliance.

Putting positive reinforcement procedures into effect can be very strategic and may enhance the child's performance during therapy sessions. Occupational therapists may use therapeutic activities that the child enjoys as reinforcement for participating in less desirable tasks. For example, the therapist may let the child play in a bubble-ball bath after he or she finishes a puzzle or does a cutting activity. The bubble-ball bath may be used as a reinforcer if it results in increasing the desired behavior. It is also a strategic therapeutic choice because it provides tactile and proprioceptive input that increase body awareness. If this activity is used to reinforce participation in an undesirable activity and is scheduled prior to a complex motor task, the child has benefited in two ways. First, his or her performance of the puzzle has been reinforced, and second, the child has received some preparatory sensory input that can enhance his or her performance of the complex motor task.

A variety of therapeutic activities can be used in similar ways to positively reinforce the child's performance of undesirable activities and to prepare him or her for the next activity. In another case, the occupational therapist may use a child's favorite food as reinforcement for using utensils. If the child enjoys chocolate pudding, the therapist may require that the child use a spoon and scoop independently to eat the pudding. In this scenario, the pudding is a natural reinforcer for using the utensil and is likely to strongly reinforce the behavior of using a spoon whenever chocolate pudding is available.

In an established program, the occupational therapist may apply his or her knowledge of sensory issues, environmental modifications, task analysis, and developmental progression to assist in selecting appropriate tasks for the child to learn. The occupational therapist may also assist in determining appropriate reinforcers according to the child's sensory needs and preferences.

Pivotal Response Training

Pivotal response training (PRT) is an intensive behavioral intervention specifically designed to enhance the development of skills such as language and play skills that are necessary for broad areas of functioning (Koegel et al., 1989). PRT is structured in a way that resembles typical adult-child interactions and creates opportunities for massed incidental trials within natural-language and play activities. PRT is designed to be used along with discrete trials and structured teaching as one component of a comprehensive behavioral program. Like many behavioral methods, PRT uses a cue → response → consequence pattern.

The pivotal skills this method was designed to teach are motivation and responsivity to multiple environmental cues. Motivation is considered to be a common problem for children with autism that must be resolved before the child will have a desire to learn new tasks and participate in social and school environments (Koegel, Koegel, Frea, & Smith, 1995). The emphasis on responsivity to multiple cues stems from a large body of research in which children with autism demonstrated stimulus overselectivity, a condition that is characterized by failure to use all of the cues available in a learning situation (Rosenblatt, Bloom, & Koegel, 1995). For example, a child with autism may attend to only one of many cues or to only a portion of a cue in his or her environment. If the child attends to visual cues but does not perceive the auditory cues, then he or she misses the opportunity to learn the association

between the visual and auditory information. Stimulus overselectivity is considered an attentional deficit that must be remediated in a child with autism to expand current learning abilities.

PRT procedures may be used in a one-to-one teaching environment or in the child's natural environment. Although PRT has no specific curriculum, skills are taught in a developmental sequence using the PRT procedures (Koegel et al., 1989). Language skills training, for example, begins by teaching prebabbling (cries, laugh, gurgling) and then progresses to babbling (ba, dada), spontaneous sounds, sound pairing (child's vocalization follows teacher's vocalization), verbal imitation, spontaneous word approximations, spontaneous one-word utterances, spontaneous phrases, and finally, concepts. The sequence of play skills is much simpler and consists of teaching functional play skills followed by teaching symbolic play skills. The lack of a specific curriculum allows for increased variability in responses and greater flexibility in teaching methods.

The teaching trials include presentation of a cue by the teacher, production of a behavioral response by the child, application of a consequence for the behavior, and a pause before the next trial so the teacher can evaluate the child's performance and determine how to present the next cue. During this process, the teacher evaluates the appropriateness of the child's response in relation to the context of the chosen activity and conscientiously applies consequences to establish a direct relationship between the response and the reinforcer. For example, to elicit a child's assistance in setting the table, the parent or teacher approaches the child, touches him or her, says his or her name, and then provides the instruction "Put the plates on the table, please." If the child does not respond, the teacher may encourage a response by repeating the instruction and either pointing to the plates or handing the plates to the child. When the task has been performed, the child's reward is the opportunity to sit down and eat his or her meal. Another step in the process may include the teacher taking a turn in the activity to provide a model of appropriate actions and language within the context of the child's chosen activity. The teacher also is responsible for ensuring that play and language tasks are interspersed with one another, simulating the flow with which those opportunities are found in the natural environment.

PRT is especially effective for teaching generalization across environments and people, maintenance of skills, and motivation (Loos, 1998). The methods decrease the prompt-dependence that often develops in children who participate in discrete trial programs and encourage typical rather than routine responses. Other benefits of using PRT include improved learning from the environment, use of existing materials and environmental conditions, as well as increased realization by the child of the meaning of spoken communication.

People who are interested in using the PRT techniques are advised to receive training in the use of cues to elicit and build on emerging skills. A training manual designed to be used by parents or professionals is available. Ordering information is listed in Appendix 9.B.

Research on PRT. Pivotal response training methodology has been shown to be effective in motivating individuals with autism to attempt to communicate with others and improve skills in play and social interaction (Koegel & Frea, 1993; Koegel, Koegel, & Surrat, 1992; Schreibman, Stahmer, & Pierce, 1996). The variables that have been identified as most powerful in effecting the changes are the child's participation to choose materials used in teaching, reinforcement of all communicative attempts, frequently interspersed maintenance tasks, and use of natural reinforcers that are directly related to the task. In addition, evidence shows that the use of the PRT methods within a natural teaching paradigm enhances the child's success.

Application of PRT Methods. Occupational therapists can readily apply the principals of PRT to their intervention services. Although occupational therapists typically do not work on communication skills per se, motivation and communication are essential for therapy services to be successful. Work on skills according to a developmental progression is the hallmark of the developmental frame of reference delineated by Llorens (1974), and work in a highly supportive, one-to-one format is typical of many occupational therapy intervention sessions. Although most occupational therapists do not conscientiously apply the cue → response → consequence sequence for working on skill development, these methods are commonly applied in an informal manner. For example, when the therapist requests that the child cut out a circle, she has introduced a cue. The child's engagement or lack of engagement in the activity is his or her response, and the therapist's reaction to the child's work is the consequence. PRT also is easily applied when working on activities of daily living. For example, the therapist may introduce a visual or verbal cue for the child to don his or her shirt. The child's interaction or lack of interaction with the shirt provides the response and leads to the consequence, which may be assistance from the therapist or successful independent dressing of the upper extremity.

In addition, occupational therapists who apply a sensory processing framework to increase a child's ability to process and use multiple sensory cues are addressing the need for the child to develop attention to multiple cues within the environment. According to the advocates of PRT methods, systematic and conscientious application of these methods to encourage the development of essential skills such as motivation, responsivity, and communication development may be beneficial in a variety of learning situations, including occupational therapy sessions.

Occupational therapists can help to develop effective PRT programs within the home or school environments by identifying developmentally appropriate skills to be taught, determining how to apply PRT for teaching functional skills, and identifying appropriate levels of assistance to be given to the child during PRT sessions.

The Miller Method®

The Miller Method®, developed by psychologist Arnold Miller and speech-language pathologist Eileen Eller-Miller, is an adult-structured approach to intervention that is designed to teach communication and cognitive skills while enhancing a child's physical organization. This approach is based on the cognitive-developmental (C-D) systems theory, conceptualized by Arnold Miller (1991).

C-D systems theory considers the body-world relationship to be paramount in the development of effective and successful functional skills. The theory states that all children are born with an inherent desire to make contact with, explore, cope with, communicate, and represent to themselves and others that which they experience. The ability to fulfill this desire is dependent on the extent to which the child experiences and participates in body-world systems that unravel in a linear progression during early childhood. If the progression of these abilities is disrupted, the child can become stalled at an early stage of development or may proceed to advanced stages in a distorted manner.

C-D systems theory describes children in early childhood as being stimulus-dominated organisms with a repertoire of part-systems (reflexive responses and rhythmic stereotypes). In the normal developmental process, children evolve into individuals who are capable of combining their part-systems to engage in increasingly complex intentional and spontaneous relations with objects and people. In this approach, a system is any organized unit of behavior. For example, the processes of opening and closing, turning on and off, and picking up and dropping are systems. Similarly, pouring water into a funnel or the sequence of picking up a farm animal, opening the barn door, placing the animal inside, and closing the door are systems. Systems such as these are the basic units of teaching in the Miller Method®.

Within the C-D framework, children with autism may exhibit either a closed-systems disorder or a systems-forming disorder. A closed-systems disorder is characterized by profound involvement with only a few objects and by the inability to detach oneself from one's interactions without great difficulty. A child with a closed-systems disorder may be preoccupied with the space immediately around his or her body, may not notice the perimeter of the room or objects moving toward him or her, or may not respond when mother calls his or her name. This child typically requires physical assistance to interrupt his or her closed system. A systems-forming disorder is present in the child who is so easily distracted by extraneous stimuli that he or she has difficulty engaging in a selected activity and also in the child who is drawn to an object but has little capacity to interact with it in a meaningful manner. A child with a systems-forming disorder may orient randomly to various aspects of his or her surroundings but is typically unable to move beyond orienting into engaging with those aspects. Figure 9.1 shows the ways in which a child with a typical reality system, a closed-system disorder, and a system-forming disorder might experience reality.

C-D systems theory holds that for children to develop and form systems, they must become aware of themselves as separate beings with the ability to make and express choices. Children with autism are perceived as lacking this awareness, an impairment that hinders their ability to engage in purposeful activity

Figure 9.1
Three different ways in which a child might experience reality.
9.1a. The child's reality system includes awareness of both the object and the person.
9.1b. Child with closed system disorder engaging only with the object.
9.1c. Child with a system-forming disorder unable to engage with either the object or the person.

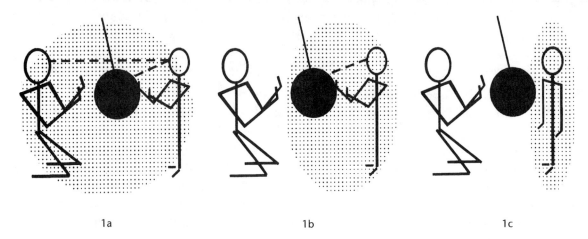

1a   1b   1c

Note. From *The Miller Method®: A new way with autistic and other children with pervasive developmental disorders* by A. Miller and E. Eller-Miller, 1999 (pp. 2) [Brochure]. Boston: Language and Cognitive Development Center. Copyright 1999 Language and Cognitive Development Center, Inc. Reprinted with permission.

because an attraction to salient stimuli drives stereotypical or random behavior. Once engaged in this stereotypical behavior, these children cannot independently detach themselves from the original activity to become involved with something else. In other words, children with autism are unable to liberate themselves from the "pull" of their immediate surroundings. However, the development in these children of a body-world awareness and the accompanying sense of possibilities is the major goal of the Miller Method®.

To foster the development of body-world awareness, the Miller Method® combines motor, cognitive, and communicative strategies (Miller & Miller, 1973). Rough-and-tumble activities and elevated structures are used to improve body organization, contact with surroundings, and social contact. Rough-and-tumble activity uses tactile contact to enhance body scheme and may take on many different forms including tickling or wrestling. Elevated struc-

tures are used to help the child organize and coordinate his or her movements. Elevated structures include boards 14–18 inches wide that are elevated 2 1/2 feet above the ground. The boards are ordered so they form a path and create a boundary within which the child interacts with people and activities. The structure may be a single board or a pair of boards, and the boards may be wide or narrow, may have a flat surface, or may be double thickness with holes like Swiss cheese on the top surface. The various boards present diverse challenges to the child, all of which are designed to enhance body organization and interaction with the environment. The child's body-world awareness is enhanced as he or she focuses attention and organizes behavior to climb and move on the elevated structures. Figure 9.2 illustrates an example of an elevated structure.

The child develops cognitive abilities as he or she moves along the boards and encounters obstacles placed in his or her path by the teacher (Miller & Miller, 1973). For example, the child may come upon a large box that must be opened so the child can move his or her body inside and through it before continuing along the path. The child may encounter a detour in which one portion of the path is removed, thus challenging the child to find an alternate route by which to reach his or her destination. Other examples of obstacles are work stations, which may have a portion of a task, an entire task, or a tool that is necessary to complete the task located at the next work station. Alternatively, the child's teacher may deliberately interfere with the child's movements along the boards. The interruption may include the presentation of a new task or the placement of a barrier over materials being used by the child. The interruptions are specifically designed to develop the child's ability to cope with unpredictable events, help him or her build intentional behavior, and generate language relevant to the situation. While on the elevated structures, children also develop language by means of verbal narration and manual signs that describe what the child is doing while he or she is doing it (Miller & Miller, 1973).

In essence, the Miller Method® structures the environment so the child is prevented from running about; places obstacles in the child's path, pressing him or her to engage in functional activities; provides narration through both spoken words and gestures; and introduces systematic task interruption to encourage child–therapist interaction. Through these methods, children develop in the areas of motor skills, communication and language, social interaction, problem solving, and coping.

Research on the Miller Method®. Empirical research to support the Miller Method® is limited. One study published in 1973 (Miller & Miller, 1973) described the performance of 19 children with autism who participated in cognitive-developmental training with elevated boards and sign language. The results of that study indicated that children with autism

Figure 9.2

Schematic of the elevated square indicating stations at which child picks up and drops objects.

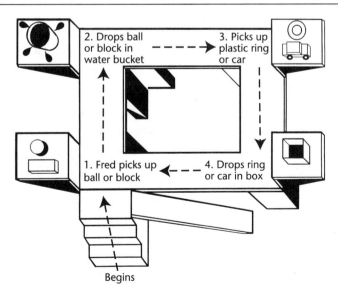

learned to understand sign language when it was paired with appropriate spoken words and that the children learned to initiate signs to request desired objects. However, the relevance of the elevated boards in learning sign language was not determined. References regarding the Miller Method® are listed in Appendix 9.C.

Application of the Miller Method®. Concepts from the Miller Method® are readily applied to occupational therapy intervention for children with autism. A variety of sensory-integration equipment can be used in the same way as the elevated board system, raising the child off the ground and providing physical boundaries that prevent the child from running about. The child may be presented with tasks while on a platform or bolster swing, while in a Lycra™ swing, or while performing the complex tasks of an obstacle course. Obstacles similar to those included in the body-awareness course also may be included to incorporate opportunities to work on concepts such as opening doors, crossing bridges, or climbing over or under objects and up or down stairs. In addition, providing narration of the child's movements and actions accompanied by gestures or sign language is a technique commonly used by speech-language pathologists who recommend the use of multimodal communication methods to enhance the child's opportunity to understand the message.

Supported Instruction Methods

Supported instruction methods include those intervention strategies that typically occur within the natural context of play. Rather than provide specific, discrete teaching scenarios, adults promote skill achievement by following the child's lead, then structuring, expanding, and elaborating on the theme of the activity that has been initiated by the child. Methods emphasize positive affect, social relatedness, initiative, and the development of functional skills. Positive aspects of supported instruction include an increase in the child's enjoyment and intrinsic motivation for social and communication skills, improvement in the child's ability to initiate and engage in reciprocal social and communicative interaction, and less need for the systematic generalization of skills.

Structured Teaching

The structured teaching approach was developed through Division TEACCH (Treatment and Education of Autistic and Related Communication Handicapped Children) at the University of North Carolina Chapel Hill that began as a state program for people with autism in 1966. In contrast to specific treatments, the structured teaching approach is designed to help people with autism better understand the world and function more successfully in it. The structured teaching approach is based on trying to understand how a child with autism sees the world, respecting the differences in perception, and altering the child's world as necessary to maximize independence. The structure in this approach includes environmental modifications, concrete and visual presentation of information, and proactive use of routines to teach skills. The structured teaching strategies are individualized according to the strengths, skills, interests, and needs of each child. Structure is established early in intervention and is maintained as the child grows and matures. The level of structure is not decreased or faded over time but, rather, is blended into the child's life to provide consistency and security.

The five distinct elements of the structured teaching approach are physical structure, the daily schedule, work systems, routines, and visual structure (Mesibov, Schopler, & Hearsey, 1994). Physical structure helps to define the layout of the classroom environment so each area has a distinct meaning and purpose. Boundaries are created with furniture, tape on the floor, and other visual means to help the child understand where each area begins and ends, and what happens in each area of the environment. Visual and auditory distractions are kept to a minimum. Basic teaching areas are developed and maintained, enabling the child to focus on the concept he or she is learning rather than on the details of the environment.

The daily schedule is a visual representation of what activities will occur and in what sequence (Mesibov, Schopler, & Hearsey, 1994). This schedule fosters anticipation, provides predictability, eliminates demands on memory, and reduces opportunities for anxiety about unknown events. Schedules may include as few as three activities or cover the span of an entire week and may consist of words, pictures, or both, depending on the abilities of the child. Two types of schedules are used: a classroom schedule and an individual schedule. The classroom schedule lists general activities in which all the children participate, including circle time, table time, break, and playground. Figure 9.3 shows a typical classroom schedule. Individual schedules may include classroom activities but also may depict specific tasks for the child to perform. Individual schedules are especially important during free-play opportunities and cognitive work stations. Visual schedules decrease the need for accurate auditory processing of spoken language and help students know what specific task they are supposed to do during the general activity listed on the classroom schedule. Systematic and regular review of the schedule with young children is important, especially while teaching the purpose and meaning of the schedule.

Work systems provide structure that helps the child with autism develop independence in routine tasks. This strategy emphasizes the concepts of where to begin a task, what to do, how much to do, what the completed task looks like, and what comes next. Work systems may include jigs, or visual maps that outline the placement of objects used for each task, and may incorporate skills such as moving in a left-to-right direction or matching colors, letters, shapes, or numbers (Schopler, Mesibov, & Hearsey, 1995). The child learns to line up his

Figure 9.3
Vertically-oriented visual schedule of classroom activities.

or her work with the visual representation and performs the steps depicted in the accompanying visual instructions. The goal is for the child to be independent in the work system, without reliance on verbal instructions or physical assistance from another person.

Routines are another component of the structured teaching approach. Routines help to establish order as well as provide understanding and security for children with autism (Mesibov, Schopler, & Hearsey, 1994). Children are taught to approach visual information from left to right and from top to bottom. These organizational patterns help the child know where to start and how to proceed with a task. Children also learn to work first, then play and to eat first, then clean up. Other critical routines involve checking the visual schedule after completing a task and following the work system. These routines help to establish behaviors that are typically needed for success in everyday life experiences.

The final component of the structured teaching approach is visual structure, which comprises three key elements: visual instructions, visual organization, and visual clarity (Faherty & Hearsey, 1996). Visual instructions show the student information about how to complete a task or organize a series of parts. Visual organization includes the organization of materials and space in the child's work environment. Visual clarity is achieved by highlighting the key materials or elements of objects through colors, pictures, numbers, or words. Rather than teach children to rely on verbal cues and instructions, visual structure helps the child with autism learn to maximize his or her visual abilities for the purposes of gathering information and clarifying expectations.

Research on Structured Teaching. Extensive research has been conducted to examine the efficacy of structured teaching methods for people with autism (Marcus, Lansing, Andrews, & Schopler, 1978; Ozonoff & Cathcart, 1998; Schopler, 1987; Schopler, Brehm, Kinsbourne, & Reichler, 1971; Schopler, Mesibov, & Baker, 1982). Studies of reported outcomes have shown (a) a low rate of institutionalization of older children and adults, (b) greater academic achievement in high-functioning adolescents and adults than was expected from previous research, and (c) substantial increases in the IQ levels of preschoolers who received TEACCH services (Lord & Schopler, 1994). Additional information about the structured teaching methods can be requested from the University of North Carolina. Contact information is listed in Appendix 9.B.

Application of Structured Teaching Methods. To adapt structured teaching techniques to the occupational therapy clinic, one first needs to organize the environment in a systematic manner. Clear boundaries need to be created to establish where each kind of therapeutic activity—sensorimotor, fine motor, gross motor, visual-perceptual, cognitive, play, self-help, and social activities—will occur. Only designated activities are to occur in each specific area.

For home use, the occupational therapist assists the parent in identifying appropriate physical locations for various activities, creating environmental structure and boundaries using available furniture and household belongings, establishing a daily schedule that matches the family's daily routines, identifying and putting into effect appropriate work systems, establishing routines that are important for the child, and using various elements of visual structure. In addition, the occupational therapist can assist the family in solving problems related to identifying, obtaining, and organizing materials that are needed for the home program.

Visual schedules are easily incorporated into occupational therapy services whether they are provided within a clinic, classroom, or home-based setting. The schedule may be posted on the wall or be available to the child in a book. Pictures should be ordered according to the sequence in which activities will occur. The organization may be vertical, with the first activity at the top of the schedule and subsequent activities below. Or, if using a schedule book, pictures are typically organized one per page. With either method, the child consults the first picture to determine what he or she is to do. After completing the task, the picture is removed or covered up or the page is turned, and the child engages in the activity depicted in the next picture.

The clinician who uses visual schedules in occupational therapy services should be responsible initially for establishing the activities to be carried out in the therapy session. He or she will arrange pictures into a visual schedule by placing them in a sequential manner in a binder, on a poster board, on a clipboard, or on some other firm, portable surface. The clinician should then present the schedule to the child, beginning with the first activity and progressing through the sequence of activities in order, saying, for example, "First, we will ____, then, we will ____" while pointing to the first and second pictures and so on. After reviewing the entire schedule, the therapist reminds the child of the first activity by pointing to it and labeling it. The child is then guided to participate in the first activity. When the first activity is completed, both the therapist and child return to the schedule. The therapist states that the activity is finished or "all done" and removes the picture, placing it in the "all done" box or in an envelope at the bottom of the schedule. The next activity is now the first picture in the sequence. The therapist points to it and says, "Now it is time for ____." As the child learns the sequence of following the schedule and removing pictures as activities are completed, he or she may begin participating in the removal of pictures and in the identification of the next activity. Eventually, the child may help set up the schedule by choosing pictures from the binder and arranging them on the schedule. The child is independent when he or she is able to establish, consult, and follow his or her schedule with minimal or no cueing or assistance when performing familiar tasks. The therapist should keep in mind that the child may still need guidance or assistance to learn the steps of new skills or activities.

Visual scheduling can be an invaluable tool in the therapy environment for children who have difficulty with transitions, who tend to be anxious, or who have difficulty selecting and initiating a task. The visual structure that is provided by the schedule helps the child know what to do and when to do it. In addition, a child who is fussing or refusing to engage in an activity may be directed to consult his or her schedule, which can help to distract the child from a behavioral outburst and move him or her on to the next activity.

Occupational therapists can assist in the carrying out of structured teaching (a) by identifying developmentally appropriate activities to be taught, problem-solving issues related to physical organization, and materials that can be effectively manipulated by the child and (b) by incorporating sensory and motor elements into the child's daily schedule and routines.

Priming

Priming is not an educational system of its own but, rather, is an adult-supported strategy developed to help parents and residential support staff provide learning opportunities that might improve a child's success in the classroom (Wilde, Koegel, & Koegel, 1992). In essence, priming gives the child a preview of a new skill or task that he or she will be required to do but is likely to find difficult. This process familiarizes the child with the materials and expectations prior to the demand for performance. Typically, priming is done to prepare a child for learning a new topic or skill in school. Often, the parent conducts a priming session at home the afternoon or evening before the skill will be taught in school. Priming is not homework or a drill but is considered to be an opportunity to expose the child to new information in a nonthreatening situation. The purpose of priming is to increase a child's familiarity with an area of potential difficulty before those difficulties arise.

Priming begins with collaboration between the teacher and parent. By working together, a program is established that articulates what information will be taught in priming sessions, what teaching methods and materials will be used, how materials will be passed between school and home, and how success will be evaluated. A routine for when and where priming sessions will take place should be established. Because the goal of the priming session is to familiarize the child with the material, sessions are typically short and concise. Parents are encouraged to approach the sessions in a relaxed and positive manner, reinforcing all attempts the child produces. When presenting difficult material, the priming session might emphasize only one portion or critical component of the material. This limited exposure helps the child to learn the critical parts of the task so they are familiar when he or she encounters them in daily life.

The benefit of priming is that the child has an opportunity to become familiar with the salient aspects of the materials, which frees him or her to have increased attention and comprehension during the lesson at school and helps the child not to busy him- or herself with gathering information about the interesting aspects of the materials. Priming also improves communication and parent-professional collaboration. This method is often effective in ensuring that the family's needs are being addressed. In addition, priming ensures the occurrence of parent-child work time on a regular basis in a positive environment.

The final step in the priming process is feedback from the teacher who informs the parent of how the child performed during the lesson (Wilde, Koegel, & Koegel, 1992). Feedback allows both the parent and teacher to evaluate the success of the priming program. If a lesson is not primed for some reason, feedback still provides a valuable way to assess the effectiveness of priming. A training manual and additional information about priming are available. The manual includes procedural information and some strategies for troubleshooting potential problems that are associated with the priming process such as what to do if priming materials do not make it home or if the lesson that was primed was not taught in class. Ordering information can be found in Appendix 9.B.

Research on Priming

Published research exploring the benefits of priming is limited. One study (Koegel, O'Dell, & Dunlap, 1988) suggested that priming that was combined with reinforcement increased language production in children with autism. Another study (Zanolli, Daggett, & Adams, 1996) applied a low-demand, high-reinforce-

ment priming paradigm to teach social interactions. In this study, each subject was taught by the classroom teacher to smile and make eye contact with a peer, touch the peer's hand, say the peer's name, and say simple phrases to the peer. Activity sessions in which the subject and peer engaged in a designated activity immediately followed the priming session. In the second phase of the study, priming and activity sessions were conducted within the typical classroom activities with all students present. The results of this study supported the use of priming as a successful method for teaching preschool children with autism to initiate interactions with peers.

Application of Priming

The concept of priming as preparation for high-demand performance situations is not directly relevant to traditional models of occupational therapy services. Occupational therapy sessions are typically conducted in a manner that maximizes the child's strengths and abilities while supporting his or her areas of deficits, thus eliminating situations that impose high performance demands on the child. However, occupational therapists may be able to foster the success of priming sessions. The occupational therapist can provide consultation regarding the priming environment, biomechanical or positioning concerns, developmental issues, or the sensorimotor components of the lessons in relation to children who are participating in priming sessions. The therapist may also find that consulting with both the parent and teacher about the use of appropriate activities to prepare a child for the learning situation is helpful. In addition, occupational therapy sessions might provide an optimal situation for priming to occur because the therapist could incorporate opportunities that would expose the child to activities or material that the child will need to learn in the near future.

Environmental Support Methods

Environmental methods use strategies in which the environment is changed and structured to increase the child's ability to understand, comply with requests, and learn. The activities typically use the least amount of adaptation necessary to include the child with autism. Environmental support strategies are useful because they foster independence; increase the child's ability to understand the environment, which often leads to a reduction in behavior problems; directly address the child's cognitive impairment; and provide a way to generalize skills learned in a direct instruction model. In addition to those presented here, other environmental modifications may be used when approaching intervention from a sensory processing perspective.

Picture Exchange Communication System

The Picture Exchange Communication System (PECS) is an augmentative communication system that requires the exchange of pictures rather than words between the communicating parties (Bondy & Frost, 1994). Children are taught to exchange small picture cards with adults and other children to express their desires, answer questions, and make comments. Pictures can be line drawings, photographs, or pictures from magazines or computers. Most often, pictures are laminated and attached by means of hook and loop fasteners to a poster board or, for easier portability, to the pages of a binder. An adult is responsible for making sure the picture source is available to the child at all times. Figure 9.4 shows a child using this system.

Initially, children receive manual assistance to help them learn the system. Later, the child gives a picture to another person when he or she wants a specific object. The person responds, "Oh, you want a ____. Here it is" and gives the child the object. No verbal prompts

Figure 9.4

Child using the Picture Exchange Communication System (PECS) to communicate his desire to the therapist.

are used in connection with the system to prevent the child from becoming dependent on them. The emphasis of the system is both to increase the initiation of communication and to improve the effectiveness of communication (Bondy & Frost, 1994). After many repetitions, the teacher, holding the desired object, moves farther away from the child so the child learns to go to the teacher to make his or her request. Some children are able to combine pictures on sentence strips to use PECS not only for requesting but also for commenting and engaging in social communication. The picture vocabulary of the child gradually increases as he or she demonstrates mastery of the picture exchange process. At the most advanced levels, the child uses a series of pictures on a sentence strip to exchange information with his or her teachers, parents, and peers.

Research on PECS. The Picture Exchange Communication System has become a widely known and used augmentative communication system for children with autism. Although many reports and anecdotal accounts about the use of PECS are available, little empirical information has been compiled about its efficacy. A study by Schwartz, Garfinkle, and Bauer (1998) explored both the rate of acquisition of the PECS system and the generalization of its use to different settings. Researchers found that, within a comprehensive early childhood education program, PECS was learned quickly by preschool-age children, providing them with an effective method of communication within an average of 14 months. In addition, all participants in the study generalized the use of PECS to various settings and to untrained communicative functions, and 44% of the participants acquired spontaneous spoken communication. These empirical findings supported Bondy and Frost (1994), who stated that PECS could effectively teach functional communication and help children acquire spoken language.

Application of PECS. The Picture Exchange Communication System is easily adapted and used within the context of occupational therapy services. Picture symbols of therapy equipment and activities can be used. After lamination and assembly into a book, the occupational therapist can use the system in many ways according to the abilities of his or her clients. For a young child who is new to PECS, the therapist may help the child learn that a picture represents an activity by placing the picture symbol in front of a desired object. As the child reaches for the object, he or she sees the picture and begins to associate its meaning. As the child becomes more skilled at using the pictures, entire therapy sessions can be structured with PECS. The therapist can preselect two or more pictures and have the child choose the activity in which he or she would like to engage. Or, at a more advanced level, the child can be allowed to select pictures independently to request activities or to establish a schedule for the session.

An extremely important part of the PECS system depends on the adult making sure that all the symbols available to the child represent objects or activities that are also available. Saying no to an activity the child has chosen can cause confusion and result in behavior problems. Both the child and the therapist have a more positive experience if the activities that are not available to the child are not represented among the child's pictures. During therapy or in the classroom environment, the child should have access to pictures representing any materials he or she may need for a craft or art project. The child uses these pictures to request necessary items. The therapist responds to the requests and helps the child access, manipulate, and use the necessary tools and materials.

Token Systems

A token system is a concrete, visual method to incorporate predictability and positive reinforcement into a teaching session. Although the way that token systems are used may vary, the basic principles are consistent: The child earns tokens for each task that he or she performs or answers correctly. A variation on this method allows the child to exchange a predetermined number of tokens for a reward.

For young children, token systems are established in a way that visually represents the amount of work to be done, the number of trials already completed versus those remaining, and what happens when the task is complete. This type of system typically uses a board or other surface with 5 or more spaces, representing the number of trials to be presented. After each trial, the child is given a token to attach to the board, filling in one space. Tokens are often attached to the board with hook and loop fasteners. When all spaces are filled, the work is complete, and the child is rewarded. Some systems include a final space on the board for a picture or other representation of the activity that will occur after the work is completed. When all spaces are filled in, the child engages in the activity that is represented by that final

Figure 9.5
A token board made from laminated stickers.

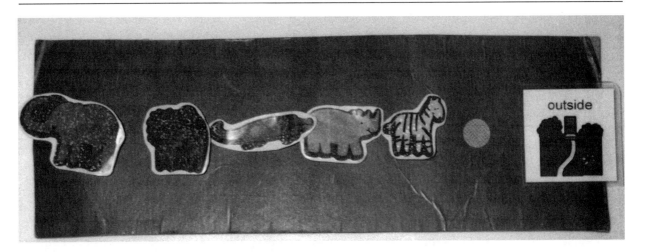

picture or object. Figure 9.5 shows a typical token board.

This strategy may be modified in many ways: changing the number of spaces to be filled in, having the child complete only one step of a task to earn the token, or requiring the child to complete more than one task before earning the token. Tokens may be plastic discs, pennies, laminated stickers of the child's favorite animals, or other small objects. The token board may or may not include a space for representation of the activity to follow the work. Tokens may be placed on the board by an adult or by the child, which adds a social component and helps the child to learn the concept and purpose of the token board.

Token systems also may be helpful to foster behaving appropriately, following classroom rules, playing nicely, or interacting appropriately with other children. The child may work throughout one day, multiple days, or an entire week to earn tokens. At predetermined times during the course of the day or week, the child may exchange his or her tokens to "purchase" a desired toy, treat, or activity. However, using the tokens in this way represents delayed grati-

fication, which can be a very difficult concept for some children with autism.

Research on Token Systems. Studies have been published supporting the effectiveness of token systems for children with disabilities (Miller & Schneider, 1970; Ruesch & McLaughlin, 1981). Detailed descriptions of token systems and information regarding how to carry out a token system is also available (Lyon & Lagarde, 1997; Sattler & Swoope, 1970).

Application of Token Systems. Token systems are readily applied within occupational therapy sessions. Because of the predictability that token systems bring to the teaching situation, they are extremely helpful when working with a child on a nonpreferred activity. At these times, a token system can be effective in helping the child direct and maintain his or her attention and energy until the task is completed. The purpose and function of token systems must be taught to the child through modeling and repetition. One suggestion is that the token system be taught within a preferred activity so the child's learning focuses on the system. Once the child understands how the tokens are earned and that completion of the token board results in concluding the task, the therapist can implement the system with a nonpreferred activity.

Peer Modeling

Another effective strategy for helping a child with autism to benefit from learning opportunities is to pair the child with a typically developing peer who is able to act as a model. The peer's role is to lead the child with autism from one activity to the next during transitions, help the child to successfully engage in play and work activities, demonstrate the appropriate use of materials, and assist the child with management of cartons and other packaging at snack time. Variations on this idea include having a different peer tutor for each type of activity or on different days of the week.

Research on Peer Modeling. Extensive research has been conducted to investigate the effectiveness of peers as models for children with autism. Beginning in the 1970s, studies exploring the effect of peer modeling of appropriate play with toys and appropriate social behaviors demonstrated increases in the appropriate play and interactions of children with autism (Guralnick, 1976). In addition, the effectiveness of peer modeling to teach sharing, problem solving, imitation, and appropriate classroom behavior has been demonstrated (Carr & Darcy, 1990; Koegel, Rincover, & Egel, 1982). Additional studies provide data that support the use of peer-mediated instruction techniques to meet individualized education plan (IEP) objectives and to increase social interaction and behavior (Garrison-Harrell, Kamps, & Kravits, 1997; Kohler, Strain, Hoyson, & Jamieson, 1997; Peck, Sasso, & Jolivette, 1997; Pierce & Schreibman, 1997).

Application of Peer Modeling. The use of peers within occupational therapy sessions is most readily applied in school system practice. Given the large body of literature substantiating the effectiveness of this method, it may be especially beneficial. To put a peer model system into effect, the occupational therapist would need to recruit and train at least one peer whose parents would support the peer tutor program. In addition, collaboration with the classroom teacher would be essential to prevent the child from missing valuable classroom time.

Initially, the therapist would need to provide direct instruction to the peer in how to model both activities and interactions in a manner that the child with autism could learn from the demonstration. Included in this direct instruction should be training that guides the peer's communication style and strategies, especially emphasizing the use of specific instructions such as "Watch me" and the use of simple, direct phrases like "Put the block in the can" or "No, do it like this." Additional training should include methods by which the peer could provide gentle physical assistance to the target child, similar to the prompting strategies described above. The peer should be instructed that his or her role is to be a "teacher's helper" in showing the target child how to do activities. Specific information about peer intervention programs and specific details regarding how to carry out these programs are available. Ordering information is in Appendix 9.B.

Transition Objects

Conscientious use of objects to direct a child from one activity to the next can be helpful. Transition objects are items that clearly represent the different activities that make up the child's day. When it is time to transition to a new activity, the child is given a representational item in addition to a simple verbal instruction that specifies the new activity. For example, to help a child transition to snack time, the therapist may give the child a plate or cup and say, "Time for snack." Consistent use of the same object and verbal instruction as a pair for a particular activity is important during training, and transition objects should be used consistently for each transition in the child's day.

Transitional objects or pictures can be used to help the child transition between activities or rooms. In these methods, the child is given a representational object or picture that communicates what he or she is to do next. For example, if the child is to work at the table, he or she may be given a pencil to represent handwriting, a picture of a table, or a small chair from a dollhouse indicating that it is time to sit.

After the child has become knowledgeable about the use of objects to represent transition, he or she can be taught to use objects to request a desired item. At first, the child must be taught to use the object in a way similar to teaching a child to use PECS. After reaching has been initiated but before it is completed, the teacher or therapist interrupts the child's reach for the object by placing the representative object in his or her way. The teacher or therapist helps the child to grasp and place the representational object in the adult's hand and then comments, "Oh, you want _____. Here it is," at which point the adult gives the object to the child. When using objects to make a request, it is important that the object always be available to the child and that the desired item or activity is an acceptable choice whenever the child gives the object to the adult.

After the child has learned to use transition objects to request and independently engages with the activity once it is given to him or her, he or she is ready to learn to make choices using objects. The therapist can hold two familiar transition objects in front of the child and encourage him or her to choose which activity he or she would prefer. Initially, a desired object should be paired with an undesirable object, for example, food (desired) and an empty soap container (undesired). If the child chooses the undesired item, he or she should be encouraged to engage with it for a few moments anyway. In this way the child learns the effects of choice making. If the child's choice is unclear, the trial can be readministered with the preferred and undesirable objects, providing prompting as

necessary. Making choices is an important step in learning the power of communication.

Research on Transition Objects. The use of objects to cue a child to transition to a new activity is one type of teacher-directed antecedent prompting. While no research examining the use of transition objects was found, research regarding antecedent prompting procedures suggests that antecedent prompting is more effective than use of consequences in facilitating transitions between activities (Sainato, 1990; Sainato, Strain, Lefebvre, & Rapp, 1987).

Application of Using Transition Objects. The methods of using transition objects both for expressive communication and for making choices are easily incorporated into occupational therapy sessions. These techniques closely parallel the PECS methods; however, objects rather than pictures are used. Objects provide the child with a more concrete representation of the task or choice because they provide a tactile element in addition to the visual cue provided by pictures.

To carry out the use of objects for transitions, expressive communication, or choice making, the therapist must first determine what activities would need to be represented. Then, representational objects would need to be purchased or created. The therapist should use systematic procedures to introduce the system to the child. He or she begins with only one object, gives it to the child while saying to him or her, "It is time to _____," and then guides the child to participate in the represented activity. At the conclusion of that activity, the therapist gives the child whatever object represents the next activity and says, "It is time for _____."

Just as with PECS, the goal is for the child to independently initiate use of the objects in an expressive manner. Often, the use of objects to represent transitions or choices is a provisional method of communication than can help to alleviate many behavioral problems. Choices can be offered at snack time by having the child choose between two snacks or items. It is important for the therapist to acknowledge each choice the child makes and to follow through accordingly. If the child chooses mustard instead of a donut, he or she receives mustard. Perhaps he or she will choose the donut the next time. If the technique proves to be effective, it is easily carried out within home, school, and community environments, provided the adult is prepared with the necessary representational objects.

Summary

Children with autism may participate in a wide array of intervention strategies designed to improve skill development. Among these strategies are those that can be classified into behavioral and educational approaches. Occupational therapists who work with children with autism should be familiar with the methods used in these programs so they can effectively participate in interdisciplinary collaboration and program planning to meet the complex needs of children with this condition.

Many of the behavioral and educational approaches described in this chapter were designed originally to stand alone as intervention methods for children with disabilities, including autism. However, recent changes in the way that intervention programs are designed support the combination of one or more of these approaches into a comprehensive program. As described above, many of the behavioral and educational approaches were designed to help develop skills in specific areas. By selecting an assortment of strategies and techniques, intervention programs can be designed that provide a variety of opportunities for children to develop a wide range of skills. Therapists can often beneficially incorporate behavioral and educational techniques with other strategies such as a developmental approach, the Affolter approach, or sensory integration, to create a program that is truly comprehensive. Occupational therapists who are well educated about the assortment of intervention options can be instrumental in helping families to identify and select those approaches that are most likely to address an individual child's complex needs.

References

Anderson, S., Avery, D., DiPietro, E., Edwards, G., & Christian, W. (1987). Intensive home-based early intervention with autistic children. *Education and Treatment of Children, 10,* 352–366.

Baer, D. M. (1993). Quasi-random assignment can be as convincing as random assignment. *American Journal of Mental Retardation, 97,* 373–375.

Billingsley, F. F., Liberty, K. L., & White, O. R. (1994). The technology of instruction. In E. C. Cipani & F. Spooner (Eds.), *Curricular and instructional approaches for persons with severe disabilities* (pp. 81–116). Newton, MA: Allyn & Bacon.

Bondy, A., & Frost, L. (1994). The picture exchange communication system. *Focus on Autistic Behavior, 9,* 1–19.

Carr, E. G., & Darcy, M. (1990). Setting generality of peer modeling in children with autism. *Journal of Autism and Developmental Disorders, 20,* 45–59.

Faherty, C., & Hearsey, K. (1996). *Visually structured tasks: Independent activities for students with autism and other visual learners.* Chapel Hill, NC: Division TEACCH, University of North Carolina.

Fenske, E., Zalenski, S., Krantz, P., & McClannahan, L. (1985). Age at intervention and treatment outcome for autistic children in a comprehensive intervention program. *Analysis and Intervention in Developmental Disabilities, 5,* 7–31.

Garrison-Harrell, L., Kamps, D. M., & Kravits, T. (1997). The effects of peer networks on social-communicative behaviors for students with autism. *Focus on Autism and Other Developmental Disabilities, 12,* 241–254.

Gresham, F. M., & MacMillan, D. L. (1997a). Autistic recovery? An analysis and critique of the empirical evidence on the early intervention project. *Behavioral Disorders, 22,* 185–201.

Gresham, F. M., & MacMillan, D. L. (1997b). Denial and defensiveness in the place of fact and reason: Rejoinder to Smith and Lovaas. *Behavioral Disorders, 22,* 219–230.

Gurlnick, M. (1976). The value of integrating handicapped and nonhandicapped preschool children. *American Journal of Orthopsychiatry, 46,* 236–245.

Harris, S., & Handleman, J. (Eds.). (1994). *Preschool education programs for children with autism.* Austin, TX: PRO-ED.

Hart, B., & Risley, T. (1968). Establishing use of descriptive adjectives in the spontaneous speech of disadvantaged preschool children. *Journal of Applied Behavior Analysis, 1,* 109–120.

Hart, B., & Risley, T. (1974). Using preschool materials to modify the language of disadvantaged children. *Journal of Applied Behavior Analysis, 7,* 243–256.

Hoyson, M., Jamieson, B., & Strain, P. (1984). Individualized group instruction of normally developing autistic-like children: A description and evaluation of the LEAP curriculum model. *Journal of the Division for Early Childhood, 8,* 157–171.

Kazdin, A. E. (1993). Replication and extension of behavioral treatment of autistic disorder. *American Journal of Mental Retardation, 97,* 377–379.

Koegel, R. L., & Frea, W. D. (1993). Treatment of social behavior in autism through the modification of pivotal social skills. *Journal of Applied Behavior Analysis, 26,* 369–377.

Koegel, R. L., Koegel, L. K., Frea, W. D., & Smith, A. E. (1995). Emerging interventions for children with autism. In R. L. Koegel and L. K. Koegel (Eds.), *Teaching children with autism: Strategies for initiating positive interactions and improving learning opportunities* (pp. 1–15). Baltimore: Brookes.

Koegel, R. L., Koegel, L. K., & Surrat, A. (1992). Language intervention and disruptive behavior in preschool children with autism. *Journal of Autism and Developmental Disorders, 22,* 141–154.

Koegel, R. L., O'Dell, M., & Dunlap, G. (1988). Producing speech use in nonverbal autistic children by reinforcing attempts. *Journal of Autism and Developmental Disorders, 18,* 525–538.

Koegel, R. L., Rincover, A., & Egel, A. L. (Eds.). (1982). *Educating and understanding autistic children.* San Diego, CA: College-Hill Press.

Koegel, R. L., Schreibman, L., Good, A., Cerniglia, L., Murphy, C., & Koegel, L. K. (1989). *How to teach pivotal behaviors to children with autism: A training manual.* Unpublished manuscript, Graduate School of Education, University of California at Santa Barbara.

Kohler, F. W., Strain, P. S., Hoyson, M., & Jamieson, B. (1997). Merging naturalistic teaching and peer-based strategies to address IEP objectives of preschoolers with autism: An examination of structural and child behavior outcomes. *Focus on Autism and Other Developmental Disabilities, 12,* 196–206.

Llorens, L. A. (1974). The effects of stress on growth and development. *American Journal of Occupational Therapy, 28,* 82–86.

Loos, L. M. (1998, June). *Pivotal response training: Enhancing acquisition, generalization and maintenance of language and play.* Paper presented at the meeting of Families for Early Autism Treatment of Washington, Bellevue, WA.

Lord, C., & Schopler, E. (1994). TEACCH services for preschool children. In S. L. Harris and J. S. Handleman (Eds.), *Preschool education programs for children with autism* (pp. 87–106). Austin, TX: PRO-ED.

Lovaas, O. I. (1987). Behavioral treatment and normal educational and intellectual functioning in young autistic children. *Journal of Consulting and Clinical Psychology, 55,* 3–9.

Lovaas, O. I., & Smith, T. (1988). Intensive behavioral treatment for young autistic children. In B. B. Lahey & A. E. Kazdin (Eds.), *Advances in clinical child psychology* (Vol. 11, pp. 285–324). New York: Plenum.

Lyon, C. S., & Lagarde, R. (1997). Tokens for success: Using the graduated reinforcement system. *Teaching Exceptional Children, 29,* 52–57.

Marcus, L. M., Lansing, M., Andrews, C. E., & Schopler, E. (1978). Improvement of teaching effectiveness in parents of autistic children. *Journal of the American Academy of Child Psychiatry, 17,* 625–639.

McEachin, J. J., Smith, T., & Lovaas, O. I. (1993). Long-term outcome for children with autism who received early intensive behavioral treatment. *American Journal of Mental Retardation, 97,* 359–372.

Mesibov, G. B. (1993). Treatment outcome is encouraging. *American Journal of Mental Retardation, 97,* 379–380.

Mesibov, G. B., Schopler, E., & Hearsey, K. A. (1994). Structured teaching. In E. Schopler and G. B. Mesibov (Eds.), *Behavioral issues in autism* (pp. 195–207). New York: Plenum.

Miller, A. (1991). Cognitive-developmental systems theory in Pervasive Developmental Disorders. In J. Beitchman & M. M. Konstonatreas (Eds.), *Psychiatric Clinics of North America: Vol. 14. Pervasive Developmental Disorders* (pp. 141–161). Philadelphia: Saunders.

Miller, A., & Eller-Miller, E. (1989). *From ritual to repertoire I: A cognitive developmental systems approach with behavior disordered children*. New York: Wiley.

Miller, A., & Eller-Miller, E. (1999). *A new way with autistic and other children with pervasive developmental disorders* [Brochure]. Boston: Language and Cognitive Development Center.

Miller, A., & Miller, E. E. (1973). Cognitive-developmental training with elevated boards and sign language. *Journal of Autism and Childhood Schizophrenia, 3,* 65–85.

Miller, L. K., & Schneider, R. (1970). The use of a token system in project Head Start. *Journal of Applied Behavior Analysis, 3,* 213–220.

Noonan, M. J., & McCormick, L. (1993). *Early intervention in natural environments*. Pacific Grove, CA: Brooks/Cole.

Ozonoff, S., & Cathcart, K. (1998). Effectiveness of a home program intervention for young children with autism. *Journal of Autism and Developmental Disorders, 28,* 25–32.

Peck, J., Sasso, G. M., & Jolivette, K. (1997). Use of the structural analysis hypothesis testing model to improve social interactions via peer-mediated intervention. *Focus on Autism and Other Developmental Disabilities, 12,* 219–230.

Pierce, K., & Schreibman, L. (1997). Using peer trainers to promote social behavior in autism: Are they effective at enhancing multiple social modalities? *Focus on Autism and Other Developmental Disabilities, 12,* 207–218.

Rogers, S. J. (1996). Brief report: Early intervention in autism. *Journal of Autism and Developmental Disorders, 26,* 243–246.

Rogers, S. J., & DiLalla, D. L. (1991). A comparative study of the effects of a developmentally based instructional model on young children with autism and young children with other disorders of behavior and development. *Topics in Early Childhood Special Education, 11,* 29–47.

Rogers, S. J., & Lewis, H. (1989). An effective day treatment model for young children with pervasive developmental disorders. *Journal of the American Academy of Child and Adolescent Psychiatry, 28,* 207–214.

Rogers-Warren, A., & Warren, S. (1980). Mands for verbalization: Facilitating the display of newly trained language in children. *Behavior Modification, 4,* 361–382.

Rosenblatt, J., Bloom, P., & Koegel, R. L. (1995). Overselective responding: Description, implications, and intervention. In R. L. Koegel and L. K. Koegel (Eds.), *Teaching children with autism: Strategies for initiating positive interactions and improving learning opportunities* (pp. 33–42). Baltimore: Brookes.

Ruesch, U., & McLaughlin, T. F. (1981). Effects of a token system using a free-time contingency to increase assignment completion with individuals in the regular classroom. *Journal of Special Education, 5,* 347–351.

Sainato, D. M. (1990). Classroom transitions: Organizing environments to promote independent performance in preschool children with disabilities. *Education and Treatment of Children, 13,* 288–297.

Sainato, D. M., Strain, P. S., Lefebvre, D., & Rapp, N. (1987). Facilitating transition times with handicapped preschool children: A comparison between peer-mediated and antecedent prompt procedures. *Journal of Applied Behavior Analysis, 20,* 285–291.

Sattler, H. E., & Swoope, K. S. (1970). Token systems: A procedural guide. *Psychology in the Schools, 7,* 383–386.

Schopler, E. (1987). Specific and nonspecific factors in the effectiveness of a treatment system. *American Psychologist, 42,* 376–383.

Schopler, E., Brehm, S., Kinsbourne, M., & Reichler, R. J. (1971). The effect of treatment structure on development in autistic children. *Archives of General Psychiatry, 24,* 415–421.

Schopler, E., Mesibov, G. B., & Baker, A. (1982). Evaluation of treatment for autistic children and their parents. *Journal of the American Academy of Child Psychiatry, 21,* 262–267.

Schopler, E., Mesibov, G. B., & Hearsey, K. (1995). Structured teaching in the TEACCH system. In E. Schopler & G. B. Mesibov (Eds.), *Learning and cognition in autism* (pp. 243–268). New York: Plenum.

Schreibman, L., Stahmer, A. C., & Pierce, K. L. (1996). Alternative applications of pivotal response training: Teaching symbolic play and social interaction skills. In L. K. Koegel & R. L. Koegel (Eds.), *Positive behavioral support: Including people with difficult behavior in the community* (pp. 353–371). Baltimore: Brookes.

Schuster, J. W., & Griffen, A. K. (1990, Summer). Using time delay with task analysis. *Teaching Exceptional Children, 22,* 49–53.

Schwartz, I. S., Garfinkle, A. N., & Bauer, J. (1998). The picture exchange communication system: Communicative outcomes for young children with disabilities. *Topics in Early Childhood Special Education, 18,* 144–159.

Sulzer-Azaroff, B., & Mayer, G. R. (Eds.). (1991). *Behavior analysis for lasting change.* San Francisco: Holt, Rinehart, & Winston.

Walls, R. T., Zane, T., & Ellis, W. D. (1981). Forward and backward chaining and whole task methods. *Behavior Modification, 5,* 61–74.

Wilde, L. D., Koegel, L. K., & Koegel, R. L. (1992). *Increasing success in school through priming: A training manual.* Unpublished manuscript, Graduate School of Education, University of California at Santa Barbara.

Zanolli, K., Daggett, J., & Adams, T. (1996). Teaching preschool age autistic children to make spontaneous initiations to peers using priming. *Journal of Autism and Developmental Disorders, 26,* 407–422.

Zelazo, P. R. (1997). Infant-toddler information processing treatment of children with pervasive developmental disorder and autism, Part II. *Infants and Young Children, 10*(2), 1–13.

Appendix 9.A
Selected References on Discrete Trial Methods for Children With Autism

Cattell-Gordon, D., & Cattell-Gordon, D. (1998). The development of an effective applied behavioral analysis program for a young child with autism: A parent's perspective. *Infants and Young Children, 10,* 79–85.

Feinberg, E., & Beyer, J. (1998). Creating public policy in a climate of clinical indeterminacy: Lovaas as the case example du jour. *Infants and Young Children, 10,* 54–66.

Gresham, F. M., & MacMillan, D. L. (1997). Autistic recovery? An analysis and critique of the empirical evidence on the early intervention project. *Behavioral Disorders, 22,* 185–201.

Gresham, F. M., & MacMillan, D. L. (1997). Denial and defensiveness in the place of fact and reason: Rejoinder to Smith and Lovaas. *Behavioral Disorders, 22,* 219–230.

Lovaas, O. I. (1987). Behavioral treatment and normal educational and intellectual function-ing in young autistic children. *Journal of Consulting and Clinical Psychology, 55,* 3–9.

Maurice, C. (1996). *Behavioral interventions for young children with autism: A manual for parents and professionals.* Austin, TX: PRO-ED.

McEachin, J. J., Smith, T., & Lovaas, O. I. (1993). Long-term outcome for children with autism who received early intensive behavioral treat-ment. *American Journal of Mental Retardation, 97,* 359–372.

Rogers, S. J. (1996). Brief report: Early intervention in autism. *Journal of Autism and Developmental Disorders, 26,* 243–246.

Smith, T., & Lovaas, O. I. (1997). The UCLA young autism project: A reply to Gresham and MacMillan. *Behavioral Disorders, 22,* 202–218.

Smith, T., & Lovaas, O. I. (1998). Intensive and early behavioral intervention with autism: The UCLA young autism project. *Infants and Young Children, 10,* 67–78.

Appendix 9.B
Contact Information

Teaching Pivotal Behaviors: A Training Manual

Robert L. Koegel, PhD
Autism Research Center
Counseling/Clinical/School Psychology
  Program
Graduate School of Education
University of California at Santa Barbara
Santa Barbara, CA 93106

Structured Teaching

Division TEACCH
University of North Carolina
310 Medical School Wing E
Chapel Hill, NC 27599-7180
Phone: (919) 966-2174

Priming

Robert L. Koegel, PhD
Autism Research Center
Counseling/Clinical/School Psychology
  Program
Graduate School of Education
University of California at Santa Barbara
Santa Barbara, CA 93106

Peer Modeling

Catherine Lord, PhD
Department of Psychiatry
University of Chicago Hospital
Chicago, IL 60637

Appendix 9.C
References for the Miller Method®

Cook, C. E. (1997). *Application of the Miller Method® with preschool children with autism or pervasive developmental disorder.* Unpublished doctoral dissertation, Kent State University, Kent, OH.

Miller, A. (1968). *Symbol accentuation—A new approach to reading.* New York: Doubleday.

Miller A., & Miller E. E. (1968). Symbol accentuation: The perceptual transfer of meaning from spoken to written words. *American Journal of Mental Deficiency, 73,* 200–208.

Miller, A., & Miller E. E. (1971). Symbol accentuation, single track functioning and early reading. *American Journal of Mental Deficiency, 76,* 110–117.

Miller, A., & Miller, E. E. (1973). Cognitive developmental training with elevated boards and sign language. *Journal of Autism and Childhood Schizophrenia, 3,* 65–85.

Miller, A., & Eller-Miller, E. (1989). *From ritual to repertoire: A cognitive-developmental systems approach with behavior disordered children.* New York: Wiley.

Further information on the Miller Method® may be obtained by contacting Dr. Arnold Miller, Executive Director, Language and Cognitive Development Center, PO Box 270, 11 Wyman Street, Boston (JP), MA 02130.

CHAPTER 10

Assistive Technology for Students With Autism

Barbaralyn Harden, MS, CCC-SP

Assistive technology devices are any simple or complex tools that enhance learning, communication, leisure pursuits, or socialization. Rapid growth in the field has created a multitude of technology options, allowing individual accommodations for special needs. Children with autism and other PDDs demonstrate significant variation of skills and abilities as well as unique characteristics across the diagnostic spectrum. These variations require an intervention approach that allows for flexibility and variability. Technology can provide that flexibility and variability. Children with a PDD may particularly benefit from the use of technology because many technology devices allow predictability, clarity, and a strong emphasis on visual stimulation. Therefore, occupational therapists who work with children with a PDD would benefit from having knowledge of and access to appropriate technology to use with this population. To best use technology with this population, one needs to understand the tools themselves, the requirements of the laws that affect the delivery of technology services, and the condition of autism. In addition, knowledge of funding issues is also beneficial.

Finally, because technology decisions are usually made by a team of professionals, the therapist should feel comfortable as a team member. The occupational therapist's knowledge base in activity adaptation and task analysis allows him or her to function as an integral member of the technology team. The practitioner must understand his or her role in using technology and how best to function within the team. The team's knowledge of specific tools that are available in assistive technology or in augmentative communication technology may influence the decisions it reaches. However, whatever devices are chosen, the team must remember to use technology as a tool to achieve a goal rather than as an end in itself.

Many books have been written on the subject of assistive technology. This chapter is not intended to give an in-depth look at all assistive technology but, rather, to provide a general discussion of assistive technology components. For the purposes of this chapter, assistive technology will be limited to computer adaptations and augmentative communication technology. Considerations for technology intervention with this specific population, information on legal requirements for technology decisions, team decision making, and the practitioner's role within the team will be included.

Legal Issues in Assistive Technology

When working with any population of children, one must consider whatever legal requirements affect intervention. The legal requirements for the use of technology in the schools have a long history. In 1975, the Education for All Handicapped Children Act (1972) [PL 94–142] was enacted, allowing for the design and use of technology for children with disabilities who receive special education services. The 1986 amendments to this law [PL 99–457] continued to support previous technology delivery and extended the reach of the law to children of younger ages. In 1990, the title of the law was changed to the Individuals with Disabilities Education Act (IDEA) [PL 101–476], and IDEA was reauthorized in 1997 [PL 105–17]. Assistive technology has been defined by the reauthorized IDEA (1997) as "any item, piece of equipment or product system, whether acquired commercially off the shelf, modified, or customized, that is used to increase, maintain, or improve functional capabilities of individuals with disabilities"(p. 300.5). A broad definition such as this one implies that assistive technology can be either a simple tool like a pencil grip or a complex device like a computer with a switch interface and adapted switches (Chambers, 1997). IDEA requires that technology be considered for all students receiving special education. In a school district, the application of technology must be related to the impact the students' disability has on his or her education.

However, if a student does not qualify for services under IDEA, he or she still may be eligible for assistive technology under section 504 of the Rehabilitation Act of 1973 [PL 93–112] and 1992 [PL 99–506] or under the Americans with Disabilities Act (1990) [PL 101–336].

Occupational Therapy and the Use of Technology

Human occupation stems from the innate urge to explore and master one's environment (Kielhofner & Burke, 1980). A person must use physical and sensory abilities to perform that exploration. When physical, sensory, or cognitive obstacles limit a person's ability to explore his or her environment, assistive technology can enable that person to overcome certain obstacles and continue his or her exploration through other means. Keeping in mind that technology is a tool, or a means to an end, technology can be used within occupational therapy intervention to achieve mastery in human occupation and allow for greater participation in life roles and performance areas. For example, technology can be used as an intervention tool to enhance learning or communication, to increase independence, to assist in peer relationship building, to provide leisure pursuits, and to provide greater job opportunities for the older student with a PDD. To effectively use technology interventions, the professional who works with this population should be familiar with the options available in technology, be knowledgeable about working on a team, and understand the characteristics of PDDs. For the occupational therapy practitioner, these competencies may require developing the following basic skills or abilities as described by Smith (1991):

- To become a technology problem solver by using assistive technology to increase a person's functional independence
- To see one's self as the human technology-environmental expert
- To gain a basic comfort level with low and high technology
- To gain basic literacy in technology-related areas
- To understand one's limits in the area of assistive technology
- To understand the ethical issues surrounding the use of assistive technology

In addition, the practitioner is encouraged to develop the ability to actively evaluate not only anticipated but also actual outcomes. Technology is rapidly advancing and each addition to the technology pool should be considered in how it may effect outcomes. Technology should be used in order to achieve outcomes not easily attained by other means. It is essential that the practitioner recognize that technology is but a tool to achieving the outcome. For example, we don't teach "pencil." Instead, we teach writing and in the process of writing, children learn how to hold a pencil, to sharpen it, to use the eraser, the pressure needed to write, etc. By evaluating actual outcomes and comparing them to anticipated outcomes, the practitioner can establish the effectiveness of the tools used and can remain focused on using the tools as a method to achieve functional goals.

Team Collaboration

Collaboration is essential when dealing with technological applications because many areas of performance cross several professional areas of expertise. Team members in technology decision making typically include therapists, educators, paraeducators, and administrators. In addition, parents should be active, participating team members in the process to decide effective intervention (Cook & Hussey, 1995). Many decisions regarding assistive technology require administrative support; therefore, an administrator also may become an important member of the team.

Collaboration among team members results in optimal assistive technology services (Beukelman & Mirenda, 1992). For collaboration to take place, team meetings must occur on a regular basis. When identifying technology applications and responding to the behaviors and the learning style of a child with autism, it is critical that team meetings occur not only consistently but also frequently.

Effective team collaboration requires skills in the areas of communication and group processes. Such skills may include active listening, negotiation, the ability to provide nonthreatening feedback, and the ability to accept criticism without becoming defensive (Dettmer, Thurston, & Dyck, 1993). Communication is built on trust. Building trust within a team takes time. Essentials for team development are regular meetings, written agendas, knowledge of team roles, productive communication, plans to deal with conflict, support for training in new skill areas, and trust building. (Fisher, Rayner, & Belgard, 1995).

Often, the human component of teaming is what creates obstacles for the child's success in learning. The breakdown of team collaboration can have disastrous consequences for a child. For example, the team may agree for a student to use a trackball instead of a mouse on a computer. However, one member does not know how to hook up the trackball and is of the opinion that the student could learn the mouse if given training. Consequently, rather than admit that he or she does not know the skill of setting up the trackball, the member struggles with the student's behavior when using the mouse. Because this member works alone with the student in the computer room, no one realizes that the trackball is not used. The student's frustration with the mouse leads to resistance at every computer work session. The resulting discussion during the next team meeting revolves around the student's dislike for the computer rather than around the confusion in using the adaptations.

One person's lack of skill and failure to communicate to the rest of the team can have a major effect on a student's success. In the area of technology, skills in setting up and troubleshooting are not innate but must be learned through experience and training for both student and staff members. All team members must be willing to function as a member of a team to be effective.

Team roles are typically defined by professional expertise. However, critical teaming roles should be filled each team meeting and any team member with the appropriate knowledge base may take on any particular role. The critical element is that at least one member of the team has information or resources in each of the following areas:
• Technology devices that are available
• Funding sources
• Availability of local lending libraries

- Mobility and portability issues as well as the effect of assistive technology devices on mobility
- Family or cultural issues related to the use of technology
- Availability of equipment through the general education environment

An occupational therapist on the technology team may take on the role of task analyzer, equipment modifier, problem solver, student, staff trainer, or consultant. He or she may be called on in the beginning to assist in the initial determination of appropriate technology intervention and again, later, to assess its effect on function once it has been obtained. In addition, he or she may be called on to teach others to correctly use the equipment. The occupational therapist may be called on to modify equipment when it is not working correctly and, in this situation, may need to collaborate with educators, other therapists, and paraprofessionals about the appropriate use of the technology for any given student. The occupational therapist may also advocate to obtain funding to purchase appropriate technological interventions. In any case, the therapist must always be a collaborator with all other team members to be effective in whatever role he or she assumes.

Team Responsibilities

The technology team has certain responsibilities regarding the delivery of assistive technology services. Those responsibilities include the following:

- Consider assistive technology for the person with disabilities as required by law
- Determine if and how assistive technology can meet the intervention needs for the person with disabilities
- Become familiar and knowledgeable with assistive technology as a tool for intervention
- Continually evaluate whether the use of technology tools is an effective means to reach desired outcomes

- Use assistive technology and appropriate strategies consistently across settings
- Evaluate student or client progress and the continued need for assistive technology

Team Decision Making

A intervention team must progress through several decision-making phases. The first is to determine if technology is an appropriate and desirable intervention. If it is, then the second phase is to complete an assessment and decide on the appropriate technology. In the third phase, the team must determine whether or not a trial period is necessary or whether the technology can be directly purchased or leased. The fourth phase requires the team to make decisions regarding funding of the equipment to be obtained and then to actually obtain the recommended device or devices.

Step One: Deciding if Technology is Appropriate. When deciding if technology is appropriate for a student, one might first consider several questions:

- Will the student be able to learn the same task if the technology is unavailable?
- Is there a way to learn the task without technology that is easier or more clear?
- Does the technology make learning easier and more clear?
- Will problems or delays in the technology create more confusion?
- Will the technology interfere with accomplishing the task once the technology is no longer necessary?
- Can staff members use the technology with this student on a daily basis? Can they troubleshoot and adjust the technology?
- Can the technology be set up quickly and efficiently?
- Can adjustments be made quickly, and who will make them?

Step Two: Determining Appropriate Technology. The next phase of decision making involves determining what technology, if any, would bring about the best outcome. Using a clearly defined decision-making process within a team has been proven effective (Dettmer, Thurston, & Dyck, 1993; Prentice & Spencer, 1985). Bowser & Reed (1998) and Zabala (1994) suggest the following tasks as key elements of effective decision making when determining what type of technology intervention might be most appropriate:

- Identify the student's abilities and difficulties related to tasks
- Determine environmental considerations and potential changes
- Identify the task and determine what the student needs to do
- Generate solutions through brainstorming
- Discuss and select the best ideas generated from brainstorming
- Determine how to carry out the plan (what assistive technology, which assistive technology services, whether to have an assistive technology trial—how long, when, which people are responsible)

Each step of the above procedure should be completed as a team, and proper documentation of the results should be provided for the entire team. During the decision-making process, several of the key elements might need to be repeated.

Once the team determines that a technology intervention should be pursued, the team can ensure success of identified outcomes by specifically determining the type of technology to be used (light or high), efficiently setting up equipment, and developing a transition plan to move from the technology intervention to application of the acquired skill in desired settings or functional activities. Many different interventions may need to be incorporated daily into the student's routine. Consequently, if a program requires technology that an educational staff must use in the absence of the therapist, then factors such as familiarity, convenience, and speed in the setup should be considered.

Step Three: Determining Whether the Equipment Should Be Obtained on a Temporary or Permanent Basis. Once the team decides on an appropriate solution, the members will need to obtain the equipment for the student. However, first, the team must decide whether or not the equipment should be obtained permanently or on a trial basis. This determination will affect the decision to (a) borrow equipment from a lending source, (b) lease equipment for a short period of time, or (c) find funding to actually purchase the equipment for a certain student. Each case must be examined carefully, and the team must identify the criteria for determining the success of the technology intervention in advance. Once through, a timeline should be set. Thus the success or failure of an intervention will be predetermined and should indicate the need of extended trial for that or other interventions. If the intervention is hardware or software (not light technology), then plans for acquisition should be made. Once the predetermined criteria has been met, pursuit of a permanent acquisition should begin.

Step Four: Funding and Obtaining Technology. Purchasing equipment can be costly, and concerns about funding are commonplace. However, assistive technology can be funded in a variety of ways. If a disability has an educational impact, and the team determines that technology intervention is the appropriate accommodation or service, then the school must provide it. School districts may use alternative funding sources such as Medicaid or private insurance to purchase the technology. Some restrictions limit the use of private insurance, however, and if private insurance is used, its use could potentially affect a family's insurance policy coverage. Additional funding may be available within the community from sources such as fraternal organizations (e.g., Elks Clubs, Moose Lodges, and Rotary Clubs) or businesses. Community service organizations may agree to assist in funding certain equipment, and for older students, the vocational rehabilitation organizations may also be of some assistance. Although the search for funding is often a tedious process, funding sources are available, varying from state to state. Occupational therapy practitioners who serve children with autism should familiarize themselves not only with the funding options that are available locally but also with any organizations that provide a lending library of equipment or software.

Technology Options and Assistive Technology as Intervention

For a therapist to participate as a team member in determining what technology options are appropriate, he or she must be knowledgeable regarding what options exist. When evaluating and selecting technology, the therapist also should be familiar and comfortable with most of the available tools. More often than not, the student's success is either hindered or helped by the comfort level of the practitioner. In addition, the more comfortable the therapist is with the technology, the more flexible he or she can be in collaborating with the team and creating appropriate interventions for the student.

Assistive technology can generally be grouped according to whether it is hardware, software, high technology, or light technology (e.g., light technology devices or no technology interventions, such as pencil grips, language boards, etc.). Hardware is the machinery itself. Hardware technology includes alternative keyboards, mouse emulation devices, word processors, switches, augmentative and alternative communication (AAC) devices, and even computers themselves (see Table 10.1 for information on hardware). Software is the program that

---

Table 10.1
Description of Hardware Technology

Alternative and augmentative communication devices (AAC)
  Devices dedicated to providing speech output or printed output for communication purposes (for more detailed description see Table 10.3). Computer software can also turn the computer into an augmentative communication device.
Alternative input methods
  Direct selection methods
  These include mouse emulators, voice input, Morse code, light pointing, head pointing, and eye pointing systems. In short, the user's selection is indicated by direct physical input.
  Indirection selection or scanning
  These devices will "scan" a set of icons/words by moving a cursor, light, or sound across the selection options until the user hits a switch or switches to identify the desired selection.
Alternative keyboards
  These are plug in or "on screen" replacement keyboards. Plug in types are either larger or smaller than the standard computer keyboard. Some expanded keyboards allow for key-size adjustments and creation or elimination of "function keys" (e.g., the "return" key, "option," or "control" key). Some keyboards allow for picture rather than letter representation.
Mouse emulators
  These are devices such as joysticks, trackballs, remote mouse emulators (such as a head mouse), touch panels, track pads, etc., that replace the computer mouse.
Switches
  Switches are separate single or multiple keys that activate the device hardware or software. Switches frequently have enlarged or reduced strike areas or have alternate forms of activation such as pulling a string or breaking a light beam. Switches must be accompanied by a switch interface for the switch to activate the desired device.
Switch interface
  This is the electronically wired device that mediates between the switch and the device it is intended to activate such as an electronic toy or computer.

Table 10.2
Types and Functions of Software Technology

Standard Software "Off the shelf"

This software has no adaptations built into it and is intended for use by typically developing individuals. The functions can be exploratory, drill and practice, leisure, reinforcement, and expansion of already developed skills or of prior learning.

Adapted Software

Software has adaptations built into it. Some companies develop software that already permits scanning of various components and that has programmed "hot spots" that will be scanned if the scanning feature is selected. This software also includes mouse training software.

Augmentative Communication Software

This software allows the computer to become an augmentative communication device through adaptations built into the software that allow for communication display development, navigation, and message activation. Such software is frequently adapted for scanning the developed displays through a variety of methods.

Specialized Software

Mouse training software usually has specific targets and rewards for successive approximations toward a target.

Talking word processors usually function exactly like any other word processor with the exception that they use speech to give feedback to the user.

Word prediction software works in conjunction with a word processing program. The user types in the first letter after which a list of words starting with that letter appears. The user can then look at the various options and select the desired word if it is there. If not, then she or he can type in the next letter and a new list of words will appear.

Picture/symbol writing software allows a student to write a story using symbols or pictures; then, using speech output, it will retell the story. These programs allow the trainer to enter a list of required words, and the software will provide the symbols necessary to generate a written story.

Concept mapping software provides the user with tools to move from semantic webs and associations to outline formats using pictures and words.

Voice recognition requires software that allows the user to speak into a special computer microphone. The computer recognizes the words that are spoken and either executes the desired command or "types" the word into a word processor. The user must "teach" the software to recognize his or her voice. With increased use both speed and accuracy improve.

Virtual reality is software and hardware technology that allows the user to place himself or herself in the environment created by the computer. This environment controls for visual, auditory, and proprioceptive input to the user.

creates the activity or function performed by the hardware of the computer. Some software requires minimal hardware adaptations whereas other software requires specific hardware to operate. Software technologies discussed in this chapter include mouse training programs, voice recognition, word prediction, AAC communication software, and virtual reality software (see Table 10.2 for more information on software). AAC devices are often an integral component of a communication system and can be grouped into three categories: light technology or Voice Output Communication Aids (VOCAs), "grow-through" technology, and "high tech" devices (see Table 10.3 for information on AAC devices). Readers who are not familiar with using

assistive technology in the educational environment are also referred to Hammel and Niehues (1998). For more information and resources on technology devices and their uses please see the resources in Appendices 10.A and 10.B.

Hardware for Children With a Pervasive Developmental Disorder

Many children with a sole diagnosis of a pervasive developmental disorder will be able to use typical hardware off the shelf with minimal modifications. What will be important, however, is the way in which the hardware devices are introduced. Whenever introducing hardware, make sure that the function is clear and the

Table 10.3

Categories and Description of AAC Devices

Dedicated or nondedicated

This category refers to the use of the device. Dedicated devices are intended solely for communication purposes and will occasionally provide for such things as environmental control (e.g., Dynavox, AlphaTalker). Nondedicated devices (usually computers) will do a variety of tasks including communication that will usually require specialized software.

Light tech/VOCAs

These devices usually have less than a 50-message vocabulary and are typically less expensive. Having only a single level display, some devices may only have one or two message keys while others may have a display of 32, (e.g., TechTalk, BigMack, CheapTalk). This type of technology, when paired with a nonvoice output, picture-word communication system, is frequently effective for an individual whose communication is emerging.

"Grow through" devices

When a student's needs and skills are not fully developed, then questions regarding vocabulary size, whether meaningful speech will yet develop, or whether spelling skills will develop do not have clear answers. In these cases, the student may need a device for communication until those skills have an opportunity to develop. In other words, a student may need a device to "grow through," implying that he or she will end up with a different device than what he or she currently needs. If spelling, speech, or vocabulary needs do not develop adequately, then the student will not "grow through" such a device, and the device would be the one of final use. These devices, having a somewhat limited vocabulary, are less sophisticated than high-tech equipment (e.g., Macaw III, SuperHawk). They often leave out a text-to-speech component (when text is entered, then decoded and spoken). "Grow through" devices may overlap into the category of "high-tech" devices.

High tech

High-tech devices are relatively sophisticated. They use an icon-word representation, have a text-to-speech component, often use both synthetic and digitized speech, and allow for linking messages together (e.g., Vanguard, Green Macaw, Liberator). Most of the computer-based augmentative software falls into this category (e.g., Speaking Dynamically, Talk:About, Dynavox software). Many such devices and software can be used in a less sophisticated way to develop simpler skills as needed.

---

cues to performance are clear also. Tasks can be explained or supported with visuals such as the written word or picture prompts. Using visual cues such as written words, pictures, and icons highlights the salient features of the task. If verbal prompts are used, they should be varied, and their use should be faded so they do not become embedded in the routine.

If a student must perform a specific motor task such as using a finger to activate a target on a computer touch screen, model it in exactly the way the task will be performed. Otherwise, the student may become confused. Consider the following scenario, for example. While showing a student how to activate a touch screen (which the student will be doing with his finger), a practitioner uses a pointer or stylus to activate the screen. The student assumes that something about the pointer is making the computer work.

He begins to grab for the pointer and then attempts to guide the practitioner's hand that is holding the pointer. When the practitioner refuses and again encourages the student to point at the screen with his finger, the student's behavior escalates. This kind of situation can be avoided if the practitioner's model is identical to the expected performance by the student.

Impulsive behavior with motor actions is common and affects the introduction of hardware. For example, while learning to manipulate a mouse, a student often will click the mouse while moving it rather than, first, finding the target and then clicking. He or she may also click the mouse too frequently or too quickly, not waiting for appropriate visual cues. Specific training may be necessary. By introducing a visual representation of the sequence to be followed (see Figure 10.1) and by demonstrating the sequence, the practitioner might help prevent confusion. Fading this type of visual cue may or may not be necessary once the student has performed the same task on several different targets.

Software for Children with a PDD

A multitude of software is available off the shelf to perform a variety of functions. However, certain of the following groups of software may benefit students with a PDD.

Mouse Training Software. A student with a PDD may need specific training in the use of a mouse and in its function. Mouse training software should be clear in its visual presentation and in the presentation of relationships between mouse action and function. Verbal instructions should be paired with visuals when possible.

Talking Word-Processing Software. Talking word-processing software allows the machine to speak what has been typed. Most talking word processors use a variety of strategies for speech output such as speaking each letter, speaking each word, or speaking by sentences, thus, giving the user feedback as to what has been generated. For children with a PDD this flexible feedback may strengthen the relationship between the written and spoken word.

Picture-Symbol Writing Software. A recent generation of software allows a student to write a story using symbols or pictures. Some software demands that the written word be entered first and then allows the student to regenerate the sentence or story using symbols. Other programs allow the trainer to enter a list of required words, and the software then will provide the symbols necessary to generate a written story. This kind of software allows students with a PDD to generate written language, establish syntactic structures, and possibly, establish a stronger relationship among symbols, written words, and spoken language.

Word Prediction Software. Word prediction software enhances typing speed by allowing the computer to provide appropriate word

Figure 10.1
Visual representation of the sequence to be followed when using the hardware.

KidPix   Move Cursor   Click Mouse

choices that are based on the first typed letter. To use word prediction software, a user must be able to generate at least the first letter of a word and identify words by sight (or in some cases by sound because some of the programs will use an auditory listing of the words being predicted). The more sophisticated the software, the more likely it will learn the user's "language," namely, that it will remember unique words or predict words that the user chooses frequently.

Concept or Mind Mapping Software. Mind mapping software allows for the association of ideas in a "mind map" versus a linear outline format. It is more complex than flow chart software but is able to develop flow charts also. The software often uses both written words and pictures or icons. What may be most useful about this type of software is that ideas can be presented pictorially to demonstrate their relationship to one another. Visual representation of this type may appeal to the learning style of those with autism (Janzen, 1996). See Figure 10.2 for an example.

The software can also support more sophisticated learners, helping students identify salient features of information in visual form. Once the visual display is completed, the software converts the visual into an outline format. This concrete and visual representation might help a student with a PDD to identify and organize information by concept. The information is all visually represented and, thus, assists students in converting to a more linear representation, which is needed to express thoughts

Figure 10.2
The association of ideas in mind mapping software.

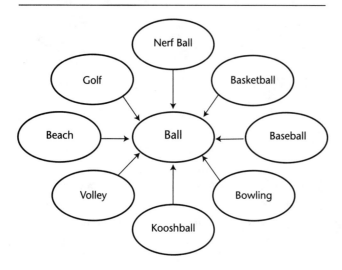

and ideas in written work such as an outline. See Figure 10.3 for an example.

Newer Technologies That May Be Appropriate for Children With a PDD

Technology that has more recently appeared on the market may have some potential benefit for children with a PDD. Such technologies include virtual reality and voice recognition. However, as there currently is little research exploring the specific benefits these types of products might provide for individuals with a PDD, we may only speculate on their usefulness.

Virtual Reality (VR). Virtual reality controls the stimulus that is presented and provides desired information in a format that looks, sounds, and feels like the real situation. For example, it can provide a "walk through" of a room. For a student with autism, learning a task with the salient features of that task visually highlighted in an unconfusing environment may be more likely to produce success with the actual task. Virtual reality could allow this type of learning. It might be used to provide a virtual-classroom view that includes only the relevant items to the task that needs to be performed. The developer might provide a controlled dialogue in which the student could participate. During this dialogue, prompts could be provided and programmed to fade over time. The advantage to virtual reality is that the developer can control the clarity of the environment, introducing only relevant information initially, then adding more stimuli as the student experiences success in reading the relevant cues in the environment. Helping the student learn to interpret different stimuli at a slow and controlled rate also increases the potential for success. However, access to the appropriate hardware and software for virtual reality is extremely limited, and little research has been done in this area.

Voice Recognition. The use of voice recognition devices has become popular in the mass market. Families with children who have speech that is not easily understood have shown increased interest. Conservative decisions should be made when considering this type of software solution. Students who use this software must understand the meaning of their own speech. A person who is proficient with the use of visual information may be a good candidate for voice recognition. The student who speaks and then sees his or her speech turned into the written word may learn more

Figure 10.3
An outline of a mind map for current events in mind mapping software.

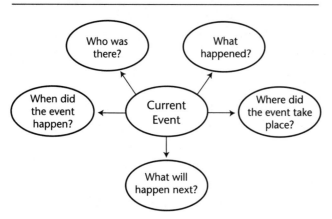

about written language and its relationship to the spoken word. However, if the student's speech lacks meaning, then voice recognition would serve only to translate meaningless speech into meaningless written words.

A child with a PDD may use a phrase that has a different intended meaning than what is actually spoken, a common behavior among children with this disorder. For example, a child may say "the monkey" to mean a request to go to the zoo. Consequently, the word *monkey* does not have the same meaning to the child as it does to the listener. If the child does not understand that the word *monkey* has a specific meaning for other people in his or her environment, then the child will not likely see the written word *monkey* as having any greater meaning than the child's spoken word.

Light-Tech Devices and Nonelectronic Interventions

Not all solutions need to involve electronic technology. When technology complicates a task rather than clarifies it, then the technology becomes an obstacle to learning. Light-tech (nonelectronic) solutions can be equally as effective and often are more so.

Visual Displays. Options such as visual displays (language boards, language books, or word displays containing symbols, pictures, or words that indicate the intended meaning) can be very effective. Information on selection and development of displays can be acquired from speech-language pathologists, speech-language professional journals, or books covering augmentative communication issues.

Facilitated Communication. Facilitated Communication (FC) is a form of communication whereby a Facilitator (usually an adult) lends physical support to the communicator either by supporting the hand in a pointing position or by providing physical support at the wrist, elbow, or shoulder. While the Facilitator is providing the support, the communicator will then point to a letter display (e.g., keyboard

or picture of a keyboard) and "spell out" a message, pointing to each letter consecutively to complete a message. It is important that the communicator look at the keyboard while composing the message. The Facilitator keeps track of the letters that would spell out a message while also giving some resistance to the pointing hand. FC is based on the notion that people with autism may have a form of apraxia whereby they have difficulty initiating certain motor movements (Biklen, 1990).

FC, begun by Rosemary Crossley (Crossley & McDonald, 1980) and expanded by Douglas Biklen (Biklen, 1990), is highly controversial. At the heart of the controversy over this method of communication is the perceived confusion with respect to who is generating the message, the user or the facilitator? Although much anecdotal evidence has been collected about the success of this method, (Biklen & Duchan, 1994; Halle, Chadsey-Rusch, & Reichle, 1994; Kaiser, 1994; Whitehurst & Crone, 1994) a multitude of single-blind and double-blind studies suggest that the facilitators are unknowingly generating the message (Green & Shane, 1994; Shane, 1994). Adding to the controversy, many people with autism have been unable to generate messages with certain facilitators but have much success with others. Several therapy associations have written position papers on FC including the American Occupational Therapy Association (AOTA) and the American Speech-Language-Hearing Association (ASHA). In addition, several courts have ruled that FC communication is unacceptable as testimony. However, if the technology team determines that this method is acceptable, the technique should be learned from a reliable and credible source that has been trained in the method. Methods for determining the origin of the message should also be put into place, such as as informal double blind checks.

Picture Exchange Communication System (PECS). The Picture Exchange Communication System allows nonverbal students to communicate by using picture symbols rather than words. The student locates a symbol, gains attention of the intended listener, gives the listener the symbol or symbols, then expects a response from the listener as the "exchange" in the communication. Several steps are required to learn this method and to acquire enough vocabulary to make it effective. The "picture exchange" is set up to help the student learn syntax and the meaning of isolated words. PECS has been particularly effective as a communication method for people with autism (Bondy & Frost, 1994) and is a good strategy for establishing intentional communication. The occupational therapist would be particularly interested in evaluating the student's ability to physically perform the exchange and in assisting the team to select appropriate symbols based on visual-perceptual qualities and physical ability to grasp and release the picture, as well as picture size needs, etc.

Considerations for Intervention Using Technology With Students With Autism

Once a practitioner is familiar with the variety of options available and the team has decided to use technology, other considerations remain. In general, the technology should be used for a specific purpose, keeping outcomes in the forefront. The team and the therapist should be knowledgeable in applying the technology and in resolving technical difficulties. Both the team and therapist should know the characteristics of autism, the specific characteristics of the particular child with whom they are working, and the way autism manifests itself. In addition, other more specific considerations related to both technology and autism must also be taken into account for intervention to be successful. These specific considerations include communication issues, motor issues, input considerations, output considerations, software considerations, AAC considerations, interface considerations, specific strategies for intervention, and troubleshooting strategies.

Communication Issues

Many students with autism learn the motor skill of selecting a switch for a voice output device as part of a routine without understanding the message of the voice output itself. This routine behavior can deceive the listener into believing that the student is intentionally communicating. Intentional communication and intentional behavior are different. If a child is near an adult who is not attending to him or her and the child sees a toy that is out of reach, he or she might stare at it and point to it. That action is an intentional behavior. However, if the child fails to get the attention of someone so he or she can get that person to retrieve the toy, communicative intent has not occurred. The adult may accidentally see the child and interpret his or her behavior as wanting the toy, and the adult may even retrieve the toy for the child. However, the adult has only interpreted the child's "behavior." The child produces intentional communication only when he or she deliberately includes a communication partner to alter the partner's behavior to obtain the toy. Especially with respect to autism, successful communication lies in the ability to intentionally communicate rather than to express intentional behaviors to which others attend and thereby interpret. Someone with a background in both language development and autism must be involved when setting up an AAC system. Basic voice output can open up many doors for people needing to communicate. However, simply providing a person with a voice output device will not automatically make him or her an effective communicator.

Students with autism may not effectively use the spoken word, and often, spoken language takes on idiosyncratic meaning. AAC technology cannot provide language and communication skills to those who do not possess them. The technology is merely a tool with which a student may express communication in an understandable manner. For an AAC device to be effective, the student must understand that communication is an exchange between two or more comprehending parties. Within that exchange, a sender must provide a meaningful message and a listener must receive and understand the message. The sender of a message must have several skills including knowing what he or she wishes to express, finding the form (verbal or visual) in which to express it, then performing the act of expressing the message using a mutually understood vehicle.

Motor Issues

Students with autism may have motor difficulties. Using technology can overcome some of the barriers created by those motor problems. Fine motor difficulties may be overcome by using alternative keyboards with larger keys or other alternative input devices (which are described later). Although many people with autism will be physically capable of walking, a few will have balance problems that would make carrying a larger or heavier communication device difficult. Consequently, the portability of any communication device becomes an issue. In general, the smaller the device, the more limited the memory and vocabulary. For many very portable devices, key size is also smaller. Some students may need a device that is portable and durable and that also can handle a large vocabulary. Although many of the smaller devices will use a "keyboard only" approach that allows a student to spell any word he or she wishes, this method is a very slow way to communicate and requires an ability to spell a message accurately and quickly. For some students, the slowness can precipitate anxiety behaviors and cause confusion when the communication breaks down because of poor spelling. Many newer devices, however, are very portable and carry significant vocabulary potential.

Input Considerations

Input is the method or device the student uses to activate or access the computer or AAC device. Typically, input methods fall into two categories: (a) expanded, or alternative, keyboards and (b) alternate input devices such as mouse emulators or switches (see Table 10.1). Input methods include direct selection and scanning.

Children with autism may have difficulty with a standard keyboard. The cause of the difficulty, whether it is cognitive, perceptual, or motoric in nature, will affect the technology support that is selected. However, some students with autism may have minimal need for hardware input adaptations. Therefore, first, attempt typical input methods for the identified age group (e.g., standard computer keyboard, standard mouse). If the standard method proves unsuccessful, then attempt simple modifications or minimal changes. If the initial adaptations are inadequate, then modifications that require specific hardware (e.g., expanded keyboard, touch panel) to overcome the input obstacles may be necessary. A common mistake practitioners make is to select a modification that is far more complex than is necessary to actually overcome the obstacle to input.

Output Considerations

Output is either the visual output of the device (what is seen on the screen or the printed paper copy) or the voice output. Speech output is of particular concern because many students with autism have difficulties attending to human speech and because the difficulties that some students have is related to the sensory input of sound. If the student is using the computer in a standard fashion, he or she may not attend to the inherent voice output messages that must be perceived to appropriately interact with the software. He or she may, instead, attend to the visual aspects of the software to determine what to do next. This behavior may deceive the practitioner who may incorrectly believe that the student understands what the computer is saying.

Often, behaviors such as increasing or decreasing the volume to the maximum are indications of problems processing the voice output. Some students may also have a strong preference for either digitized or synthetic speech output, especially when using AAC devices. These children may need time to adjust to speech output because they may have sensory difficulties in processing sounds or they may fail to connect the speech output to the intended meaning.

Calling an individual's name in an angry voice means something very different than when using a beckoning tone. As mentioned earlier, students with autism have difficulty identifying meaning carried in inflection; consequently, they may perform better with high quality synthetic speech in which a single word is spoken in the exact same manner each time rather than with the different inflections that occur in digitized speech. However, they may also ignore the speech while accomplishing the motor task of selecting the switch or picture.

The user of a voice or speech output device needs not only to attend to the speech output but also, more importantly, to understand that output. Although most adults prefer digitized speech, some high-end synthetic speech is often more understandable than poor quality digitized speech. AAC devices with synthetic speech weigh less and cost less than those having digitized speech because digitizing takes more memory (which increases the cost and often the weight of a device). For some students with autism, portability may be a more important issue.

Once the team determines that the student will tolerate voice output, the team should consider where voice output is necessary, where the student prefers voice output, and where voice output runs the risk of disruption for the student or others, keeping in mind the student's right to communicate (see Appendix 10.C). Voice output is usually desirable over non-voiced systems when other competing distractions exist or where the "speaker" and the "listener" are separated by distance. Be aware, however, that the voice output can become a distraction to the meaning of the communication. The student can become fascinated with getting the device to "talk" rather than with communicating what is intended. On the one hand, this behavior can be an indication of high motivation to use the device. On the other hand, the device may need to be reintroduced in a more meaningful way and its function may need to be clarified for the student.

Software Considerations

When choosing software, the purpose of the software should be easily identified. Software can be used to provide a leisure activity, to introduce new concepts and ideas, to reinforce concepts that have already been taught, to conduct drill and practice sessions, and to help the student explore. Students with autism need to see the function to understand the purpose of what they are doing. If the purpose of the software is not clear to the practitioner, it also will be unclear to the student. For the student with autism, the lack of clarity often brings confusion and invites inappropriate responses and behaviors. If the student can see that performing task A gets to task B, which results in a response in task C, he or she is more likely to persist in the activity.

Another consideration for software is the hardware it requires (e.g., knowledge of the keyboard, use of the mouse, use of a touch window, use of the return key or space bar, and so forth). A student who is proficient with a touch window but unable to use a mouse will need software that runs with a touch window only.

Several additional considerations that are exclusive of the content should be taken into account when selecting and using software. These considerations include screen clarity, pre-

Table 10.4
Considerations for Evaluating Software

Area of Consideration	Description of Term
Clarity of learning objectives	Refers to the targeted learning objectives for which the software was designed
Visual clarity	The number of images on the screen and their relationship to each other within the display itself (A clean or visually clear screen: A display that provides clear discrimination between foreground and background, contains items to be activated that are clearly delineated from those with no activity, contains items to be activated that have a clear relationship to one another, and makes the means and reason for activating an item self evident)
Predictability	The ability of the software to establish a routine of activation that is predictable by the user in its expected outcome; also, consistency in entering or exiting a part of the program
Auditory sensitivity and voice output	The amount of ambient noise, synthetic speech output for instruction, and noise level for auditory rewards
Data keeping	The tool section of a software program that allows the computer to keep track of correct and incorrect responses by one or several users.

dictability of events, auditory sensitivity, data keeping, and the clarity of learning objectives that are embedded in activities. The practitioner will want to keep these considerations in mind when looking at software (see Table 10.4 for additional information).

Because software should be selected to reinforce or in other ways enhance learning, the clarity of the software objectives becomes important. Software that is exploratory in nature (i.e., software that has no right or wrong answers) can promote a student's misperception of a series of unrelated cause-and-effect responses. The student may not be attending to the content of the animation but, rather, to the initiation of animation (e.g., a screen where some objects just move and other objects launch a mini-movie). The student may miss the content of the movie, which is needed to answer the next question, because he or she believed the task was to activate each object rather than attend to the content and apply the information to the next task.

Because students with autism tend to learn holistically (Janzen, 1996) they are often unable to sort out the relevant features of a picture to determine the meaning. Consequently, a busy

screen that produces a multitude of unconnected responses may be confusing to a student with a PDD. The less cluttered the screen display is, the more likely the student will make the right associations between the expected task and the expected response. An unclear display increases the likelihood that the student will incorporate incorrect responses into a routine of getting to the correct response.

Students with autism also show a preference for repetitive and predictable activities (Janzen, 1996). Therefore, software that provides predictability is likely to be more successful. If the software provides a routine of interaction, it will capitalize on the student's strength.

Many students with autism have auditory sensitivity (Janzen, 1996). Consequently, the type of voice output that the software will use (digitized or synthetic speech) and what the student's response is to sound and voice output in general are important to consider. As mentioned before, intonation and inflection can affect student performance.

Because students with a PDD often "know" a task one day then fail to "know" it on another day, data keeping is important. Without consistent monitoring of progress, data can become sketchy or absent. Software that tracks a student's responses also maintains a student's independence and provides the practitioner with a tool to check for understanding of the content.

For some students, other considerations may include the type of reinforcement visuals a software provides and the length of the delay between the computer request for a response and the student's actual response. Some software provides animation as a response to incorrect student responses. At times, the animation for incorrect responses can be more motivating than the animation for correct responses, which encourages the repetition of errors and the reinforcement of the wrong response. In addition, verbal cues can be confusing. Consider the delay between the computer's request of a task and the student's response. Often, software will request a task to be performed and then pause, allowing time for the student to complete the task. When the time has run out, the software may be programmed to repeat the request or offer a prompt. Students with a PDD may need additional time to process auditory information (Frith, 1989; Janzen, 1996). Consequently, if the response time is brief and a prompt is offered too quickly, the student may become confused because he or she may need to reprocess the new instruction or prompt.

AAC Considerations

When developing a communication system, a team will generally settle on a primary mode of communication, implying that additional parts of a system will need to be determined as necessary. For example, if a family already has begun to use a manual signing system in the home, it would not be efficacious to eliminate it as a functional part of a communication system. Although the manual signing system may not be desirable as a primary mode of communication, it may be beneficial as a secondary mode or as an environment-specific mode. By the time students with a PDD have reached the elementary grades, they often have experienced use of low-tech communication systems such as a picture exchange system. However, expecting that new people the student meets will understand manual signing or will quickly understand a picture exchange would be unrealistic. In certain circumstances, an electronic communication device would be more effective. The key is to find and use methods of effective communication that enable the student to fully participate in a variety of activities. It is unnecessary to identify a single device that would meet all needs in all situations (Beukelman & Mirenda, 1992). Because students with a PDD often do not generalize across settings, they may use one device or system at home and use another for school.

Often, the first decision is to determine a primary mode of communication and other support modes or secondary modes. A primary mode for many students with a PDD is a picture-based system such as a picture exchange with a secondary support of voice output in specific environments where a voice is needed to fully participate (e.g., show-and-tell activities or calling for help). Additional secondary modes could be signing, pointing, and routinely spoken phrases. Another decision involves whether to include voice output as a part of the communication system. For a student who is nonverbal, a complete system that includes flexible ways to express communication is necessary. Electronic devices do not easily go into swimming pools, yet the need to communicate still exists.

Typically, speaking adults use the term *right* while meaning "wrong" by just changing facial expression and vocal inflection. We may also use the word *no* to mean both "no, thank you" and "No!" (implying anger and protest). The only distinguishing feature is the vocal quality added to the word and the accompanying facial expression. These nonverbal characteristics of language are part of our system of communication. The nonverbal signals such as inflection and facial expression can often be confusing to a person with autism (Janzen, 1996). Consequently, the ability of a person to use voice output that incorporates vocal inflection to distinguish meaning will influence the decision on whether a voice output device will be a primary mode of communication or a secondary mode.

Other decisions include evaluating where a student needs to communicate. A light-tech, laminated picture system might be less effective in a setting where communication must occur from a distance (e.g., across a room) but might be more effective in an inclusionary classroom during a time when a voice output device could be disruptive (e.g., during silent reading, state assessments). In the first case where distance is a factor, a voice output device would be more effective, but it would be less effective in the second case where sound is a factor. Both light-tech and electronic methods will be necessary to meet communication needs. A comprehensive system may reflect both the use of several devices and a determination of settings in which they are to be used. A system might include a low-tech picture board, gestures, vocalizations, some speech, light technology such as VOCAs for quick reprogramming, some manual signs, and an electronic speech output device for more comprehensive vocabulary.

In determining whether or not to use voice output, consider first whether or not the student can tolerate the voice itself. If the student has auditory aversions, the device will likely go unused. The student may need several exposures to the voice output device, however, before the practitioner will be able to determine tolerance or preference for the voice output.

Occasionally, other students or even the teacher may find the inappropriate use of a device to be a distraction and may discourage its use. An important perspective to remember is that the distraction of the device may be no greater than that of a student who verbally blurts out comments without permission and is dealt with in a systematic manner. The student with a PDD who uses a voice output device should be treated as though the voice output were the student's real voice rather than responded to by removing the method of communication. Remember that the communication system becomes the student's voice, and he or she has the right to communicate (see Appendix 10.C).

Additionally, when choosing AAC devices, consider the system that is represented on the message keys. For the user, the symbol that is seen becomes the visual link between the input and output. Many students with a PDD may not yet be literate or they may be hyperlexic but not yet understand the meanings of the words they can decode. Therefore, a keyboard that displays only alphabet letters would be an inappropriate tool for a student who is not yet literate. This kind of keyboard usually cannot be altered to represent whole words or to manage a picture-based or word-based system.

People change throughout their lives. What may be functional at one point may no longer prove effective during another time. The child's age, rate of learning, rigidity of learning style, and motor skills can affect the choice of AAC devices. For example, a younger child may need to have access to a broad vocabulary that can grow as he or she develops. However, the same child, when older, may have acquired very functional speech and the ability to effectively communicate using speech, and, thus, may no longer need a comprehensive vocabulary selection.

Interface Considerations

Interfaces are the connections between input and output. Interfaces for computer adaptations are almost always a hardware component such as a cable from the keyboard to the computer. Interfaces are usually transparent; that is, the user does not need to learn to manipulate the interface itself but interacts only with the device through the interface. However, message compilation is one type of interface that is not transparent and that may be difficult for students with a PDD. Compiling a message from several keys and several locations on a device is dependent on memory skills, social appropriateness, and sometimes, the ability to navigate through several screens or boards to locate a specific message. Students may be motorically proficient at compiling the message but may lack an understanding of the message itself.

The nature of the autism may profoundly affect the selection of the method of message compilation. For example, when using a dynamic display device, liquid crystal display (LCD) screens may be too reflective or too visually distracting for the student to navigate efficiently to a desired page. A device that uses multiple levels to compile a message can also be difficult for a student with autism. If an overlay, or level, is not quickly or easily available, the potential for confusion exists. In addition, the student may see the act of changing the overlay as somehow essential to the meaning of the message he or she is attempting to communicate.

Specific Strategies for Students With a PDD

A key issue is to determine how to teach the prerequisite skills that are required for any piece of technology or software while making sure that the separate skills still relate to the activity in which those skills will be used. Because of the nature of PDDs and the potentially rigid learning style that is part of these disorders, a task may be learned as a rote motor skill without an understanding of its function or purpose. For example, if a student will be learning to operate a mouse so he or she may independently operate highly motivating software for leisure time, the practitioner might consider some of the following skills and determine what may need to be either taught separately or

taught within the activity in which the child will use the skill. In addition, the practitioner might determine which of the skills may be most likely affected by characteristics of the student's PDD that may cause faulty understanding:

- Physically moving the mouse across the screen
- Physically clicking the mouse
- Moving the cursor to a desired location
- Identifying the desired software logo on the screen
- Identifying the need for a single click or double click
- Watching the screen while moving the mouse
- Identifying his or her name on the software to gain entry
- Attending to the voice output instructions
- Following the voice output instructions
- Determining how to exit one screen and enter another

Task components can be identified by means of simple task analysis. If the student is weak in more than one of the skills required, the practitioner must adapt the activity appropriately to maximize independence.

Practitioners are often hampered by time constraints that minimize their opportunities to learn the technology. Consequently, they may be learning along with the student. However, if the practitioner takes the time to learn at least the part of the task that the student will be expected to perform so it can be presented to him or her problem free, the student will be more successful in learning the tools of technology. Therefore, prior to engaging the student, the practitioner should test the software, boot up the application, test the switches, and make sure that any batteries are charged.

With technology, the function of each specific task is not always apparent. If the student tends to respond positively to explanations, the practitioner should take some time to explain or demonstrate the function of each task the student is expected to perform. For example, all the particular skills that are needed to manipulate the mouse may not be relevant to being able to independently select his or her favored computer activity. Rather than complete all mouse training activities, a more effective plan might be to create an alias of the student's favorite computer activity in a folder with the student's name and then conduct mouse training with this favorite activity. Therefore, the function is evident and the motivation is inherent in the task. To expand the training display, the practitioner can create another alias from other activities that are less motivating and add them to the folder. The task becomes using the mouse to accurately locate and activate the desired program logo.

When instructing the student in the use of technology, the visual and physical setup should clearly indicate what item does which task. The practitioner can take a shoebox lid and cut out holes that would reveal only the specific keyboard keys that activate options available to the student. Another adaptation is to use colored labels on the appropriate keys. Both of these adaptations create a clear visual setup for the student and minimize potential confusion.

In addition to learning to make simple choices and process general communication, students with a PDD may use AAC devices for self-cueing. They may learn to follow a sequence of instructions by selecting keys on a voice output device that will speak a series of instructions. Students may also self-cue by selecting a key with an icon that represents the desired message, hearing the message spoken by the voice output device, and then speaking the message themselves. The device provides an appropriate model to imitate.

Troubleshooting

Using technology with students with a PDD may present unique obstacles. Problem solving is therefore an essential skill. Technology interventions need to be constantly evaluated and reevaluated. The practitioner needs to ask this question: Is the intervention accomplishing the target goal? If the answer is no, then changes need to be made.

For example, consider the following scenario. A student learns to use a computer joystick effectively in a simple mouse-training situation but has yet to independently use it to select an icon that launches his or her favorite software. The student loves simply to click the joystick button to make something happen. The therapist then provides exploratory software that requires no mouse click to show the student that clicking does not always do something. The therapist then introduces highly motivating software as an alias icon in a folder with two other nonfunctioning icons. When the student clicks on anything but the desired target, nothing happens.

Often, a student will exhibit unusual behaviors during a routine or task that has become familiar. We begin to question whether the student understands the task or whether he or she is bored with the task. When new behaviors arise during the use of technology with which the student was previously comfortable, observe what is visually or physically different about the setup of the hardware or materials to be used with the technology. A student with a PDD may respond adversely to materials that are in a different position as well as to missing equipment or visual cues.

Problem solving should be driven by the student's needs and learning characteristics. Consider the following situation. A student has the motor skills to operate a standard computer mouse but has yet to make the connection between the mouse movement and its relationship to the cursor on the computer screen. The student demonstrates an interest in watching other students but does not attempt to play on the computer. The student resists any attempts to lure him to play on the computer. Arrangements are made for him to watch others successfully operate the mouse. He watches, and then, when left alone, he attempts to explore on his own terms. When he attempts play on the computer, software that uses only mouse movement without an accompanying "click" is made available to him. He is then allowed to explore mouse function on his own.

Such a solution was based on an understanding of how this student with was learning by visual example. A different student was already touching the computer screen whenever something exciting happened but resisted all use of the mouse and did not understand the connection between the mouse movement and the cursor location. Because he was already pointing to the screen, use of the touch window was the simplest adaptation. The solutions for both students were driven by the skills and demonstrated readiness of the students.

Conclusion

A practitioner who provides services to children with a PDD must be aware of the benefits and limitations of assistive technology. Technology can assist a child with autism in a variety of student roles and tasks if it is incorporated into that child's life in appropriate ways. Technology can enhance learning, communication, play, and vocational options; however, it can also become a hindrance if not used properly. The technology team must remain focused on the outcomes they hope to achieve with a student and must continually reevaluate whether those outcomes are being reached.

References

Americans with Disabilities Act of 1990. Pub. L. 101–336, 42 U.S.C. § 12101.

Beukelman, D. R., & Mirenda, P. (1992). *Augmentative and alternative communication: Management of severe communication disorders in children and adults.* Baltimore: Brookes.

Biklen, D. (1990). Communication unbound: Autism and praxis. *Harvard Educational Review, 60,* 291–314.

Biklen, D., & Duchan, J. D. (1994). "I Am Intelligent": The social construction of mental retardation. *Journal of the Association for Persons with Severe Handicaps (JASH), 19*(3),173–184.

Boardmaker. [Computer software]. Solana Beach, CA: Mayer-Johnson Company.

Bondy, A. S., & Frost, L. A. (1994). The picture exchange system. *Focus on Autistic Behavior, 9*(3), 1–19.

Bowser, G., & Reed, P. (1998). *Education tech points: A framework for assistive technology planning.* Winchester, OR: Coalition for Assistive Technology in Oregon.

Chambers, A. C. (1997). *Has technology been considered? A guide for IEP teams.* Reston, VA: Council of Administrators of Special Education and The Council for Exceptional Children, Technology and Media Division.

Cook, A. M., & Hussey, S. M. (1995). *Assistive technologies: Principles and practice.* St. Louis, MO: Mosby.

Crossley, T., & McDonald, A. (1980). *Annie's coming out.* New York: Penguin.

Dettmer, P., Thurston, L., & Dyck, N. (1993). *Consultation, collaboration, and teamwork for students with special needs.* Newton, MA: Allyn & Bacon.

Education for All Handicapped Children Act of 1975. Pub. L. 94–142, 20 U.S.C. §1400 *et seq.*

Education for All Handicapped Children Amendments of 1986. Pub. L. 99–457, 20 U.S.C. § 1401, Part H, Section 677.

Fisher, K., Rayner, S., & Belgard, W. (1995). *Tips for teams: A ready reference for solving common team problems.* New York: McGraw-Hill.

Frith, U. (1989). *Autism: Explaining the enigma.* Oxford, England: Blackwell.

Green, G., & Shane, H. C. (1994). Science, reason, and facilitated communication. *Journal of the Association for Persons with Severe Handicaps (JASH), 19*(3),151–172.

Halle, J. W., Chadsey-Rusch, J., & Reichle, J. (1994). Editorial introduction to the special topic on facilitated communication. *Journal of the Association for Persons with Severe Handicaps (JASH), 19*(3),149–150.

Hammel, J., & Niehues, A. (1998). Integrating general and assistive technology into school based practice. In J. Case-Smith (Ed.), *Making a difference in school system practice* (pp. 1–54). Bethesda, MD: American Occupational Therapy Association.

Individuals With Disabilities Education Act of 1990. Pub. L. 101–476, 20 U.S.C., Ch 33.

Janzen, J. (1996). *Understanding the nature of autism: A practical guide.* San Antonio, TX: Therapy Skill Builders.

Kaiser, A. P. (1994). Invited commentary. The controversy surrounding facilitated communication: Some alternative meanings. *Journal of the Association for Persons with Severe Handicaps (JASH), 19*(3),187–190.

Kielhofner, G., Burke, J. P. (1980). A model of human occupation: Part I, conceptual framework and content. *American Journal of Occupational Therapy, 34,* 572–581.

Prentice, R., & Spencer, P. (1985). *Project BRIDGE: Decision-making for early services: A team approach.* Elk Grove Village, IL: American Academy of Pediatrics.

Reauthorization of the Individuals With Disabilities Education Act. (1997). Pub. L. 105–17.

Rehabilitation Act Amendments of 1992. Pub. L. 99–506.

Rehabilitation Act of 1973. Pub. L. 93–112, 29 U.S.C. § 701 *et seq.*

Shane, H. (1994). *Facilitated communication: The clinical and social phenomena.* San Diego, CA: Singular.

Smith, R. (1991). Technological applications for enhancing human performances. In C. Christensen & C. Baum (Eds.), *Human performance deficits* (pp. 747–788). Thorofare, NJ: Slack.

Whitehurst, G. J., & Crone, D. A. (1994). Invited commentary: Social constructivism, positivism, and facilitated communication. *Journal of the Association for Persons with Severe Handicaps (JASH), 19*(3),191–195.

Zabala, J. (1994). *The SETT framework: Critical questions to ask when making informed assistive technology decisions.* Paper presented at Closing the Gap, St. Paul, MN.

Appendix 10.A
Web Site Resources

Alliance for Technology Access

http://www.ataccess.org/

Autism Society

http://www.autism-society.org/

Communication Aid Manufacturers Association (CAMA)

http://www.aacproducts.org/

Disability-Specific Web Sites: Autism Link

http://www.disserv.stu.umn.edu/disability/Autism/

Rehabilitation Engineering and Assistive Technology Society of North America (RESNA)

http://www.resna.org/resna/hometa1.htm

TEACCH Program of University of North Carolina at Chapel Hill

http://www.unc.edu/depts/teacch/

The Autism/PDD Society of Mainland Nova Scotia

(contains excellent links)
http://cnet.windsor.ns.ca/Health/Autism/links.html

Trace Center

http://trace.wisc.edu/

Pictures from Boardmaker (by Mayer-Johnson)

http://www.mayer-johnson.com

Appendix 10.B
Additional Information

Alm, N. (1993). The development of augmentative and alternative communication systems to assist with social communication. *Technology and Disability, 2*(3), 1–18.

Anson, D. K. (1997). *Alternative computer access: A guide to selection.* Philadelphia: F.A. Davis.

Biklen, D., Morton, M. W., Goal, D., Berrigan, C., & Swaninathan, S. (1992). Facilitated communication: Implications for individuals with autism. *Topics in Language Disorders, 12*(4), 1–28.

Blackstone, S. W., & Bruskin, D. M. (1986). *Augmentative communication: An introduction.* Rockville, MD: American Speech-Language-Hearing Association.

Church, G., & Glennen, S. (1992). *The handbook of assistive technology.* San Diego, CA: Singular.

Crossley, R., & Remington-Gurney, J. (1992). Getting the words out: Facilitated communication training. *Topics in Language Disorders, 12*(4), 29–45.

Inspiration. [Computer software]. (1999). Portland, OR: Inspiration Software.

Katzenbach, J. R., & Smith, D. K. (1993). *The wisdom of teams.* Boston: Harvard Business School Press.

Phillips, B., & Zhao, H. (1993). Predictors of assistive technology. *Assistive Technology, 5*(1), 36–45.

Quick, T. L. (1992). *Successful team building.* New York: AMACOM, American Management Association.

Schmuck, R., & Runkel, P. (1994). *The handbook of organization development in schools.* Palo Alto, CA: Mayfield.

Smith, R. O. (1991). Technological approaches to performance enhancement. In C. Christiansen & C. Baum (Eds.), *Occupational therapy: Overcoming human performance deficits* (pp. 746–796). Thorofare, NJ: Slack.

Swinth, Y. (1994). The role of the special education team in selecting and implementing assistive technology. *School Systems Special Interest Section Newsletter, 1*(3), 1–2.

Torres, C. (1994). *The tao of teams: A guide to team success.* San Diego, CA: Pfeiffer.

Appendix 10.C
Basic Communication Rights

1. The right to request desired objects, actions, events, and persons and to express personal preferences or feelings.
2. The right to be offered choices and alternatives.
3. The right to reject or refuse undesired objects, events, or actions, including the right to decline or reject all preferred choices.
4. The right to request and be given attention from and interaction with another person.
5. The right to request feedback or information about a state, an object, a person, or an event of interest.
6. The right to active treatment and intervention efforts to enable people with severe disabilities to communicate messages in whatever modes and as effectively and efficiently as their specific abilities will allow.
7. The right to have communication acts acknowledged and responded to, even when the intent of these acts cannot be fulfilled by the responder.
8. The right to have access at all times to any needed augmentative and alternative communication devices and other assistive devices and to have those devices in good working order.
9. The right to environmental context, interactions, and opportunities that expect and encourage persons with disabilities to participate as full communicative partners with other people, including peers.
10. The right to be informed about the people, things, and events in one's immediate environment.
11. The right to be communicated with in a manner that recognizes and acknowledges the inherent dignity of the person being addressed, including the right to be a part of communication exchanges about an individual that are conducted in his or her presence.
12. The right to be communicated with in ways that are meaningful, understandable, and culturally and linguistically appropriate.

CHAPTER 11

Interactive Guiding: The Affolter Approach

Karin Berglund Bonfils, OTR

The Affolter treatment approach, or "interactive guiding," uses nonverbal manual cueing to assist people in completing daily living skills. The emphasis is on helping the tactile-kinesthetic system to receive and process information that can then be combined with other sensory systems to perceive events appropriately. Interactive guiding has been used with a variety of people who have brain processing problems such as cerebral vascular accident (CVA), traumatic brain injury (TBI), coma, and Alzheimer's disease, as well as developmental processing problems such as a Pervasive Developmental Disorder (PDD). This chapter will discuss the use of the Affolter interactive guiding techniques with the child who has autism or autistic-like symptoms.

Dr. Felicie Affolter, the creator of the technique, is a Swiss speech and language pathologist with degrees in psychology, education, audiology, and language pathology and speech sciences. She has been performing innovative research with her partner, Dr. Walter Bischofberger, on perceptual-cognitive processing for more than 35 years. She has studied with developmental theorist Jean Piaget and has based her theoretical model of the Affolter approach on his developmental framework. Dr. Affolter is also one of the founders of The Center for Per-

ceptually Disturbed Adults and Children in St. Gallen, Switzerland.

The Affolter Approach

The Affolter approach focuses on the perception of tactile and kinesthetic input and uses these sensations in intervention as movement is guided. Therefore, a discussion of perception and the importance of the tactile and kinesthetic senses is necessary before further information on the technique is provided (Affolter, 1991).

Perception

Perception, in its broadest sense, can be defined as the input of stimuli by means of different sensory modalities that allows us to relate to our surroundings (Affolter, 1987). Webster's dictionary defines perception as "a mental image: awareness of the elements of the environment through physical sensation: an impression of an object obtained by the use of senses: physical sensation interpreted in the light of experience" (Webster, 1988). For a person to interpret physical sensation in relation to experience, he or she must interact with the environment. Interaction is therefore a key element in the Affolter approach. One needs to interact with the environment to know where he or she is in relation to the world, to the situation, or to the activity

(Bonfils, 1996). Perception involves the simultaneous processing of more than one sensation, whether those sensations arise from different modalities or from within one modality (Nelson, 1984). Perception helps us make sense out of the potentially overwhelming richness and variety of different sensations. Perceptual processes organize, or integrate, sensations into meaningful gestalts, or wholes. Past experiences with sensation help in the integration of new sensations (Nelson, 1984).

How people touch and interact in their environment appears to be absolutely critical to their ability to process information adequately (Affolter & Stricker, 1980). People are continually using their collection of experiences to compare and contrast gathered sensory data from actual situations. In other words, people may not be able to perceive something without having some experience on which to base the perception (Davis, 1992). Affolter and Stricker (1980) maintain that "interaction between the environment and the person requires contact. Contact means to be 'in touch with.' To be in touch, or in contact with, can be achieved via the tactile kinesthetic system" (p. 11). The tactile-kinesthetic sensory system provides the information that is essential for interaction, and the process of interaction leads to more complex performances (Affolter & Stricker, 1980).

The Importance of Tactile-Kinesthetic Information

The tactile-kinesthetic system senses, regulates, and evaluates pain, pressure, temperature, and body position by integrating information from millions of receptors throughout the entire body. This information is critical for our normal development. Babies initially learn about themselves and their environment by moving, searching, and exploring, thus, providing input to this system. Touch is also a significant factor in the development of the relationship between the parent and child.

In careful observations of infants and children who range from 3 months to 3 years old, Affolter has noted that the tactile-kinesthetic system offers unique information about environmental qualities that the other sensory systems are not able to provide. The receipt of environmental information by means of perceived changes in resistance during activities leads to cause-and-effect relationships (Bonfils, 1996).

The tactile-kinesthetic system is unique among the sensory systems in the sense of being the only one that relates directly to reality. One's looking at the world does not alter it. Listening does not change the world either. However one can scarcely touch the world without changing it. This phenomenon is related to the fact that the tactile-kinesthetic system combines receiving, as well as, exploratory functions (Affolter & Stricker, 1980, p. 115).

Affolter believes that the tactile-kinesthetic sense is of primary importance. Research findings support the hypothesis that tactile-kinesthetic information is absolutely essential for adequate interaction with the environment (Bonfils, 1996). Having received, processed, and evaluated input, a person has the opportunity to take an active role in the world through motor output. Motor responses inevitably result in sensory feedback, which provides new opportunities to assess the environment.

Deficits in Tactile-Kinesthetic Processing

People with poor perception of tactile-kinesthetic information have difficulty with movement and exploration as well as difficulty with adaptation of muscle tone in response to environmental demands (Bonfils, 1996). Motor processes are strongly dependent on and interrelated with perceptual processes. Learning or relearning of rules for posture and movement in relation to new situations takes place through the tactile-kinesthetic channel (Affolter &

Stricker, 1980). Often, people are unable to explore the environment effectively or efficiently. People with inadequate tactile-kinesthetic processing may have peculiar hand and finger movements or abnormal body movements. Grasping an object in appropriate ways (providing tactile and proprioceptive input) provides information about its characteristics (haptic perception) (Nelson, 1984). People with perceptual processing deficits are more likely to grasp inappropriately or to use inappropriate manipulation patterns. Inappropriate manipulation patterns or unsuitable grasps (such as grossly squeezing or pinching) provide greater resistance, which is then perceived. The intensity of the resistance helps provide information to the person about his or her body in relation to the environment, but it is also profoundly inadequate. Situations in which information from touching and moving is insufficient may indicate an overreliance on the visual sense.

People with perceptual deficits may also revert to sensory-specific behaviors that are similar to those of an infant 0–3 months old who has not yet developed the ability to integrate multisensory experiences. For example, a person may close his or her eyes during an activity to reduce visual stimulation and enhance the perception of the tactile-kinesthetic sense. The emphasis in today's environment on visual stimulation (e.g., television and video games) leads easily to an overload of the visual system. Constant overloading may lead to visual accommodation and overfunction that possibly results in further underfunctioning of the other sensory modalities.

Tactile-Kinesthetic Deficits of Children With Autism

Difficulties in processing tactile-kinesthetic information can be noted in many children with autism. Many of these children are observed frantically touching their environment with their fingertips. Although this touch provides them with the instant resistance nec-essary to perceive where their bodies are in relation to the environment or object, it does not provide them with enough information; hence, they continue the search with hectic touching. Self-stimulatory behavior such as finger twiddling, hand flapping, or hand posturing is often associated with a reduction in visual stimulation (Nelson, 1984) and may be related to a search for information. Toe walking, seen in many children with autism, may be related to proprioceptive self-stimulation or to an interaction among proprioceptive, tactile, and vestibular sensations (Nelson, 1984). Self-injurious behaviors such as head banging, self-striking, biting, and hair pulling have a tactile component (Nelson, 1984) and may also indicate intense information seeking. Finally, children with autism are commonly overreliant on their visual systems, perhaps because of inefficient tactile-kinesthetic processing.

Intervention With Interactive Guiding

Affolter developed the technique of nonverbal interactive guiding as a means to provide a person with information that may be missing. The therapist's hands are placed directly over the hands or body part of the person. If hand-to-hand guiding is used, hands should be placed fingertip to fingertip (as if the hands were a pair of gloves). The amount of pressure used is entirely dependent on the amount of resistance the person needs to interpret the tactile input appropriately. The pressure therefore varies from maximal to very minimal resistance. Whenever possible, the therapist guides both hands of the person. Guiding is possible with all body parts and can be used also to enhance mobility. (See Table 11.1, which provides guidelines for using the Affolter approach.)

Perception is a whole-brain experience. Therefore, alternating input between the left and right sides of the body to provide input to both of the cerebral hemispheres is important. Any bilateral activity should be guided bilaterally. While guiding, the therapist is not teach-

Table 11.1

Guidelines for Affolter Interactive Guiding Techniques

- Therapy is geared toward emphasizing appropriate input through a problem-solving process rather than focusing on output and successful completion of a product.

- Real-life events and activities in daily living are a necessity in treatment planning. No special equipment is required.

- The setting can be anywhere that includes a problem to be solved. For example, guiding can occur during a meal, during self-care, in the classroom, in the clinic, or at home.

- Hand-over-hand "guided interaction" occurs as the situation presents itself. Some people need intensive guiding, and some need only brief guiding. A person typically may not appreciate being touched; however, when the problem to be solved requires some assistance, guiding is often accepted.

- The hand-over-hand approach is "fingertip to fingertip," as if the hands were gloves. The left and right sides of the body are alternated when possible; perception has no dominance, and guiding needs to be a whole-body, whole-brain experience.

- Guided interaction is nonverbal. No words are used during guiding to allow for maximal sensory processing. Language is definitely incorporated after the guided input to assess integration of information, retention, memory, retrieval, and articulation.

- Length of treatment may be as brief as a few seconds (opening a door) or as intense as an hour (preparing something to eat). The length is determined by the problem to be solved, the sequences involved, and the input offered.

ing a person how to perform. He or she is providing the person with the sensory experience of performing a real-life event. If the person learns and performs the task, the motor output resulting from the sensory input was appropriate, and the information was organized. The person must be challenged enough so learning occurs yet assisted enough to minimize frustration and failure (Bonfils, 1996).

During guiding, the therapist's responsibility is to assist people in obtaining their optimum level of performance, or the "performance ceiling" as described by Affolter. One reaches the performance ceiling when one is working at or near peak ability with an appropriate challenge (Bonfils, 1996). The following characteristics may be observed when people are working at their performance ceiling: silence during guiding, intent facial expression, appropriate eye contact for the task, and normalization of muscle tone (Bonfils, 1996). Occupational therapists must learn to observe situations, environments, and people carefully; interpret individual behavior; and rapidly modify the guiding accordingly. (See Table 11.2 for information on assessing the effectiveness of guided interaction.)

The Significance of Problem-Solving Events

The Affolter approach to intervention is unique in that it requires the use of nonverbal problem-solving events. Problem-solving events may consist of any activity that offers the possibility of logical sequencing, for example, dressing, grooming and hygiene skills, opening containers and packages, preparing food, or cleaning up after a task. A true problem-solving event is created with the limited use of verbal instruction during the task or activity. The person must think through the steps as he or she interacts during each step in the process. The traditional approach to assisting a client in functional activity is to begin with verbal instructions. In contrast, the Affolter approach requires that the search for information be nonverbal, with communication occurring mainly through the tactile-kinesthetic senses.

This nonverbal characteristic of the approach may be unusual, particularly as designed by a speech-language pathologist; however, it is one of the most important aspects of using the approach correctly. By refraining from speaking while guiding, the therapist gives the person the opportunity to process information without extra stimuli. Silence allows the person to wonder about what is happening. What will we do first? What will be next? Verbal instructions are either followed or not followed. Instructions that are not followed may make the instructor frustrated. Nonverbal guiding captures the client's attention, if only for a second. Initial attention may be followed by a reaction of increased tone or by refusal if the situation is not familiar or expected. However, with appropriate information at the appropriate time, guiding may invite a person to participate in an experience not otherwise available or conceivable.

Although giving instructions is not necessary before guiding, the therapist may say, "I am going to guide you by moving your hands (or body) with my hands. I am not going to tell you with words what it is I want you to do. Listen to my hands." Often, however, guiding is just a matter of seizing an opportunity to assist the person at just the right time to complete the task together without the necessity of verbal input. The session should flow; at one point, the therapist is observing, and at the very next point, the therapist guides with direct hands-on input. The result is a nonverbal understanding between the person and the therapist (Bonfils, 1996). The success of the interaction often depends on the timing of the therapist. Verbal information is often incorporated after guiding has taken place and after a task or sequence has been completed. Having had the experience of the interactive event, the person may have improved comprehension of the situation and be better able to comprehend verbal information regarding the activity.

Planning During Problem-Solving Events

Problem solving requires specific planning. Affolter emphasizes two hierarchical levels of planning. The first level is step-by-step plan-

Table 11.2
Assessing the Effectiveness of Guided Interaction

Signs of perceptual processing and progress may include improvements in the ability to do the following:

- Attend, focus, or initiate
- Take over purposeful movement in a sequence of events
- Adapt body tone appropriately for the situation
- Anticipate what step may be coming up next in a sequence during a task
- Recall and retrieve information about a guided event
- Use spontaneous language
- Articulate and form ideas
- Assimilate learned information into other events

ning. A person must recognize that there is a problem to be solved and must be able to carry out a step-by-step series of sequences to solve the problem. The second level of planning is higher level planning. Higher level planning includes planning for an event without visual, verbal, or other cues. The person must be familiar with the task and able to organize, plan, prepare, and execute the necessary sequences to achieve the goal. This second level is, consequently, a very demanding level of performance. A person may therefore revert to the step-by-step level and perhaps seek assistance to achieve the goal.

Guiding to Assist Planning

Lack of initiation is a key symptom in perceptual processing problems. If a person does not recognize that there is a situation or problem to be solved, he or she will not take the necessary steps to initiate a plan of action. Perhaps a person will be able to initiate the first or second step in a sequence of steps but then get stuck, not knowing what might come next. Difficulty following through with sequencing is another key symptom of perceptual processing deficits.

Through careful observation, a therapist can instantly intervene with guiding at the exact moment when the process begins to break down. If the person has difficulty initiating, the therapist may be able to guide the person to begin the process. Often, the person will then recognize what to do and "take over" the process. The therapist may then step back. At other times, the person will begin a process and get stuck in a sequence at which point the therapist is able to immediately assist by guiding the person through the sequence until the information is received or the sequence is complete.

Resistance or refusal should be noted as a sign that the person has been asked to work on a level of planning that is too difficult. Without realizing that the inappropriateness of the complex activity produces frustration and consequent behavior patterns, therapists can inadvertently create behavior issues. Often, children with autism are not actively resisting learning but are merely unable to do or understand the task at hand.

Meaningful Activity: A Prerequisite for Success

Life is made up of a series of activities or events such as getting dressed. Each of these events is actually a routine with a common sequence of steps that flow from beginning to end to achieve a goal. These routines are functional and practical, and they allow a person to take care of daily needs. In normal development, much of what a person does is motivated by the activity itself. The exploring child is reinforced by the changes that he or she makes in the environment, and the mastering child is reinforced by his or her own productions.

Affolter emphasizes the use of real-life situations or events and avoids contrived activities. Tasks involving the everyday problem solving within life events are the only appropriate activities for Affolter's interactive guiding techniques. These activities make sense and have

productive meaning and value. Real-life events do not necessarily require special tools or equipment, and activities are easily adapted and variable.

The location and timing of an event or activity may make a significant difference. Kitchen activities are best performed in a kitchen, bathroom tasks in a bathroom. Simulated situations that use cones and pegs or that involve cutting plastic food with a knife (instead of real-life situations that use real food) need to be avoided. Tasks should be varied to promote assimilation and generalization of information to other events. The slightest change in a task or activity could mean a slight change in the performance of the person also. "Performance inconsistency is simply a part of the learning process. No one does all occupational performance at a 100% level of success, trial and error is an essential feature of learning new activities" (Nelson, 1984, p. 98). It is important to go with the natural rhythm of the activity, which means that, if a mistake is made, it may provide the perfect opportunity to deal with a new problem-solving experience together.

Because those with autism learn routines quite easily, teaching functional skills in the context of these important natural routines is efficient (Janzen, 1996). At whatever level a child with autism begins therapy, the therapist should try to gradually encourage a sense of pleasure in activity for its own sake (Nelson, 1984). A problem that is solved either by the child alone or by the therapist and the child is a natural reinforcer if the activity is purposeful (Nelson, 1984).

Use of Interactive Guiding as a Comprehensive Approach

The Affolter technique allows health care providers, educators, caregivers, and family members to involve people with autism in a unique opportunity to interact with the environment. Communication with all of the significant people who are involved in the child's daily life is essential to ensure that the positive aspects of the therapeutic relationship can be transferred to all environments. The Affolter approach can be taught to families, teachers, and caregivers by guiding them through a simple problem-solving process. Allowing people to participate in an actual event involving interactive guiding provides them with the opportunity to experience the technique and feel the powerful input that can take place. Experiential learning encourages a different perspective, although observing others being guided can also be very beneficial for those who are being trained. With a multidisciplinary team approach to interactive guiding, problem-solving events can be interspersed throughout the day, and multiple skills can be enhanced.

The effect of interactive guiding is readily observed in improved planning and problem solving, but language skills also may improve. Although guiding is nonverbal, language skills are supported by means of enhanced comprehension of objects and events through touch and perception. Perception leads to the ability to form symbols for language. The unique advantage of using the Affolter approach with this population is that, when the information is adequate, symbols are developed and language evolves. What better way to prepare to discuss the properties of an orange than by first seeing it, cutting it, squeezing it, and drinking the juice? The brain will have already had the advantage of the experience.

Research

Over the last 40 years, Dr. Affolter has conducted extensive research to contribute to the understanding of perceptual performances of people who are hearing impaired, visually impaired, or language impaired; children who demonstrate reading and writing difficulty (dyslexia); adults with aquired language distur-

bances secondary to brain damage; and children exhibiting a PDD (Affolter & Stricker, 1980). All of the studies are motivated by the general hypothesis that, often, inadequate complex human performances are accompanied by inadequate perceptual performances. Affolter has proposed that Austistic Disorder results from primary intermodal (sensory integrative) deficits (Affolter & Stricker, 1980). The subsequent research findings suggest a relationship between (a) disturbances of language and other complex performance and (b) disturbances of perceptual processes on a high level of organization (Affolter & Stricker, 1980). Findings also reveal that children with language disturbances and dyslexia as well as adults with left- or right-sided brain damage perform significantly more poorly in forms recognition and successive pattern recognition than control subjects without disabilities. Perceptual difficulties accompany inadequate acquisition of spoken and written language in children. This relationship can also be found in adults who have sustained brain damage. Given this relationship, one can further hypothesize that the observed perceptual difficulties are primary to the problems of language disturbances. That is, people fail in complex human performances such as language because of more basic perceptual problems. In this sense, adequate perceptual functioning seems to be a prerequisite for adequate language performance and for other complex nonverbal performances (Affolter & Stricker, 1980). Dr. Maureen Levine, neuropsychologist, and Lynn Sweeney, speech and language pathologist, are conducting research on the efficacy of guided interaction therapy for improving language in children with PDDs, attention deficit, or cerebral palsy.

The results of using interactive guiding with a small group of children with autism and cerebral palsy have been presented (Sweeney, 1996). All eight of the children in the project were nonverbal. Each child had been receiving consultant-based language intervention in the classroom prior to the project. Teachers, family members, or caregivers were trained to use Affolter interactive guiding techniques for a minimum of 15 minutes 3 times per week. Dramatic changes were noted in the development of basic language skills after using Affolter's method. Every child who received guided interaction therapy made progress ranging from 1 month to more than 23 months of developmental improvements in basic developmental language skills after only 6 months of intervention with Affolter techniques. Prior to beginning the guided interaction therapy, gains of only 0–3 months of developmental progress had been reported in the same time frame (Sweeney, 1996).

Additional research studies on the effect of tactile experience using interactive guiding have included children and adults with Attention Deficit Disorder (ADD) and Attention Deficit Disorder with Hyperactivity (ADD/H) involving the variability of reaction and movement time (LeVine, VanHorn, Sweeney, Pallas, & Mullin, 1998).

Affolter's Techniques and Occupational Therapy

Affolter's treatment technique of integrating interactive guiding within normal daily living skills is readily adapted to occupational therapy intervention. Assisting others in the completion of tasks and activities that are fundamental to the formation of habits and to participation in important roles is an integral facet of occupational therapy. Affolter's techniques provide occupational therapists with another treatment option while using human occupation during intervention. (See Case Studies 11.1 and 11.2, which describe the use of Affolter techniques within occupational therapy intervention for children with autism or a PDD). Affolter techniques are also readily used in combination with a variety of other techniques commonly

used by occupational therapists such as sensory integration and neurodevelopmental treatment, which provides an eclectic approach. One should note that Affolter's concept of the performance ceiling is similar to Ayre's conceptualization of the adaptive response. In addition, Affolter's use of meaningful activity during guiding fits very well within an occupational therapy framework's use of human occupation during intervention. Within this occupational therapy framework, progress is easily documented using traditional terminology, such as "The client required moderate tactile cues to initiate the activity, attending and focusing for 4 minutes while being guided through three sequences."

The use of interactive guiding has been successfully used with many children with autism. However, because tactile defensiveness is common in this population, the therapist should be cognizant of any aversive reactions the child may be having to the guiding experience and modify the intervention as needed. This approach may not be possible with all children with a PDD.

Conclusion

Children with PDDs demonstrate many characteristics of disordered perceptual processing, particularly within the tactile-kinesthetic system. Affolter's interactive guiding techniques provide a unique opportunity to assist the child in organizing himself or herself within an activity that has a normal sequence of events. The Affolter approach not only is appropriate for use with children with a PDD but also is extremely compatible with occupational therapy in general. The most recent research findings suggest that we are only beginning to learn about the tremendous potential of the human brain and body to respond to appropriate and meaningful tactile input. This area of research and practice is of great importance to the field of occupational therapy.

Case Study 11.1
Dominick

Dominick was a 4 year old who had a Pervasive Developmental Disorder and significant sensory processing issues. He had difficulty tolerating household noises, particularly those of small household appliances and the vacuum cleaner. He also had difficulty tolerating touch. Dominick received occupational therapy services two times a week for 30- to 40-minute sessions in an outpatient setting.

For one particular session, the therapist had strategically planned an event involving a large box placed up high on a shelf—almost within Dominick's reach. "Let's see what I have in that box, Dominick. I have brought something new today." Dominick was interested. He tried to get at the box by jumping up and reaching on his tiptoes. The therapist, who had been trained in Affolter techniques, wondered specifically, Would he assess the situation correctly? Would he process the verbal and visual information and use feedback if he could not get the box? Would he come up with an alternative solution or get frustrated and give up?

Dominick looked around the room, and the therapist was able to seize the searching moment as an opportunity to assist. She took her hand over his hand and gently but firmly guided it to a nearby chair without telling him what to do. She also guided the other hand to begin moving the chair. Dominick got the message right away and took over the task to move the chair. The therapist could back away and allow him to continue to solve the problem. Dominick set the chair up next to the shelves and climbed up to reach the box. The therapist determined just the right moment that Dominick needed assistance and moved close to be able to guide him to get the box safely off the shelf. Dominick was able to carry it with assistance until he got off the chair and, then, carried it independently to the table.

The box had been taped shut with packing tape. Dominick examined the box closely, looking at all sides of the box, turning it over and looking at the sides. He spontaneously went to get a pair of scissors. He had assessed the situation and had come up with a solution. Although it was not necessarily the correct solution, he had initiated and executed a plan. Dominick took the scissors and tried to cut the box as if it were paper. The moment he appeared to have realized this would not produce the desired results, the therapist guided him to open the scissors wide to use them as a scoring tool. Dominick had no problem with the closeness of the therapist or with the assistance she provided. He continued to be focused on the task to see what was in the box.

When the scoring was complete, Dominick opened the box on his own. Inside, he found a lot of tissue and newspaper, which was wrapped around a variety of toy monsters. Dominick enjoyed unwrapping and discovering each monster. The speech therapist had quietly arrived, joined the activity during the unwrapping process, and began to participate in the therapy session. The speech therapist and Dominick discussed and demonstrated to each other the noises that the monsters made as well as talked about their sizes, shapes, and colors. The situation was a wonderful opportunity to work on articulation, sentence structure, and pragmatic speech. At the end of the session, each monster was again wrapped in paper and put away.

At each session that followed, Dominick wanted the opportunity to check the monsters in the box. Activities were planned that involved tools or small appliances such as a small hand-held vacuum, an electric orange juice squeezer, and an electric mixer that made noises similar to monster noises. All tasks would include hand-over-hand guiding to explore and assemble the piece of equipment and to learn its purpose. Dominick tolerated these sessions well. Knowing the purpose of the appliance and how it was used made a dramatic difference in the way he was able to handle the associated noise. He stopped covering his ears and began enjoying the experiences, including showing his mother that he could vacuum all by himself.

Dominick's family became very enlightened with respect to the realm of possibilities that existed with guided activities. The family was trained to guide Dominick at home, and interactive guiding became a way for them to have bonding experiences. Dominick was guided to set up activities and could then be allowed to take over parts of the tasks independently. Dominick became an integral part of not only getting a job accomplished but also contributing to helping his family. His auditory sensitivity became manageable in his everyday environment.

Case Study 11.2
Greg the Terrible Eater

Greg was an 8 year old from a large family. He rarely spoke in sentences, and his speech consisted primarily of television jargon. He demonstrated poor eating habits, difficulty with social skills, and inappropriate behavior during meals. His parents complained of his lack of desire to eat and his difficulty in using utensils.

An observation of the situation prior to intervention revealed that, at home, Greg appeared to be given special advantages during meals because of his autism. His siblings were encouraged to participate in meal preparation, but he was not. His parents felt he did not have the ability to attend to kitchen tasks well enough for those activities to be safe for him. They also believed he was not capable of completing tasks without repeated prompting.

Greg's family did not often sit down to the table and eat together. Greg had a difficult time sitting still, so most of their meals were eaten in the television room. Greg and his younger siblings usually ate off of television lap trays or at the coffee table. Often, the food was served to Greg on paper plates or lightweight, nonbreakable dinnerware, in plastic cups with a lid and straw, and at times, with plastic uten-sils. Greg had the tendency to get easily agitated and throw or smear his food or upset his tray, and this type of dinnerware prevented breakage. He was given a fair amount of finger foods such as hot dogs, sandwiches, chips, and cut fruit so he would not require utensils. He was not allowed to cut his own food or handle a knife because of his unpredictable behavior.

In planning the intervention, the therapist decided that the first area to be addressed was the eating environment. Few social skills are learned by sitting in front of the television, and children are commonly distracted and overstimulated by the television to a point where they are unable to attend to the meal. Television trays do not provide the same stability as a sturdy table. If the eating surface does not provide for adequate stability and resistance, it may also be difficult to use a fork or spoon. In addition, sitting on one's knees at a coffee table seems to encourage continual requirements for body repositioning.

The therapist recommended that Greg's family begin by turning off the television and sitting at the dinner table together. The seat that the therapist recommended for Greg was one next to the wall where he would have some clearly defined space and where the stimulation from at least one side would be limited. Because Greg was constantly moving and fidgeting, he needed distinct boundaries. He was given a chair that had armrests and a washable cushion, and he was seated close to the table. The seating system was not meant to restrain Greg but to allow him the opportunity to restrain himself. Although Greg was assigned a specific seat, the main purpose was to provide him an opportunity for stability, resistance, and support so he could attend to a task. The seat was not assigned to establish a routine. Establishing a routine is important, but not as important as providing the best possible environment.

Training was necessary for the family to learn interactive guiding techniques. Greg needed to be given the opportunity to practice using regular utensils and to cut his own food. The amount of food presented to him could be limited to only one or two items at a time. Breaks could be provided after each food item as necessary. Paper cups, paper items, and lightweight dinnerware were not recommended because these items neither had enough weight or substance nor provided enough resistance to give the body and brain spatial information. The therapist recommended that Greg be given the opportunity to be guided while using heavy glassware and real utensils. If his tendency was to throw the object when he was not being guided, then the person who performed the guiding would be responsible to remove the object when it was not being used.

Prior to making any changes at home, several sessions of guided interaction occurred in the clinic. Greg was guided to cut pieces of fruit with a sharp paring knife that had a large thick handle for easier gripping. He was encouraged to bring in items that he was interested in cutting and eating as well as to eat what he had cut with stainless steel utensils. Some of the utensils had solid, built-up handles to provide additional information through resistance in the hand. Guiding began with hand-over-hand, gross-grasp grip and progressed to a lateral pinch grip. Greg demonstrated motivation by beginning to gesture requests to be guided when he was challenged. He also began thinking of new and different items to try cutting and

Case Study 11.2
Continued

preparing. He was guided to grate, peel, and mash various foods and to squeeze oranges and other fruits for juice. His parents were instructed in hand-over-hand interactive guiding techniques, and meal preparation was a suggested activity at home. Greg and his parents agreed to begin a home program.

The family was asked to pick one task or one part of a sequence that they could devote their undivided attention to during meal preparation. Of importance to note, the therapist did not recommend that Greg be expected to do meal preparation on his own without someone assisting. He had not been "taught" to use a knife in therapy sessions; he had been given the opportunity only to have the perceptual sensory experience of the event.

Home intervention began with peeling and cutting one cucumber. A parent set up the activity and guided Greg to hold the knife and to cut slices. The parent would finish by allowing Greg the opportunity to put all of the pieces into the bowl on his own. They were surprised to discover, after only several days, that Greg enjoyed the experience of being trusted to work with a knife, even if it meant being guided for safety and quality during cutting. His parents soon discovered that they could actually allow him to do some of the cutting on his own as long as they remained close by and paid complete attention to Greg and his activity. Greg began to show the desire to move on to the next sequence, instead of just completing one part of the task. After he had completed his initial contribution, he automatically began to initiate adding additional vegetables to a salad, as he had seen his family do.

Greg and his parents expanded the experiences by working on opening and emptying containers of food into bowls, taking off lids, and opening jars and packages. As Greg participated in even the most simple tasks (in terms of sequences to be performed), he was more apt to be motivated to eat what he had participated in preparing. Greg had the added experience of watching his family enjoy his culinary contributions. It became naturally rewarding. He became motivated to speak in appropriate short phrases, classifying foods and colors. He showed an improved willingness to try different flavors and textures of foods.

Three months after the initial therapy evaluation, Greg was able to make juice from a can and pour it into glasses to serve the entire family. It was a task that he had learned in the clinic and had been able to generalize to his own environment with very little assistance. This task incorporated adding a specific amount of water to the juice concentrate, stirring with a large utensil, estimating of the amount of liquid for each glass, anticipating when to stop pouring, transporting the glasses to each place setting, and even counting ice cubes to add to each glass. Although the task involved a small set of calculated sequences, it took a great amount of attention and focus, equaling a big responsibility. Greg had blossomed into a productive family member who adapted to his environment by interacting in normal everyday events.

References

Affolter, F. D. (1987). The development of perceptual processes and problem solving activities in normal, hearing impaired and language disturbed children. In D. S. Martin (Ed.), *Cognition, education, and deafness: Directions for research and instruction* (pp. 44–46). Washington, DC: Gallaudet University Press.

Affolter, F. D. (1991). *Perception, interaction and language: Interaction of daily living as the root of development*. Berlin, Germany: Springer-Verlag.

Affolter, F. D., & Stricker, E. (Eds). (1980). *Perceptual processes as prerequisites for complex human behavior: A theoretical model and its application to therapy*. Bern, Switzerland: Hans Huber.

Bonfils, K. (1996). The Affolter approach to treatment: A perceptual-cognitive perspective of function. In L. Pedretti (Ed.), *Occupational therapy: Practice skills for physical dysfunction* (4th ed., pp. 451–461). St. Louis, MO: Mosby.

Davis, J. Z. (1992). The Affolter method: A model for treating perceptual disturbances in the hemiplegic and brain injured patient. *Occupational Therapy Practice, 3*(4), 30–38.

Janzen, J. (1996). *Understanding the nature of autism: A practical guide.* San Antonio, TX: Therapy Skill Builders.

LeVine, M. J., VanHorn, K. R., Sweeney, L. A., Pallas, D. M., & Mullin, J. P. (1998). Reaction and movement time variability in ADD/H: Effect of tactile experience. *Pediatric Rehabilitation, 2*(2), 57–63.

Nelson, D. (1984). *Children with autism and other pervasive disorders of development and behavior: Therapy through activities.* Thorofare, NJ: Slack.

Sweeney, L. A., Stockman, I. J., Hayden, D., Sweeney, L., Parham, D., & Bonfils, K. (1996, November). *Augmented sensory input in managing pervasive developmental disorders: Efficacy of guided interaction therapy for improving language.* Seminar presented at the National Convention of the American Speech-Language-Hearing Association: Seattle, WA.

Webster's new world dictionary (3rd college ed.). (1988). New York: Simon & Shuster.

CHAPTER 12

Alternative and Complementary Approaches in the Treatment of Autism

Patricia S. Lemer, MEd, NCC, MS, BUS

The primary care for children with a Pervasive Developmental Disorder (PDD) occurs in both the health-care and educational arenas. These two environments provide occupational therapists with opportunities to work as members of multidisciplinary teams that evaluate and treat each child. A variety of traditional and commonly used interventions have been presented in earlier chapters of this book. However, many less well-known options may also be effective. Readers should be cautioned that, as with many intervention approaches included within this text, the validity and effectiveness may be considered questionable until each is thoroughly investigated through research. However, with that caution in mind, many options are available to families that practitioners should be familiar with because parents searching for alternatives to the traditional approaches may ask about them.

This chapter will present an overview of both some traditional interventions and a large variety of nontraditional approaches. Where possible, research regarding effectiveness will be provided. Additional information and resources will also be provided in Appendix 12.A for those clinicians who wish to gather further information about any of the included approaches.

Traditional Treatments

Traditional approaches, which focus on language, psychological, neurological, and behavioral issues, include pharmaceutical intervention, special education, counseling, and applied behavior management. These interventions constitute the first-line multidisciplinary approach usually recommended by physicians, mental health professionals, and educators. Educational and behavioral approaches are discussed elsewhere in this text and will not be repeated here.

The ultimate goal of treatment is to eliminate undesirable behaviors such as hyperactivity, poor attention, perseveration, and impulsivity while increasing desirable outcomes such as relatedness, eye contact, self-control, attention span, and confidence. Although traditional treatments certainly have palliative effects, they often do not address some of the most basic physiological difficulties. In addition, they are frequently accompanied by undesirable side effects.

Medications

Since they were introduced 60 years ago, medications for behavioral and learning problems have become more specialized and powerful. At the present time, five classes of drugs are being

Table 12.1

Common Medications Prescribed for Children With Autistic Spectrum Disorders

Class	Drugs	Effects
Psycho-stimulants	Ritalin	Affects dopamine
	Dexedrine ®	Monitors arousal system
	Cylert ®	Causes better regulation
	Adderall ®	Causes better regulation
Antidepressants	Prozac ®, Paxil ®	Affects serotonin
	Luvox ®	Reduces anxiety
	Anafranll, Tofranil, Wellbutrin ®, Elavil ®, Zoloft ®	Reduces inappropriate and ritualistic behaviors
Hypertensives	Clonidine, Tenex ®	Lowers blood pressure Calms and improves sleep
Anticonvulsants	Depacote, Phenobarbital, Tegretol ®, Dilantin	Calms behavior
Antipsychotics	Mellaril, Thorazine ®	Reduces agitation, aggression, and hallucinations

prescribed for children who have conditions within the autistic spectrum of disorders: psycho-stimulants, antidepressants, hypertensives, anticonvulsants, and antipsychotics (see Table 12.1).

Although pharmaceutical preparations certainly alleviate many attentional and behavioral symptoms, significant temporary side effects are inevitable with most drugs (*Physician's Desk Reference*, 1998). Minor secondary health problems include rashes, headaches, palpitations, and nervousness. Visual side effects such as lack of focus or abnormal eye movements can also occur. Long-term effects that are

extremely troubling are tics, loss of inhibitions, and interference with sleep, appetite, and growth (Konopasek, 1997). Often, all five types of medications are used together to balance out one another's side effects. For instance, Ritalin can cause sleeping problems, so Clonodine may be added to induce sleep.

Since 1967, the Autism Research Institute has been collecting parent ratings of the behavioral effects of more than 40 drugs and 10 nutrients. Figure 12.1 depicts these findings. For instance, giving Prozac, a serotonin booster with considerable side effects, resulted in improved behavior in only about one-third of the cases. That means the drug demonstrated no effect on or worsened the conditions of two-thirds of the children. With the majority of drugs, the same was true. The best results were noted with the antifungal drug Nystatin. (See the section on probiotics and antifungals under "Nutritional Supplementation" in this chapter.)

Special Education, Counseling, and Behavior Management

In addition to the use of medication in traditional treatments, placement in special education and the delivery of counseling or behavioral management services from mental health professionals are frequently recommended as a part of a traditional treatment plan. Unquestionably, children with autism require specialized teaching, and their parents require psychological support to address the social and emotional issues of raising a child with special needs. However, these treatments and this support may produce additional problems. For example, providing external methods of monitoring and handling behavior may prevent children from learning how to develop internal controls.

Although medications, special education, and counseling clearly help, these traditional treatments may be treating the symptoms of autism rather than addressing the underlying

Figure 12.1
Parent ratings of behavioral effects of drugs and nutrients.

Autism Research Institute □ 4182 Adams Avenue □ San Diego, CA 92116

PARENT RATINGS OF BEHAVIORAL EFFECTS OF DRUGS, NUTRIENTS, AND DIETS

The parents of autistic children represent a vast and important reservoir of information on the benefits—and adverse effects—of the large variety of drugs and other interventions that have been tried with their children. Since 1967 the Autism Research Institute has been collecting parent ratings of the usefulness of the many interventions tried on their autistic children.

The following data have been collected from the more than 18,500 parents who have completed our questionnaires designed to collect such information. For the purposes of the present table, the parents responses on a six-point scale have been combined into three categories: "made worse" (ratings 5 and 6), "no effect" (ratings 1 and 2), and "made better" (ratings 3 and 4).

% WORSE[A]   % NO EFFECT   % BETTER

Note: For seizure drugs: The first line (beh) shows the drug's behavioral effects; the second line (seiz) shows effects on seizures.

DRUG	Parent Rating: % (Worse / No Effect / Better)	NO. OF CASES[B]	BETTER/WORSE
Aderall	32 / 22 / 46	81	1.4:1
Amphetamine	48 / 28 / 24	1059	0.5:1
Anafranil	31 / 36 / 33	294	1.1:1
Antibiotics	29 / 62 / 9	1366	0.3:1
Antifungals[C]			
Diflucan	8 / 26 / 66	38	8.3:1
Nystatin	5 / 48 / 47	460	9.3:1
Atarax	25 / 53 / 22	390	0.9:1
Benadryl	24 / 51 / 25	2200	1.1:1
Beta Blocker	19 / 45 / 36	219	1.9:1
Buspar	26 / 41 / 33	178	1.3:1
Chloral Hydrate	42 / 32 / 26	297	0.6:1
Clonidine	20 / 32 / 48	796	2.4:1
Clozapine	40 / 40 / 20	45	0.5:1
Cogentin	17 / 56 / 27	121	1.5:1
Cylert	46 / 33 / 21	523	0.5:1
Deanol	15 / 55 / 30	186	2.0:1
Depakene (beh)	24 / 43 / 33	700	1.4:1
Depakene (seiz)	11 / 29 / 60	450	5.6:1
Desipramine	32 / 13 / 55	38	1.8:1
Dilantin (beh)	29 / 47 / 24	1047	0.8:1
Dilantin (seiz)	13 / 35 / 52	325	4.0:1
Felbatol	25 / 33 / 42	24	1.7:1
Fenfluramine	21 / 50 / 29	432	1.4:1
Halcion	36 / 25 / 39	36	1.1:1
Haldol	38 / 27 / 35	1039	0.9:1

DRUG	Parent Rating: % (Worse / No Effect / Better)	NO. OF CASES[B]	BETTER/WORSE
Klonapin	21 / 29 / 50	86	2.4:1
Lithium	26 / 43 / 31	331	1.2:1
Luvox	17 / 29 / 54	41	3.1:1
Mellaril	28 / 38 / 34	1927	1.2:1
Mysoline (beh)	46 / 38 / 16	120	0.3:1
Mysoline (seiz)	17 / 57 / 26	46	1.5:1
Naltrexone	23 / 43 / 34	169	1.5:1
Paxil	18 / 28 / 54	61	3.0:1
Phenergan	34 / 41 / 25	197	0.7:1
Phenobarb. (beh)	47 / 37 / 16	994	0.3:1
Phenobarb. (seiz)	15 / 43 / 42	397	2.8:1
Prolixin	29 / 31 / 40	68	1.4:1
Prozac	31 / 32 / 37	697	1.2:1
Risperdal	14 / 30 / 56	124	4.1:1
Ritalin	44 / 27 / 29	3082	0.7:1
Stelazine	28 / 44 / 28	401	1.0:1
Tegretol (beh)	23 / 45 / 32	1180	1.4:1
Tegretol (seiz)	11 / 33 / 56	613	5.3:1
Thorazine	36 / 40 / 24	863	0.7:1
Tofranil	31 / 37 / 32	597	1.0:1
Valium	35 / 42 / 23	728	0.7:1
Zarontin (beh)	32 / 44 / 24	113	0.8:1
Zarontin (seiz)	17 / 53 / 30	66	1.8:1
Zoloft	32 / 30 / 38	103	1.2:1

NUTRIENTS/SUPPLEMENTS	Parent Rating: % (Worse / No Effect / Better)	NO. OF CASES[B]	BETTER/WORSE
Calcium[D]	2 / 59 / 39	522	18.4:1
DMG	7 / 50 / 43	3687	6.4:1
Folic Acid	3 / 53 / 44	724	13.8:1
Melatonin[E]	— / 33 / 67	46	—
Vit. B3	5 / 53 / 42	307	8.6:1
Vit. B6/Mag.	4 / 50 / 46	4059	10.9:1
Vit. C	3 / 57 / 40	811	15.3:1
Zinc	3 / 54 / 43	453	14.8:1

DIET	Parent Rating: % (Worse / No Effect / Better)	NO. OF CASES[B]	BETTER/WORSE
Candida Diet	2 / 45 / 52	398	23:1
Feingold Diet	2 / 48 / 50	527	22:1
Rotation Diet	2 / 52 / 46	565	20:1
Rem. Chocolate	1 / 53 / 46	1156	38:1
Removed Dairy	1 / 54 / 45	3989	33:1
Removed Eggs	1 / 64 / 35	605	52:1
Removed Sugar	2 / 52 / 46	3000	27:1
Removed Wheat	1 / 58 / 41	2022	32:1

A. "Worse" refers only to behavior. Drugs, but not nutrients, typically also cause physical problems if used long-term.
B. No. of cases is cumulative over several decades, so does not reflect current usage levels (e.g., Haldol is now seldom used).
C. Antifungal drugs are used only if autism is yeast-related.
D. Calcium effects not due to dairy-free diet; statistics similar for milk drinkers and non-milk drinkers.
E. Caution: While melatonin can benefit sleep and behavior, its long-term effects on puberty are unknown.

From Autism Research Institute, October 1994, San Diego, CA. Copyright October 1994 by Autism Research Institute. Revised September 2000. Reprinted with permission.

causes. Thus, benefits are short-term at best. At worst, certain issues are alleviated while other significant problems result. For instance, Ritalin helps attention, but it could possibly create a tic disorder such as Tourette's syndrome in vulnerable children (Gadow, Nolan, Sverd, 1995). Also of great concern is the huge financial burden placed on both the health-care and the educational systems, which are not designed to manage so many children with special needs.

Alternative Treatments

Although mainstream medical practitioners have historically questioned alternative treatments, these approaches are now receiving a great deal of attention. The merging of traditional medicine with other therapies has been enhanced by the addition of an Office of Alternative Medicine (OAM) to the National Institutes of Health (NIH). As of October 1998, the OAM is a separate entity, with a budget of $50 million to be distributed to researchers who are evaluating a host of alternative treatments for both adults and children.

Alternative treatments generally focus on addressing causes rather than treating symptoms. This approach is difficult with autism because many possible etiologies of the condition are being examined. The bulk of research into the etiology of autism focuses on the brain and body-based clues. Autism is believed to be a neurologically based problem (Kemper & Bauman, 1993). Researchers, however, are now paying attention to other "emerging" symptoms that have been noted but were previously unreported or ignored (Gupta, Aggarwal, & Heads, 1996; Panksepp, 1979; Rimland, 1985; Shaw, 1998; Wakefield, 1998). Iverson (1996) has listed some of these symptoms:

- Digestive problems including chronic constipation, diarrhea, reflux, or a combination of the problems
- Self-limited diets, often consisting primarily of wheat and dairy products

- Allergy symptoms such as red ears and cheeks, black circles under the eyes, and puffy face
- Food and air-borne allergies
- Sleep problems
- Hyperactivity
- Hypotonia

The big question is what happens to the body that causes the development of these systems to go awry?

Dr. Bernard Rimland, a psychologist and father of a son with autism, has been addressing this question of etiology since 1967 when he founded the Autism Research Institute (see Appendix 12.A). For the past 30 years, Dr. Rimland has worked to understand the causes of autism. In January 1995, with Doctors Sidney Baker and Jon Pangborn, he created Defeat Autism Now! (DAN!), a think tank made up of eminent autism researchers worldwide. They have published the DAN! protocol (Baker & Pangborn, 1997), which documents specific tests and procedures that are needed to exhaustively evaluate vascular, immunologic, autoimmune, metabolic, iatrogenic, and genetic issues surrounding the etiology of autistic symptoms. Each year since 1995, DAN! doctors meet to discuss new research findings, which they share with the public. In October 1998, when more than 1,200 parents and professionals attended their conference, possible links between the physical and neurological problems were first highlighted.

Parents and physicians of children with autism frequently relate that their youngsters passed their developmental milestones appropriately. Almost all sat, walked, and related as toddlers. Many developed some speech and language. At some point, usually between 15 and 24 months, behavior became unmanageable, or it regressed. Although many case histories of "classic" or Kanner's Syndrome autism suggest sequences of events similar to these, today's researchers agree that the autism they are seeing today is qualitatively different

(Greenspan & Wieder, 1998; Iverson, 1996; Ritvo, et al.,1990; Shaw, 1998).

Some families can recall the exact date and event when their toddlers first changed and some even have home videos to show. They know it happened at approximately the same time the child developed colic, ear infections, allergies, asthma, eczema, or seizures; reacted negatively to an immunization; became a picky eater; or stopped sleeping through the night. Sometimes, the change was gradual. Perhaps Grandma noticed that the baby no longer looked and smiled at her. Perhaps Mom and Dad realized that they no longer heard the single words the child used at approximately the age of 1 year and that the child was not adding words to his or her vocabulary. In other cases, the change was sudden and followed an ear infection, high fever, immunization, or routine surgery. After days, weeks, or even months of anxiety, experts were consulted and the diagnosis made: a PDD.

The Total Load Theory

Children who have conditions on autistic disorders have an important commonality: a huge total load. Total load theory is a multifactorial approach to describe the cumulative effect of the individual assaults of each problem on the body as a whole (Dorfman, 1996). The cluster of symptoms that eventually leads to one of the diagnoses on the autistic spectrum is the result of many organ, muscle, and sensory systems of the body being stressed to their limits. Each person has a personal load limit, as does a bridge. When that limit is exceeded, then skin, respiratory, digestive, immunological, language, motor, and attention problems occur. These problems coexist with developmental, cognitive, and sensory problems, and their relationship is very complex.

Children are far more susceptible to a load of stressors than adults because their small, less mature systems cannot handle the assault. The end of the second year of life is a particularly vulnerable period when vision, language, and social skills are maturing at a rapid rate. This period is the crucial developmental stage when the child moves out of "near" space, increasing visual-motor manipulation and interaction with the "far" environment. As self-awareness expands to other-awareness, language develops and social skills emerge (Kavner, 1985).

Many prenatal conditions may contribute to the total load. Babies who have endured complications of pregnancy or have had subtle birth trauma, including oxygen deprivation or breech presentation, and who are born to parents who have conditions such as thyroid problems, severe allergies, chronic fatigue syndrome, or fibromyalgia are much more at risk for later developmental problems (Dorfman, 1996). Additional factors that occur in the first year of life and that are red flags include colic, allergies to cow's milk, projectile vomiting, reflux, eczema, chronic ear infections, repeated use of antibiotics, immunization reactions, or sensory deprivation. The developmental histories of children with most delays show one or more of these problems. According to a study of almost 700 children done by Developmental Delay Resources (DDR) in 1994, children who had more than 20 rounds of antibiotics were more than 50% more likely to have delays. Affected children were nearly four times as likely to have had negative reactions to an immunization (Dorfman, Lemer, & Nadler, 1995).

Difficulties That Add to the Total Load: The Structural Connection

According to Dr. Viola Frymann, an osteopathic physician in California, birth trauma is the most common cause of developmental problems, including autism. At least 80% of children with developmental problems have a history of a traumatic birth (Frymann, 1996). Problems during delivery, resulting from temporary compression that occurs while passing through the birth canal (problems from which the skull and sacrum do not recover fully), can affect the brain, spinal column, and the fluids inside these organs. If any of the organs, fluids, bones, and connective tissues are out of balance, for any reason, their function can be affected. Many of the underlying health issues are experienced by children with a PDD and these issues are clustered into specific organ and muscular systems. The nervous and digestive systems are particularly vulnerable. In addition, some children have seizure disorders and obvious motor problems such as cerebral palsy (Frymann, 1996).

Immune System Connection

Of all the possible causes associated with autism, the breakdown of the immune system is the one that has received the most attention. The immune system is the body's defense against disease. It is on the alert to protect against all invaders: bacteria, toxins, viruses, pollen, parasites, molds, and incompletely digested particles of food. A defense such as the immune system that is exhausted from continuous efforts to ward off repeated assaults is a vulnerable system. Immune system problems can be divided into two types: those related

specifically to immune system dysfunction and those related to problems with detoxification pathways. Table 12.2 details signs of immune system dysfunction, and Table 12.3 details symptoms of problems with detoxification pathways (Dorfman, 1997; Shaw, 1998). Many children have both types of problems because the immune and detoxification systems overlap and load onto each other. The larger the total load of problematic factors on the child's overall system, the more severe the attention, behavior, and cognitive difficulties.

In a newborn, the immune system is still immature. If the baby is born compromised in any way, the immune system might also be affected (Dorfman, 1995a). If that baby develops an ear infection, fighting it may be a fight for life itself. Nonetheless, if the baby's immune system is permitted to fight its first ear infection, the process appears to strengthen the immune system in the long term (Schmidt, 1996). The next time an invader comes around, the body is better prepared. In children with a PDD, assaults to the immune system may occur during a critical period of development when the body may not have enough vital force to fight infection and to process touch, sound, sights, thoughts, and feelings simultaneously to fight infection. The body may be putting all its energy into staying alive. The immune system becomes hypervigilant and irritated. This internal sensitivity can be observed outwardly as distractibility and hyperactivity. Also, this hypervigilance and irritation severely affect sensory processing (Dorfman, 1995a).

The Antibiotic Connection. Nature intended us to use our immune systems. So what happens to a baby's immune system if an antibiotic takes over its job? Some believe that the immune system becomes suppressed (Schmidt, Smith, & Sehnert, 1994) and might respond less vigorously to the next infection. By the fourth or fifth infection, the immune system might not even recognize an invader as a threat because it now depends on the antibiotic to do its job.

Table 12.2
Signs of Immune System Dysfunction

- Allergies
- Frequent ear, sinus, or strep infections
- Respiratory problems, including asthma and bronchitis
- Skin problems, including excema and poor color
- Digestive problems, including constipation, chronic diarrhea, or reflux
- Deep circles under the eyes (allergic shiners)
- Red ears or apple cheeks
- History of an extended immunization reaction
- Sudden decline in function between 15 and 30 months
- Chronic, unexplained fevers
- Yeast infections

Note. From *Biological treatments for autism and PDD,* by William Shaw, 1998, Lenexa, KS: The Great Plains Laboratory. Copyright 1998 by William Shaw. Adapted with permission.

Antibiotic, when translated literally, means "against life." Antibiotic creams work topically to combat external infections. If a child has an ear or strep infection, however, a systemic product must be used. These powerful agents not only kill infections but also they knock out virtually all of the bacteria in the gut, including beneficial varieties. Many people experience digestive problems when taking an antibiotic for this reason. The gut is a host to thousands of types of flora that live together cooperatively in the healthy person. After ingestion of antibiotics, however, this symbiotic environment is disrupted. The good bacteria, which are sacrificed to combat infection, serve to control the growth of yeasts and other fungi in the digestive tract. In their absence, yeasts colonize and their usually small colonies proliferate. Although yeasts interfere with the body's ability to regulate absorption of essential fatty acids, their by-products of metabolism are very toxic to children with a PDD (Crook, 1996).

Today's antibiotics are like atom bombs compared to the water-pistol varieties of the previous generation of antibiotics, including penicillin. Recently, physicians have become concerned about drug-resistant infections that develop because of antibiotic overuse. Is it possible that these lifesaving miracle drugs, which are essential to combat infection, are also negatively affecting some children's nervous and digestive systems?

The Yeast Connection. Dr. William Crook, a country pediatrician since 1949, has written extensively on the relationship between ear infections, antibiotics, and autism (Crook, 1986, 1994, 1996). Dr. Crook believes that many children with autism have problems connected to yeast (*Candida albicans*). Dr. Rimland also suspected a relationship between yeast and autism (Rimland, 1985). Yeast needs sugar to grow. Children who crave sweets are highly suspect because yeasts feed on sugar from candy, soft drinks, fruit juices, and baked goods. The following scenario is common to children with yeast-related problems. The mother has recurrent yeast infections, menstrual irregularity, and bladder infections. Her child has thrush in infancy; recurrent and persistent diaper rash; colic; recurrent ear infections with repeated or prolonged antibiotic use; chronic allergies including rashes, wheezing, and coughing; headaches; muscle aches; abdominal pain or digestive problems; irritability; depression; mood swings; hyperactivity; and attention problems. Many children with autism initially demonstrate these occurrences prior to diagnosis.

Dr. William Shaw, the former director of clinical chemistry and toxicology at Children's Mercy Hospital in Kansas City, confirmed Dr. Crook's suspicions with highly sophisticated laboratory testing. Dr. Shaw, a biochemist who previously had no experience with autism, identified very high levels of abnormal by-products of yeast overgrowth in the gut flora of children who, he later learned, were autistic brothers (Shaw, Kassen, & Chaves, 1995). A follow-up study of other children who had been diagnosed with autism confirmed his findings, but he was prohibited from sharing his results and was fired for speaking in public about his research. He subsequently founded the Great Plains Laboratory and is a member of DAN!.

Leaky Gut. A "leaky gut" occurs when undigested food particles and toxins produced

Table 12.3
Signs of Problems with Detoxification Pathways

- Hyperactivity
- Agitated sleep
- Wild swings in mood and function
- Self-injurious or violent behaviors
- Regressive behavior after eating food with additives
- Sensitivity to dyes, chemicals, perfumes, or medications
- Craving for apple juice

Note. From "Improving detoxification pathways" by K. Dorfman, 1997, *New Developments, 2,* p. 3. Copyright 1997 by Developmental Delay Registry. Adapted with permission.

in the digestive process pass through the intestinal wall. The intestines are lined with a thin mucosal membrane barrier that becomes weakened by both antibiotic overuse and the yeasts taking root. Picture this phenomenon as similar to ivy attaching itself to a brick house and slowly destroying the mortar. The tiny holes made by the yeast allow the toxins to enter the bloodstream. The body's immediate reaction is to clear these incompletely digested particles. IgG antibodies are produced by the immune cells, which attach themselves to oversized food particles. "Allergies" are a result of the white blood cells working overtime to combat these invaders. If the immune system is compromised because of any of the other factors of the total load, it cannot purge the system completely. The toxins thus travel around the body, affecting other systems, including the brain, and produce inflammation, distress, and dysfunction (Braly, 1992).

Allergies, Asthma, Constipation, Diarrhea, and Reflux. Many children with autism have early health-related issues such as chronic ear infections, food and seasonal allergies, asthma, chronic constipation, or diarrhea. In some of the most severe cases, both the digestive and respiratory problems persist. In others, they gradually disappear. Parents think that because their children no longer have colic, stomachaches, reflux, constipation, diarrhea, or vomiting, their offspring have "outgrown" early allergies such as those to cow's milk. However, many of these digestive, respiratory, and cognitive problems, although seemingly unrelated, can also be the result of immune dysfunction (Braly, 1992). These problems may persist, and as the child's body matures, the physical illnesses are then manifested as cognitive problems, behavioral problems, or both (Rapp, 1991).

Wheat and Dairy. Two of the most common food allergies in young children are allergies to wheat and cow's milk. Problems with cow's milk and wheat are probably lifelong and have been related to many chronic health problems such as eczema, asthma, childhood diabetes, constipation, diarrhea, and reflux, as well as behavioral and learning problems (Oski, 1983). Because of these problems, pediatricians often recommend rice cereal first and are against introducing cow's milk into a baby's diet until after the first birthday.

Yet, many children with a PDD eat a very limited diet consisting almost entirely of wheat and dairy food in every imaginable combination. Breakfast may be cereal and milk or a bagel and cream cheese; lunch might consist of macaroni and cheese or a grilled cheese sandwich; and dinner might typically be pizza. Many parents report this diet using words like "addicted" and "craves." These children appear to need their next "fix" of wheat and dairy food as much as an addict needs his drug. Research that is described in the next section may begin to explain the "need" that these children have for foods containing wheat and dairy products.

Gluten, Casein, and the Opioid Excess Theory. Milk may not be the culprit with respect to food allergies, but rather, the dairy protein, casein, may be problematic. Likewise, it may not be wheat, but gluten—a protein common to many cereal grains, including wheat, rye, oats, and barley—that is the culprit in the foods eaten by children with autism (Panksepp, 1979; Reichelt, Ekrem, & Scott, 1990). This discovery was made from studying the results of specially designed urine tests on people with autism whose samples also included fragments of incompletely digested proteins from cow's milk and wheat (Sinaiko, 1996). A major reason that cow's milk is a problem for humans is that it has seven times as much casein as human milk (cows have more stomachs to digest their food).

Noting similarities between the behavioral effects of opioid-based drugs on animals and the symptoms of autism, biochemists Kalle Reichelt and Paul Shattock were not surprised to find that 90% of children with autism have abnormally high urine levels of certain opioid peptides (Reichelt et al, 1990). It is believed that the gluten from the wheat and the casein from the dairy combine chemically to make these opioid peptides. The brain has receptors for opioids and many other different types of peptides. The role of these peptides is to switch on a neuron's sensitivity to other neurotransmitters. Some opioid peptides are useful, but too many are harmful. Excessive peptides can mimic some of the good hormones and transmitters, thus disturbing perception, behavior, mood, emotions, brain development, and immune function (McCrone, 1998).

Dr. Rosemary Waring discovered that many children with autism who have trouble digesting gluten and casein also have low levels of phenol-sulfotransferase-P. This chemical is an enzyme that is needed to process certain foods containing a phenyl ring in their structure and to detoxify certain intestinal bacteria. She conjectures that the intact phenyls and bacteria act as internal irritants, which cause bizarre and hyperactive behavior. Dr. Waring and the DAN! committee are convinced of a definite connection between deficiencies of phenol-sulfotransferase-P and autism (Waring, 1990).

Additives. Today's children are the third generation who ingest artificially manufactured food products. Almost everything they ingest on their limited diets is "unnatural." The root beer of their grandparents' era was made with sarsaparilla root, and the grape flavored ices were made with grape juice. Today's "root beer" and "grape" products are made entirely from chemicals, technologically produced colors and flavors, and preservatives that extend their shelf life. Dr. Waring's discovery that many children with autism are deficient in pheno-sulphotransferase-P and, thus, cannot digest gluten and casein products is important because the production of pheno-sulphotransferase-P is inhibited by food dyes (Brostoff & Gamlin, 1989).

Twenty-five years ago, Dr. Benjamin Feingold, working at the Kaiser Permanente Medical Center in San Francisco, became concerned about the behavior of children in his pediatric practice. He noticed that some became hyperactive after ingesting aspirin and specific food products. He traced the behavior to salicylates, an ingredient found in aspirin and occurring naturally in apples, oranges, tomatoes, peppers, berries, and cucumbers. He also traced unusual behaviors to artificial dyes, colors, flavors, and the preservatives butylated hydroxyanisole (BHA), butylated hydroxytoluene (BHT) and tertiary butyl hydroquinone (TBHQ) (Feingold, 1975).

Look at the few "real" foods that children with autism eat, and you will often find that most contain salicylates: apple and orange juice, raw cucumbers, green peppers, pizza with tomato sauce, and strawberries. Parents who are taking comfort in the fact that their children are getting some healthy products may have to think again. Although many controlled, double-blind studies linking diet and hyperactivity have been conducted (Boris & Mandel, 1994; Egger, Stolla, & McEwen, 1992; Kaplan, McNicol, Conte, & Moghadam, 1989; Rowe & Rowe, 1994), for the most part, they have been ignored or refuted by the medical community.

The Secretin Connection. Parker Beck is a child whose development regressed in the second year of life and who also had chronic diarrhea. After the traditional medical evaluations revealed little, his parents requested an endoscopy, a thorough examination of the digestive tract. Part of this procedure included a secretin challenge test, used diagnostically to evaluate pancreatic function. Secretin is an amino acid that aids in regulating gastric function. In addition to its role in digestion, it is intimately involved in many activities of the brain, including the production and use of the neurotransmitter serotonin. In a secretin challenge test, secretin is infused by IV to see what effect this has on the system. When Parker had a secretin challenge test, the first major change noted was a normal bowel movement. Within a few weeks, he demonstrated improved eye contact, a decrease in self-stimulatory behavior, and a marked jump in vocabulary development. However, these improvements wore off quickly. A second and then a third infusion of secretin showed similar results. Each time, Parker improved but then plateaued. He maintained the gains he made, but his rate of development slowed again as his body used up the secretin from the infusion, unable to produce any of its own.

How does secretin work? It enhances intestinal fluid production, which, in turn, allows the normal metabolism of protein. When secretin is present in the digestive tract, casein and gluten are no longer problems. The end products of digestion are formed stools and a rise in blood serotonin levels that stimulate the production of other neurotransmitters, leading to increased attention, language production, and socialization.

Estimates suggest that about 3,000 children with autism have been given secretin by about 250 physicians. The vast majority have received it by IV injection, though a few have had transdermal applications or sublingual drops. Reactions such as hyperactivity and aggressiveness seem to grow worse in about 5–10% of the children. Two cases of grand mal seizures have been documented. However, most reports are positive, describing improvements in eye contact, interest in the environment, better sleep patterns and accelerated language development (Rimland, 1999b).

In short, secretin is a link between the gut and the brain. Its discovery is one of the most exciting in the autism field to date because it relates physical symptoms with cognitive and behavioral problems. The link has created an interest in research to determine which children are good candidates, what is an appropriate dosage, and how often it should be administered for optimal effectiveness. At the time of this writing, the demand for secretin is greater than the supply. The product is being extracted from pigs by a pharmaceutical company that obtains the enzyme to be used as a diagnostic tool to assess pancreatic disease. Doctors are thus searching for other sources, perhaps from humans, and for alternative methods of delivery such as patches, lozenges, sprays, or salves (Rimland, 1998).

The Vaccine Connection. Those who see the connection between immune system deficiencies and autism believe that immunizations play a role. As early as 1971, Dr. Chess noted an association between congenital rubella and autism (Chess, 1971). Since the early 1980s, parents have reported a possible link between the onset of autism and a rubella or a DPT (diphtheria, tetanus, pertussis) immunization. Researchers have confirmed these suspicions (Warren, Foster, & Margaretten, 1986; Zimmerman, Frye, & Potter, 1993).

Vaccines work by triggering an immune response. Vaccines are now being given to babies in "cocktails," and, often, within the first 24 hours of life. According to a *USA Today* article (Manning, 1999), most of the 11,000 children born each day in the United States will get at least 21 vaccinations before they start first grade—more than twice as many as a decade ago.

What happens when a premature infant or one with a low Apgar score is immunized with the measles, mumps, rubella (MMR) vaccine? Some children, later diagnosed as autistic, had inconsolable crying, an extremely high fever, or a seizure within 24 hours of the vaccine (Fudenberg, 1996). In addition, if the reaction occurs in that crucial second year of life, many parents report the sudden loss of eye contact and language as well as the onset of sterotypical behaviors, temper tantrums, and general agitation (Dawbarns, n.d.).

Barbara Loe Fisher, cofounder of the National Vaccine Information Center (NVIC) (see Appendix 12.A), coauthor of *DPT—A Shot in the Dark* (Coulter & Fisher, 1985), and the mother of a vaccine-damaged child, has devoted the past 15 years to advocating for freedom of choice. Because of her work, many parents are able to choose to not give the pertussis in the DPT shot or to delay immunizations until a child enters school. The NVIC maintains a registry and publishes a newsletter on this subject.

Congress is now listening to Fisher and the parents who have told her their stories. U.S. Representative Dan Burton, himself the grandfather of a child who developed autism shortly after receiving a DPT shot, held hearings in August 1999. He wanted to ensure that what is being done for the good of society outweighs the risks.

Even at the time of this writing, the campaign to immunize every child earlier and earlier and for more and more diseases has escalated. "Be Wise and Immunize," the radio and television slogans beg. The newest thrust is for a mandatory Hepatitis B vaccine worldwide. However, the Association of American Physicians and Surgeons came out with a statement in August 1999, which was critical of school districts requiring vaccinations for school entry (Rimland, 1999a). The NVIC and others fear an even greater increase in the numbers of children with a PDD as new vaccines are introduced.

The Vaccine-Gut Relationship. Until two years ago, no concrete evidence had shown that gut problems and vaccine-related autism are connected. Andrew J. Wakefield, MD, chairman of the Inflammatory Bowel Study Group in London, was investigating children with Crohn's disease and colitis, a population unknown to the medical community prior to 1975. Like William Shaw, Wakefield had no prior knowledge of autism. One of his subjects, however, was a child who had experienced normal development until age 4 1/2. Within 24 hours of receiving an MMR (measles, mumps, rubella) booster, this boy lost all acquired skills and became unable to control urine or bowels.

Wakefield studied the digestive tracts of this child and 59 other children with autism who also had inflammatory bowel disease and compared the findings to those of 36 typically developing children with the same consistent gastrointestinal symptoms: chronic diarrhea and constipation, alternating diarrhea and constipation, undigested food particles in the feces, bloating, and abdominal pain. Using an endoscope, a camera that can see inside the digestive tract, he made the following astounding observations:

- Children with autism had inflammation all through their bowels whereas those with inflammatory bowel disease and no symptoms of autism showed inflammation that got progressively worse toward the lower end of the bowel.

- Children with autism had huge, tonsil-like swellings of lymphoid tissue in their bowels. Some had red rings surrounding these swellings where the tissue had broken down and ulcerated. Only one case of the control group had even mild inflammation of this type.

- The inflammatory bowel disease in the children with autism appeared to be triggered by a virus.

- Biopsies of the lymphoid follicles found the measles virus present in low amounts in five of seven cases and in a very specific location: the follicular dendridic cells, the gatekeepers of the immune system.

Wakefield's conclusions are that, in many children with autism, the gut is the source of the problem, and the target organ is the brain. He named this syndrome "autistic entero-colitis." It is characterized by an autoimmune response to the brain that is caused by exposure to the measles vaccine in susceptible children (Wakefield, 1998). Wakefield's findings have been duplicated twice (Singh, Lin, & Yang, 1998; Zecca, Graffino, Lania-Howarth, Passante, & Oleske, 1997).

Approaches to Reduce the Total Load

Alternative and complementary treatments that focus on physiological relationships occurring in the body neurologically, metabolically, and psychologically can be categorized as follows:

- Structural therapies including osteopathy, cranial-sacral therapy, and chiropractic
- Treatments that boost the immune system, including dietary modification, nutritional supplementation, homeopathy, and immunotherapy
- Treatments that address the processing of sensory information, including sensory-integration therapy, auditory training, and vision therapy

Please refer to Appendix 12.A for references providing further information.

Structural Therapies

Practitioners from many disciplines are trained in manipulative techniques, and it thus can be confusing when evaluating which type of structural therapy might be beneficial for a particular child. Because the underlying cause of the problem, rather than the diagnosis, is what is important, an in-depth developmental history is essential to making this determination.

A number of alternative treatments take into account the structural and skeletal systems of the body and their relationship to each other. These include osteopathy, cranial-sacral therapy, chiropractic, and massage. Structural therapies serve to realign the body's internal parts. The therapist applies pressure, addressing each dysfunctional system with procedures designed to reactivate that system and bring its function back into balance (Caskey, 1996). These therapies are believed to correct the reduced flow of impulses.

Osteopathic physicians, health professionals trained in craniosacral techniques, massage therapists, chiropractors, and other "bodyworks" people can provide precise, gentle, restorative, manipulative treatment. These procedures have been shown to be particularly beneficial for treating those who have chronic ear infections (Anderson & Peiper, 1996; Block, 1996). If structural dysfunction resulting from birth trauma is corrected early, neurological development can progress satisfactorily. Then motor, sensory-motor, language, social-emotional, cognitive, and behavioral problems can be averted by establishing or restoring optimal anatomic-physiologic integrity.

Many therapists combine techniques and disciplines because there is no clear-cut, single cause to the problems on the autism spectrum. More and more, occupational therapists are learning how to integrate cranio-sacral therapy and massage techniques into their practice because of the synergistic benefits that emerge. These benefits are especially evident when manipulation is used in conjunction with dietary modification and allergy treatments (Upledger, 1991). The Upledger Institute provides training courses in many locations throughout the year for clinicians to learn cranio-sacral techniques. See Appendix 12.A for organizations that can provide referrals to osteopathic physicians, chiropractors, massage therapists, and those trained in cranio-sacral techniques.

Treatments That Boost the Immune System

To determine how dysfunctional a child's immune system is, the clinician must take an extensive medical and developmental history. This history must be an exhaustive look at prenatal, natal, environmental, and social factors such as exposure to medications; vaccine reactions; use of pesticides, chemicals, or tobacco; toxic building materials; pet products; travel; changes in environment; and water. Some factors may be obvious, for example, moving into an older house with lead paint, but others may be more subtle, for example, toxic lawn treatments that daily are tracked into the home. One family became sick when the fertilizer they had been using on their farm was unknowingly "cut" with recycled radioactive material. The effort to trace the cause of illness and developmental problems in children to this source was extraordinary.

Treatment for immune system problems will depend on whether symptoms are related to simple immune system dysfunction, problems with detoxification pathways, or both. Although history taking alone is sometimes adequate to determine an appropriate treatment plan, laboratory testing is frequently necessary to confirm suspicions about gut flora, nutritional deficiencies, or the presence of toxic agents.

Laboratory Testing

Many children with PDDs have had traditional laboratory testing for allergies. However, these usually yield negative results. Several opinions have been proposed about why these negative results occur. Some believe that the reactions children's bodies are having are not true allergies but, rather, subtle sensitivities (Crook, 1987; Rapp, 1991). Although many reactions such as hives and obvious respiratory or intestinal symptoms are immediate, some reactions can be delayed, taking hours, days, or even weeks to appear, and they may involve a cumulative exposure. Making the picture even more complicated is the fact that some foods do not trigger a reaction on their own but may do so only when ingested with another food substance (Baker & Pangborn, 1999).

Fortunately, some very sophisticated blood, urine, and stool tests have lately been designed to pinpoint exactly what has gone awry with the immune, digestive, and respiratory systems as well as with the detoxification pathways. These tests, detailed in the DAN! protocol (Baker & Pangborn, 1997), measure the following factors:

- Strength of both immediate and delayed systemic responses to various common foods
- Gluten and casein sensitivity
- The presence of abnormal organic acids associated with yeast and fungal metabolism
- Undesirable invaders such as intestinal parasites and toxic metals, including lead, cadmium, mercury, and aluminum
- Amino acid abnormalities
- Unusually high antibody titers resulting from markedly abnormal responses to childhood immunizations, including rubella, DPT, and oral polio

The DAN! protocol includes a flow chart for health care professionals to follow in the search for causes of the difficulties known as autism. It is reprinted here as Figure 12.2 with permission from the Autism Research Institute.

Be aware that these tests can be quite expensive and require a physician's interaction, but they may be invaluable diagnostic tools that are often reimbursable. After the tests have been run, specific recommendations can be made. Some interventions can be tried without doing any laboratory testing at all. However, many parents may prefer to have concrete evidence that a significant change is indicated before trying an elimination diet or nutritional supplementation because both can be challenging with a child who is a picky eater.

Immune system and detoxification problems can be dealt with in two ways: (a) lessening the toxic burden by removing some of what is ingested and (b) increasing the efficiency of the body's functioning by adding missing factors using supplementation.

Dietary Modification

This intervention has shown considerable benefits for children with attention, behavior, and learning problems. Parents report increases in the understanding and use of language, better eye contact, and more relatedness (Rapp, 1991). Dr. Talal Nsouli, an allergist at Georgetown University Hospital, has shown that 78% of early childhood ear infections are related to food allergies. By eliminating the offending food from the diet over a 16-week period, he ameliorated the infections in 86% of these children. Reintroduction of the food caused a recurrence. By limiting the diet of his patients, Dr. Nsouli avoided the unnecessary use of antibiotics or insertion of ear tubes, often seen as panaceas to

Figure 12.2
Flow sheet of possible clinicial choices in evaluating children with autism spectrum disorders.

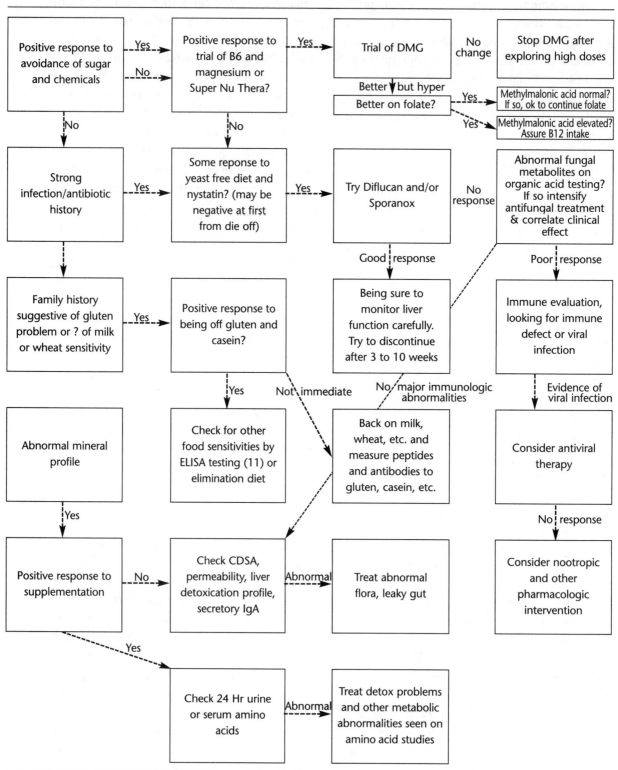

the chronic nature of the problem (Nsouli, Linde, Scanlon, & Bellanti, 1991). General dietary guidelines recommend that the child adhere as closely as possible to a diet based on whole grains and varied protein sources, including beans, fresh fruits and vegetables, as well as nuts and seeds.

The following sections include additional dietary recommendations and tips for children with PDDs.

Eat a Diet That is Unrefined, Varied, and Free of Artificial Colors, Flavors, Additives, and Naturally Occurring Salicylates. Unprocessed foods are less likely to cause problems than those with additives. A rotation diet that alternates grains, meats, fruits, nuts, seeds, and legumes is also less likely to cause reaction. Young bodies cannot tolerate a consistent assault of single unvaried food products.

The Feingold diet, free of additives and salicylates, and developed by Dr. Benjamin Feingold 25 years ago, may be helpful to children with a PDD. For a small yearly fee, the Feingold Association of the United States (FAUS) can provide an extensive booklet that shows, by brand, products that are acceptable and those that are not (see Appendix 12.A). Families who are members of FAUS give impassioned testimonials about how the Feingold diet has changed their children's lives. The organization has evaluated every product in most grocery stores, and parents can use the food list to shop, thus, avoiding having to read every label. This list is kept up-to-date with monthly addenda as new products come on the market and old ones are modified.

Eat a Diet That Is Gluten and Casein Free. Removal of gluten and casein from the diet can make a marked and often immediate difference. However, identifying offensive products can be rather complex. Gluten and casein sometimes masquerade under other names and appear as by-products in other forms such as barley malt (a sweetener) or as an additive to baked goods. Help is available from the Autism Network for

Dietary Intervention (ANDI) (see Appendix 12.A).

Eat a Diet That Is Yeast, Mold, and Sugar Free. Foods containing yeasts and molds include breads, crackers, pastries, pretzels, cakes, cookies, enriched flour, rolls, mushrooms, cantaloupes, peanuts, all cheeses (including cottage cheese), buttermilk, vinegar, catsup, mayonnaise, olives, pickles, some salad dressings, alcohol, malted products, many commercial vitamins, and anything aged or fermented. Reading labels is essential, and even then, products containing yeast can sneak in. Follow guidelines detailed in books by Doctors Doris Rapp, William Crook, or James Braly. Another excellent resource is *Special Diets for Special Kids* by the founders of ANDI (see Appendix 12.A).

Because sugar is the food of yeast, restricting sugar is an important component of dietary modification. Yeasts ferment sugars into alcohol, leaving a child acting drunk, hung over, unfocused, or hyperactive (Crook, 1991). More than 100 recognized substances are described as sugars (Braly, 1992). These include, but are not limited to, sucrose, turbinado, honey, fructose, barley malt, rice or yinnie syrup, dextrose, sorbitol, xylitol, aspartame, saccharine, mannitol, and lactose.

One of the most common and overlooked sources of sugar is fruit juice. Many children consume quarts of juice each day. Fruit juices should be diluted and rotated. Apple and grape juice both contain salicylates, so these products are particularly troublesome for susceptible children.

Filter Water. Water is a better choice than fruit juice as a beverage for most children because it has no sugar, salicylates, or allergens. However, water contains other substances that may contribute to hyperactivity or lack of relatedness. Chlorine, fluoridation, aluminum, lead, and parasites are all potential problems. Chlorine reacts with organic matter to spawn cancer-producing substances such as chloroform (Morris, Audet, Angelillo, Chalmers, & Mosteller, 1992). Fluoridation increases the possibility that the water will leach aluminum from cookware into food (Tennakone & Wickramanayake, 1987). Elevated aluminum from cookware and lead from old plumbing are often overlooked as possible causes of hyperactivity and subtle learning disabilities (Howard, 1984). Parasites such as *Giardia* are becoming more and more common in the water sources of large cities (Galland, 1997).

Paying attention to the quality of the water children are drinking is imperative. Filtering all water through activated charcoal can remove chlorination and fluoridation as well as decrease the possibility of parasite contamination (Galland, 1997).

Nutritional Supplementation

"The key to a strong, healthy immune system for all children is optimal nutrition" (Galland, 1988, p. 2). What constitutes good nutrition, however, is a matter of great controversy. Although, in the past, people were confident that they could obtain all the nutrients their bodies needed through the foods they ate, this expectation is no longer true. The soil has become depleted, eating habits have changed, and more foods are processed. Even those who eat a wide variety may not be obtaining good-quality nutrition. For the picky eater with a PDD, a diet consisting primarily of processed foods that are made of wheat and dairy products is hardly adequate, let alone optimal.

A logical step in closing the nutritional gap between what is eaten and what the body needs is the therapeutic use of supplements. Unfortunately, many commercial vitamins for children may be low in important trace minerals, and they often contain colors, flavors, preservatives, and fillers to which children with autism react negatively.

The use of nutritional aids is becoming increasingly accepted, especially for children with behavioral and developmental problems. According to Kelly Dorfman, a nutritionist who works with families of children diagnosed with a PDD and autism, these youngsters need more nutrients than typical children do because of poor absorption, self-restricted diets, impaired ability to detoxify environmental chemicals and pollutants, and inherited nutrient deficiencies (Dorfman, 1996). Health-care providers can suggest customized formulas designed to fit a child's unique nutritional needs. Several pharmacies produce these mixtures without colors, flavors, preservatives, or fillers (see Appendix 12.A). Nutritional aids include vitamins and minerals, essential fatty acids (EFAs), amino acids, probiotics and antifungals, and various other supplements.

Vitamins and Minerals. Like medications, some vitamins and minerals can enhance cognition, improve speech and language, help sleeping patterns, lessen irritability, and decrease self-injurious and self-stimulatory behavior, without side effects. Minerals are perhaps the most important of the body's nutrients because vitamins, proteins, enzymes, amino acids, fats, and carbohydrates all require minerals for activity.

Mineral deficiencies are very common in children who eat high carbohydrate and processed foods. Balance is the key because if a shortage or overabundance of just one mineral exists, then the function of the whole body can be thrown off (Weintraub, 1997). For instance, adequate zinc protects against adverse effects from heavy metals, including lead, cadmium, and copper, and adequate calcium neutralizes excess aluminum. Children on dairy-free diets and others with calcium deficiencies may be irritable, hyperactive, sleep-disturbed, and inattentive. They may also have stomach and muscle cramps as well as tingling in arms and legs. These symptoms often disappear with properly balanced supplements of calcium and magnesium (Smith, 1990).

Vitamins have long been used to increase immunity and cognitive function. Both deficiencies and toxic levels can contribute to poor learning and aberrant behavior. The supplements used therapeutically most often are combinations of vitamins B complex, C, and E along with important trace minerals such as zinc, chromium, selenium, and calcium (Smith, 1990).

Dr. Rimland has shown for the past 25 years that supplements can improve functioning in children with autism and prevent birth defects (Rimland, 1972). (See Figure 12.1.) He recommends a combination of folic acid, dimethyl glycine (DMG), vitamin B6, and magnesium, packaged as "Super Nu-Thera" and sold by Kirkman Labs (see Appendix 12.A).

DMG has been shown to improve language, but it can also increase self-stimulatory behavior. Folic acid acts as an antidote to the DMG, allowing it to work without agitating the nervous system. In a double-blind research study, high doses of vitamin B6 were shown to work better than Ritalin in reducing hyperactivity in a controlled group of boys (Coleman et al., 1979).

The newest interest in vitamin supplementation centers on vitamin A. Dr. Mary Megson, a developmental pediatrician in Richmond, Virginia, noted that many of the children in her practice regressed after receiving a vaccine. She theorized that some vaccines may act as an "off switch" to genetically weakened receptors for the processing of language, vision, and perception and that natural vitamin A may switch these receptors back on. She is currently studying the use of cod-liver oil as a supplement of vitamin A and her results with approximately 70 children are promising (Lindsey, 1999).

Essential Fatty Acids (EFAs). EFAs are crucial to maintaining a healthy immune system. These substances must be ingested because the body cannot produce them. Because parents have consciously eliminated fats from their families' intake, some children's diets have become depleted of omega 3 and omega 6 fatty acids. Fortunately, both are found in a variety of foods, including nuts and seeds, fish, and oils such as flaxseed, borage, and cod-liver. However, these products are very fragile; overprocessing or exposure to air or high temperatures eradicates the valuable EFAs. Furthermore, nonessential fatty acids such as the hydrogenated vegetable oils that are used to make margarine and to fry fast food interfere with a child's ability to make use of the marginal amounts of EFAs that are consumed (Schmidt, 1997).

Children with yeast overgrowth are particularly vulnerable to EFA deficiencies. The large quantities of sugar they ingest also weaken the enzymes of EFA metabolism. When vitamin and mineral balance is off, metabolism is further disturbed. Signs of EFA deficiencies are dry, scaly skin and lusterless hair, brittle nails, excess thirst, and in older girls, menstrual problems (Galland, 1997). Studies of hyperactive children reveal improvement in almost two-thirds of the children after they took evening primrose oil (Stevens, & Burgess, 1995). Evening primrose oil is a particularly popular treatment in England and has also been shown to be effective in reversing some of the secondary health symptoms of these children, including asthma, allergies, and eczema. Supplementing an EFA-deficient diet with omega-rich oils has been shown to be safe and to be without side effects (Galland, 1988).

Amino Acids. Amino acids are subunits of protein molecules that result from completed digestion. When absorbed into the bloodstream, they aid in ridding the body of toxins that are by-products of normal metabolism and toxins that come from bowel germs, impure waste, and food.

Many individuals with a PDD show two types of amino acid abnormalities. One is the result of incomplete digestion, and the other is an amino acid deficiency. Glutamine, glycine, gamma-aminobutyric acid (GABA), and taurine are free-form amino acids that have an inhibitory effect on hyperkinetic movements. When any of these amino acids is absent or deficient, many behavioral symptoms can occur. The DAN! protocol describes this problem in depth and provides information about laboratories that can run a urine amino acid analysis (Baker & Pangborn, 1999).

Tryptophan is an essential amino acid necessary to maintain protein balance. Many people with a PDD have profiles showing low tryptophan, low serotonin (a neurotransmitter formed from tryptophan), and low B6. This deficiency is especially apparent in those who have dairy sensitivities because dairy products are a major source of tryptophan. One study on adults with autism found a significant increase in whirling, flapping, banging, and hitting when tryptophan levels were depleted (McDougle, Holmes, Carlson, Pelton, Cohen, & Price, 1996). Combining tryptophan with B vitamins and magnesium can have remarkable results in reducing these self-stimulatory behaviors (Sahley, 1996).

Amino acid supplements combined with other nutrients are available in many over-the-counter products such as Kids Plex, Jr., and Calm Kids, available from The Pain & Stress Therapy Center in San Antonio (see Appendix 12.A). Tryptophan, however, can be obtained only by prescription.

Probiotics and Antifungals. To reestablish intestinal integrity and to mend the leaky gut, over-the-counter and prescribed supplements are often recommended. These fall into two categories: probiotics, meaning "in support of life," and antifungals, or drugs that kill the yeasts and fungi. Probiotics, including acidophilus and lactobacillus, replace the good bacteria in the gut; they are available over the counter. Antifungals, needed to wipe out the yeasts, include Nystatin, Nyzoral, and Diflucan; these require a doctor's prescription. These products are often used together and in conjunction with the elimination of all sugars, including fruits, from the diet (Chaitow, 1988).

Miscellaneous Supplements. Herbs, digestive enzymes, and plant extracts, including algae, can also be taken in combination with vitamins, minerals, antifungals, amino acids, and probiotics in the treatment of hyperactivity and autistic-like symptoms. Echinacea (a plant antibiotic), chamomile, skullcap, certain botanical scents, and pycnogenol are some other supplements that have also been shown to be beneficial (Anderson & Peiper, 1996). Pycnogenol is a nontoxic, water-soluble product occurring in grape-seed extract and pine bark. It is increasingly being used as a nonprescription alternative to improve focus, memory, fine motor skills, and eye contact (Dorfman, 1995b).

Homeopathy

Homeopathy is a 200-year-old approach to healing that has historically been rejected by the traditional medical community. Homeopathic practitioners, who can be traditional MDs, naturopathic or osteopathic physicians, or laypeople, use substances from nature that may cause a group of symptoms in a healthy person but that cure the same symptoms in a sick person by stimulating the body's own ability to heal itself. This approach follows the Law of Similars, where "like cures like" whereas traditional or allopathic medicine uses the Law of Opposites (Ullman & Ullman, 1996).

Many physicians combine traditional and homeopathic treatments, depending on the patient's symptoms and history. A patient's history provides the most important information because homeopathy, like other treatments that have been mentioned, focuses on the person, not the diagnosis. Thus, children with similar diagnoses may be given very different treatments or "remedies," as they are called, depending on what symptoms cluster together. For instance, a thin, excitable, anxious child may be given one remedy whereas a devilish child who is shy but plays tricks may be given another, and a fidgety child who becomes so hyperactive that he or she starts to cry may be given yet another (Zand, Walton, & Rountree,

1994). Physical, mental, and emotional states are evaluated together and treated as the person's system is brought into balance.

Homeopathic practitioners believe that the symptoms representing a particular imbalance develop hierarchically, with physical problems, which are least severe, appearing first, followed by mental and emotional illness, which is more problematic. Disease manifests itself first on the outside and then moves to internal organs. Thus, when a baby's diaper rash or eczema clears up externally, it often reemerges as an internal problem in the digestive or respiratory tract. Constipation, diarrhea, bronchitis, and asthma commonly precede the onset of hyperactivity and autistic-like symptoms in children with a PDD. A homeopathic doctor may see all these problems as having the same cause and treat the patient accordingly. Healing occurs in a sequence that is opposite to the sequence of illness, with the cognitive and behavioral symptoms clearing before the physical ones and with skin issues being the last to subside (Ullman & Ullman, 1996).

A pharmacist, Dr. Allen Krantz, and a specialist in clinical nutrition, Dr. Gregory Ellis, are combining homeopathic remedies with enzymes and other nutritional supplements in a program called "Homeovitics," which enhances the immune system while detoxifying the body (Ellis & Krantz, 1995). An enthusiastic group of parents in the Northeast has documented significant changes in the blood chemistry, behavior, and learning abilities of their children with autism who are using this approach (see Appendix 12.A for this resource).

Homeopathy is making a huge comeback today for many acute and chronic illnesses because people are becoming disillusioned with and fearful of the long-term effects of drugs. Most homeopathic practitioners are open-minded about combining their treatments with other therapies, especially nutritional supple-

mentation and dietary modification. To find a homeopathic practitioner, contact The National Center for Homeopathy listed in Appendix 12.A.

Immunotherapy

Parents of some children with a PDD report an onset of autistic symptoms and hyperactivity after an immunization. If, as suspected, autism and related disorders have an immunological basis, developing treatments to enhance immune system function is the obvious next step. Blood tests show high titers for months and even years after a vaccine has been administered. The immune system is still in high gear acting against an invader. A technique called intravenous immune globulin (IVIG) therapy is currently being used with children who are diagnosed with a PDD. This technique was found to be helpful after a mother, Cindy Goldenberg, would not accept her doctor's disinterest in her son's high rubella titer. She sought out further medical advice until she found Dr. Sudhir Gupta at the University of California at Irvine. He tried IVIG with her son Garrett, and it resulted in immediate changes in Garrett's behavior and in the ultimate reversal of his autism and hyperactivity (Gupta, Aggarwal, & Heads, 1996). IGIV therapy is now being used more widely. To find a doctor who uses this methodology, contact the National Vaccine Information Center (NVIC). (See Appendix 12.A.)

Treatments That Affect Sensory Processing

Our senses allow us to process, organize, and give meaning to our world. In addition to the five senses of vision, hearing, touch, smell, and taste, occupational therapists are familiar with other important senses of body position, of gravity, and of movement that send vital information to our brains. The bodies of children with autism do not process sensory information efficiently. Thus, the children have difficulty simultaneously organizing different types of sensory input while, at the same time, trying to meet the demands of their environment. The following are a variety of approaches that attempt to improve sensory processing.

Sensory-Integration Therapy

The late A. Jean Ayres, PhD, an occupational therapist, has described many of the identical symptoms of children with a PDD and autism as occurring in those who have sensory-integration dysfunction. Her belief is that the body's ability to process and interpret information coming in through touch, movement, balance, and body position is essential for sustaining attention, understanding and using language, and participating in social interaction (Ayres, 1985). If a child is suspected of having sensory-integration dysfunction, a specially trained and certified occupational or physical therapist can conduct an evaluation. Tests and observations study a child's response to sensory stimulation, posture, balance, coordination, and movement activities. These reactions are compared to norms established for the child's age. After carefully analyzing data and putting them in the context of the child's home and school environments, the therapist can make recommendations. Therapy consists of guided activities that challenge and enhance the body's ability to respond appropriately to sensory input. Efficient, organized responses, in turn, heighten a child's ability to pay attention, relate, sit still, organize language, and focus. Training of specific skills is not usually done because the body then does not learn how to adapt to future similar activities but, rather, how to do only that single task. Certification is required to perform The Sensory Integration and Praxis Test but not to do therapy. Sensory Integration International (SII), listed in Appendix 12.A, can locate practitioners around the world who are knowledgeable and qualified in sensory-integration techniques.

The Squeeze Machine

Dr. Temple Grandin, probably the most well-known and successful adult with autism, was a child with severe tactile defensiveness. During regular childhood visits to a relative's farm, she tried out the machine that is used to restrain cows while they are branded. She loved the deep pressure that the machine provided her body and found that it calmed her and decreased her anxiety. This experience led to her career as the world's authority on livestock handling equipment. Today, a similar machine that she designed called the squeeze machine is available for people to use in homes and schools (see the Therafin Corporation in the Appendix 12.A).

Auditory Integration Training (AIT)

Good listening requires that the various components of each ear and the two ears themselves work together. The coordination of sounds allows the ear to send messages to the brain to be interpreted and stored. The vestibular system is also important to the efficient processing of sound. Difficulties with sound sensation have been associated with autism since Kanner defined the disability in 1943. These difficulties very well could be related to the repeated inner-ear infections that many children with autism experienced as babies.

Both over- and undersensitivities are reported. Many children hear distortions of and experience delays in processing the signals that come into their ears. The distorted messages that are sent to the brain negatively affect the ability to focus on and give meaning to what they hear. The result may be an inconsistency in hearing the various frequencies of sound or lack of synchronicity of the ears, resulting in behavior that is distractible, avoidant, hyperactive, inattentive, or bizarre (Stehli, 1991). Common symptoms include crying, covering the ears, running from the sound source, and temper tantrums. Many children with autism "tune out." It is unclear from their behavior whether they are experiencing actual pain or fear.

Several types of auditory training have been developed to normalize the way people with autism process sound, and they all require specialized electronic equipment. The first type was developed by Dr. Guy Berard in France. He believed that children with autism hear some sound frequencies more clearly than others. This hypersensitivity to sound in turn affects the development of phonological awareness and language. The end product is delayed or decreased comprehension, poor articulation, decreased or inappropriate expression, or some combination of these effects.

Intervention begins with an audiogram to determine specific needs. Then the person listens to music for 30 minutes twice a day for 10 days through a special instrument called an AudioKinetron. The music is modified and may also be filtered to meet the child's specified profile. The modified music stimulates the vestibular system, located in the inner ear, which in turn, activates the language centers of the brain, eye movements, and the digestive system. Thus, far more than hearing may be influenced.

For most of the 1990s, the FDA has prohibited distribution of the AudioKinetron in the United States. However, since November 1998, the FDA ruled that AIT equipment was not subject to the agency's regulation, so practitioners can now use their AudioKinetrons freely. Digital Auditory Aerobics (DAA) is the most up-to-date equipment, and it requires special training to use. Information on how to access this program is available from the Georgiana Institute (see Appendix 12.A).

Guy Berard's AIT is based on a physiological approach that is designed to reduce hypersensitivity to sound and equalize the perception of all frequencies. Alfred Tomatis developed a different method that takes a psychological approach designed specifically to improve listening and communication skills directly.

The Tomatis method is based on the idea that the ear integrates auditory information at every level of the nervous system. Listening is considered an active process that is accomplished with intention and desire whereas hearing is the passive reception of sound. The goal of a Tomatis listening program is to establish good functional use of the auditory system. Successful Tomatis therapy could take as long as 100 hours, done in "loops" of 8 hours at a time. This therapy is far more time consuming and expensive than Berard's training.

The Tomatis method has several variations. Samonas Sound Therapy is a home-based program that can be purchased on compact discs and listened to through high quality headphones on any standard CD player. This therapy should be used only under the direction of a qualified auditory training practitioner. This technique was developed by Ingo Steinbach in Germany and has been used in Europe since the mid-1980s. For short periods of time every day, this technique extends Tomatis therapy by exposing the listener to classical chamber music (primarily Mozart) and to nature sounds. These sounds stimulate the ears and brains of people of all ages, from infants to mature adults. More information on this type of AIT is available from www.samonas.com.

Don Campbell, the world's foremost authority on the connection between music and healing, has taken the music of Mozart and used it to affect the body, mind, and spirit not only of people with a PDD and autism but also of infants and typically functioning people (Campbell, 1997). The Mozart Effect is an extension of Tomatis therapy, which also uses Mozart's music because its high frequency range is like sonic vitamin C for the brain. The Mozart Effect tapes and CDs are available through the Mozart Effect Resource Center (see Appendix 12.A).

According to the Society for Auditory Intervention Techniques (SAIT), at least 15 studies have investigated the effectiveness of AIT with people with autism. Training is given to children as young as 3. In 12 of these studies, improvement was noted (Society for Auditory Intervention Techniques). One study suggests that for those with abnormally high levels of serotonin (about one-third of the people with autism), AIT may lower these levels (Panksepp, Rossi, & Narayanan, 1995). Parents report a reduction in temper tantrums, sound and tactile sensitivity, hyperactivity, impulsivity, and distractibility. Increased eye contact and the ability to follow directions, pay attention, remember, speak, socialize, move, draw, and play independently are reported. Sometimes sleep and other activities are disturbed temporarily, but a return to normality is usually seen in a short time (Rimland, 1995).

The newest types of auditory training incorporate the technology of computers with earphones. Fast ForWord (formerly called HAILO), a program based on 20 years of brain research, allegedly enhances the auditory timing mechanism of the brain, thus rapidly building language competence in children ages 4 through 12. This type of auditory training focuses on having a child discriminate and recognize phoneme differences, which are delivered at increasing speeds (Tallal, et al., 1996). Some practitioners recommend that traditional auditory integration training be attempted first. To find a Fast ForWord practitioner, contact Scientific Learning Corporation (see Appendix 12.A).

Although music therapy is not a form of AIT, it works by enhancing both the auditory and vestibular functions. Many people with autism are intrinsically attracted to music, and some, like David Helfgott, featured in the movie *Shine*, are musically gifted and communicate through music rather than through language. Singing, dancing, and rhythmic movement are natural ways to interact with people in this group because these musical activities require no verbal interaction, have inherent structure, can be playful, and can promote the desired outcomes of increased language, socialization, and appropriate behaviors (Gerlach, 1998).

Certified music therapists use a variety of instruments and also have training in the behavioral sciences. To find a music therapist, contact the National Association of Music Therapy (see Appendix 12.A). Some therapists practice rhythmic entrainment, which uses drum rhythms that are said to improve brain functioning by altering the body's processing of the beats. For more information about this therapy, contact the REI Institute (see Appendix 12.A).

Vision Therapy (VT)

Vision is not the same as eyesight. Eyesight is the act of seeing; vision is the ability to focus on and give meaning to that which is seen. Clarity is important, but a person must also be able to identify, interpret, and understand what is seen. Vision is a set of abilities that is learned from birth and acquired in tandem with movement. Developing good visual skills includes learning to effectively use both eyes together. Having both eyes move, align, fixate, and focus as a team enhances the ability to interpret and understand visual information.

It is important for occupational therapists to take a functional rather than a structural approach to vision, just as they do with the movement senses. Therapists can then understand that people with autism have visual, spatial, and perceptual deficits that can be alleviated, just as vestibular and proprioceptive deficits can be reduced.

Developmentally, babies start at a motor stage where they are moving without purpose. Next, toddlers move to a motor-visual level where their movements enhance and drive their vision. They move toward an object or person and then give it meaning. Children should next move to a visual-motor stage where their vision drives their movement. This ability allows them to walk into a room with a purpose or to write what their brain tells them. We know when children are ready to write because they make purposeful strokes with their pencils. The final stage is using vision alone without movement. Because two-thirds of all information we receive is visual, vision must become the body's primary sense. If it does not, then compensations using other senses are always necessary.

Many children with autism are stuck in the motor-visual stage. They are inefficient at seeing and giving meaning to people and objects. They may walk into a room aimlessly, appearing not to be paying attention. Their lack of attention is a symptom of their poor visual skills. Most children with a PDD are not able to use their vision without moving. The admonition to "sit still and pay attention" is a disservice to these children. They truly cannot look or listen without moving. Many symptoms of autism have visual components. Poor eye contact, attention, and focus; excessive visual scanning; and visual defensiveness are common behaviors that may be caused by visual dysfunction. As visual demands at home, play, and school increase, so does the degree of dysfunction. Mild problems with these skills may contribute to academic or coordination problems; moderate dysfunction adds visual disorientation, which leads to panic and anxiety disorders, emotional disturbance, and Obsessive-Compulsive Disorder (OCD); and severe visual problems may be a contributing cause of autistic symptoms.

The first step in vision therapy is to identify the problem. A functional vision exam takes into account more than eye health and visual acuity at a distance. It looks at the person as a whole and at how that person uses his or her vision to direct his or her behavior. Of the different types of eye care professionals, the one who is most likely to take a functional approach is an optometrist (OD). The optometrist is able to change sensory input through the use

of lenses, prisms, filters, and occlusion. These tools, unique to the practice of optometry, have the potentiality to break through the inflexible world of even the child with the most severe autism and to assist the child with attention problems in focusing (Schulman, 1994). Unlike his medical colleague, the ophthalmologist, the optometrist has extensive training in how the eyes function with the rest of the body. Some optometrists have gone on for further specialty training and are certified Fellows of the College of Optometrists in Vision Development, FCOVD. See Appendix 12.A (College of Optometrists in Vision Development) to find one nearby.

Vision is to eyesight what listening is to hearing. Efficient vision assumes good ocular health and refractive status, aspects that are a part of most eye exams. However, just as good audition requires coordination not only of several parts of the ear but also of both ears themselves, vision requires the components not only of each eye but also of the two eyes themselves to work together. Other visual skills that must also be evaluated are listed as follows:

- Binocularity—the ability to use both eyes together as a team. If one eye turns in, out, up, or down by just the smallest amount, vision is affected. A very high incidence of a turned eye (strabismus) occurs in people with autism. One study found that 21% of a sample showed an eye turning out at distance and 18% at nearpoint (Scharre & Creedon, 1992). Another found 50% of 34 autistic 7 to 19-year-olds had a strabismus. Of that group, 65% demonstrated an exotropia (outward turning of one or both eyes) and 35% demonstrated an esotropia (turning in of one or both eyes) (Kaplan, Rimland, & Edelson, 1999). Even if one or both eyes have been corrected surgically, they may not be working as a team, and binocularity may not be stable.
- Tracking—the ability to follow a moving object smoothly with both eyes, independent of the head.

- Fixation—the ability to quickly and accurately locate and inspect with both eyes a series of stationary objects such as words. Efficiency is reduced if a reader moves the head or body with the eyes.
- Focus change—the ability to look quickly from far to near and vice versa without momentary blur, as is required when looking at a book, the blackboard, and the teacher. Inattention may be the symptom of difficulties with focus change.
- Visual Form Perception—the process of receiving, integrating, and interpreting that which is seen. Noting likenesses and differences of size, shape, texture, and position in space lays the foundation for reading and spelling.
- Visualization—the ability to form mental images in the "mind's eye," retain them, and use them as references in the future. As the highest level visual skill, its efficiency thus depends hierarchically not only on the other essential visual skills but also on the lower level senses. Listening, following directions, reading comprehension, and paying attention all require good visualization.

The optometrist evaluates each of these visual skills by observing performance on a variety of visual tasks, both with and without selected lenses and prisms. Using these tools, the doctor makes judgments about how to improve the person's ability to use his or her vision more efficiently to deal with movement, light, and thought.

After the evaluation is complete, the doctor then prescribes a training or therapy program. This training or therapy includes the use of lenses and prisms as well as activities to increase visual arousal, disrupt inaccurate visual perception, and increase visually directed movement.

Prisms reorient the eyes to look at an image in a new position in space. When the eyes see this new image, the motor system readjusts, sending information to the brain, which then comprehends that the person must adapt himself or herself to this new position in space. This readjustment causes a reorganization of the motor and sensory data in the cortex. Success in making the shift in motor orientation occurs not only because the eye muscles change in alignment but also because the information is matched and reestablished between the sensory component of vision, the motor component of vision, the vestibular process, the kinesthetic process, and the proprioceptive inputs to the brain. The prisms thus serve to establish balance among all the senses (Kaplan & Flach, 1985).

Dr. Melvin Kaplan, an optometrist in New York, has been at the forefront of using prisms with children who have and autism. He reports a case of a 5-year-old boy who had never spoken but who interacted using Facilitated Communication. When he donned his corrective lenses for the first time, he verbalized, "What a bright, sunny day!" When his mother asked, "What color is my dress," he verbally responded, "Your dress is blue!" which caused great surprise (Kaplan, Carmody, & Gatdos, 1996, p.87). Occasional breakthroughs such as this dramatic one serve to emphasize the importance of the visual system in language and behavior.

Vision therapy (VT) activities vary and are individualized for each child. Typically, one begins with simple visual arousal activities such as playing visually directed games with balloons or flashlights in a darkened room because improved awareness of the peripheral visual world is a prerequisite to good eye contact and social skills (Rose & Torgeson, 1994). Next, more difficult visually directed tasks such as completing mazes or putting pegs in a rotating board are performed as the child learns to use his or her eyes more efficiently.

Educational Kinesiology (E-K)

Also known as Brain Gym, EK is a therapy that purportedly improves sensory function by enhancing neuropathways. Developed in the 1970s by Dr. Paul Dennison, an educator who was trying to understand his own learning and visual problems, EK is based on an understanding of the interdependence of physical development, language acquisition, and academic achievement. Dr. Dennison synthesized the pioneering work of optometrists, chiropractors, and learning specialists.

Brain Gym movements can be incorporated into the school program for a few minutes several times a day to wake up the body to learn. The regimen starts with a readiness routine called PACE, for Positive, Active, Clear, and Energetic, which includes drinking ample water (to nourish the neuropathways) and then doing a number of techniques with catchy names such as Brain Buttons, Cross Crawls, and Hook-Ups. Carla Hannaford has written an understandable discussion of this interesting technique (Hannaford, 1995), and Cecilia Freeman has shown how it can be used with children who have various types of special needs, including children with autism (Freeman, 1998). For referrals to Brain Gym practitioners, see Edu-Kinesthetics in Appendix 12.A.

The Miller Method®

The Miller Method® focuses on developing cognition within interactional activities while respecting the rituals that children with autism use to understand and relate to the world. The primary goal of this therapy is to expand play, socialization, and routines through sensorimotor activities. Using platforms with play stations; large and small objects such as boxes, blocks, and cups; obstacles; and interpersonal interaction, children learn to orient and attend to people and activities. As they become more engaged, the demands become more complex. Eventually, children become more functionally engaged, choosing activities independently. Language is elicited as awareness and engagement increases (Cook, 1998). Dr. Arnold Miller,

the mind behind this ingenious program, is based in Boston. However, through the use of videoconferencing, he monitors Miller Method® programs in several sites around the world. For more information about this intervention, see the Language and Cognitive Development Center in Appendix 12.A.

The Son-Rise Program

One alternative therapy that does not fit neatly into any category is Son-Rise, developed by Barry Kaufman and his wife, the founders of The Option Institute. Like many other programs, this one was born out of a need to help their own son, who was diagnosed with autism at 18 months and who later went on to attend an Ivy League college. The Son-Rise program is based on a loving, trusting, respectful, nonjudgmental attitude, and encourages parents to follow the child's lead or actions while simultaneously directing him or her into an expanded world. The unique feature of this program is the commitment to happiness. Parents are encouraged to explore their own belief systems and to question judgments that are limiting them. They stay at the Option Institute and are trained to use skills that allow them to accept their child and become his or her teacher. Son-Rise is an intensive program that requires an enormous commitment of time and money. However, many families who use it report that their children recover from autism. For more information, see the Option Institute in Appendix 12.A.

Conclusion

Some exciting new treatment options for children with a PDD both address causes and treat symptoms by removing individual stressors contributing to the total load that may produce autism. In addition to social, academic, and language benefits, long-standing health problems often are also alleviated. The occupational therapist who works with children with a PDD has a professional obligation to become aware of and conversant about some of these new programs and how to access them in the community to provide parents with many options for intervention.

References

Anderson, N., & Peiper, H. (1996). *A.D.D.: The natural approach.* East Canaan, CT: Safe Goods.

Ayres, A. J. (1985). *Sensory integration and the child.* Los Angeles, CA: Western Psychological Services.

Baker, S., & Pangborn, J. (1999). *Biomedical assessment options for children with autism and related problems.* A consensus report of the Defeat Autism Now! (DAN!) Conference, Dallas, TX, January 1995. San Diego, CA: Autism Research Institute.

Block, M. A. (1996). *No more ritalin: Treating ADHD without drugs.* New York: Kensington Books.

Boris, M., & Mandel, F. (1994). Foods and additives are common causes of the attention deficit hyperactive disorder in children. *Annals of Allergy, 72,* 462–468.

Braly, J. (1992). *Dr. Braly's food allergy and nutrition revolution.* New Canaan, CT: Keats.

Brostoff, J., & Gamlin, L. (1989). *Food allergy and intolerance.* London: Bloomsbury.

Campbell, D. (1997). *The Mozart effect.* New York: Avon Books.

Caskey, R. (1996, March). *Treating Candida with chiropractic kinesiology.* Lecture delivered at the Developmental Delay Registry Conference, Stamford, CT.

Chaitow, L. (1988). *Candida albicans: Could yeast be your problem?* Rochester, VT: Healing Arts Press.

Chess, S. (1971). Autism in children with congenital rubella. *Journal of Autism and Childhood Schizophrenia, 1,* 33–47.

Coleman, M., Steinberg, G., Tippett, J., Bhagavan, H. N., Coursin, D. B., Gross, M., Lewis, C., & DeVeau, L. (1979). A preliminary study of the effect of pyridoxine administration in a subgroup of hyper-kinetic children: A double-blind crossover comparison with methylphenidate. *Biological Psychiatry,141,* 741–751.

Cook, C. E. (1998). The Miller Method: A case study illustrating use of the approach with children with autism in an inter-disciplinary setting. *The Journal of Developmental and Learning Disorders, 2*(2), 231–263.

Coulter, H. L., & Fisher, B. L. (1985). *DPT: A shot in the dark.* Orlando, FL: Harcourt Brace Jovanovich.

Crook, W. G. (1986). *The yeast connection.* New York: Vintage Books.

Crook, W. G. (1987). *Solving the puzzle of your hard-to-raise child.* Jackson, TN: Professional Books.

Crook, W. G. (1991). *Help for the hyperactive child.* Jackson, TN: Professional Books.

Crook, W. G. (1994). *The yeast connection and the woman.* Jackson, TN: Professional Books.

Crook, W. G. (1996). *The yeast connection handbook.* Jackson, TN: Professional Books.

Dawbarn's Solicitors Fact Sheet. (n.d.). *Mumps, measles, and rubella (MMR) vaccines and measles rubella (MR) vaccines.* Norfolk, Great Britain: Dawbarn's Solicitors.

Dorfman, K. (1995a, January). High functioning autism. *The Townsend Letter for Doctors and Patients, 140,* 98–101.

Dorfman, K. (1995b, Summer). Pycnogenol and developmental delays. *New Developments Newsletter, 1,* 1–4.

Dorfman, K. (1996, Winter). Why so many children have developmental problems: The total load theory. *New Developments Newsletter, 1,* 3–4.

Dorfman, K. (1997). Improving detoxification pathways. *New Developments Newsletter, 2,* 3–4.

Dorfman, K., Lemer, P., & Nadler, J. (1995). *What puts a child at risk for developmental delays?* Unpublished survey of the Developmental Delay Resources (DDR), Bethesda, MD.

Egger, J., Stolla, A., & McEwen, L. M. (1992, May). Controlled trial of hyposensitization in children with food-induced hyperkinetic syndrome. *The Lancet, 339,* 1150–1153.

Ellis, G., & Krantz, A. (1995). Homeovitic clearing and detox. *Alternative Health Practitioner, 1*(3), 195–203.

Feingold, B. (1975). *Why your child is hyperactive.* New York: Random House.

Freeman, C. (1998). *I am the child.* Ventura, CA: Edu-Kinesthetics.

Frymann, V. M. (1996). Birth trauma: The most common cause of developmental delays. *New Developments Newsletter, 1,* 4–6.

Fudenberg, H. (1996). Dialyzable lymphocyte extract in infantile onset autism: A pilot study. *Biotherapy, 9,* 144.

Gadow, K., Nolan, E., & Sverd, J. (1995). School observation of children with attention-deficit hyperactivity disorder and comorbid tic disorder: Effects of methylphenidate treatment. *Journal of Developmental and Behavioral Pediatrics, 16,* 167–176.

Galland, L. (1988). *Superimmunity for kids.* New York: Delta Books.

Galland, L. (1997). *The four pillars of healing.* New York: Random House.

Gerlach, E. (1998). *Autism treatment guide.* Eugene, OR: Four Leaf Press.

Greenspan, S. I., & Wieder, S. (1998). *The child with special needs.* Reading, MA: Addison-Wesley.

Gupta, S., Aggarwal, S., & Heads, C. (1996). Brief report: Dysregulated immune system in children with autism. *Journal of Autism and Developmental Disorders, 26*(4), 439–452.

Hannaford, C. (1995). *Smart moves: Why learning is not all in your head.* Arlington, VA: Great Ocean Publishers.

Howard, J. M. H. (1984). Clinical import of small increases in serum aluminum. *Clinical Chemistry, 30,* 1722–1723.

Iverson, P. (1996, July). *Emerging symptoms in autism.* Lecture delivered at CAN conference, New York, NY.

Kanner, L. (1943). Autistic disturbances of affective contact. *Nervous Child, 2,* 217–250.

Kaplan, B. J., McNicol, J., Conte, R. A., & Moghadam, H. K. (1989, January). Dietary replacement in preschool-aged hyperactive boys. *Pediatrics, 83*(1), 7–17.

Kaplan, M., Carmody, D., & Gaydos, A. (1996). Postural orientation modification in autism in response to ambient lenses. *Child Psychiatry and Human Development, 27*(2), 81–91.

Kaplan, M., & Flach, F. (1985, April). The magic of yoked prisms. *Optometric Extension Program Foundation* (Series 1, No. 7, 15–19). Santa Ana, CA: Optometric Extension Program Foundation.

Kaplan, M., Rimland, B., & Edelson, S. (1999). Strabismus in autism spectrum disorder. *Focus on Autism and Other Developmental Disabilities. 14*(2), 101–105.

Kavner, R. S. (1985). *Your child's vision.* New York: Simon & Schuster.

Kemper, T., & Bauman, M.(1993). The contribution of neuropathologic studies to the understanding of autism. *Behavioral Neurology, 1*(1), 175–187.

Konopasek, D. E. (1997). *Medication "Fact Sheets": A medication references guide for the non-medical professional.* Anchorage, AK: Arctic Tern Publishing.

Lindsey, A. (1999, August 5). Treatment spurs breakthrough for child. *Richmond Times-Dispatch,* B1.

Manning, A. (1999, August 3). Are vaccines safe for our kids? *USA Today,* p. 1.

McCrone, J. (1998). Gut reaction: Is food to blame for autism?. *New Scientist,* (June 20), 42–45.

McDougle, C. J., Holmes, J. P., Carlson, D. C., Pelton, G. H., Cohen, D. J., & Price, L. H. (1996). Effects of tryptophan depletion in drug-free adults with autistic disorder. *Archives of General Psychiatry, 53,* 993–1000.

Morris, R. D., Audet, A. M., Angelillo, I. F., Chalmers, T. C., & Mosteller, F. (1992). Chlorination, chlorination by-products, and cancer: A meta-analysis. *American Journal of Public Health, 82,* 955–963.

Nsouli, T. M., Nsouli, S. M., Linde, R. E., Scanlon, R. T., & Bellanti, J. A. (1991). The role of food allergy in serious otitis media. *Annals of Allergy, 66,* 91.

Oski, F. (1983). *Don't drink your milk.* Syracuse, NY: Mollica Press.

Panksepp, J. (1979). A neurochemical theory of autism. *Trends in Neuroscience, 2,* 174–177.

Panksepp, J., Rossi III, J., & Narayanan, T. K. (1995, November). *An animal model of auditory integration training (AIT).* Presentation to the annual meeting of the Society for Neuroscience, San Diego, CA.

Physician's Desk Reference. (52nd ed.). (1998). Oradell, NJ: Medical Economics.

Rapp, D. (1991). *Is this your child?* New York: Quill Books.

Reichelt, K. L., Ekrem, J., & Scott, H. (1990). Gluten, milk proteins and autism: Dietary intervention effects on behavior and peptide secretion. *Journal of Applied Nutrition, 42*(1), 1–11.

Rimland, B. (1972). *Megavitamins, hypoglycemia and food intolerances as related to autism.* San Diego, CA: Autism Research Institute.

Rimland, B. (1985). Candida-caused autism. *Autism Research Review, 2*(2), 3.

Rimland, B. (1995). Auditory integration training update: Scientific clues, FDA obstruction. *Autism Research Review, 9*(4), 2.

Rimland, B. (1998). The autism-secretin connection. *Autism Research Review, 12*(3), 3.

Rimland, B. (1999a). Major medical, political developments fuel furor over vaccines. *Autism Research Review International, 13*(3), 1,7.

Rimland, B. (1999b). Secretin update: March 1999. *Autism Research Review, 13*(1), 3.

Ritvo, E. R., Jorde, L. B., Mason-Brotners, A., Freeman, B. J., Pingree, C., Jones, M. B., McMahon, W. M., & Peterson, P. B. (1990). The UCLA-University of Utah epidemiologic survey of autism prevalence. *American Journal of Psychiatry, 146*, 194–199.

Rose, M., & Torgeson, N. (1994). A behavioral approach to vision and autism. *Journal of Vision Development, 25*, 269–275.

Rowe, K. S., & Rowe, K. J. (1994). Synthetic food coloring and behavior: A dose response effect in a double-blind, placebo-controlled, repeated-measures study. *The Journal of Pediatrics, 125*(5), 691–698.

Sahley, B. J. (1996). *Control hyperactivity/A.D.D. naturally*. San Antonio, TX: Pain & Stress.

Scharre, J. E., & Creedon, M. P. (1992). Assessment of visual function in autistic children. *Optometry and Vision Science, 69*(6), 433–439.

Schmidt, M. A. (1996). *Healing childhood ear infections: Prevention, home care, and alternative treatment*. Berkeley, CA: North Atlantic Books.

Schmidt, M. A. (1997). *Smart fats: How dietary fats and oils affect mental, physical and emotional intelligence*. Berkeley, CA: Frog.

Schmidt, M. A., Smith, L. H., & Sehnert, K. W. (1994). *Beyond antibiotics*. Berkeley, CA.: North Atlantic Books.

Schulman, R. (1994). Optometry's role in the treatment of autism. *Journal of Vision Development, 25*, 259–268.

Shaw, W. (1998). *Biological treatments for autism and PDD*. Overland Park, KS: Great Plains Laboratory.

Shaw, W., Kassen, E., & Chaves, E. (1995). Increased excretion of analogs of Krebs cycle metabolites and arabinose in two brothers with autistic features. *Clinical Chemistry, 41*, 1094–1104.

Sinaiko, R. (1996, July). *The biochemistry of attentional/behavioral problems*. Lecture delivered at the conference of the Feingold Association of the United States (FAUS), Orlando, FL.

Singh, V. K., Lin, S. X., & Yang, V. C. (1998). Serological association of measles virus and human herpes virus-6 with brain auto-antibodies in autism. *Clinical Immunology and Immunopathology, 89*(1), 105–108.

Smith, L. H. (1990). *Hyperkids*. Santa Monica, CA: Shaw/Spelling Association.

Society for Auditory Intervention Techniques. From the World Wide Web: http://www.teleport.com/~sait

Stehli, A. (1991). *The sound of a miracle*. New York: Doubleday.

Stevens, L. J., & Burgess, J. (1995). Essential fatty acid metabolism in boys with attention deficit hyperactivity disorder. *American Journal of Clinical Nutrition, 62*, 761–768.

Swanson, J. M., McBurnett, K., Wigal, T., Pfiffner, L.J., Lerner, M.A., & Williams, L. (1993). Effect of stimulant medication on children with attention deficit disorder: A review of reviews. *Exceptional Children, 60*, 154–162.

Tallal, P., Miller, S. L., Bedi, G., Byma, G., Wang, X., Nagarajan, S., Schreiner, C., Jenkins, W. M., & Merzenich, M. (1996). Language comprehension in language-learning impaired children improved with acoustically modified speech. *Science, 271*(January), 81–84.

Tennakone, K., & Wickramanayake, S. (1987). Aluminum leaching from cooking utensils. *Nature, 325*, 270–272.

Ullman, J., & Ullman, R. (1996). *Ritalin-free kids: Safe and effective homeopathic medicine for ADD and other behavioral and learning problems*. Rocklin, CA: Prima Publishing.

Upledger, J. (1991). *Your inner physician and you*. Berkeley, CA: North Atlantic Books.

Wakefield, A. (1998). Ileal-lymphoid-nodular hyperplasia, non-specific colitis, and pervasive developmental disorder in children. *The Lancet, 352*(7), 234–235.

Waring, R. (1990). Enzyme and sulfur oxidation deficiencies in autistic children with known food/chemical intolerances. *Xenobiotica, 20*, 117–122.

Warren, R. P., Foster, A., & Margaretten, C. (1986). Immune abnormalities in patients with autism. *Journal of Autism and Developmental Disorders, 16*, 189–197.

Weintraub, S. (1997). *Natural treatments for ADD and hyperactivity.* Pleasant Grove, Utah: Woodland Publishing.

Zand, J., Walton, R., & Rountree, B. (1994). *Smart medicine for a healthier child.* Garden City, NY: Avery.

Zecca, T., Graffino, D., Lania-Howarth, M., Passante, M., & Oleske, J. (1997, February). *Elevated rubella titers in autistic children* (UMDNJ Study at NJMS Children's Hospital of New Jersey, Newark, NJ). Presented at Journal of Allergy and Clinical Immunology Scientific Session, San Francisco, CA, Abstract #768.

Zimmerman, A. W., Frye, V. H., & Potter, N. T. (1993). Immunological aspects of autism. *International Pediatrics, 8*(2), 199–204.

Appendix 12.A
Resources

American Massage Therapy Association (AMTA)

820 Davis St. Suite 100
Evanston, IL 60201-4444
Phone: (847) 864-0123
Fax: (847) 864-1178
www.amtamassage.org

Apothecary Pharmacy

Pathways Custom Compounding Pharmacy
Phone: (800) 869-9160
www.the-apothecary.com
Produces vitamins and prescriptions without colors, flavors, or fillers.

Autism Network for Dietary Intervention (ANDI)

P.O. Box 17711
Rochester, NY 14617-0711
Fax: (716) 544-7864
www.AutismNDI.com
Publishes newsletter and distributes products related to the elimination of gluten and casein products.

Dr. Bernard Rimland, Director

Autism Research Institute
4182 Adams Avenue
San Diego, CA 92116
Publishes the DAN! protocol; available for $25.

College of Optometrists in Vision Development (COVD)

243 N. Lindbergh Blvd. Suite 310
St. Louis, MO 63141-7851
Phone: (888) COVD770 (268-3770)
www.covd.org
Referrals to behavioral optometrists.

Developmental Delay Resources (DDR)

4401 East West Highway, Suite 207
Bethesda, MD 20814
Phone: (301) 652-2263
Fax: (301) 652-9133
www.devdelay.org
Publishes quarterly newsletter on all aspects of treatments. Referral directory of families and professionals worldwide.

Edu-Kinesthetics, Inc.

P.O. Box 3395
Ventura, CA 93006-3395
Phone: (888) 388-9898
www.braingym.com
Information about Brain Gym and E-K.

Feingold Association of the United States (FAUS)

127 East Main St. #106
Riverhead, NY 11901
Phone: (800) 321-FAUS (3287) or (631) 369-9340
www.feingold.org

The Georgiana Institute

P.O. Box 10, 137 Davenport Rd.
Roxbury, CT 06783
Phone: (860) 355-1545
www.georgianainstitute.org
Berard method of auditory integration training.

The Great Plains Laboratory

Dr. William Shaw, Director
11813 W. 77th St.
Lenexa, KS 66214
Phone: (913) 341-8949
www.greatplainslaboratory.com

Great Smokies Diagnostic Laboratory

63 Zillicoa Street
Asheville, NC 28801
Phone: (800) 522-4762
www.greatsmokies-lab.com

Healing Arts

www.healing-arts.org/children
Web page of treatment approaches for autism and developmental disorders.

HomeoViticS

3427 Exchange Ave.
Naples, FL 34104
Phone: (800) 521-7722
http://www.hvlabs.com

Hyperactive Children's Support Group

Sally Bunday
71 Whyte Lane, Chichester
West Sussex, PO19 2LD United Kingdom
Phone: 019-03-725-182
http://www.demon.co.uk/charities/AIA/aia.htm

Immuno Laboratories

1620 West Oakland Park Blvd.
Fort Lauderdale, FL 33311
Phone: (800) 231-9197

International Chiropractic Pediatric Association (ICPA)

5295 Highway 78 D362
Stone Mountain, GA 30087
Phone: (770) 872-5437

Kirkman Laboratories

P.O. Box 1009
Wilsonville, OR 97070
Phone: (800) 245-8282
www.kirkmanlabs.com
Distributors of Super Nu-Thera

The Language and Cognitive Development Center, Inc.

11 Wyman Street
Jamaica Plain, MA 02130
Phone: (800) 218-LCDC (5232)
www.millermethod.org
The Miller Method

Mozart Effect Resource Center

3526 Washington Ave.
St. Louis, MO 63103-1019
Phone: (800) 721-2177
www.mozarteffect.com

National Association of Music Therapy

8455 Colesville Rd. Suite 1000
Silver Spring, MD 20910
Phone: (301) 589-3300

National Center for Homeopathy

801 N. Fairfax Street #306
Alexandria, VA 22314
Phone: (703) 548-7790

National Vaccine Information Center (NVIC)

512 W. Maple Ave. #206
Vienna, VA 22180
Phone: (800) 909-SHOT (7468)
www.909shot.com

Nutri-Chem

1303 Richmond Rd.
Ottawa, Ontario, Canada
K2B 7Y4
Phone: (613) 820-9065
www.nutrichem.com
Produces customized nutritional supplements. Has Parent network and free newsletter for professionals.

Option Institute

2080 South Undermountain Rd.
Sheffield, MA 01257
Phone: (413) 229-2100
Information about the Son-Rise Program.

Osteopathic Center for Children

4135 54th Place
San Diego, CA 92105
Phone: (619) 454-2200
www.osteopathic-ctr-4child.org

Pain and Stress Therapy Center

5282 Medical Center Drive, Suite 160
San Antonio, TX 78229-6043
Phone: (800) 669-CALM (2256)
Distributes vitamins.

REI Institute

HC 75 Box 420
Lamy, NM 87540
Phone: (800) 659-6644
www.reiinstitute.com
Musical recordings for calming people with disabilities.

Scientific Learning Corporation

1995 University Ave.–Suite 400
Berkeley, CA 94704
Phone: (888) 665-9707
www.scientificlearning.com
Produces Fast ForWord

Sensory Integration International (SII)

1602 Cabrillo Ave.
Torrance, CA 90501
Phone: (310) 320-9986
www.sii.org

Society for Auditory Integration Training (SAIT)

1020 Commercial St. SE #306
Salem, OR 97302
http://www.teleport.com/~sait/

Therafin Corporation

19747 Wolf Rd.
Mokena, IL 60448
Phone: (708) 479-7300
Manufactures the squeeze machine.

The Upledger Institute, Inc.

11211 Prosperity Farms Rd. D325
Palm Beach Gardens, FL 33410
Phone: (407) 622-4771
Trains cranio-sacral practitioners.

CHAPTER *13*

Transition From School to Adult Life for Students With Autism

Lois Hickman, MS, OTR, FAOTA, and Meira L. Orentlicher, MA, OTR/L

The transition from school to adult life can be defined as the life changes, adjustments, and cumulative experiences that occur in the lives of young adults as they move from the school to the work environment and, eventually, to independent living (Wehman, 1996). This transition includes changes in self-awareness, sexuality, work, financial needs, and the need for independence in travel and mobility. Transition, therefore, means change, and change of any kind can be difficult for students with autism. Although the transition from school to adult life presents many challenges to all students, students with autism often face additional difficulties. Indeed, the more severe symptoms of autism do appear incompatible with independent adult life. These symptoms involve the severe issues related to language, social interaction, and behavior that can include self-stimulation, aggression, self-injury, and property destruction (Smith, Belcher, & Juhrs, 1995). Therefore, these students require a continuum of support services and an effective and committed team to assist them in achieving full citizenship.

The occupational therapy practitioner should be an integral member of that team. As a team member, the occupational therapist must not only be familiar with topics related to transition from school to adult life but also be famil-

iar with the specific needs of people with autism. The occupational therapy practitioner's expertise in person-environment-task fit and his or her ideological belief in full inclusion and self-determination provide a beneficial addition to the transition team (Dunn et al., 1995). The occupational therapy practitioner is ready, by education and by inclination, to advocate for the individual student's needs, evaluate that student's interests and skills, explore and evaluate job sites within the community, and help the student prepare for the most appropriate work setting possible. In addition, occupational therapy's unique focus on human performance is critical in providing supports for students who are seeking opportunities for independent living and community integration. For the occupational therapist to function effectively on the transition team, he or she must be familiar with the legislation that guides practice in this arena.

Legislation Pertinent to Occupational Therapy and Transition Services

The passage of the Education for All Handicapped Children Act (EHA) of 1975, [PL 94–142] (EHA, 1975) provided for special education services for all children with disabilities within the public education system. Over time, however, professionals and parents realized that special education services alone did not necessarily lead to positive postschool outcomes (Edgar, Levine, & Maddox, 1986; Hasazi, Gordon, & Roe, 1985; Wagner, 1989). Despite special education, many young adults with disabilities remained unemployed as well as dependent on public aid and services after graduation (Halloran, 1992). Therefore, in 1990, amendments to EHA included legal mandates to provide specific transition services to aid in increasing employment and the assumption of adult life roles. With these amendments, the name of the law was also changed. The EHA became the Individuals With Disabilities Education Act (IDEA) [PL 101-476] (IDEA, 1990). IDEA was reauthorized in 1997 [PL 105–17] (Reauthorization of IDEA, 1997). Currently, IDEA (1990) defines transition services as following:

> Transition services comprise the coordinated set of activities for a student, designed within an outcome oriented process, which promotes movement from school to post school activities including post-secondary education, vocational training, integrated employment, including supported employment, continuing adult education, adult services, independent living or community participation. The coordinated set of activities shall be based upon the individual student's needs taking into account the student's preferences and interests and shall include instruction, community experiences, employment development, and other post school adult living objectives, and when appropriate acquisition of daily living skills and functional vocational evaluation. (PL 101-476, 20 U.S.C., Ch 33)

Under IDEA, each student's Individualized Education Plan (IEP) must include annual statements of the needed transition services and must focus on transition planning from age 14 and annually thereafter as well as on the delivery of services from age 16 and annually there-

after. The emphasis on transition planning that begins at age 14 brings increased attention to the need for planning appropriate transition services within the context of secondary education.

The IDEA amendments of 1997 put a greater emphasis on lifelong outcomes, team collaboration, and interagency cooperation. To effectively design services that focus on lifelong outcomes, IEP teams must initiate transition planning in accordance with the student's preferences and long-range transition goals. If, for example, the long-term goals include postsecondary education, then the student has to meet academic prerequisites such as successfully completing the given number of credits dispersed across math, science, and English for graduation. If the student's goals encompass competitive employment, supported employment, and supported living outcomes, transition goals should emphasize knowledge, skills, and attitudes related to employment, job-seeking skills, and community participation.

Transition services are developed and planned by the student and his or her family in collaboration with a professional team. Team members may include school administrators, general and special educators, related service providers, adult service providers, community-based service providers, and community members. IDEA defines occupational therapy as a necessary related service that is provided to help a student with a disability benefit from special education. Therefore, occupational therapy practitioners may be involved with transition planning and services.

Additional related legislation that can enhance and promote transition services is provided by the following legal mandates with which occupational therapists should be familiar:

• Rehabilitation Act Amendments (RAA) of 1992 [PL 102–569]—These amendments describe the role of the adult rehabilitation services in transition from school to adult life and require each state rehabilitation program to specify within its state plan how transition services will be coordinated with the educational agencies. The plan must establish policies to ensure that students receive required services with no break as they exit school and that students with disabilities are active participants in their own rehabilitation programs (RAA, 1992).

- School-to-Work Opportunities Act (STWOA) of 1994 [PL 103–239]—This act established a national framework for states to create school-to-work systems for all youth. STWOA is intended to prepare youth for high-skilled jobs, and it outlines that school-to-work programs must incorporate school-based learning, work-based learning, and connecting activities into transition systems (STWOA, 1994).
- Americans With Disabilities Act (ADA) of 1990 [PL 101–336]—ADA guarantees equal access for people with disabilities to critical transition target settings such as employment, public accommodations, state and local government services, transportation, and telecommunications (ADA, 1990).
- Goals 2000: Educate America Act of 1994 [PL 103–227]—Commonly referred to as Goals 2000, this law contains two inextricably linked components: (1) a system for helping states establish high academic standards and (2) a system to support business, labor, educators, and the public in developing occupational standards (Goals 2000, 1994).
- The Technology Related Assistance Act for Individuals with Disabilities Amendments of 1994 [PL 103–218]—Commonly referred to as the Tech Act, this law provides access to assistive technology services and devices for people of all ages who have disabilities (Tech Act, 1994).

Guiding Principles for Occupational Therapy's Role in Transition Services

Social integration and inclusion in the mainstream of life are the primary goals of the transition process. The changes in the IDEA reauthorization of 1997 are intended to provide students who have disabilities greater access to the general education curriculum to ensure more successful employment and independent living outcomes after graduation. Similarly, the Developmental Disabilities Act Amendments (DDAA) of 1984 [PL 98–527] (DDAA, 1984) stipulate that the focus of supported employment for workers with diverse abilities is integration with their coworkers without disabilities. Moreover, as a country, the shift toward full inclusion and opportunities for people with disabilities was reaffirmed with the passage of the ADA in 1990. In fact, we now view disability as

> a natural part of human experience and [it] in no way diminishes the right of individuals to (a) live independently; (b) enjoy self-determination; (c) make choices; (d) contribute to society; (e) pursue meaningful careers; and (f) enjoy full inclusion and integration in the economic, political, social, cultural, and educational mainstream of American society. (Rehabilitation Services Administration, 1992, p. 1)

As a profession, occupational therapy has stated its support for full inclusion of people with disabilities in our schools and in our communities (Dunn et al., 1995). Full inclusion means fully participating in the interactions that occur within an environment to the same extent as do other people who are a part of that environment. By participating fully in the interactions in the environment, people gain access to a myriad of benefits such as friendships, opportunities to learn, and personal satisfaction. Social integration occurs when individual differences are accepted and individual competencies are supported and maximized.

Wehman (1996) identified nine guiding principles for carrying out transition. They are self-determination and student choice; level and intensity of support; family and student attitudes; person-centered planning; secondary curriculum reform; inclusion; career development; longitudinal curricula; and business connections and alliances. The following sections discuss these guiding principles and their applications to occupational therapy practice.

Self-Determination and Student Choice

Ward (1988) defined self-determination as the "attitudes [that] lead people to define goals for themselves and their ability to take initiative to achieve these goals" (p. 8). Vreeburg Izzo, Johnson, Levitz, and Aaron (1998) argue that the emergence from adolescence to adulthood may be characterized as a quest for self-determination. In essence, "self-determination is *the* transition experience for the adolescents emerging into adulthood" (p. 254). Employment, independent living, access to the community, and social integration are important and valued outcomes, but they are only as important as they are determined and directed by the person achieving them.

The changes in the IDEA reauthorization of 1997 require the IEP team to involve the student in determining his or her desired postschool outcomes. In fact, the IEP team must invite the student to participate in any IEP meeting when the purpose of the meeting is to determine transition services. If the student does not attend, the team must take other steps to ensure that the student's preferences and interests are taken into account. The intent of IDEA is evident: Students with disabilities must be invited to become active participants whose interests, preferences, and needs drive the IEP process. As Mitchell Levitz testified,

> I requested to be part of my own IEP meeting. It really helped me to speak up for myself . . . to make my own decisions and choices. It is something that many people with disabilities should be doing in the future. We will become the next generation of leaders (as cited in Vreeburg Izzo et al., 1998, p. 259).

Students with autism are not typically provided with opportunities to exert social influence, participate in decisions, and exercise control over their lives. Too often, choices about everyday living such as what to wear or eat, how to spend free time, or where to live or work are made by parents, teachers, or service providers. Many of the students experience such powerlessness and lack of self-direction that they become passive, or they resort to problem behavior as an expression of choice and self-direction (Brown & Gothelf, 1996). Learning how to make good choices and express them effectively requires experience with the process of decision making. Service providers must, therefore, take responsibility for teaching students with autism to take control of their lives. Opportunities to learn and practice skills of choice and decision making must be made available early in life and must exist across multiple environments.

Philosophically, the focus on self-determination requires professionals to question the goals and objectives of education and rehabilitation as well as the role of agencies and professionals in addressing the needs of students with disabilities. Professionals are traditionally trained to perceive themselves as experts whose primary role is to impart content knowledge to youth and others. Occupational therapists must now realize, however, that achieving success in life also demands self-confidence, striving, coping, and perseverance. Transition planning, therefore, should be about the processes of listening and supporting students as they explore their gifts and dreams, make choices, and follow through to achieve their desired goals (Orentlicher & Michaels, 2000; Powers et al., 1996; Sands & Wehmeyer, 1996).

Level and Intensity of Support

The Office of Special Education and Rehabilitative Services (OSERS) describes transition from school to adult life as a bridging process. It presents the need for two strong foundations to support the transition bridge: a strong secondary special education and related services program on the one side and a variety of adult services and employment options on the other. It describes three levels of supports that are available to students in crossing the bridge from school to adult life:

- Generic Support—those supports available to all students, not just those with disabilities (i.e., the service provided by a high school guidance counselor)
- Time-Limited Support—those support services provided just for students with disabilities (i.e., vocational training prior to job placement at a vocational rehabilitation facility)
- Intensive and Continuous Support—ongoing support specifically provided to people with the most severe disabilities (i.e., job placement provided through supported employment) (Will, 1984)

Within the focus of self-determination, supports are ways to help students with disabilities become more independent and capable of controlling their own lives, not ways to "cure" their disabilities. The transition process, therefore, involves determining what types and levels of supports are needed to ensure that students with autism experience the most normalized lifestyle possible (Jacobs, 1991; Michaels, 1998; Orentlicher & Michaels, 2000; Texas Collaborative Transition Project, 1993).

Families' and Students' Attitudes

Parents play an extremely important, even critical, role in the transition process. Parents are an excellent source of information about their sons and daughters as well as about the types of situations in which they will most likely be successful. Parents have spent more time than anyone else (including anyone professional or any single professional discipline) learning about and successfully meeting the needs of their sons and daughters. Moreover, most of the transition goals initiated at the secondary level will not be attained until after students leave the secondary system. Thus the parents, as primary advocates for their children, are left to ensure that transition goals are realized.

> If the goals are more a reflection of what the professionals think are best and most appropriate for the student rather than what is desired by the youth and the family, then it is likely that achievement of the targeted outcomes will fail. (Wehman, Moon, Everson, Wood, & Barcus, 1988, p. 96)

A student's family is one of the most important elements in the adjustment to community life. For example, the family has been seen as one of the most powerful sources of influence on the student's attitude, motivation, and behavior related to work. Parents can influence their child's general motivation to learn and perform the tasks and behaviors required by a job. Their willingness to assist their children in getting to work on time and wearing appropriate clothing can also determine job success (Sowers & Powers, 1991). Michaels (1998) argues that "quality will be built into the transition planning processes we create in direct proportion to our ability to empower parents to serve as 'equal partners'" (p. 24). Falvey (1989) offers principles for promoting full partnerships with parents:

- The emotional reactions of families of people with disabilities are normal, necessary, and protective reactions.
- Families are capable of solving their own problems; their solutions may not be "our" solutions, but they may be more effective for a particular family than our solutions.
- Professionals can learn to work effectively within the family system.
- The progress and needs of the son or daughter with disabilities may not be the most important issue for a family at a given time.
- The family is the best, most committed, long-term advocate for the child.
- There is no such thing as a family that cannot be actively and productively involved in the

educational process of a son or daughter with disabilities.

• Families have information about their sons or daughters with disabilities that is critical to the development of a sound educational program.

Service providers must assist family members to identify their role in supporting the student during the transition process. Support for family participation can take many forms, including allowing families to participate directly in the transition planning as well as providing information and assistance that helps families gain access to adult services.

Person-Centered Planning

Person-centered planning is a term used to describe a group of approaches that are intended to organize and guide the efforts of a person with a disability, his or her family members, friends, and service providers as they work collectively to assist the person in pursuing his or her interests, desires, and goals. Person-centered planning approaches are based on the belief that the student and those close to him or her are best able to plan for and meet future needs (Kregel, 1998; Mount, 1994).

Snow (1994) suggests that the focus of services should be about helping people to express their giftedness:

> Everyone has gifts—countless ordinary and extraordinary gifts. A gift is anything that one is or has or does that creates an opportunity for a meaningful interaction with at least one other person. Gifts are the fundamental characteristics of our human life and community (pp. 18–19).

Gifts can be made tangible and can be shared through conducting a functional assessment, identifying needed skills and training, and developing individualized accommodations in real environments.

All person-centered strategies share a common process. First, planning is based on the student's vision of life in the community after graduation. This vision is based on the student's personal hopes and dreams, including the kind of job the student would like, where he or she wants to live, and the relationships that he or she wants to maintain or develop. Second, the vision is shaped by the needs, interests, and abilities of each student as well as by the opportunities that will be available to him or her in home, school, work, and community settings. Third, the activities necessary to meet the goals are identified. Finally, the people who will assist the student in carrying out his or her plan are identified and their responsibilities are assigned. These people could include the student, his or her parents or other family members, peers, community members, and as necessary, representatives of educational and community service agencies. The planning process attempts to blend all of these potential sources of support as the student moves into the community (McDonnell, Hardman, McDonnell, & Kiefer-O'Donnell, 1995).

However, the most important common principle of person-centered planning reflects an attitudinal adjustment that is much more important than the use of any specific process:

> We all have ideas about what we want to achieve in life and how we eventually want our lives to look. Sometimes these are vague visions of careers and lifestyles, other times they are more specific. Many times our life's goals relate to what we would like to change in our current situation. Today's relationships, living situations, careers, and other factors influence how we want the future to be. People with disabilities are no different. Listening and learning about a person with a disability and discovering aspects about his or her personality are necessary first steps to helping the person to think about the future (DiLeo, 1994, p. 25).

Without a coherent vision of where someone is heading or what his or her "personal plan" entails, those who are coordinating whatever supports might be needed along the way face a difficult task. All too often, however, a student with a disability has a vision that professionals dismiss as being unrealistic. How can he or she possibly be a singer, a boss, an artist, or a doctor? Immediate rejection of dreams, however unrealistic they seem to be, denies the student a means of communicating important information that should be respected. These dreams provide critical information about the student's future paths and how these relate to his or her quality of life (DiLeo, 1994). When considering life goals, occupational therapy practitioners are encouraged to think of how best to help the student approach the realization of a life's dream. For example, if a student expresses a desire to be a musician, the occupational therapy practitioner should seek creative ways to help the student enter a field in which music is involved. Working in a music store, in a theater, or at a radio station may help the student be close to his or her dream. Students should be provided opportunities to develop and maintain skills of both interest and use in their lives by discovering and expressing their unique gifts and capacities.

Secondary Curriculum Reform

The goal of education is to prepare students with disabilities to live and to work in their communities (Wehman, 1996). This focus expands the role of education to include making initial placements and providing practical experiences in appropriate community settings before the students actually exit school. This functional community experience is described by the commonly used terms functional-skill training and community-based instruction.

Edgar (1987) noted that a close relationship must be established between instruction in the schools and the requirements of business and the workplace. Schools must alter their curricu-

---

Table 13.1
Five Abilities Needed to Succeed in the Modern Workplace

1. The ability to identify, organize, plan, and allocate resources, including budgeting, keeping records, following schedules, distributing work, evaluating others' performance, offering feedback and managing time.

2. The ability to work with others, including working in teams, experiencing leadership, negotiating and being able to work well with people from diverse backgrounds.

3. The ability to acquire and evaluate information, including using computers, interpreting and communicating data.

4. The ability to understand how various parts of a system fit together. This includes knowing how social, organizational and technological systems work and how to make them more efficient.

5. The ability to work with various technologies. This includes choosing the right tools or equipment for each job as well as maintaining and troubleshooting equipment.

Note. From U.S. Department of Labor, Commission on Achieving Necessary Skills, 2000.

---

la to include functional-skill training that reflects those skills required for success in business and industry. Table 13.1 lists the abilities required to succeed in the modern workplace that are identified by the U.S. Labor Department—Commission on Achieving Necessary Skills.

Brown and Lehr (1993) suggest that for functional-skill training to be meaningful, the student must participate in daily routines according to his or her strengths. Functional-skill training must also lead to the student having more meaningful control over personal routines and events in the environment.

Functional-skill training and community-based instruction lead to several important outcomes for students and families. First, students who learn to carry out personal management and leisure activities enhance their immediate participation in their homes, schools, and communities (McDonnell et al., 1995). Second, students who have access to community-based instruction are exposed to the range of employment alternatives available to them after graduation (McDonnell, Hardman, Hightower, & Kiefer-O'Donnell, 1991; Wehman, 1996). Finally, community-based instruction involves real-life conditions so service providers can develop alternative performance strategies and can identify the level of program support that will ensure that students are able to successfully participate in home, school, work, and other community settings (McDonnell et al., 1995). This information will ultimately assist the student and the family to select employment and residential programs that will meet the student's needs and preferences.

Inclusion

Schools are responsible not only for the education that students receive but also for what students are prepared to do once they graduate. That is, schools are responsible for providing services in ways that ensure their graduates' success (Wehman, 1996). For the typical student, success is measured in outcomes such as meaningful work, a place to live, and personal fulfillment that includes a social network of friends and family—full participation and inclusion in American society. These goals are equally valid for students with autism.

Living successfully and being fully included in the community require that we develop and maintain social relationships (McDonnell et al., 1995). The quality of the relationships that we develop significantly influences our satisfaction with our lives (Belle, 1982). These relationships also provide important sources of support in meeting the demands and challenges of adult life (Unger & Wandersman, 1985). This support can range from having someone to talk to after a tough day at work to having someone to provide a ride to the store when one's car is in the shop. Although we often do not think about the effect these relationships have on our lives, ultimately, they may be the most important factor in promoting successful community living (O'Brian & O'Brian, 1992). Transition serv-

ices, therefore, should foster the process of building, nurturing, and sustaining relationships. Snow (1994) highlights this critical friendship component of transition-to-community membership:

> When I am in relationship with other individuals and if these others are networked with each other and especially if these others are different from each other, the possibility exists for all of us to have a rich life, drawing on each other's gifts (p. 12).

A sense of belonging in a community provides the comfort and security that is needed to explore and use one's gifts (Grady, 1995; Snow, 1994). Occupational therapy as a profession believes that

> people belong together regardless of real or perceived differences. All people have the right to choose where they wish to live, work, learn, and play and with whom they wish to spend time. On a deeper level, we believe people belong together because of differences. (Grady, 1995, p. 301)

Regular and frequent opportunities to interact with typical peers in school and community settings is one of the most important things that schools can do to promote the postschool adjustment of students with autism (Hasazi, Johnson, Hasazi, Gordon, & Hull, 1989; Rusch, Destefano, Chadsey-Rusch, Phelps, & Szymanski, 1992; Wehman, 1996). The opportunity to interact with typical peers allows students with autism to develop the communication, social skills, and relationships that are so important to successful community living (Haring, 1992). Certainly, critical factors of postschool adjustment are that secondary transition instruction occur in the environments in which students will ultimately live their lives—in the community, in the home, and on the job—and that all students be included in school activities and classes alongside their general education peers. However, an equally critical factor of this adjustment is that students be socially accepted into these environments as full participants (Hughes & Carter, 2000). Occupational therapy practitioners must take an active role to promote acceptance of students as equal members in general education classrooms, in employment environments, and in the community.

Career Development

Most people see employment as a major and essential means to gain income, enhance self-esteem, and increase quality of life as well as options and opportunities. To a large extent, a job influences where people live, what activities they engage in, and what relationships they develop. Michaels (1998) suggests that the benefits of work for people, even those with the most severe disabilities, should not be underestimated. Bates (1989 as cited in Butterworth & Kiernan, 1996) states that

> work should be valued for its contributions to an individual's self-sufficiency and for its benefit to the individual's community, regardless of the pay level, or the nature of the work itself. By placing greater value on work as a personal and social contribution, there is . . . a greater likelihood that a system that values the unique contributions of all citizens will be created (p. 244).

Employment, therefore, is a critical focus of the transition process (Michaels, 1998; Orentlicher & Michaels, 2000; Wehman, 1996). Research shows that students who are successful in obtaining and maintaining paid work in community settings after high school are those who (1) receive ongoing opportunities for direct training in community employment sites throughout their high school career and (2) obtain a paid job before graduation (Hasazi et al., 1985; Hasazi et al., 1989; Wehman et al., 1988). However, preparation for employment or career should also include training in work-related skills such as social skills, career aware-ness, and self-advocacy training. The Division on Career Development and Transition of the Council for Exceptional Children (CEC) has listed key aspects of career development and transition education that should begin at the elementary school level. They are listed in Table 13.2.

As a society, we tend to limit the social and vocational experiences of students with autism by excluding them from participation in extracurricular activities or, worse, by placing them in sheltered environments such as day activity centers. Community-based experiential learning opportunities are needed to encourage the typical development of career exploration, preparation, and maturity.

Longitudinal Curricula

A longitudinal curriculum maintains a focus on career education during a student's entire education. Children begin developing not only a general personality but also a work personality in early childhood. Work attitudes, values, interests, motivations, needs, habits, and be-

---

Table 13.2
Key Aspects of Career Development and Transition Education at the Elementary Level

1. Career development and transition education is for individuals with disabilities at all ages.

2. Career development is a process that begins at birth and should continue throughout life.

3. Early career development is essential for making satisfactory choices later.

4. Significant gaps or periods of neglect in any area of basic human development affect career development and the transition from one stage of life to another.

5. Career development is responsive to intervention and programming when the programming involves direct instruction for individual needs.

Note. From "Career Development for Students with Disabilities in Elementary Schools: A Position Statement of the Division of Career Development and Transition," by G. Clark, B. Carlson, S. Fisher, I. Cook, and V. D'Alonzo, 1991, *Career Development for Exceptional Individuals, 14,* p. 109–120. Copyright 1991 by the Council for Exceptional Children. Reprinted with permission of the authors.

haviors develop early and are susceptible to the influence of parents, teachers, peers, and experiences (Brolin, 1993). Thus, Wehman (1996) stresses the importance of all elementary and middle school programs having an active vocational component, making career and vocational education a fairly prominent role in the students' daily educational programs. Brolin (1993) conceptualizes career development as a process that occurs in three stages:

- Career awareness stage: During the elementary school years, students should be provided with instruction and experiences that will make them more aware of themselves, of the world of work and its requirements, and of how they might fit into it someday.
- Career exploration stage: During the junior high or middle school years, students should be provided with career awareness opportunities and opportunities to explore areas of interest and aptitude, which is important because, during this stage, students can begin to determine their future roles as citizens, family members, employees, and participants in productive avocational activities.
- Career preparation stage: During high school, the focus is on career planning and preparation for the world of work after high school.

Longitudinal curricula integrate career education that responds to these three stages. These curricula allow students to develop satisfactory work personalities and career maturity. The education of students with autism, therefore, must focus on the development of life skills, affective skills, and general employability skills. These students should be provided with opportunities for hands-on experiences such as real-life work experiences, visits, and career-oriented field trips throughout their school years.

Business Connections and Alliances

Findings from many studies show that students are most likely to be employed after leaving school if they held paid jobs while they were in school (Edgar, 1987; Frank, Sitlington, Cooper,

& Cool, 1990; Hasazi, 1985; Hasazi et al., 1985; Levine & Edgar, 1995). McDonnell, Hardman, and Hightower (1989) suggest that emphasis on employment outcomes can be achieved through the use of two approaches:

- Job sampling: Placements in a number of nonpaid positions at actual job sites during high school, which not only provide students with training in specific work skills but also provide practitioners and family an opportunity to observe a student's performance in a wide range of employment possibilities.
- Specific job training and placement: Placements in jobs that match a student's interests and needs and that train the student to complete assigned job tasks to employers' standards.

These approaches require the use of and partnerships with community resources and employers. Accordingly, cooperation, coordination, and collaboration at the community level are necessary to fully support the transition efforts of students with autism. The Texas Collaborative Transition Project (1993) calls for a new philosophy for serving students with disabilities. In this new and evolving philosophy, the community holds the responsibility to provide the supports that are necessary for the full inclusion of students with disabilities. When students leave school, they become part of the community. The community's role is to provide the services and supports that each student will need to function independently and productively after leaving school. In practice, schools are encouraged to develop partnerships with local businesses. These local businesses can be used as sites for internships and for paid work experiences.

The Process of Providing Transition Services

The actual process of providing transition services includes three steps: evaluation, planning, and service delivery. While completing each of these steps, the occupational therapist must keep the previously described principles in mind to ensure that the services remain centered around the needs of the student.

Evaluation

The first step of transition is to determine the desired outcomes for a particular student and the needs of that student. The step of evaluation provides three challenges (DiLeo, 1994):

- Students with autism often have had limited opportunities to explore their full potential. As a result, service providers can only guess at the possibilities for their futures.
- Students with autism who have had limited life experiences are often unaware of the range of choices before them. They have difficulty discovering interests when they have not had diverse interactions with environments, activities, and other people.
- Students with autism have difficulty with communication, and others must make sensitive efforts to learn when a student is motivated, happy, involved, or disinterested. If language is not easily used, then these personal states may be communicated by facial expression, behavior, attentiveness, or other means.

The evaluation process must overcome these challenges by using a variety of approaches and assessment tools. One approach uses person-centered planning tools, which provide an alternative to traditional testing. The process of person-centered planning results in a plan of action that is based on preferences and strengths of the student and is developed so specifically that IEP goals, objectives, and action statements are easily completed (Clark, 1998). Appendix 13.A includes examples of self-evaluation forms for students. These forms were developed within the philosophy of person-centered planning and self-determination. However, they may need adaptation for students with limited language skills. Other forms of assessment for students with autism include functional and situational assessments, ecolog-ical inventories, formal and informal observations, community-based job-site analysis, and task analysis. Appendix 13.B provides sample assessment tools and checklists that might be beneficial in guiding observations. One of the major contributions that occupational therapists can make is to target the most appropriate tasks for evaluation in specific environments such as the work site.

The term *functional assessment* refers to the measurement of purposeful behavior in interaction with the environment (Riches, 1993). In the vocational arena, for example, functional assessment can be described as the process of obtaining information about a worker's skills and performance to make appropriate training or placement decisions. The specific tasks, activities, and skills required for various jobs can be identified, and assessment and training on these specific tasks can be carried out in the natural work or community environments.

Moon, Inge, Wehman, Brooke, and Barcus (1990) defined *situational assessment* as "behavioral assessments in real settings" (p. 68). Students in this evaluation approach are observed in an actual work, home, or recreation setting as they perform tasks demanded by that environment. Tasks in which students have difficulty are identified and become the focus of training. Environmental cues, consequences, and supports can also be identified through this approach and, ultimately, can be capitalized on in designing intervention strategies and, ultimately, can be built into the design of intervention strategies.

Planning

Once a comprehensive evaluation is completed, planning occurs by means of designing the IEP goals and objectives. These goals and objectives are designed to bridge the gap between where the student wishes to end up (desired outcomes) and where the student currently is (current strengths and weaknesses). Transition planning needs to include several important areas (McDonnell et al., 1995):

- Employment: The planning should specify the type of placement or program that will be most appropriate for the student and should determine how the resources among the school and postschool service programs will be coordinated to ensure not only that appropriate jobs are identified but also that the student is trained for the placement. Appendix 13.C includes examples of ITP Annual Goals for a student in 9th grade in the area of employment and career exploration.
- Living Arrangement: The team should determine which residential alternative is the most appropriate for the student and identify the specific residential programs to be contacted when the student is ready to move away from home.
- Leisure Activities: Activities should be planned to ensure that the student has the necessary resources and skills to participate in leisure alternatives that are most important to him or her. Ensuring these resources and skills may involve determining financing and transportation for the activity or establishing a peer to attend the activity with the student.
- Income and Medical Support: The team should make certain that the student is enrolled in a social service program (i.e., Medicaid, SSI), which is necessary to ensure the student's financial stability and good health.
- Transportation: The specific transportation needs for access to vocational, residential, and leisure alternatives should be determined. The team should identify the specific alternatives for each activity, the method of financing transportation, and the strategies to coordinate transportation between school and adult service providers.
- Long-Term Support and Care: The team should identify the need for guardianship, specific trusts or wills, or both.

Before the student leaves school, as many components of the transition plan as possible should be carried out. For example, the student may be placed full time in his or her target employment setting. Transportation from home to work should be arranged, and potential difficulties should be examined.

Service Delivery

Who will provide services and in what way must be determined. Services may include specific training and education; the establishment of appropriate linkages among the school and adult service providers or community agencies; consultation and collaboration with other team members or agencies; or coordination of services. Service delivery, therefore, can be either direct or indirect. Education may include academic, vocational, or community experiences.

Specific Roles for Occupational Therapy in the Transition From School to Adult Life

Occupational therapy practitioners may be involved throughout the transition process from evaluation through service delivery. The occupational therapist may perform analysis of anticipated roles and requirements, job task analysis, assessment of skills and needs in relation to specific job tasks, and environmental or task adaptation to improve student effectiveness. The occupational therapist may also be involved in training students for specific tasks or in the establishment of plans that address behavior or social issues of concern. In addition, with the greater emphasis that the reauthorization of IDEA (1997) places on independent living, the occupational therapist may be involved in the delivery of services to address self-care, household management abilities, and leisure skills. Table 13.3 summarizes potential roles of occupational therapy in transition services. Appendix 13.D provides additional resources and references to assist the practitioner in providing transition services.

Transition planning is often perceived to be an activity that occurs only when a student begins high school. In fact, to be most effective, it should be viewed as a longitudinal process, beginning when students are in elementary school, proceeding through middle school and high school, and culminating in a paid job and community integration before the student leaves school (Brolin, 1993; Sowers & Powers, 1991; Wehman, 1996). As a part of the team, an occupational therapist should be involved in early planning.

Elementary School

From the very beginning of the student's school experience, collaboration among team members is important. The consultation, treatment, and guidance that is given in preschool and elementary school will affect the direction a student takes at the close of the high school experience. The occupational therapy practitioner needs to be aware of the budding interests of the young student and ready to support parents in thinking of the future and of the possible vocations that might suit their child's distinct gifts. Case Study 13.1 profiles one young student's interests and abilities and describes how those might translate into various vocations.

For this early planning to happen, continuity of care is crucial. However, as often occurs in the schools, occupational therapy services are not continual nor is the therapist typically the same person throughout the school years. Therefore, the documentation done by all therapists who have contact with the student is critical as is the continual sharing of information by all team members. Without this information sharing, an in-depth understanding of the child's personality, abilities, and needs will not be possible.

Specific issues that can begin to be addressed as early as elementary school include the following:

- Discussion with parents about household chores for the student to develop work habits and skills
- Discussion about the student's potential future living environments
- Development of the student's self-determination skills

Table 13.3
The Occupational Therapist's Roles in Transition

Transition Service	Occupational Therapist's Role
Evaluation	Determine desired outcomes as well as future dreams and plans.
	Assist in determining a student's unique gifts and abilities.
	Assist in the completion of appropriate functional assessments.
Planning	Collaborate with team members by providing information gained during evaluation and by assisting in the creation of appropriate IEP goals and objectives to bridge the gap between abilities and needs.
Service Delivery	Provide specific community or school based instruction.
	Coordinate services between agencies.

- Discussion about the student's possible vocational opportunities and career options
- Inclusion of IEP goals related to the ability to remain on task, become more independent, and increase responsibility

Middle School or Junior High

When a child reaches middle school or junior high, teachers and therapists on the child's IEP team need to begin working with parents on

Case Study 13.1
Tommy

Tommy, an 8-year-old student, has exceptional abilities in music, is very good with animals, loves to categorize and organize numbers and written material, has a wonderful memory for facts, prefers to work in a quiet environment, and is beginning to enjoy helping people one-on-one. His occupational therapist has begun to explore the possibility with his parents that he might develop job interests in library science, might work in a music library, or possibly be an assistant in a veterinarian's office.

specific transition goals. If this preparation is done, the high school experience and final transition planning will be much more smooth and effective. Case Study 13.2 describes how this process was carried out for one student.

Specific activities or discussions that can occur during middle school or junior high include the following:

- Discussion of community-supported work options
- Greater involvement of the student in household chores with increased independence
- Increased independence of the student with respect to communicating to others about his or her disability and specific needs
- Increased responsibility for the student at home and at school
- Initial exploration of the student's specific aptitudes and abilities
- Simple paid work for the student such as a paper route or assisting with farm, horticulture, veterinary office, or humane society chores

High School

When the student reaches high school, the occupational therapist's role may become more complex. The occupational therapist may assist with the functional vocational evaluation to determine the student's specific skills, abilities, and needs; appropriate work environments and work tasks; requirements of specific work tasks by means of task analysis; and the discrepancy between the student's abilities and the task requirements. During the secondary education years, the student needs to gain skills that will enable him or her to live and work as independently as possible (Rusch & Chadsey, 1998). The occupational therapist, therefore, may also be involved in teaching appropriate life skills and work habits. Moreover, independent living requires a multitude of skills and abilities that fall within the realm of occupational therapist. Tasks such as shopping, using the phone, doing the laundry, paying bills, preparing a meal, using public transportation, and finding community leisure opportunities could require specific education and training as well as the delivery of appropriate modifications or assistance.

Communicating preferences, learning how to access resources, being able to identify and solve problems, advocating for one's self, and managing one's time are goals that need to be addressed throughout the high school experience and into adulthood (Wehmeyer, 1993–94). Additional areas of intervention for students with autism include teaching appropriate social and communication skills, establishing community recreational and leisure activities,

---

Case Study 13.2
Umi

The interests that Umi demonstrated as a young child, and that his mother recognized and used in home activities, were used to his advantage in middle school. His interest in cooking became a helpful focus in improving math and reading skills, and in the pre-vocational training that eventually led to meaningful self-employment.

There were no services for Umi as a child, and his mother was advised to institutionalize him. She refused, feeling that there must be a means to reach her son and to teach him. This means was through the kitchen. Umi always loved to be involved in his mother's cooking, and this interest was capitalized on to teach him reading and math through the steps that are required in following a recipe. He learned each meticulous step involved in making delicious cookies and cakes until he became totally independent in all the measuring, mixing, baking, and packaging of the baked goods. The long-term goal was to prepare Umi to own his own bakery and to market the baked products to become financially self-sufficient. Umi's transition plans included not only his need for independent living and work situations but also his need for leisure pursuits. The team acknowledged his interest in music and his desire to develop his inherent talent for singing. The occupational therapist collaborated with his mother to find a teacher to provide voice lessons who would understand Umi's learning style. He now enjoys performing for friends and for more formal public functions.

and teaching independent mobility and transportation.

In addition to the functional vocational evaluation and the learning of tasks, skills, and work habits, other issues such as the following directions need to be addressed during high school:

- The education of the student and parents regarding community opportunities
- Discussion with parents about their rights and responsibilities
- Determination of how the student will be involved in his or her own transition planning
- Determination of the student's specific aptitudes, interests, and desires
- Emphasis on the student's greater involvement with chores and responsibilities
- Discussion of available adult services and funding

Identifying Community Resources. Many high schools provide students with community-based vocational experiences and job tryouts as part of the secondary transition program. Usually, a teacher or a vocational counselor will be responsible for seeking these job opportunities. However, as suggested by Sowers and Powers (1991), occupational therapists can provide consultation to teachers or vocational trainers when work experience sites are being sought and established for students. In these consultations, the occupational therapist should discuss task and work-related skill performance issues as they relate to specific students.

Optimally, an occupational therapist should accompany the teacher or vocational trainer to the site when instructional strategies or when task completion modifications or accommodation strategies may be required. However, if the therapist is not able to go along, he or she should discuss specific details that the teacher or other vocational trainer should note during the analysis that may be particularly relevant to the student. Before a job placement is finalized, the occupational therapist should complete a job analysis to determine whether a good match exists between the individual student and the targeted job. Once a placement is made, the therapist can suggest job design and adaptation strategies. Task analysis can be used to divide a set of activities or skills into smaller components for the student to learn. Therapists can also arrange the sequence of activities to be learned in a functional manner. Appendix 13.E includes procedures and forms for Task Analysis and Ecological Inventory. The job placement process does not always progress smoothly. Often, as job placements are attempted, the client and therapist discover new insights and information that direct future plans, which is illustrated in Case Study 13.3.

Employment Options and Opportunities. Employment is a critical focus of the transition process. Work and employment options for students with autism can be divided into two major categories: (1) integrated, competitive employment, including supported employment options; and (2) segregated, noncompetitive options, including day treatment, work activity centers, and sheltered workshops (Michaels, 1998).

Although segregated, noncompetitive options are still available across the country, the transition amendments of the IDEA clearly do not recognize segregated options as acceptable transition outcomes for students with disabilities. According to Wehman (1995),

> The time has well passed for individuals with autism to be sitting in segregated schools, residential facilities, or adult activity centers all day long, performing meaningless tasks. ... The time has passed for individuals with autism to be relegated to earning a dollar a day in a sheltered workshop or to be confined to a "day treatment" center. (p. x)

Therefore, segregated, noncompetitive options are not discussed here.

Supported employment emerged as an alternative to segregated training centers. Sup-

Case Study 13.3
Kyle

Kyle experimented with several work settings before finding the right fit. He had been involved with special education services, had attended summer camps for children with developmental delays, and had received speech and occupational therapy. He could read well but had difficulty with sequencing thoughts or work plans. As a young adult, his family moved to another state, and he enrolled in a training program with a sheltered workshop program in his county, packaging small parts for a local company. A caseworker, social worker, and job trainer were on the workshop team, but no occupational therapist was in the program. Behavioral problems, such as refusal to work, arguments with other clients, and a generally negative attitude led the team to request the consultation of an occupational therapist in private practice. The one aspect of Kyle's program which he did enjoy was volunteering at a local nursing home where he said he "liked helping the ladies in the wheelchairs go to dinner."

Goals for Kyle were to follow through at the therapist's clinic on a predictable sequence of jobs in which he had indicated an interest. These jobs included watering plants, washing dishes, and learning to file charts alphabetically. Each therapy session concluded with a social time. He gradually developed the ability to do most chores with no or minimal supervision, and he always enjoyed the social times, which for him, were a definite reward for work well done.

However, these skills did not translate well into other work settings where he was expected to work independently without much interaction with others, settings that could not provide the social time that Kyle had come to expect. Being paid for his work was not a real incentive for him. Something was missing. His occupational therapist was aware of his need for socialization with trusted, consistent coworkers and of his interest in the speech therapist's "therapy dog" who would often accompany her to work. The occupational therapist became more creative in searching for the right work setting for Kyle. She discovered a small farm that was willing to have Kyle participate in caring for animals and to do light farm chores. Collaborating with an animal-assistive therapist as well as with his caseworker and social worker, the occupational therapist initiated a training program of animal care and work safety. The work was predictable, and the animals as well as the other farm workers gave Kyle the calm and personal interaction he needed. Arrangements were made for Kyle to work on the farm for a half day two times a week. Arrangements also were made to have Kyle participate in the planning to have people from a nearby nursing home visit the farm. Kyle would be the official greeter and "tour guide."

---

ported employment is defined as paid employment in which students with autism are provided with support such as supervision and training that enables them to work in settings where people without disabilities are employed (Smith, Belcher, & Juhrs, 1995; Wehman & Kregel, 1998). Supported employment is grounded in the assumption that all people can work and that we, as a nation, need to create the formal and informal long-term support mechanisms that are required to realize this assumption. In other words, the question is not whether a student with autism is capable of being employed but, rather, what kinds of support services are needed to ensure successful work performance.

Supported employment is grounded in a place-and-train approach (Michaels, 1998). This approach focuses on teaching work behaviors and skills within the actual work environment. In the place-and-train approach,

performance criteria in the natural environment are based on the demands of natural settings rather than arbitrary standards of a classroom setting. . . . [Specifically, instruction in the natural learning environment offers] exposure to the natural stimuli (cues), reinforcements, and corrections that can facilitate performance (Artesani, Itkonen, Fryxell, & Woolcock, 1996, p. 5).

In contrast, the traditional approach of train-and-place requires that students, first, be trained in a classroom setting and, only when they achieve a predetermined level of "readiness," enter the competitive world of work. This traditional approach assumes that students are able to generalize skills learned in the classroom to a new or different work environment.

Westling and Fox (1995) list the major characteristics of supported employment:

- Supported employment means competitive work in an integrated setting with ongoing support services.
- Supported employment may be provided to students with autism who traditionally have been unable to perform competitive work.
- Competitive work means work that is performed on a full-time or part-time basis for which the student is compensated.
- Integrated work settings are job sites where most employees do not have disabilities and where the student with autism interacts on a regular basis with other employees who do not have disabilities.
- If a student with autism is placed in a work setting as a member of a group of students with disabilities, then no more than eight students with disabilities should be in that group.
- Ongoing support services are the services needed to support and maintain the student in employment.
- Ongoing support services must include at a minimum twice-monthly monitoring at the work site of the student.

In a supported employment approach, a job coach helps the student through all phases of the job search process. The job coach then stays with the student in the employment setting, helping the student to learn all facets of the job, negotiate accommodations, and develop appropriate social interactions with coworkers (Michaels, 1998; Moon & Griffin, 1988). As the student becomes more independent, the job coach begins to "fade," that is, to decrease the level of support and physical presence at the work site. However, as job requirements or demands change, the level of job-coach support and direct job-coach intervention also may need to change as well. Appendix 13.F includes forms for on-going evaluations of a student's performance at work.

Normalization, integration, and real work for real pay are but a few of the concepts that underline the way employment programs for students with autism are being viewed. Supported employment is designed to increase the community integration and inclusion of students with autism, and it should be viewed as the most important outcome of the transition process.

Specific Issues for Students With Autism

In teaching or coaching people with autism, whether early in their school careers or later as they prepare for employment, the occupational therapist, other members of the team, and the potential employer should be aware of several important principles (Moreno & O'Neal, 1999). These principles include the following:

- Organizational skills may be a challenge for people with autism.
- Tasks that need to be learned should be broken down into small specific steps.
- When assessing skills, one cannot assume that having one skill automatically transfers into a related skill; for example, math skills do not necessarily equate with cash-register skills. Uneven skill development is a hallmark of autism.
- One should avoid asking vague questions and should be as concrete as possible during interactions.
- Speech should be literal and should avoid idioms, double meanings, sarcasm, nicknames, or "cute" names.
- Communication with people with autism should be clear, should avoid verbal overload, and should involve shorter sentences.
- A person with autism may not be able to recognize the meaning in facial expressions and other social cues.

- Levels of auditory and visual input that are acceptable for most people can be too much or too little for the person with autism.
- A person with autism should be prepared in advance if changes in environment or other life situations or routines will be occurring.
- Misbehavior should not be taken personally or be seen as manipulative because people with autism have extreme difficulty reading the reactions of others.
- If the frequency of unusual or difficult behaviors increases, it may indicate increased stress. A person with autism may need to retreat to a "safe" place or be with or near a "safe" person to reduce stress.
- Behavioral management, if used correctly, can be effective. Procedures should be positive and appropriate to the chronological age of the person.
- Everyone working with the person with autism must be consistent in treatment and expectations.
- If the person with autism uses repetitive verbal arguments or questions, others should respond with logical interruptions and avoid arguing. The person may be upset about a subject quite different from the subject he or she is perseverating on and may be calmed by being directed to write down both the repetitive question or argument and then a logical reply for him or herself. Role-playing and reversing roles may also help the person discover a logical answer.

Community Involvement

Independent living after high school will require some level of community involvement with individuals and organizations outside the immediate circles of family, friends, and service providers. Living independently also requires making choices and taking risks. As stated earlier, a critical element of service planning is listening to client choices and encouraging the risk taking necessary for personal growth, employment, and independence. Choice making and risk taking may be made easier and less stressful for the student at the time of transition

if community involvement has been ongoing since childhood. Visiting the neighborhood library, the fire or police station, local small businesses, or even community health spas can assist children in feeling comfortable in their environment, while providing a sense of belonging to a community. Community interactions such as these allow early opportunities for choice making and risk taking and may also foster the development of appropriate social skills.

Social Skills

Autism is a disorder in which difficulties in social relationships are prominent. Learning appropriate social skills before transitioning to work is, therefore, a crucial component of learning for the student. Early planning by means of appropriate IEP goals that address social abilities should be given priority throughout the educational experience. Once transitioning has begun, specific social skills that are necessary for the workplace may need to be taught. Social issues that might arise in the work place include the following:

- Knowing suitable greetings
- Keeping appropriate personal space
- Conversing with coworkers, employers, and possibly customers (answering questions; using appropriate volume, rate, and intensity; allowing others time to respond; and if possible, observing others' body language for their interest in the topic)
- Maintaining some level of eye contact with others
- Maintaining suitable hygiene
- Knowing ways to handle workplace conflict with composure

As parents and practitioners review the desired social skills that have been identified to successfully interact in the public arena, they must be careful about what they expect of the person with autism. Expecting a person with autism to be aware of what others convey by facial expression or body language may or may not be appropriate. People with autism often have difficulty reading these cues and need verbal explanations of the reasons for the reactions of others. Expecting eye contact, likewise, may or may not be realistic. Recognizing these limitations, fitting the job setting to the person, and preparing the person for the job setting are important actions. Social skills curricula are available to guide specific training (Goldstein et al. 1980; Walker et al. 1993; Varenhorst, 1980; & Gibbs, 1987).

Behavioral Concerns

Students with autism may demonstrate unusual and challenging behaviors that can hinder their ability to remain on task and function in certain employment settings. Occupational therapists may be involved in determining appropriate job placements or task modifications to deal with behavioral issues. In addition, the occupational therapist may provide specific intervention to reduce or eliminate problem behaviors. See Table 13.4 for a suggested format to teach replacement behaviors. PROPP is an acronym that stands for Praise Review, Offer Help, and Practice a Plan, the three major

---

Table 13.4
Support Plan for Replacement Behaviors

The following process is a suggested format to teach "replacement behaviors," or other ways for individuals to express messages or meet needs that they currently accomplish by engaging in inappropriate or challenging behaviors. This process should be more beneficial if the support person has a functional understanding of the individual's challenging behavior (what purpose the behavior serves, what the "payoff" is). Use this process regularly at a scheduled time, preferably daily. Have the session at a neutral time when both parties are calm and nothing disruptive is occurring in the environment.

A. Provide feedback that praises.
Goals: To make a positive connection, build self-esteem, and promote bonding.

1. Give praise and thanks for appropriate behavior and effort.

2. Express positive affirmation. Examples include "You're really a neat guy (kid, lady, etc.)" and "I really enjoy working with you."

3. Affirm specific positive qualities (e.g., sense of humor, kindness, tries hard, etc.).

B. Offer help.
Goal: To make the challenging behaviors a source of alliance with the person rather than a source of division.

1. Identify the behavior and the need it may be expressing. However, talk more about the feeling associated with the behavior rather than the behavior itself.

2. Ask something like "How can I help things go better?"

3. Talk about helping the person to change the behavior in terms of reasons that benefit him or her rather than the other people in the person's environment (e.g., to feel better about self, so other people will like you better).

C. Practice a plan.
Goal: To create together and practice a strategy for what to do when the feelings or physical signs that precede problem behaviors occur or when difficult environmental situations cannot be avoided.

1. Explore a variety of options (e.g., move away from stressful situation, take some deep breaths, come to support person for help, talk about it, use planned relaxation techniques, make a verbal or signed request for a break or attention).

2. Choose an option (or options) together. If possible, the person with the challenging behavior should try to suggest his or her own options or choose from acceptable options.

3. Review and practice. Role-play if appropriate (but make it fun).

4. Reaffirm the plan and your desire to help.

5. Express confidence that the person will be successful.

Note. Adapted From *PROPP: Support Plan for Teaching Replacement and Coping Techniques* by B. Maly, 1995, monograph. Copyright 1995 by B. Maly. Adapted with permission of the author.

Case Study 13.4
Brett

Brett was good, even obsessive, with numbers. He could become very agitated or violent, however, if other people made errors in dates, measurements, or in counting money. He had been dismissed from two sheltered workshops for self-abusive behavior and for kicking holes in walls when fellow workers made these mistakes. The occupational therapist on the transition-to-work team recognized his gifts in computation and consulted with the caseworker who, in this situation, was also responsible for finding Brett a job. The two agreed that Brett should have work that accentuated his abilities but that would involve low-level stress or very controlled interaction with other employees.

The first placement that Brett's caseworker arranged for him was employment in the community with a large computer company where he was on a two-person team (himself and a trainer, initially), hanging pictures and shop boards. This employment had to be terminated because Brett could become extremely upset if a picture was the slightest bit out of alignment. Behavior management with calming techniques to modify these outbursts was only marginally successful.

Subsequently, after further consultation with the occupational therapist and exploration of job sites in the community, a more appropriate placement was found—a coin processor for a large local bank. This job has been the perfect match for Brett's interest in numbers. Bags of coins are delivered to the bank from the city's parking meters, and Brett is responsible for accurately totaling the contents of these bags by the end of each workday. He has been successful in this position for more than 5 years, and his employer has been pleased with the quality of his work.

Even though the job builds on a skill that might be judged to be an obsession, this job has capitalized on a talent that Brett has especially enjoyed. Through his work, Brett can make a beneficial contribution to the community and satisfy his interest in numbers. Brett is extremely conscientious, and even a small error can be very upsetting to him. His coworker is sensitive to any warning of frustration from Brett and will remind him to go to a quiet room specifically provided for him, which allows Brett to have cool-down time whenever he might need it.

---

points in Maly's support plan for teaching replacement behaviors and coping techniques. Maly (1995) developed the PROPP plan out of his deeply felt personal philosophy that the client with challenging behaviors should be an active participant in developing a plan to change these behaviors. He stated that:

> Positive accountability to the individual's own plan, that they have been a part of designing, promotes intrinsic motivation. It doesn't rely on reward or punishment from an outside source but instead relies on the individual's own sense of self-worth and sense of accomplishment in reaching a goal they have committed to themselves. PROPP continues to be effective in helping clients understand and change the behaviors that are troublesome to them. (Personal communication, Feb. 27, 2001)

Case Studies 13.4 and 13.5 describe situations in which job modifications and interventions to change inappropriate behaviors helped two clients to function better on the job.

Conclusion

The occupational therapist's knowledge of human occupation and function as they relate to the individual skills and interests of the person with autism can make an important difference in that person's quality of life. The wide variation of interests, intellectual abilities, personality characteristics, and job placements described in the case studies illustrates the varied skills of people with autism. The occupational therapist can be an important leader and team collaborator as he or she works with the community, the family, and the person with autism to obtain appropriate placements and services that aid the person with autism in the transition from school to adult roles.

References

Americans with Disabilities Act (ADA) of 1990. PL 101–336, 42 U.S.C. § 12101 *et seq.*

Artesani, A. J., Itkonen, T., Fryxell, D., & Woolcock, W. W. (1996). Community instruction. In W. W. Woolcock & J. W. Domaracki (Eds.), *Instructional strategies in the community: A resource guide for community instruction for persons with disabilities* (pp. 1–16). Austin, TX: PRO-ED.

Belle, D. (1982). Social ties and social support. In D. Doled (Ed.), *Lives in stress: Women and depression* (pp. 133–144). Beverly Hills, CA: Sage.

Brolin, D. E. (1993). *Life centered career education: A competency based approach.* Reston, VA: The Council for Exceptional Children.

Brown, F., & Gothelf, C. R. (1996). Self-determination for all individuals. In D. H. Lehr & F. Brown (Eds.), *People with disabilities who challenge the system* (pp. 335–353). Baltimore: Brookes.

Brown, F., & Lehr, D. H. (1993). Making activities meaningful for students with severe multiple disabilities. *Teaching Exceptional Children, 25,* 12–16.

Butterworth, J., & Kiernan, W. J. (1996). Access to employment for all individuals: Legislative, systems, and service delivery issues. In D. H. Lehr & F. Brown (Eds.), *People with disabilities who challenge the system* (pp. 243–281). Baltimore: Brookes.

Clark, G. M. (1998). *Assessment for transition planning: A guide for special education teachers and related service personnel.* Austin, TX: PRO-ED.

Developmental Disabilities Act Amendments of 1984. PL 98–527, 98 §§ 2662–2685.

DiLeo, D. (1994). *Reach for the dream! Developing individual service plans for persons with disabilities.* St. Augustine, FL: Training Resource Network.

Dunn, W., Foto, M., Hinojosa, J., Boyt-Schell, B., Thompson, L., & Hertfelder, S. (1995). Occupational therapy: A profession in support of full inclusion. *American Journal of Occupational Therapy, 49,* (10), 855.

Case Study 13.5
Tony

Tony loved coffee—really loved coffee. His obsessive attraction to coffee created havoc in the Community Living Office. He would drink his own coffee and anyone else's coffee left sitting around. He would even go into neighboring offices to empty all the coffee cups there. The challenge was to honor this desire but to help him control his obsession while working at a coffee packaging company in his community. He now works 3–4 hours a day, 3 days a week, surrounded by the sight and the smell of coffee. If a fellow worker gives him almost constant redirection, he can stay with the task of packaging rather than drinking coffee. The occupational therapist on the transition team suggested that a closed-loop verbal audiotape reminder be developed for Tony to hasten his achievement of the goal to accomplish complete self-direction. She also recommended varying the voice levels used for the reminders and varying the intervals between the reminders to avoid monotony and habituation.

Edgar, E. (1987). Secondary programs in special education: Are many of them justifiable? *Exceptional Children, 53,* 555–561.

Edgar, E., Levine, P., & Maddox, M. (1986). *Statewide follow-up studies of secondary special education students in transition.* Working paper of the Networking and Evaluation team, University of Washington, Seattle.

Education for All Handicapped Children Act of 1975. PL 94–142, 20 U.S.C. § 1400 *et seq.*

Falvey, M. A. (1989). *Community-based curriculum: Instructional strategies for students with severe handicaps* (2nd ed.). Baltimore: Brookes.

Frank, A. R., Sitlington, P., Cooper, L., & Cool, V. (1990). Adult adjustment of recent graduates of Iowa mental disabilities programs. *Education and Training in Mental Retardation, 25,* 62–75.

Gibbs, J. (1987) *Tribes: A process for social development and cooperative learning.* Santa Rosa, CA: Center Source Publications.

Goals 2000: Educate America Act of 1994. PL 103–227, U.S.C. § 5801 *et seq.*

Goldstein, A. P., Sprafkin, R. P., Gershaw, N. J. & Klein, P. (1980) *Skillstreaming the adolescent.* Champaign, IL: Research.

Grady, A. P. (1995). 1994 Eleanor Clarke Slagle Lecture: Building inclusive community: A challenge for occupational therapy. *American Journal of Occupational Therapy, 49,* 300–310.

Halloran, W. (1992). *Transition services requirement: Issues, implications, challenge.* Washington DC: U.S. Department of Education.

Haring, T. G. (1992). Social relationships. In L. H. Meyer, C. A. Peck, & L. Brown (Eds.), *Critical issues in lives of people with severe disabilities* (pp. 195–218). Baltimore: Brookes.

Hasazi, S. B. (1985). Facilitating transition from high school: Policies and practices. *American Rehabilitation, 11*(3), 9–16.

Hasazi, S. B., Gordon, S., & Roe, R. (1985). Factors associated with the employment status of handicapped youth exiting high school from 1979–1983. *Exceptional Children, 51,* 455–469.

Hasazi, S., Johnson, R. E., Hasazi, J., Gordon, L. R., & Hull, M. (1989). Employment of youth with and without handicaps following school: Outcomes and correlates. *Journal of Special Education, 23,* 243–255.

Hughes, C., & Carter, E. (2000). *The transition handbook: Strategies high school teachers use that work!* Baltimore: Brookes.

Individuals With Disabilities Education Act (IDEA) of 1990. PL 101–476, 20 U.S.C., Ch 33.

Jacobs, K. (1991). *Occupational therapy: Work-related programs and assessments* (2nd ed.). Boston: Little, Brown.

Kregel, J. (1998). Developing a career path: Application of person-centered planning. In P. Wehman & J. Kregel (Eds.), *More than a job: Securing satisfying careers for people with disabilities* (pp. 71–91). Baltimore: Brookes.

Levine, P., & Edgar, G. (1995). An analysis by gender of long-term postschool outcomes for youth with and without disabilities. *Exceptional Children, 61,* 282–300.

Maly, B. (1995). *PROPP: Support plan for teaching replacement and coping techniques.* [Monograph].

McDonnell, J. J., Hardman, M. L, & Hightower, J. (1989). Employment preparation for high school students with severe handicaps. *Mental Retardation, 27,* 396–404.

McDonnell, J. J., Hardman, M. L., Hightower, J., & Kiefer-O'Donnell, R. (1991). Variables associated with in-school and after-school integration of secondary students with severe disabilities. *Education and Training in Mental Retardation, 26,* 243–258.

McDonnell, J. J., Hardman, M. L., McDonnell, A. P., & Kiefer-O'Donnell, R. (1995). *An introduction to persons with severe disabilities: Educational and social issues.* Newton, MA: Allyn & Bacon.

Michaels, C. A. (1998). *Transition to employment.* Austin, TX: PRO-ED.

Moon, M. S., & Griffin, S. L. (1988). Supported employment service delivery models. In P. Wehman & M. S. Moon (Eds.), *Vocational rehabilitation and supported employment* (pp. 17–30). Baltimore: Brookes.

Moon, M. S., Inge, K. J., Wehman, P., Brooke, V., & Barcus, J. M. (1990). *Helping persons with severe mental retardation get and keep employment: Supported employment issues and strategies.* Baltimore: Brookes.

Moreno, C., & O'Neal, C. (1999). *Tips for teaching high functioning people with autism.* Crown Point, IN: MAAP Services.

Mount, B. (1994). Benefits and limitations of Persons Futures Planning. In V. J. Bradley, J. W. Ashbaugh, & B. C. Blaney (Eds.), *Creating individual supports for people with developmental disabilities: A mandate for change at many levels* (pp. 97–108). Baltimore: Brookes.

O'Brian, J., & O'Brian, C. L. (1992). Members of each other: Perspectives on social support for people with severe disabilities. In J. Nisbet (Ed.), *Natural supports in school, at work and in the community for people with severe disabilities* (pp. 11–16). Baltimore: Brookes.

Orentlicher, M. L., & Michaels, C. A. (2000). Some thoughts on the role of occupational therapy in the transition from school to adult life: Part 1. *School-Systems Special Interest Section Quarterly, 7,* 1–4.

Powers, L. E., Wilson, R., Matuszewski, J., Phillips, A., Rein, C., Schumacher, D., & Gensert, J. (1996). Facilitating adolescent self-determination. In D. J. Sands & M. L. Wehmeyer (Eds.), *Self-determination across the life span* (pp. 257–284). Baltimore: Brookes.

Reauthorization of the Individuals With Disabilities Education Act of 1997. PL 105–17.

Rehabilitation Services Administration. (1992). *The Rehabilitation Act of 1973 as amended by the Rehabilitation Act Amendments of 1992.* Washington, DC: U.S. Department of Education.

Riches, V. C. (1993). *Standards of work performance: A functional assessment and training manual for training people with disabilities for employment.* Artarmon, Australia: MacLennan & Petty.

Rusch, F. R., & Chadsey, J. (Eds.). (1998). *Beyond high school: Transition from school to work.* Belmont, CA: Wadsworth.

Rusch, F. R., Destefano, L., Chadsey-Rusch, J., Phelps, L. A., & Szymanski, E. (1992). *Transition from school to adult life: Models, linkages, and policy.* Sycamore, IL: Sycamore.

Sands, D. J., & Wehmeyer, M. L. (1996). Future directions in self-determination: Articulating values and policies, reorganizing organizational structures, and implementing professional practices. In D. J. Sands & M. L. Wehmeyer (Eds.), *Self-determination across the life span* (pp. 331–344). Baltimore: Brookes.

School-to-Work Opportunities Act of 1994, PL 103–239. 20 U.S.C. § 6101.

Smith, M., Belcher, R., & Juhrs, P. (1995). *A guide to successful employment for individuals with autism.* Baltimore: Brookes.

Snow, J. (1994). The power in vulnerability. In J. O'Brien & C. L. O'Brien (Eds.), *A little book about person-centered planning* (pp. 11–13) Toronto, Canada: Inclusion Press.

Snow, J. A. (1994). *What's really worth doing and how to do it.* Toronto, Canada: Inclusion Press.

Sowers, J. A., & Powers, L. (1991). *Vocational preparation and employment of students with physical and multiple disabilities.* Baltimore: Brookes.

Technology-Related Assistance for Individuals with Disabilities Amendments of 1994, PL 103–218. 29 U.S.C. § 2201 *et seq.*

Texas Collaborative Transition Project. (1993). *Transition planning: A guide for systems change in Texas.* Austin, TX: Texas Rehabilitation Commission, Texas Education Agency, and Texas Commission for the Blind.

Unger, D. G., & Wandersman, A. (1985). The importance of neighbors: The social, cognitive, and affective components of neighboring. *American Journal of Community Psychology, 13,* 139–169.

U.S. Labor Department, Commission on Achieving Necessary Skills. (2000, April). *Abilities needed to succeed in the modern work place.* Retrieved from the World Wide Web: www.dol.gov.

Varenhorst, B.B. (1980). *Curriculum guide for student peer counseling.* Palo Alto, CA: Author.

Vreeburg Izzo, M., Johnson, J. R., Levitz, M., & Aaron, J. H. (1998). Transition from school to adult life: New roles for educators. In P. Wehman & J. Kregel (Eds.), *More than a job: Securing satisfying careers for people with disabilities* (249–286). Baltimore: Brookes.

Wagner, M. (1989). The transition experiences of youth with disabilities: A report from the national longitudinal transition study. Menlo Park, CA: SRI International.

Walker, H.M., Todis, B., Holmes, D. & Horton, G. (1993). *Adolescent curriculum for communciation and effective social skills.* Austin, TX: PRO-ED.

Ward, M. J. (1988). The many facets of self-determination. *Transition Summary, 5,* 2–3.

Wehman, P. (1995). Foreword. In M. D. Smith, R. G., Belcher, & P. D. Juhrs. *A guide to successful employment for individuals with autism* (pp. ix–x). Baltimore: Brookes.

Wehman, P. (1996). *Life beyond the classroom: Transition strategies for young people with disabilities* (2nd ed.). Baltimore: Brookes.

Wehman, P., & Kregel, J. (1998). Supported employment: Growth and impact. In P. Wehman, P. Sale, & W. Parent (Eds.), *Supported employment: Strategies for integration of workers with disabilities* (pp. 3–28). Austin, TX: PRO-ED.

Wehman, P., Moon, M. S., Everson, J. M., Wood, W., & Barcus, J. M. (1988). *Transition from school to work: New challenges for youth with severe disabilities.* Baltimore: Brookes.

Wehmeyer, M. (1993–1994). Self-determination as an educational outcome. *Impact, 4*(Winter), 6–7.

Westling, D. L., & Fox, L. (1995). *Teaching students with severe disabilities.* Englewood Cliffs, NJ: Merrill.

Will, M. (1984). *OSERS programming for the transition of youth with disabilities: Bridges from school to working life.* Washington, DC: Office of Special Education and Rehabilitative Services (OSERS), U.S. Department of Education.

Appendix 13.A
Who Are You? Worksheets Identifying Your Strengths, Interests, Hobbies, Accomplishments & Achievements, Top Skills, Career Areas of Interest

Strengths Inventory Worksheet

From the following list check the words that describe you. These are just a few of the many words that may describe you. You can use others if you wish.

☐ Thoughtful	☐ Conservative	☐ Funny
☐ Serious	☐ Polite	☐ Calm
☐ Impatient	☐ Nervous	☐ Happy
☐ Angry	☐ Outgoing	☐ Shy
☐ Impulsive	☐ Cautious	☐ Friendly
☐ Unfriendly	☐ Professional	☐ Casual
☐ Hardworking	☐ Lazy	☐ Motivated
☐ Uninterested	☐ Laid Back	☐ Energetic
☐ Confident	☐ Organized	☐ Honest
☐ Disorganized	☐ Mature	☐ Adaptable
☐ Intelligent	☐ Trustworthy	☐ Reliable
☐ Conscientious	☐ Decisive	☐ Assertive
☐ Fair	☐ Independent	☐ Artistic
☐ Curious	☐ Dependable	☐ Punctual
☐ Cooperative	☐ Patient	☐ Loyal
☐ Personable	☐ Persuasive	☐ Flexible

When you're finished, look at your list. Pick three that best describe you.

1. _____

2. _____

3. _____

Identifying Hobbies and Interests Worksheet

The next activity will help you to identify your interests and the ways that you fulfill them.

In the chart below, list ten (10) ways you like to spend your time. Think of things that you enjoy doing, things that you would choose to do if you did not have other demands on your time, things that interest you the most.

Ways I like To Spend My Time	**Have I Done This In The Past Month?**
1. _____	1. _____
2. _____	2. _____
3. _____	3. _____
4. _____	4. _____
5. _____	5. _____
6. _____	6. _____
7. _____	7. _____
8. _____	8. _____
9. _____	9. _____
10. _____	10. _____

Now look at your list. Answer the following question.

Do your interests match your list of strengths? How?

_____

_____

_____

_____

_____

_____

_____

_____

_____

_____

_____

_____

_____

Your Most Satisfying Accomplishments And Achievements Worksheet

What are you really proud of?

_____

_____

_____

_____

_____

_____

_____

Your Top Skills

Name your top skills and state whether they seem work-related.

_____

_____

_____

_____

_____

_____

_____

Career Areas or Jobs That Interest You

No limit to your imagination here.

_____

_____

_____

_____

_____

_____

_____

_____

Occupational Strengths Groupings Worksheet

Directions: Below are the same words used in the Strengths Inventory Worksheet. Here they are grouped under several categories. Find the words you chose and circle them.

In which group did you circle the largest number of words? In which group did you circle the least number of words?

Communication Skills

well-spoken

friendly

patient

personable

organized

persuasive

assertive

dynamic

Interpersonal Skills

open-minded

flexible

patient

cooperative

outgoing

confident

dynamic

Managerial Skills

organized

decisive

independent

assertive

dynamic

fair

objective

Investigative Skills

analytical

curious

follow-through

persistence

resourceful

innovative

Creative Skills

artistic

innovative

resourceful

imaginative

General Work Skills

conscientious

punctual

trustworthy

dependable

intelligent

adaptable

Previous Work Experience Worksheet

List every job and work experience you ever had, and what you did and did not like about each one.

_____

_____

_____

_____

_____

_____

_____

_____

_____

_____

_____

_____

_____

_____

_____

_____

_____

_____

_____

_____

_____

_____

_____

_____

_____

Student's Strengths Inventory Worksheet

Directions: Read the list below and circle the words that you feel describe your strengths.

sensitive	artistic	friendly
organized	well-spoken	cooperative
outgoing	honest	confident
independent	intelligent	assertive
dependable	trustworthy	fair
personable	reliable	caring
flexible	patient	

Choose three of the words you circled. Write the word and state one thing you have done that shows that strength.

Example: Dependable: I walk my dog every day.

_____

_____

_____

_____

_____

_____

_____

_____

_____

_____

_____

_____

_____

_____

_____

_____

_____

_____

_____

Student's Self-Evaluation Worksheet

Student's Name: _____   Date: _____

1. My hobbies and interests: _____

_____

_____

_____

2. Career areas or jobs that interest me: _____

_____

_____

_____

3. My top skills: _____

_____

_____

_____

4. My short- and long-range goals:

Personal: _____

_____

_____

_____

_____

Educational: _____

_____

_____

_____

_____

Professional: _____

_____

_____

_____

Job Characteristics I Like Worksheet

Name: _____   Job Site: _____   Date: _____

Directions:
What I Like column: Circle the job characteristic that you like best in each box.
What is Here column: Circle the job characteristic in each box that best describes what is at this job.
Matches column: Circle YES if the first two columns are the same. Circle NO if they are not.

	What I Like	**What is Here**	**Matches**	
1.	work alone lots of people around	work alone lots of people around	Yes	No
2.	quiet workplace noisy workplace	quiet workplace noisy workplace	Yes	No
3.	work close to home distance to job doesn't matter	work close to home distance to job doesn't matter	Yes	No
4.	weekdays only weekends too	weekdays only weekends too	Yes	No
5.	easy job challenging job	easy job challenging job	Yes	No
6.	dress up for work do not dress up	dress up for work do not dress up	Yes	No
7.	standing up sitting down moving around	standing up sitting down moving around	Yes	No
8.	work mornings work afternoons work nights	work mornings work afternoons work nights	Yes	No
9.	co-workers my age co-workers' age doesn't matter	co-workers my age co-workers' age doesn't matter	Yes	No
10.	thinking work physical work	thinking work physical work	Yes	No
11.	detail important detail not important	detail important detail not important	Yes	No
12.	job same every day job different every day	job same every day job different every day	Yes	No
13.	work with people work with things	work with people work with things	Yes	No

Job Characteristics I Like Worksheet *(continued)*

	What I Like	What is Here	Matches	
14.	important to work fast not important to work fast	important to work fast not important to work fast	Yes	No
15.	little supervision a lot of supervision	little supervision a lot of supervision	Yes	No
16.	work outside work inside	work outside work inside	Yes	No

Percent of Matches

Directions:

Place the total number of matches from your "MATCHES" column on line (a).

Enter (a) into your calculator and push the "÷" button.

Enter "16" into your calculator and push the "=" button.

Push the "x" button, enter "100," and push the "=" button.

This tells you your percentage. Place your percentage in the oval marked (b).

Draw a line where your "% Matches" falls on the scale. Color from 0% to your percentage to see how well the job matches what you like.

Number of matches: $\dfrac{\text{(a)} \underline{\hspace{2cm}}}{16} \times 100 = \text{(b)} \bigcirc \text{ \% Matches}$

not many	few	some	many
25%	50%	75%	100%

Appendix 13.B
Sample Assessment Tools and Checklists

Vocational Training/Employment Evaluation: Transition Program

Worker: _____ Supervisor: _____ Business: _____

Write in the job tasks assigned to the job position. Check the number to indicate current level of job performance.

1=Very good 2=Good 3=Acceptable 4=Fair 5=Needs help N/A=Not applicable or not observed

	Dates															
Job Tasks (Skills) and Date Introduced	1	2	3	4	5	1	2	3	4	5	1	2	3	4	5
1															
2															
3															
4															
5															
6															
7															

Check the number corresponding to the worker's demonstrated skills using the key above.

	Personal Traits	1	2	3	4	5	1	2	3	4	5	1	2	3	4	5
1	Daily grooming & hygiene															
2	Suitable clothes for the job															
3	Good eating manners															
4	Positive attitude															
5	Flexible & cooperative															
6	Demonstrates common sense															
7	Willingness to learn															
8	Honesty															
9	Takes pride in work															

Vocational Evaluation (*continued*)   Dates

Job Tasks (Skills) and Date Introduced															
Social/Communication	1	2	3	4	5	1	2	3	4	5	1	2	3	4	5
10 Polite & considerate of others															
11 Appropriate work conversation															
12 Appropriate level of friendliness															
13 No inappropriate behaviors															
14 Works well with co-workers															
15 Works well with supervisors															
16 Can understand and can be understood at the job site															
Work-Related Skills	1	2	3	4	5	1	2	3	4	5	1	2	3	4	5
17 Use of time clock/time sheet															
18 Arrives and leaves on time															
19 Maintains good attendance															
20 Calls in when absent															
21 Takes breaks appropriately															
22 Maintains neat work/break area															
23 Independent getting to/from work area															
24 Independent setting up own work materials															
25 Follows company's rules & regulations															
26 Team player															
27 Conscientious work habits															
28 Responds to constructive criticism															
29 Asks questions when unclear															
30 Manages money (snacks, bus, etc.)															
31 Handles own transportation to/from work															

Vocational Evaluation (*continued*)   Dates

Work Skills		1	2	3	4	5	1	2	3	4	5	1	2	3	4	5
32	Quality of work; accuracy															
33	Quantity of work; productivity															
34	Follows instructions of supervisor															
35	Works carefully & safely															
36	Improves with repetition; remembers tasks															
37	Able to transfer learning; generalizes															
38	Works without close supervision															
39	Works at a constant rate without reminders															
40	Able to correct own errors															
41	Accepts & learns new tasks															
42	Initiates work on own															

Trainee/Employee is: a. ___ a good worker b. ___ an average worker c. ___ a below-average worker

School staff is present: a. ___ full time   b. ___ part time

Please note any specific job skills or social skills employee needs to improve or additional supports that s/he needs in order to be more successful on the job:

_____   _____   _____

Date   Supervisor   Worker

RTD Bus Riding Training: Task Analysis

Goal: Gain independence in riding public transportation

Student: _____

Staff: _____

Key: I = independent, VP = verbal prompt, GP = gestural prompt, PP = physical prompt, NA = needs assistance

Steps:	Date → Initials →										
1. Walk to & locate appropriate bus stop Bus Route # →											
2. Locate appropriate place to wait											
3. Wait at stop appropriately											
4. Prepare to get on bus (watch for bus, line up, get out money or pass)											
5. Wait in line & enter bus appropriately											
6. Hold on to railing and walk up steps											
7. Deposit correct change in fare box or show pass. Obtain transfer if necessary.											
8. Hold on to seats and move down aisle to locate empty seat.											
9. Sit & watch for correct exit stop; do not talk to passengers (or exchange only brief greeting)											
10. Signal driver to stop in enough time; be ready to exit; have belongings gathered											
11. Exit bus quickly and through correct door											
12. Move safely away from bus											

Street Safety Evaluation/Training: Task Analysis

Goal: Demonstrate safety skills for crossing streets; 18–21 Transition Program

Student: _____

Staff: _____

Steps:	Key: I = independent, VP = verbal prompt, GP = gestural prompt, PP = physical prompt, NA = needs assistance									
Date →										
Initials →										
1. Preparedness: 1a. Carries change for emergency phone call										
1b. Carries 2 forms of ID										
1c. Carries or knows phone numbers. Home phone number = Family work phone number = Emergency contact number =										
2. Sidewalks: 2a. Uses sidewalks when available										
2b. Identifies and uses safest walking alternative when sidewalks are not available										
3. Streetlight knowledge: 3a. Identifies red as "stop" and responds										
3b. Identifies green as "go" and responds										
3c. Identifies yellow as "caution" or wait and responds										
4. Cross walk knowledge: 4a. Identifies white "person" light as "go" & responds										
4b. Identifies orange "hand" as "stop" & responds										
4c. Identifies flashing sign as "wait" & responds										
5. Stop sign: Identifies red stop sign as a sign for cars to stop										

Date →											
6. Intersections: 6a. Walks to & crosses streets at intersections											
6b. Identifies when it is safe to cross and crosses only when it is safe											
7. Intersections with pedestrian lights: 7a. Locates & pushes "walk" button											
7b. Watches "walk" signal & is aware when it changes											
7c. Crosses quickly when it signals "walk"											
7d. Completes crossing within the time alloted											
7e. Watches for cars that might be turning											
8. Intersections with traffic lights (no walk signal): 8a. Focuses on traffic light in direction wants to cross & is ready to cross when it turns green											
8b. When light turns green, looks for turning cars & evaluates whether it is safe to cross											
8c. When light turns green, crosses quickly											
9. Intersections without lights: 9a. Stops at intersection and looks for oncoming traffic											
9b. Identifies whether it is safe to cross											
9c. Crosses street quickly											
9d. Checks for cars turning from behind											
9e. Identifies stop sign as meaning car will plan to stop											
9f. If car is approaching stop sign, waits for indication that it is stopping before stepping into street											

	Date →										
10. Crossing driveways & parking lots: 10a. Stops and looks for traffic before crossing driveways, alleys and other auto exits/entrances											
10b. In parking lots, avoids walking in traffic lanes & watches for backing or turning cars											
10c. In parking lots, checks for traffic before stepping into a traffic lane											

Appendix 13.C
Annual Goals

Annual goal: Angel will discuss career opportunities, training requirements, his interests, and his strengths and weaknesses in relation to these careers.

Short term objectives:

1) Angel will name and explain 3 potential careers in which he might be interested.
Timeline: October

2) Angel will describe the training requirements and income potential for the 3 careers identified.
Timeline: October

3) Angel will complete an interest inventory.
Timeline: September

4) Angel will identify his 3 best employee characteristics and 3 he needs most to work on.
Timeline: October-November

Annual goal: Angel will increase his understanding of post-secondary employment options.

Short term objectives:

1) Angel will identify at least two private/state/federal agencies he could access for assistance in planning for post-secondary options.
Timeline: January

2) Angel will identify at least three examples of post-secondary employment options available to him.
Timeline: January

Annual goal: Angel will acquire skills necessary to obtain a job (completing applications, resumes, and interviews).

Short term objectives:

1) Given instruction in job-seeking skills from the teacher/job coach, Angel will demonstrate ability to complete an application form.
Timeline: April

2) Angel will obtain at least two applications from possible job sites.
Timeline: May-June

3) Given instruction in job-seeking skills from the teacher/job coach, Angel will demonstrate the ability to write a resume.
Timeline: March

4) Given instruction in job-seeking skills from the teacher/job coach, Angel will demonstrate interview skills by completing a successful mock interview.
Timeline: March

Annual goal: Angel will participate in modified in-house work-experience to practice and improve variety of work skills, such as speed, endurance, and stamina.

Short term objectives:

1) Given support as necessary from the job coach, Angel will choose optional four to five work tasks/samples to be practiced throughout the year.
Timeline: September

2) Given support as necessary from the job coach, Angel will perform the identified work tasks/samples successfully with at least 50% of the task components completed independently.
Timeline: April

3) Given support as necessary from the job coach, Angel will perform the identified work tasks/samples successfully with at least 100% of the task components completed independently.
Timeline: The end of the school year.

Appendix 13.D
Suggested Readings on Transition and Related Topics

Brollier, C. B., Shepherd, J., & Markley, K. F. (1994). Transition from school to community living. *American Journal of Occupational Therapy, 48,* 346–353.

Forest, M. (2000). Captain A1: A unique teacher in a unique school. *Inclusion News, 9.*

Michaels, C. A. (1992). *Transition strategies for persons with learning disabilities.* San Diego: Singular.

O'Brien, J. & O'Brien, C. L. (Eds.). (1999). *A little book about person-centered planning.* Toronto: Inclusion Press.

Rainforth, B., & York, J. (1987). Integrated related services in community instruction. *Journal of the Association for Persons with Severe Handicaps, 12,* 190–198.

Rusch, F., DeStefano, L., Chadsey-Rusch, J., Phelps, L. A., & Szymanski, E. (Eds.). *Transition from school to adult life: Models, linkages, and policy.* Sycamore, IL: Sycamore.

Spencer, K. (1989). The transition from school to adult life. In S. Hertfelder & C. Gwin (Eds.), *Work in progress: Occupational therapy in work programs* (pp. 157–179). Bethesda, MD: American Occupational Therapy Association.

West, L. L., Corbey, S., Boyer-Stephens, A., Jones, B., Miller, R., & Sarkees-Wircenski, M. (1992). *Integrating transition planning into the IEP process.* Reston, VA: Council for Exceptional Children.

Woolcock, W. W., & Domaracki, J. W. (Eds.). *Instructional strategies in the community: A resource guide for community instruction for persons with disabilities.* Austin, TX; PRO-ED.

York, J., Rainforth, B., & Dunn, W. (1990). Training needs of physical and occupational therapists who provide services to children and youth. In A. P. Kaiser & C. M. McWhorter (Eds.), *Preparing personnel to work with persons with severe disabilities* (pp. 153–179). Baltimore: Brookes.

Appendix 13.E
Voices National Center for Disability Services

Educational Services Work Experience Appraisal

Date of appraisal _____

Student employee's name _____

Age _____ Grade _____ School _____

Job title _____

Department _____

Start date _____

Hours per week: Mon. _____ Tues. _____ Wed. _____ Thurs. _____ Fri. _____

Immediate supervisor _____

Use the following scale to rate participants in each category. Be fair and objective. Concentrate on one factor at a time.

Excellent   5
Above average   4
Average   3
Below average   2
Poor   1
Not applicable   N/A

Appearance	_____	Attitude toward job	_____
Disposition	_____	Relations with public	_____
Punctuality	_____	Initiative	_____
Ability to learn	_____	Judgment and common sense	_____
Quantity of work	_____	Enthusiasm	_____
Quality of work	_____	Reliability	_____
Cooperation with supervisor	_____		
Cooperation with co-workers	_____		

Supervisor's comments: _____

_____

_____

Signature _____ Date _____

National Center for Disability Services Research and Training Institute
Vocational Options in Community Employment Settings: Hear Our Voices

Procedure for Ecological Inventory

Prior to your potential trainee walking in the door, an ecological inventory should be conducted.

An ecological inventory is simply a series of lists. It is done for each potential job site, whether or not you have a student in mind. It is particularly important if you do have a student in mind for that particular site.

If you have a particular job training site in mind for a particular student, it is of critical importance for you and your fellow job coaches to have an idea of important physical characteristics of the student's place of employment.

Important information in an ecological inventory includes the locations of fire/emergency exits, hot stoves, toilets, stairs, water fountains, employee break areas, and other interesting or necessary physical characteristics.

These, along with the name and address of the establishment and names of important coworkers, should be on page one. After the list of important characteristics there should be a list of jobs or tasks that a trainee would need to learn.

The second page of the ecological inventory should be a crude map, rough floor plan, or a perfectly drawn fire map obtained from the prospective employer. Exits and toilets should be clearly visible, as should any obstructions or potential hazards. The place to which the trainee will report should be marked so a substitute job coach would have no trouble finding it.

The third and following pages of the ecological inventory should be a task analysis for each job or task the trainee will perform, would perform, or could someday perform at that location.

National Center For Disability Services Task Analytic Recording Sheet
Vocational Options in Community Employment Settings: VOICES

Student's Name: _____   Job Coach: _____

Job Site: _____   Antecedent Cue: _____

Prerequisite Steps:
Component Steps:

Total Correct Steps:												
Percent Correct Steps:												

Code: + = independent/correct   P = physical prompt
          − = incorrect   M = model/visual cue   V = verbal prompt

Appendix 13.F
Voices: Work Experience Progress Report

Student's Name: _____ Date: _____

Work Site: _____ Hours Per Week: _____

Job Coach: _____ Immediate Supervisor: _____

1. Achievement and Performance:

List task(s) student performs:

Task(s)	**Rating**	Use one of the following for performance rating:
1. _____	_____	
2. _____	_____	Independent 1
3. _____	_____	
4. _____	_____	Job coach supervision 2
5. _____	_____	Job coach assistance 3
6. _____	_____	Job coach support 4

Comments:

2. Use number to indicate the statement which best applies:

(1) Student manages independently.
(2) Student manages with job coach support
(3) Student needs training/practice in this area.

	Number
1. Observance of rules	_____
2. Acceptance of supervision	_____
3. Acceptance of criticism	_____
4. Relationship with co-workers	_____
5. Following instructions	_____
6. Speed in completing work	_____
7. Accuracy in completing work	_____
8. Ability to work with others	_____
9. Works neatly/effectively	_____
10. Ability to do quality work	_____

3. Have situations occurred during this training period, which may affect employment of this student? _____

_____

_____

_____

4. Comments and recommendations: _____

_____

_____

_____

Job coach's signature: _____   Date: _____

14

Occupational Therapy Research on Children With Autism

Jane Case-Smith, EdD, OTR/L, FAOTA, BCP

In the 1980s and 1990s, the research literature about autism proliferated, greatly expanding our knowledge of this disorder and appropriate interventions. Although psychological and medical research has expanded, occupational therapy research on autism remains minimal. The purpose of this chapter is to examine how occupational therapy research complements and contributes to the broader body of research on autism, to identify research questions of interest and relevance to occupational therapists, and to define appropriate methods for occupational therapists to accomplish autism research.

For purposes of this discussion, examples of published research on autism are categorized into two distinct research questions: (1) What is autism? and (2) How effective are interventions for children with autism? These questions require two different levels of research design: a more basic level of descriptive research for the first question and a more sophisticated level of predictive research for the second. Predictive studies require greater design complexity, experimental control, and researcher manipulation than descriptive studies. See Table 14.1 for examples of descriptive and predictive research questions.

The first category of descriptive and correlational studies helps health care professionals

and consumers understand a diagnosis and its implications for functional performance. When asking the question, What is it?, control and manipulation of the subjects is not expected or desired. Descriptive research on autism includes the following goals: (a) to explain the phenomenon of autism, (b) to define behaviors and characteristics associated with autism, (c) to investigate possible etiologies, and (d) to identify variables and outcomes associated with autism. Basic descriptive research uses observations, surveys, inventories, questionnaires, or interviews to describe children with autism. Data are combined and descriptive analyses are used to discover trends and commonalities across children, thereby developing a clinical picture of autism.

Correlational studies relate two or more concepts or variables. For example, the behaviors or characteristics of children with autism can be correlated with other personal and contextual variables. Correlational studies require more control because specific behaviors or contextual variables are measured. Inferential statistical analyses such as Pearson correlation coefficient analysis are applied to determine how variables influence one another. These analyses estimate how much variability is shared by two or more measures.

Table 14.1

Examples of Research Questions Related to Children With Autism

Descriptive Research Questions	Predictive Research Questions
1. What sensory processing problems are exhibited by children with autism? Do contextual variables relate to behaviors indicating sensory processing difficulties?	1. Do deep pressure and linear vestibular stimulation techniques improve eye contact and attention in children with autism?
2. Does hyper-responsiveness or sensory defensiveness correlate with motor planning skills?	2. Do consultative models of occupational therapy in inclusive settings improve play skills in children with autism?
3. Does poor sensory modulation relate to stereotypical use of objects in play?	3. When preschool environments are modified to match the sensory needs of children with autism, are more social interactions with peers observed?

The second level of research, predictive research, determines cause-and-effect relationships. Experimental designs are needed to answer cause-and-effect questions. These designs require that subjects be manipulated by the researcher and that as many variables as possible are controlled. To determine cause and effect, a sample of children with autism who have similar ages and demographic characteristics is divided into two or more groups. Different or contrasting interventions are applied to the groups and must be well defined and applied uniformly to the participants in each group. The intervention is termed the independent variable because it is determined and manipulated by the researcher. To estimate the effects of the independent variable, performance of the participants is measured.

The measured effect of the intervention is the dependent variable. The dependent variable is carefully selected to ensure the internal validity of the study; that is, the performance measured must be a meaningful and logical outcome of the intervention. For example, if sensory integration is the independent variable, appropriate dependent variables include sensory responsiveness, assessed through the Sensory Profile (Dunn, 1999), or playful behaviors, assessed using the Test of Playfulness (Bundy, 1997). To study the effects of social stories (Gray & Garand, 1993), behaviors during transitions between activities at preschool could be evaluated using a scale that rates whether or not the child's behaviors were socially appropriate. Tests used as dependent variables should be reliable; that is, scores for a child should be stable over short periods of time or when different therapists administer the test. They should also have established validity or evidence that they accurately measure the constructs or behaviors that they claim to measure.

To determine the effects of an intervention, inferential statistical analyses are computed. Analysis of variance and t tests are examples of statistical tests that can determine the probability that differences between groups are either real (i.e., significant) or simply what would be expected by chance given the inherent variability within the sample groups.

These two research levels (descriptive and predictive) provide an organizational frame for this chapter. For each level section, the general body of research literature and the occupational therapy research that answers the questions at that level are described. Then guidelines and recommendations are made regarding future autism research by occupational therapists.

What is Autism?—Descriptive Research

Because autism is such an enigma, much of the research on autism is descriptive in nature. Primary goals of descriptive research are to identify possible etiologies and to define associated behavioral patterns.

Genetic and Neurological Research

Although autistic disorders are behaviorally defined, clinicians and researchers concur that the bases for these disorders are neurological or neurochemical differences that can be measured. In certain children, autism has also been linked to specific genetic disorders.

Genetic Studies. Genetic disorders have been associated with autism, and children with certain genetic syndromes demonstrate autistic-like behaviors. For example, children with Angelman's Syndrome, Fragile X, and Rett's Disorder exhibit autistic-like behaviors that include poor eye contact, stereotyped movements, and very limited language. People with Down's Syndrome, William's Syndrome, and tuberous sclerosis are at high risk for a concurrent diagnosis of Autistic Disorder. A number of the syndromes linked to autism have associated abnormalities with genes of the seventh chromosome. Ongoing research explores the linkage between chromosome 7 and autism (Fisher, Vargha-Khadem, Watkins, Monaco, & Pembrey, 1998; International Molecular Genetic Study of Autism Consortium, 1998). Whether or not autism has a genetic association remains an important research question.

Neurological Studies. Although inconclusive, studies of the brains of people with autism have revealed differences in brain structure and function. Brain abnormalities have been observed using magnetic resonance imaging (MRI) and functional MRI (Rapin, 1999). Brain histology studies suggest that the phenomenon that causes autism occurs very early in fetal development. The brains of people with autism are often larger than normal, and between 20–24% of people with autism have macrocephaly (Bailey et al., 1998; Lainhart et al., 1997). Studies of brain cell composition have demonstrated differences in the numbers of brain cells. People with autism have reduced numbers of Purkinje cells in the cerebellum (Rapin & Katzman, 1998). In addition, hypoplasia in the cerebellar vermis and brain stem has been reported. Cerebellar cells are smaller and more dense (Huebner, 1992).

Seizures are among the known neurological problems associated with autism. The incidence of seizures is much higher in children with autism than in typically developing children. Approximately 20–35% of people with autism have a seizure disorder (Bailey, Phillips, & Rutter, 1996; Fisher et al., 1999). It appears that seizures co-occur with autism rather than cause autism. Often, the onset of seizures is not until adolescence or young adulthood, although a small number of children develop seizures in the preschool years. Seizures do not appear to relate to intelligence or to the severity of the autism (Bailey et al., 1996). Because medical professionals lack evidence of a single genetic or neurologic causative factor, the diagnosis of Autistic Disorder is reached by exclusion and requires clinical assessment.

Neurochemical Differences. Information about the brain's chemistry may provide more promise than the imaging and electroencephalogram (EEG) techniques. Neurotransmitters, the chemicals that transmit a signal of inhibition or excitation across the neural synapse, have been found to differ in children with autism (Mesibov, Adams, & Klinger, 1997). Neurotransmitter abnormalities suggest that drug or nutritional therapies may help relieve the symptoms of autism.

A consistent neurochemical finding is that people with autism have elevated levels of platelet serotonin (Mesibov et al., 1997). Serotonin influences mood, aggressive behavior, repetitive movements, sleep, memory, pain, and anxiety. Between 30% and 50% of children with autism have elevated blood serotonin levels. In a recent clinical study, medication was given to people with autism to inhibit the uptake of serotonin. The decreased uptake in those who had taken the medication was associated with improved behavior (Fisher et al., 1999).

Other researchers have investigated the association between dopamine and autism. Dopamine is a neurotransmitter linked to motor activity and repetitive behaviors. Excessive dopamine levels have been related to stereotypical behaviors in animals. Research on neurotransmitters appears to be expanding as the relationships shed light on behaviors and also may lead to pharmaceutical therapies (Fisher et al., 1999; Rapin & Katzman, 1998).

Summary. Researchers have yet to establish definitive neurological and genetic causes of autism; however, neurological impairment has been hypothesized from the behaviors observed in people with autism. Research using functional MRI will continue to expand our understanding of how brain centers activate and integrate during specific functional activities. These studies have shown that neuronal activation during specific activities is more localized in people with autism. These studies in conjunction with continued neurochemical studies show promise in revealing the neurological bases for autistic disorders.

Behavioral

Behavioral research can be organized according to the basic diagnostic criteria of autism (American Psychiatric Association, 2000). The three primary diagnostic criteria for autism are lack of social interactions, limited language, and stereotyped, restrictive-repetitive patterns of behavior.

Lack of Social Interaction. Children with autism have limited use of nonverbal behavior, fail to develop peer relationships, and lack social-emotional reciprocity. These characteristics have been explored by researchers from different theoretical perspectives.

In 1986, Sigman, Mundy, Sherman, and Ungerer found that children with autism responded to verbal commands as did typically developing children and children with mental retardation. However, they infrequently shared attention with their caregivers, and they infrequently gestured to adults. Eye contact was diminished, and avoidance was common. Mars, Mauk, and Dowrick (1998) found that the lack of joint attention was the strongest early marker of autism and PDDs. In their home video-

tapes, the children with autism did not show or share objects to nearby adults and did not simultaneously interact with objects and their caregivers. Facial regard and alternating gaze were minimal.

As an explanation for their poor eye contact and limited attention to social stimuli, Dawson and Lewy (1989) proposed that children with autism are generally overaroused. In a study of affective exchanges between young children with autism and their mothers, the children differed significantly in frequency of smiles with eye contact. They failed to combine emotion and eye contact in a single act that conveys communicative intent. Most of the children never smiled in response to the mother's smile. The mother's smile may be overstimulating and cause the child to lose interest (Dawson, Hill, Spencer, Galpert, & Watson, 1990).

In contrast, nonsocial stimuli are more predictable and more easily assimilated. Objects and nonsocial stimuli may have an arousal-reducing function. The ability to share an object of interest typically develops during the first year of life, and its absence is one of the earliest symptoms of autism (Osterling & Dawson, 1994). These studies support the theory that the lack of social interaction relates to difficulty with sensory processing.

To regulate their own arousal levels, children with autism often choose one stimulus and screen out all others. By selecting one stimulus at a time, children with autism have a specific style of problem solving. Frith (1989) proposed that children with autism focus on details rather than gestalts. They perform well on the Block Design of the WISC-R (Wechsler Intelligence Scale for Children-Revised) (Wechsler, 1974). However, children with autism appear to view the designs as segmented parts rather than gestalts. Shah and Frith (1993) concluded that people with autism are not inattentive; rather, they attend to what they see as meaningful and salient. What is salient may be narrowly defined.

In summary, as set forth by Dawson and Lewy (1989), children with autism fail to establish affective contact with others, in part, because they are easily overaroused from social stimulation. Because social stimuli are intense, unpredictable, and complex, these stimuli are particularly arousing and therefore easily exceed the child's low tolerance for unpredictability. Although this relationship remains hypothetical rather than proven, the research of Dawson and some of the clinical findings of Greenspan support this concept.

Greenspan and colleagues have documented sensory modulation and processing problems in children with autism. Although Greenspan and Wieder (1997a, 1997b) have produced minimal experimental research, they have extensively documented descriptions of the children seen in their practice. A great majority of the children who were diagnosed with Autistic Disorder demonstrated difficulties in sensory reactivity, sensory processing, motor tone, and motor planning. These problems appeared to be highly associated with limitations in the children's abilities to socially interact, engage with others, and demonstrate appropriate affect.

Correlational research that relates measures of the child's sensory processing abilities and social interaction can further our understanding of the perceptual demands of social interaction. As occupational therapists gain an in-depth understanding of these relationships, they can develop interventions to decrease overarousal, improve attention, and increase engagement in social play.

Limited Language. The second criterion of autism has also been researched in an effort to understand the basis for and extent of the language impairment. Some children with autism have no or minimal functional speech and gestural, or nonverbal, language. These children either may not develop language as infants or toddlers or may begin their first words on time and then lose their verbal language between 24

and 30 months (Mesibov, Adams, & Klinger, 1997). Greenspan and Wieder (1997a) found that almost two-thirds of their clinic population regressed at the second or third year, and about one-third demonstrated a gradual onset in the first year. Almost 40% of all children with autism did not develop speech; those who did develop speech had difficulty with semantic and pragmatic aspects of language. Other researchers report that when the child acquires speech, it is almost always deviant and is often echolalic. About 85% of children with autism demonstrate echolalia (Schuler & Prizant, 1985).

Semantic problems are evidenced in that the language of children with autism is rigid and often inappropriate to the situation. Pragmatic use of language is also delayed or deviant. These children's conversations include tangential detail or unrelated speech. They may single-mindedly pursue a topic. Research of language is of interest to occupational therapists but is not central to the research focus of the occupational therapy field. The third criterion (the restrictive repertoire of activities), like the first (lack of social interactions), is of more immediate relevance to occupational therapists and has been the focus of occupational therapy descriptive research.

Restrictive Repertoire of Activities. The third defining characteristic of people with autism is a restrictive repertoire of activities, originally defined as an insistence on sameness. Children with autism exhibit an "encompassing preoccupation with one or more stereotyped and restricted patterns of interest" (APA, 2000, p. 71). Although this trait can be interesting, most behaviors associated with this criterion are difficult to accommodate in everyday life.

People with autism have an inflexible adherence to specific routines and rituals. They may eat only particular foods and may demand specific routines through the day. They often exhibit stereotyped behavior or body movements such as rocking, hand flapping, spinning, or head banging. These behaviors are believed to be related to sensory disturbances or sensory deprivation (Lovaas, Newsom, & Hickman, 1987; Ornitz, 1974, 1985). Lovaas et al. (1987) theorized that the self-stimulation behaviors were the child's efforts to maintain arousal. Self-stimulation was inherently rewarding; therefore, Lovaas used the self-stimulation behaviors to engage the child's cooperation. Although Lovaas felt that the self-stimulation behaviors helped to arouse the child, King and Grandin (1990) theorized that the self-stimulation behaviors helped to calm the child.

The concept that children with autism use self-stimulation to regulate arousal is a logical extension of the research of Dawson (e.g., Dawson & Lewy, 1989). She proposed that autism involves dysfunction of the cortical-limbic-reticular system that mediates arousal and attention. The orienting response to sensory input does not habituate, which causes a flood of sensory input, or overarousal. Ornitz (1985) helped to establish these concepts through his physiological research of the vestibular system. His findings demonstrated that children with autism had abnormal visual-vestibular interactions, prolonged time constants, and reduced secondary nystagmus after vestibular stimulation. These findings supported the concept that the problems of social relating, attending, and stereotypical as well as bizarre behaviors observed in autism relate to disturbances in sensory processing. In children with autism, sensory input becomes distorted information and the basis for deviant social behaviors and stereotypes. Hence, Ornitz (1989) proposed that sensory modulation disturbances are primary symptoms of autism. The disturbance of sensory modulation involves all sensory modalities and is manifested both as under- and over-reactivity to sensory stimuli and as self-stimulation (Ornitz, 1989). The increased autonomic responses and overarousal that has been found by a number of researchers may reflect an inability

to filter sensory stimulation. The theories relating self-stimulation and stereotyped behaviors to sensory processing problems have provided a basis for occupational therapy descriptive research.

Occupational Therapy— Descriptive Research

In the occupational therapy literature, most descriptive studies of autism have examined sensory processing and sensory modulation problems. Occupational therapy knowledge and skills in sensory integration stem from the evolutionary work of Jean Ayres. In the late 1970s, Ayres developed great interest in children with autism, sensory processing, and praxis, and the research she initiated has continued in recent years.

Several research methods have been applied to describe the sensory-processing problems of children with autism. To identify the behaviors that are indicative of difficulty in sensory modulation, the Sensory Profile (Dunn, 1999) or a similar inventory or questionnaire on sensory reactivity has been used. Basic descriptive and correlational research has been completed that explores differences between children with autism and typically developing children. Other occupational therapy research has investigated the relationships between sensory processing and stereotyped behaviors.

To explore differences in sensory processing, the Sensory Profile (Dunn, 1994) was completed by parents of 32 children with autism and then compared to the normative sample (Kientz & Dunn, 1997). Of the 32 subjects, 15 were considered to have mild to moderate autism and 17 had severe autism. The children with autism were significantly different in every sensory category. Effect sizes of the categories were moderate to high (ranging from .41 to .89). Kientz and Dunn (1997) concluded that the Sensory Profile distinguishes between children with and without autism and can identify the specific differences in sensory processing of children with autism.

In a second descriptive study, Baranek, Foster, & Berkson (1997) investigated the relationship between stereotyped behaviors and tactile defensiveness in children with autism and related developmental disorders. This study used behavioral measures to further investigate the relationship between sensory modulation and stereotyped behavior that was proposed by Ornitz (1974) and Greenspan (1992). Tactile defensiveness, as measured by the Touch Inventory of Preschoolers (Royeen, 1987), correlated with three of eight factors of stereotyped behavior: Rigidity-Sameness, Auditory-Repetitive Verbalizations, and Abnormal Focused Affection. No significant relationships were found between tactile defensiveness and motor or object stereotypes. Baranek et al. (1997) suggested that the relationship between rigid behaviors and sensory defensiveness warrants further study.

In a survey of occupational therapists regarding their practice with children with autism (Case-Smith & Miller, 1999), 95–97% of the respondents indicated that sensory processing, social-emotional function, and play were the problems observed often or always. These problems were often addressed in occupational therapy intervention, and 95% of the respondents indicated that they often or always provide service to improve sensory modulation (Case-Smith & Miller, 1999). The respondents also observed problems in cognition, motor function, and social-emotional behaviors. These problems endure, particularly when they present as severe difficulties, a characteristic that other researchers have acknowledged (Fisher et al., 1999; Mesibov et al., 1997). The respondents reported that children with autism made significant improvements in every performance domain, with the least improvement in cognition and learning, pretend play, and social play and the greatest improvement in sensory processing. In a similar survey study, Watling, Deitz, Kanny, and McLaughlin (1999)

found that 99% of occupational therapists used sensory-integration approaches with these children. Other theoretical approaches were also used (developmental [88%] and behavioral [73%]). Taken together, these studies demonstrate that occupational therapists are eclectic in their approach to children with autism but almost universally apply sensory-integration approaches as one of a combination of theories used.

The research of occupational therapists and professionals of other disciplines has established the nature of sensory-processing problems in children with autism. Further research is needed to identify the relationships among sensory processing, motor behaviors (including stereotypes), attention, arousal, and social interaction. If strong relationships exist between sensory processing and these functional behaviors, intervention approaches are suggested.

Strategies for Future Descriptive Research

Research areas that match the interest and expertise of occupational therapists include sensory processing, motor planning, play, and social behaviors. To expand the body of descriptive research literature in these areas, however, occupational therapists need to further develop their measurement tools. Although new assessments such as the Test of Playfulness (ToP) (Bundy, 1997) and the Sensory Profile (Dunn, 1999) show promise as tools to evaluate play and sensory processing, additional instrument development is needed. For example, additional measures of praxis are needed. Because children with autism experience difficulties in language, tests should measure motor performance from visual cueing (e.g., a picture card) or from physical modeling. Evaluations should include a child's performance of an activity when given an object or tool and the same child's performance when given an activity picture without a concrete object. Measures of play are also needed, recognizing that assessment should include object play and social play as well as distinguish between engaged and non-engaged behaviors (see Case-Smith & Bryan, 1999).

Children with autism have difficulty following the instructions that are required in most norm-referenced tests. Valid measures of behavior need to be based on naturalistic observations and reports of the caregivers. The instruments described above, the Sensory Profile and the ToP, are suitable for children with autism and offer an occupational therapy perspective. Continued development of instruments that are applicable to this population remains an important area for occupational therapy research. Additional measures will contribute to the body of descriptive research and will answer the question making up the second research category: How effective are intervention approaches for children with autism?

How Effective Are Intervention Approaches for Children With Autism?

A number of the intervention programs that have been researched demonstrate some level of effectiveness. These results, although not universally positive, are encouraging and allow professionals to state that beneficial outcomes can be achieved with intervention.

A primary intervention advocated by many psychologists, educators, and medical professionals is Applied Behavior Analysis (ABA). The Young Autism Program (Lovaas, 1987) is one example of a program that uses a strict behavioral approach. Efficacy studies of the Lovaas method have been published in educational and psychological journals during the 1980s and 1990s. Other programs based on applied behavioral techniques—for example, LEAP, Douglas Developmental Center, May Institute (Dawson & Osterling, 1996)—are well established in certain areas of the country but lack the substantial research of the Lovaas method. The Young Autism Program (Lovaas, 1987) uses discrete trial formats in intensive daily training. The one-on-one training is required 30–40

hours a week. The training is provided at home rather than at school. In a quasi-experimental study, 19 children with autism received the Lovaas protocol of 40-hour-a-week, one-on-one intervention for about 2 years. Children in two control groups received 10 hours of one-on-one behavioral interventions per week. Of the 19 children who received intervention, 9 reportedly recovered from autism and achieved a normal IQ. None of the control group recovered. A follow-up study in 1993 reported that subjects in the experimental group had maintained the positive effects of the training (McEachin, Smith, & Lovaas, 1993). Gresham and MacMillan (1998) critiqued this research, claiming that major threats to internal and external validity were present. They noted that measurements were inconsistent across children and included both parent reports and standardized tests. They argued that the Lovaas and the McEachin studies had selection bias and lacked representation of the population of children with autism. In addition, Gresham and MacMillan maintained that the program, as administered in the study, probably could not be replicated in other locations of the United States.

Ozonoff and Cathcart (1998) evaluated the effectiveness of a TEACCH-based home program intervention for young children with autism. Parents taught activities to promote cognitive skills of their preschool children. Two matched groups of 11 children were compared; only group one received the home-based program. After 4 months of home programming, the children were tested with the Psycho-Educational Profile-Revised (PEP-R). When compared to the children in the control group, the children who participated in the TEACCH program improved significantly more on the PEP-R subtests of imitation, fine motor, gross motor, and nonverbal conceptual skills. Progress in the treatment group was three to four times greater than that in the control group on all outcome tests (Ozonoff & Cathcart, 1998). Other outcome studies of TEACCH have demonstrated positive results when using this approach (Schopler, Mesibov, & Hearsey, 1995).

The efficacy of Greenspan's model (Greenspan, 1992) of "Floor Time" has not undergone rigorous experimental design research; however, case studies and a chart review of 200 children who had received intervention at the Greenspan clinic provide evidence of the effectiveness of this approach (Greenspan & Wieder, 1997a). All of the children had been diagnosed with a Pervasive Developmental Disorder and received differing amounts of consultation, intervention, or both by an interdisciplinary team, which included an occupational therapist. Individualized home programs were provided to each family that included intense Floor Time and interactive sessions ranging from 2 to 5 hours a day. The speech therapy, occupational therapy, and education that was provided emphasized an individualized interactive approach that centered on building relationships. The Floor Time approach organizes intervention around the child's affects and relationships as well as his or her developmental level, challenges, and individual differences. The rationale for this intervention approach is that the child's symptoms are secondary to underlying biologically based processing difficulties, including auditory, motor planning, and sensory modulation difficulties. Therefore, this approach, which includes sensory integration as one aspect, is probably the intervention approach most compatible with occupational therapy.

Greenspan and Wieder (1997a) reported that of the 200 children who participated in Floor Time and the services offered by their clinic, 116 (58%) were in the "good to outstanding" outcome group, 50 (25%) were in the "medium" outcome group, and 34 (17%) continued to have significant difficulties. Twenty of the children in the good-to-outstanding group were studied in-depth to understand the types of changes and the potential among some children with Pervasive Developmental Disorders.

Most of the 20 children scored above normal on standardized tests of cognitive abilities. On a measure of attention, emotions, engagement, interaction, and problem solving, the 20 children who had received intervention with outstanding results scored at the top of the scale, comparable to the results for typically developing children. In conclusion, Greenspan and Wieder concurred with other researchers (e.g., Lovaas) that children who did best tended to learn complex imitations quickly. Children with low IQs were generally poor responders; however, in children without language, IQ is difficult to assess. Difficulties in motor planning were the most significant indicator of prognosis, perhaps because praxis is a better indicator of overall intelligence than language.

As guidance for future research of intervention efficacy, Freeman (1997) summarized the findings of outcome studies of autism. Approximately 50% of all people with autism function in the moderate and severely mentally retarded range throughout life. Initial measures of cognition are highly predictive of later outcomes. Approximately 25% of children with autism who function in the mild mentally retarded range develop language before 5 years of age and can later function in supported employment and supported living conditions. The remaining 25% have normal intelligence and may raise families. Freeman indicated that the use of current intervention models seems promising in raising the percentage of children with autism who have a prognosis of fitting into the normal population.

Several authors have summarized the results of the efficacy studies that have been completed. Children who receive specific clinical intervention using ABA or Floor Time models achieve better outcomes than children who attend traditional educational programs. Mesibov and Shea (1996) present a strong argument that segregated educational environments hold advantages over integrated, inclusive environments. Children with autism often have sensory and perceptual difficulties; therefore, the regular education environment leads to disorganization, agitation, and possibly aggression. An important educational strategy is to structure environmental conditions so students can attend to and learn the information presented. Students with autism may actually be more dependent on adult supervision in an inclusive setting because they have more difficulty functioning. An environment structured for students with autism that includes routines to enable independence can enhance function more than inclusive settings.

Dawson and Osterling (1996) summarized the outcome data of various educational and clinic programs for children with autism. Elements of an intervention program that seem important to achieving good outcomes emphasize the child's ability to (a) attend to elements of the environment (focus on shared attention), (b) imitate others (focus on motor imitation), (c) comprehend and use language, (d) play with toys (focus on imaginative play), and (e) socially interact with others (focus on peers).

Other authors believe that inclusive models are optimal for all children, including those with autism. Schwartz, Billingsley, and McBride (1998) recommend that educational programs for children with autism (a) teach communicative and social competence, (b) use instructional strategies that maintain the natural flow of classroom activities, (c) teach and provide opportunities for independence, (d) proactively and systematically build a classroom community that includes all children, and (e) promote generalization and maintenance of skills (Schwartz et al., 1998).

How Effective are Occupational Therapy Intervention Approaches?

Efficacy research by occupational therapists is minimal. In the first study published, Ayres and Tickle (1980) acknowledged the difficulties incurred in research with children with autism. These researchers used a pre-experimental de-

sign. The sample included 10 children (3–13 years) who had sensory modulation problems and demonstrated varying degrees of hypo- or hyperresponsiveness. None of this sample could complete standardized testing, and each had unique problems that warranted an individualized approach. After a year of occupational therapy emphasizing sensory integration, the children were categorized into good or poor responders, according to the changes they demonstrated in interactional play, language, or motor skills. The children who responded well tended to have normal or hyperresponsiveness. The poor responders tended to be hyporesponsive. These results suggest that the children with hyperresponsivness (with low neural thresholds) respond more to sensory-integration therapy than those who are under-responsive (with high neural thresholds).

This first clinical study had numerous threats to validity. Of importance, it lacked standardized measures and a control group. The intervention was described in general; therefore, the study would be difficult to replicate. Despite a relatively weak experimental design, the results have clinical validity. Clinicians concur with the results indicating the hyperresponsiveness seems to have a better clinical outcome than hypo-responsiveness, particularly when it is severe.

Since the Ayres and Tickle (1980) study, a number of case studies have been reported in occupational therapy literature. Case studies of children with autism have some merit given the unique strengths and limitations observed in each child with autism. Frick and Lawton-Shirley (1994) reported the results of auditory integrative training with two sets of identical twins. The first set, who exhibited autistic-like behaviors, received auditory integration training at age 13. At the end of a 2-week treatment, they exhibited increases in ability to listen, attention, eye contact, calmness, self-initiation, and activity level. Language also improved and continued to improve for months after the training. The second set of twins were 3 years old and were diagnosed with a Pervasive Developmental Disorder and severe sensory defensiveness. They received auditory integration training combined with a sensory diet. At the end of 2 weeks of therapy, they had improved in engagement in purposeful play, initiation of social interaction and activity, independence, responsiveness to directions, and eye contact (Frick & Lawton-Shirley, 1994). Case studies provide ideas for more structured and better controlled experimental designs; however, generalizations should not be made from case study results. In addition, these studies did not provide sufficient detail regarding the intervention for replication, although a standard program of Auditory Integration Training was used (Berard, 1993). Further research is needed to clarify which children benefit most from this training and what functional results can be expected.

Case-Smith and Bryan (1999) used an A-B design to examine the results of sensory-integration therapy as part of a preschool program. The participants were five boys, each 5 years old and each diagnosed with a Pervasive Developmental Disorder. After a 3-week baseline of preschool programming without occupational therapy, a 10-week occupational therapy intervention using a sensory-integration approach was implemented. Weekly baseline and intervention measurements of the frequency of adult and peer interactions, mastery play, and nonengaged behaviors were compared. During the 10 weeks of intervention, the children demonstrated increased frequency of mastery play and decreased frequency of nonengaged behaviors. One child exhibited increased interaction with adults, but none of the children improved in peer interaction. Despite consistent improvement in play and engaged behaviors (attention to the environment), the social skills with peers remained quite low. In concurrence with other research, the children responded to adults who initiated interaction; however, they did not initiate interaction with peers and remained limited in their responsiveness to peers. These results of occupational therapy intervention provided in an integrated preschool setting are similar to those of other research studies and other types of intervention.

Recommendations for Occupational Therapy Efficacy Research

The research by occupational therapists reported to date regarding the effects of intervention have used pre-experimental designs. Each has reported individual rather than group results, reflecting the individualized needs of children with autism and the unique types of progress that they make. Although the results of these studies have been positive, they cannot be generalized.

Karnes and Johnson (1988) made recommendations for future research, based on the current foundation of efficacy research (see Table 14.2).

Table 14.2
Future Research of Children With Autism

1. The social validity of research questions and research results should be examined. Are research questions and findings meaningful for practice and current intervention systems?

2. Research designs should include triangulation of measures. Results should be measured by using multiple methods and by combining qualitative and quantitative data. Synthesizing the results of multiple evaluations will promote validity (truth value) of results.

3. Studies must be replicated in a variety of naturalistic settings, using different groups of children.

4. The family and the child should be the focus of the intervention effort and of the measured effect.

5. Interventions need to be well defined and explicitly described so the findings can be generalized.

6. The results should be disseminated using a variety of methods and media.

Note. Adapted from "Considerations and Future Directions for Conducting Research with Young Handicapped and At-Risk Children," in S. L. Odom & M. B. Karnes (Eds.), *Early Intervention for Infants and Children with Handicaps: An Empirical Base*, pp. 287–298. Copyright 1988 Paul H. Brookes. Adapted with permission.

These goals in Table 14.2 should be embraced by occupational therapy researchers. Because standardized testing is often not feasible to administer, triangulation in measurement will improve the validity of the results. Triangulation means that skills and behaviors are evaluated several different ways, and information is gained from different sources. For example, the child's behaviors may be observed in different environments, and his or her parents and teachers may be interviewed. When all of the data provide the same picture, the validity of the evaluation is greatly increased.

Because sensory responsivity is an elusive ability, it should be evaluated using naturalistic observation, parent reports, teacher reports, and standardized tests of sensory reactivity. When these sources agree, confidence in the assessment increases. If the measurement shows inconsistent results, additional observations or retesting is warranted.

Occupational therapists need to accomplish efficacy studies of children with autism using experimental group designs. Reports of case studies no longer satisfy the research needs of occupational therapists, families, children, and other disciplines. Case studies and single-subject design research can never provide definitive evidence of efficacy. To support the efficacy of occupational therapy approaches, experimental designs using relatively large sample sizes must be used. In addition, efforts should be made to obtain control samples that are matched in diagnosis and age. Intervention strategies should be standardized and well described (while accommodating to children's individual needs). In an effort to recruit a sample of children with similar development skills and characteristics, multisite, collaborative designs should be considered. In a multisite efficacy project, a number of investigators apply the same research design, using the same methods and measures. Careful attention must be given to controlling extraneous variables such as amount and type of parent involvement, home and school environments, and the inter-vention strategies. Because sample sizes can be large, a multisite research project can have good generalizability and strong effect sizes (confidence in effects). These projects require that faculty and practitioners collaborate, linking university and clinical resources. Occupational therapy faculty can help design the project, secure funding, as well as input and analyze data. The clinician can provide expertise in designing the intervention, can help to recruit subjects, can carry out interventions, and can gather data. Studies that combine university and clinical resources should produce highly meaningful results and provide information that will improve intervention with children with autism.

Conclusion

Occupational therapists have developed important intervention approaches for children with autism. They have helped professionals and families understand sensory processing issues and their effect on behavior and play interactions. Understanding performance problems associated with difficulties in sensory processing has led to the development of intervention approaches using sensory-integration techniques. Although occupational therapists have gathered evidence of the effectiveness of sensory-integration approaches, they have not engaged in experimental research of its efficacy. To help the legitimacy of our profession and to improve the quality of services to people with autism, occupational therapists need to evaluate and document the effectiveness of their interventions.

References

American Psychiatric Association. (2000). *Diagnostic and statistical manual of mental disorders* (4th ed., rev.). Washington, DC: Author.

Ayres, J. A., & Tickle, L. S. (1980). Hyper-responsivity to touch and vestibular stimuli as a predictor of positive response to sensory integration procedures by autistic children. *American Journal of Occupational Therapy, 34,* 375–381.

Bailey, A., Luthert, P., Dean A., Harding, B., Janota, I., Montgomery, M., Rutter, M., & Lantos, P. (1998). A clinicopathological study of autism. *Brain, 121*(5), 889–905.

Bailey, A., Phillips, W., & Rutter, M. (1996). Autism: Towards an integration of clinical, genetic, neuropsychological, and neurobiological perspectives. *Journal of Child Psychology and Psychiatry, 37*(1), 49–126.

Baranek, G. T., Foster, L. G., & Berkson, G. (1997). Tactile defensiveness and stereotyped behaviors. *American Journal of Occupational Therapy, 51,* 91–95.

Berard, G. (1993). *Hearing equals behavior.* New Canaan, CT: Keats.

Bundy, A. (1997). Play and playfulness: What to look for. In L. D. Parham & L. Primeau (Eds.), *Play in occupational therapy for children.* (pp. 52–66). St. Louis, MO: Mosby.

Case-Smith, J., & Bryan, T. (1999). The effects of occupational therapy with sensory integration emphasis on preschool aged children with autism. *American Journal of Occupational Therapy, 53,* 489–497.

Case-Smith, J., & Miller, H. (1999). Occupational therapy with children with pervasive developmental disorders. *American Journal of Occupational Therapy, 53,* 506–513.

Dawson, G., Hill, D., Spencer, A., Galpert, L., & Watson, L. (1990). Affective exchanges between young autistic children and their mothers. *Journal of Abnormal Child Psychology, 18,* 335–345.

Dawson, G., & Lewy, A. (1989). Arousal, attention, and the socioemotional impairments of individuals with autism. In G. Dawson (Ed.), *Autism: Nature, diagnosis, and treatment* (pp. 49–74). New York: Guilford.

Dawson, G., & Osterling, J. (1996). Early intervention in autism. In M. Guralnick (Ed.), *Effectiveness of early intervention* (pp. 307–326). Baltimore: Brookes.

Dunn, W. (1994). Performance of typical children on the sensory profile: An item analysis. *American Journal of Occupational Therapy, 48,* 967–974.

Dunn, W. (1999). *Sensory Profile.* San Antonio, TX: Psychological Corporation.

Fisher, S. E., VanDyke, D. C., Sears, L., Matzen, J., Lin-Dyken, D. C., & McBrien, D. M. (1999). Recent research on the etiologies of autism. *Infants and Young Children, 11*(3), 1–9.

Fisher, S. E., Vargha-Khadem, F., Watkins, K. E., Monaco, A. P, & Pembrey, M. E. (1998). Localization of a gene implicated to a severe speech and language disorder. *Nature Genetics, 18,* 168–170.

Freeman, B. J. (1997). Guidelines for evaluating intervention programs for children with autism. *Journal of Autism and Developmental Disorders, 27*(6), 641–651.

Frick, S. M., & Lawton-Shirley, N. (1994). Auditory integrative training from a sensory integrative perspective. *Sensory Integration Special Interest Section Newsletter, 17*(4), 1–3.

Frith, U. (1989). *Autism: Explaining the enigma.* Oxford, England: Blackwell.

Gray, C., & Garand, J. (1993). Social stories: Improving responses of students with autism with accurate social information. *Focus on Autistic Behavior, 8,* 1–10.

Greenspan, S. (1992). Reconsidering the diagnosis and treatment of very young children with autistic spectrum of pervasive developmental disorder. *Zero to Three, 13*(2), 1–9.

Greenspan, S., & Wieder, S. (1997a). Developmental patterns and outcomes in infants and children with disorders in relating and communication: A chart review of 100 cases of children with autistic spectrum diagnoses. *Journal of Developmental and Learning Disorders, 1*(1), 87–142.

Greenspan, S., & Wieder, S., (1997b). An integrated developmental approach to interventions for young children with severe difficulties in relating and communicating. *Zero to Three, 17*(5), 5–17.

Gresham, F. M., & MacMillan, D. L. (1998). Early intervention project: Can its claims be substantiated and its effects replicated? *Journal of Autism and Developmental Disorders, 28*(1), 5–12.

Huebner, R. A. (1992). Autistic disorder: A neuropsychological enigma. *American Journal of Occupational Therapy, 46,* 487–501.

International Molecular Genetic Study of Autism Consortium. (1998). A full genome screen for autism with evidence for linkage to a region on chromosome 7q. *Human Molecular Genetics, 7*(3), 571–578.

Karnes, M. B., & Johnson, L. T. (1988). Considerations and future directions for conducting research with young handicapped and at-risk children. In S. L. Odom & M. B. Karnes (Eds.), *Early intervention for infants and children with handicaps: A empirical base* (pp. 287–298). Baltimore: Brookes.

Kientz, M. A., & Dunn, W. (1997). A comparison of the performance of children with and without autism on the Sensory Profile. *American Journal of Occupational Therapy, 51,* 530–537.

King, L. J., & Grandin, T. (1990, October). *Attention deficits in learning disorder and autism: A sensory integrative treatment approach.* Workshop presented at the Conference Proceedings of the Continuing Education Programs of America, Milwaukee, WI.

Lainhart, J. E., Piven, J., Wzorkey, M., Landa, R., Santangelo, S. L., Coon, H., & Folstein, S. (1997). Macrocephaly in children and adults with autism. *Journal of the American Academy of Child and Adolescent Psychiatry, 36*(2), 282–290.

Lovaas, O. I. (1987). Behavioral treatment, normal education, and intellectual functioning in young autistic children. *Journal of Consulting and Clinical Psychology, 55,* 3–9.

Lovaas, O. I., Newsom, C., & Hickman, C. (1987). Self stimulatory behavior and perceptual reinforcement. *Journal of Applied Behavior Analysis, 20,* 45–68.

Mars, A. E., Mauk, J. E., Dowrick, P. W. (1998). Symptoms of pervasive developmental disorders as observed in prediagnostic home videos of infants and toddlers. *Journal of Pediatrics, 132*(3), 500–504.

McEachin, J., Smith, T., & Lovaas, O. I. (1993). Long-term outcome for children with autism who received early intensive behavioral treatment. *American Journal of Mental Retardation, 97,* 359–372.

Mesibov, G. B. (1996). Division TEACCH: A program model for working with autistic people and their families. In M. C. Roberts (Ed.), *Model practices in service delivery in child and family mental health* (pp. 215–230). Hillsdale, NJ: Erlbaum.

Mesibov, G. B., Adams, L. W., & Klinger, L. G. (1997). *Autism: Understanding the disorder.* New York: Plenum Press.

Mesibov, G. B., & Shea, V. (1996). Full inclusion and students with autism. *Journal of Autism and Developmental Disorders, 26,* 337–346.

Ornitz, E. M. (1974). The modulation of sensory input and motor output in autistic children. *Journal of Autism and Childhood Schizophrenia, 1,* 197–215.

Ornitz, E. M. (1985). Neurophysiology of infantile autism. *Journal of the American Academy of Child Psychiatry, 24,* 251–262.

Ornitz, E. M. (1989). Autism at the interface between sensory and information processing. In G. Dawson (Ed.), *Autism, nature, diagnosis and treatment* (pp. 174–207). New York: Guilford.

Osterling, J., & Dawson, G. (1994). Early recognition of children with autism: A study of first birthday home video tapes. *Journal of Autism and Developmental Disorders, 24,* 247–257.

Ozonoff, S., & Cathcart, K. (1998). Effectiveness of a home program intervention for young children with autism. *Journal of Autism and Developmental Disorders, 28,* 25–32.

Rapin, I. (1999). Appropriate investigations for clinical care versus research in children with autism. *Brain & Development, 21,* 152–156.

Rapin, I., & Katzman, R. (1998). Neurobiology of autism. *Annals of Neurology, 43*(1), 7–14.

Royeen, R. (1987). TIP—Touch inventory for preschoolers: A pilot study. *Physical and Occupational Therapy in Pediatrics,7*(1), 29–40.

Schopler, E., Mesibov, G., & Hearsey, K. (1995). Structured teaching in the TEACCH system. In E. Schopler & G. Mesibov (Eds.), *Learning and cognition in autism* (pp. 243–268). New York: Plenum.

Schuler, A., & Prizant, B. (1985). Brief report: The relationship of learning disabilities and higher-level autism. *Journal of Autism and Developmental Disorders, 15,* 423–435.

Schwartz, I. S., Billingsley, F. F., & McBride, B. M. (1998). Including children with autism in inclusive preschools: Strategies that work. *Young Exceptional Children, 1*(2) ,19–26.

Shah, A., & Frith, U. (1993). Why do autistic individuals show superior performance on the Block Design test? *Journal of Child Psychology and Psychiatry, 34,* 1351–1364.

Sigman, M., Mundy, P., Sherman, T., & Ungerer, J. (1986). Social interactions of autistic, mentally retarded and normal children and their caregivers. *Journal of Child Psychology and Psychiatry, 27,* 647–656.

Watling, R., Deitz, J., Kanny, E. M., & McLaughlin, J. F. (1999). Current practice of occupational therapy for children with autism. *American Journal of Occupational Therapy, 53,* 498–505.

Wechsler, D. (1974). *Manual for the Wechsler Intelligence Scale for Children-Revised.* San Antonio, TX: Psychological Corporation.

Index

Page numbers in boldface refer to tables.
Page numbers in italics refer to figures.

331